THE SOUND OF THE ANCESTRAL SHIP

THE SOUND OF THE ANCESTRAL SHIP

Highland Music of West Java

Sean Williams

2001

OXFORD
UNIVERSITY PRESS

Oxford   New York
Athens   Auckland   Bangkok   Bogotá   Buenos Aires   Cape Town
Chennai   Dar es Salaam   Delhi   Florence   Hong Kong   Istanbul   Karachi
Kolkata   Kuala Lumpur   Madrid   Melbourne   Mexico City   Mumbai   Nairobi
Paris   São Paulo   Shanghai   Singapore   Taipei   Tokyo   Toronto   Warsaw

and associated companies in
Berlin   Ibadan

Copyright © 2001 by Oxford University Press, Inc.

Published by Oxford University Press, Inc.
198 Madison Avenue, New York, New York 10016

Oxford is a registered trademark of Oxford University Press

All rights reserved. No part of this publication may be reproduced,
stored in a retrieval system, or transmitted, in any form or by any means,
electronic, mechanical, photocopying, recording, or otherwise,
without the prior permission of Oxford University Press.

Library of Congress Cataloging-in-Publication Data
Williams, Sean, 1959–
The sound of the ancestral ship : highland music of West Java / Sean Williams.
p. cm.
Includes bibliographical references and index.
ISBN 0-19-514154-7; ISBN 0-19-514155-5 (pbk.)
1. Sundanese (Indonesian people)—Music—History and criticism.
2. Music—Indonesia—Jawa Barat—History and criticism.
3. Jawa Barat (Indonesia)—Social life and customs.
I. Title
ML3758.153 W55   2001
781.62'99220582—dc21   00-065202

1 3 5 7 9 8 6 4 2

Printed in the United States of America
on acid-free paper

Daweung ménak Pajajaran
Now we will consider the noblemen of Pajajaran

ACKNOWLEDGMENTS

I would like to offer my deepest gratitude to everyone who has helped me through the process of researching and writing the results of my work. In particular, Euis Komariah and Gugum Gumbira took me into their home and taught me not only the inner workings of *tembang Sunda* but also how to be Sundanese. Apung Wiratmadja and his wife A. Tjitjah spent many hours with me toward the end of my stay in Indonesia, discussing the history and other details of tembang Sunda each week. Burhan Sukarma—a kind and dedicated teacher not only of *suling* but also of *kacapi*—put me in contact with most of my primary teachers. My primary teacher for the kacapi, Rukruk Rukmana, was particularly helpful in discussing aspects of innovation and development in tembang Sunda.

I was fortunate to have frequent contact with the vocalists Yayah Rochaeti Dachlan, Mamah Dasimah, Tintin Suparyani, Rina Oesman, Enah Sukaenah, Ida Widawati, Didin Badjuri, and the late Dadang Sulaeman (d. 1989), all of whom were very kind and helpful. Neneng Dinar Suminar was my constant companion during my vocal lessons and performances; I was proud to receive a copy of her first tembang Sunda recording. Several instrumentalists were essential to the completion of my research. The late Uking Sukri (1925–1994) and Dacép Eddy (1923–1990) were master musicians on the kacapi and *rebab*; they generously shared their time and their exceptional talent with me. Gan-Gan Garmana and Tatang Subari increased my awareness of the scope of kacapi styles and the lore surrounding the kacapi. Ade Suandi obtained copies of several fine recordings of tembang Sunda radio broadcasts from the 1960s. For increasing my understanding of tembang Sunda and Sundanese music in general, I would also like to express my deep appreciation to Nana Suhana, Gardea Soegeng, Nano Suratno, Tatas Tasripin, and the late Mang Suarna (d. 2000).

None of the research would have taken place had I not received a doctoral dissertation award from Fulbright-Hays, a research visa from the Lembaga Ilmu Pengetahuan Indonesia, and a sponsorship from the Sekolah Menengah Karawitan Indonesia. I was fortunate to receive a Ford Foundation Fellowship to prepare my doctoral dissertation. I would like to thank Nelly Polhaupessy at the United States Embassy in Jakarta for her help and good humor.

I owe a great debt to the people at home and in the Netherlands. Ter Ellingson, Christopher Waterman, Lorraine Sakata, and Daniel Lev were all very helpful in their reading of the original dissertation from which this book was derived. I would like to thank Ter Ellingson in particular for his diligence and care in weekly meetings with me. My sincere thanks go to Laurel Sercombe and Pamela Costes at the University of Washington Ethnomusicology Archives for the transfer of my field recordings to CD format. Their efforts greatly facilitated the creation of the compact disc recording for this book.

In the Netherlands, I have had three fine allies. Wim van Zanten has been a strong advocate of continued research on tembang Sunda, and was not only very encouraging but also very helpful as he gave me concrete suggestions for conducting my research. His pioneering research on tembang Sunda provided essential information about the genre and functioned as a springboard for my own research. Ernst Heins proved an invaluable resource, sending photographs and copies of commercial recordings of tembang Sunda from the Ethnomusicologisch Centrum "Jaap Kunst," and carefully critiquing my writing. Robert Wessing was my Dutch teacher in 1986; as one of the few Western scholars to discuss Sundanese culture and cosmology in print, he has been an inspiration to my work and a very helpful colleague.

Among the many ethnomusicologists of Indonesian music in the United States, the following have been influential: Andrew Weintraub, Henry Spiller, Philip Yampolsky, Endo Suanda, Sumarsam, R. Anderson Sutton, David Harnish, Michael Bakan, René Lysloff, Marc Perlman, Michael Tenzer, Benjamin Brinner, and others. Their articles and books on Indonesian music have been an inspiration, and their critiques of my dissertation, articles, and conference presentations have been instrumental in shaping the present work. In particular, Andrew Weintraub, Philip Yampolsky, and David Harnish served as readers for this book, and I am immensely grateful for their insightful suggestions.

ACKNOWLEDGMENTS

The good people at Oxford University Press-USA have been unfailingly professional and supportive at each stage of the publication process. As editor of music books at Oxford, Maribeth Payne was encouraging and enthusiastic from our initial contact onward. The production editors, Cynthia Garver and Robert Milks, oversaw the process of turning manuscript pages into a bound volume, and I am grateful to them for doing a fine job. Laura Lowrie was the copyeditor, and I thank her for her close attention to detail. Any errors in content are, of course, entirely mine.

My family and friends have provided encouragement, support, and criticism at all the right stages of my work. My parents, Alan and Julian Williams, have truly inspired me; my mother's exhilarating joie de vivre and my father's elegant sense of logic, order, and beauty inform everything I do. My brother, Guy Williams, and his partner Antonio Navas-Rufino made a special trip to Indonesia to visit me in 1988, and I appreciate their traveling all the way from their home in Spain. My late grandparents, Julius and Marian Williams, sped up my work time by giving me a computer in the 1980s. My late grandmother, Dorothy Gonzenbach, inspired me through her own travel adventures.

Since 1991, I have worked at the Evergreen State College in Olympia, Washington, and it has been my great pleasure to enjoy the unfailing support, kindness, and humor of my colleagues and friends there. Among these good people are Patrick Hill, Charles Teske, Arun Chandra, Doranne Crable, Meg Hunt, John Cushing, Sarah Williams, Ratna Roy, Terry Setter, Andrew Buchman, Rose Jang, Chris Yates, and Jacinta McKoy. Arun Chandra painstakingly set my handwritten music notation into print, for which I am very grateful. My 1998–1999 teaching partner Joe Feddersen helped to develop the kind of team-taught curriculum that would allow me the time, inspiration, and impetus to finish this book in a timely manner. I am happy to acknowledge the fine efforts of my students Jenefer Bertucci, Keaton Simons, Leone Reinbold, Vaughn Shoot, and Senayit Tomlinson for graciously learning to perform tembang Sunda. My friends Gloria Hatch, Laurie Bonilla, Julie Biskie, Lyndon Haviland, Tamara Kohn, Roy Hamilton, and Gage Averill have supported me in countless ways before, during, and after the entire process. My daughter Morgan (born in 1994), whose genuine enjoyment of Sundanese music from *gamelan degung* to tembang Sunda to *angklung buncis* brings me great happiness, keeps me connected to both the sublime and the mundane. My husband, Cary Black, has been my companion and kindred spirit for my entire adult life, and deserves more thanks for his support, love, critical eye, and compassion than can be conveyed in writing.

This book is for the musicians.

CONTENTS

Introduction, 3

I The Transformation of the Past in Politics and Music
    1 Sundanese Culture in Transition, 19
    2 The Antecedents of Tembang Sunda, 37

II Tembang Sunda in the Urban Environment
    3 Contexts for Performance, 51
    4 Musical Interactions between Men and Women, 81
    5 The Mediation of Sound, 93
    6 Learning the Craft, 121

III The Music of Tembang Sunda
    7 The Parameters of Style, 141
    8 Instrumental and Vocal Characteristics, 164

IV The Meaning of Tembang Sunda
    9 A Name Is All That Remains, 197
    10 Connecting with the Ancestors, 211

Notes, 233
Glossary, 247
Bibliography, 251
Discography, 261
Index, 262
Notes on the CD, 273

A section of photographs appears after p. 92.

THE SOUND OF THE ANCESTRAL SHIP

INTRODUCTION

A few months prior to my most recent departure from Bandung, Indonesia, I was attending a wedding of two seventeen-year-olds. Sitting among the perhaps two thousand guests near a busy, noisy road, I overheard the people in front of me gaily placing bets on how long the marriage might last. "Ten months!" said the first man. "As soon as the child is born, he's out of there." "Ten thousand rupiah says that it's going to be after the second son is born," reasoned the next man. "They spent all this money on the wedding, so they have to have some proof that it was worth it to get married." "At least the music is good," returned the first man. "The bridal couple can pretend that they're members of the aristocracy today. Tomorrow, they're just regular Sundanese people."

At this particular wedding, the event was seasoned with the music of *tembang Sunda*, an ensemble associated with highland Sundanese people of aristocratic descent. Featuring one or more vocalists accompanied by bamboo flute (*suling*) and two boat-shaped zithers (one large and one small *kacapi*), the ensemble performs song lyrics that amplify feelings of nobility and the longing for an idealized rural past. At this particular event, the group provided an élite sonic atmosphere, allowing the connubially doomed young couple to imagine an entirely different life for themselves than the one expected by the crowd of urban wedding guests. Indeed, the staged representation of their future life was one of connection to the aristocratic past.

The boat shape of the kacapi zither (and the *rincik*, its smaller, high-pitched companion zither) is a cultural metaphor for the use of tembang Sunda to aurally transport its audience into a different time and place. As the main instrument in a performance of tembang Sunda, the kacapi functions as an ancestral ship for urbanites of the early twenty-first century. Carrying people back to a time of aristocrats, ancestors, and gods, the kacapi locates its listeners in the ancient kingdom of Pajajaran (1333–1579), as both a historical kingdom and an imagined paradise. My primary kacapi teacher, Rukruk Rukmana, noted that "the kacapi is much better now that we live in the city. We have good materials with which to build it, and we wouldn't have any way to reach Pajajaran if it wasn't for the boat. Village people don't need a boat because they are already there" (Rukmana, personal communication, 1988).

In most performance settings, tembang Sunda songs generally occur in small groups, each set lasting approximately fifteen or twenty minutes. The first section of each set is performed in free rhythm with each song (*mamaos*) related to the others, through either similar textual themes or melodic structure. After each group of free-meter songs, the ensemble begins a fixed-rhythm *panambih* (or "addition") to close the set. Panambih are cyclical in nature; they are performed only by women vocalists and are generally accompanied by male instrumentalists. The bamboo flute, which generally plays in heterophony with the singer's melody during the free-rhythm section of each set, has a vocal-like quality that has great appeal to audience members.

From its beginnings as a very localized tradition in the small regency of Cianjur (where it was known as *Cianjuran*), tembang Sunda spread across West Java and eventually was relocated in Bandung, a large urban center in the highlands of West Java. This book is a study of the effects of the subsequent urbanization of the genre on both practitioners and audience members. Current ideas in urban ethnomusicology allow an exploration of audience and performer perception of tembang Sunda, as well as the subsequent alteration of the music in order to conform to, and firmly establish, the primarily urban setting of the music. Examining a particular tradition may lead not so much to a profound understanding of the tradition itself but, rather, to an understanding of it "as a *site* for the examination of how locality emerges in a globalizing world, of how colonial processes underwrite contemporary politics, of how history and genealogy inflect one another, and of how global facts take local form" (Appadurai 1996:18). The lives of tembang Sunda musicians were strongly affected by the increasingly rapid urbanization of West Java in the latter half of the twentieth century, and the music they perform reflects these changes and the increasing influence of foreign elements. This introduction provides a theoretical framework through which the rest of the book may be viewed.

INTRODUCTION   5

The book is divided into four main sections. Part I, "The Transformation of the Past in Politics and Music," introduces the area and people of Sunda and includes the early development of tembang Sunda. Part II, "Tembang Sunda in the Urban Environment," discusses the genre in the regional capital city of Bandung, including the urban institutions responsible for its support and promotion since the early part of the twentieth century. The continuing development of tembang Sunda through these institutions has resulted in specific alterations to musical performance practice. Part III, "The Music of Tembang Sunda," explores the musical features of the genre, including the different styles used, the instruments, and the tuning systems. In the two chapters of Part III, I emphasize the ways in which the presence of tembang Sunda in the city has affected its performance practice. Lastly, Part IV, "The Meaning of Tembang Sunda," examines Pajajaran as a mythical place, discusses the symbolism of the kacapi, and briefly describes the poetry of tembang Sunda. It also explores the emotional and spiritual connection for the urban Sundanese between modern tembang Sunda in its urban setting and its early rural roots in the homes of the Sundanese aristocracy.

Tembang Sunda is performed most frequently in the cities of West Java, particularly in the regional capital city of Bandung. Although many definitions of the word *city* exist in the literature on urban studies, the different types of cities found throughout the world defy broad generalization beyond a listing of attributes. The terms *urban* and *rural* are abstract constructs in a continuum; features that occur in a city may be transplants from a rural setting, and characteristics usually attributed to urban life may be found in situations far from the city. In the broadest theoretical sense, the features that distinguish city life from country life fall under the rubric of *urbanism*, and the process leading to the acquisition of those features is referred to as *urbanization*. The following pages clarify some of the ideas in the literature on urbanism and urbanization.

URBAN ETHNOMUSICOLOGY AND
THE MUSIC OF WEST JAVA

The process of musical urbanization is complicated due to the lack of a unified theory of urbanization in general, and to the lack of clarity regarding which musical features may be claimed as urban. In a rural area, a battery-operated synthesizer may easily sample and reproduce the sound of a shepherd's flute. Is the music to be classified as urban because of the origin of its instrument, or is it rural because of the melody performed? It is necessary to make a distinction between "music *of* the city" (music that originates in the urban environment) and "music *in* the city" (music that has been brought to, and developed in, the city). Modern tembang Sunda began *in* the city and evolved into music *of* the city. The distinction between rural and urban settings is no clearer today than in the early part of the twentieth century, when these issues were first being sorted out.

Researchers have long studied cultural responses to urban conditions, beginning with the Chicago school of sociology in the early twentieth century. In the study of their own city, these early researchers developed concepts about urbanism that could be applied to other cities in America and Western Europe. The followers of American urban sociology at that time were divided into two subfields: those who attempted to understand the fundamental features of human society in the city, and those who based their work on surveys in order to better understand the social problems associated with cities (Hannerz 1980:21). The ferreting out of social ills and the explanation of their presence in regard to the urban environment was to become a standard topic of writings in urban studies later in the twentieth century (Mitchell 1966:39–40).

In these early writings it was posited that certain societal changes always took place under the influence of urbanism. One of the most significant changes was said to be the gradual dissolution of social ties, which, under rural conditions, were based on the location of the individual, kinship, and status differences between people (Hannerz 1980:24). The dissolution of these ties was believed to be brought about by an increase in the division of labor and a greater density of population, making human relationships more superficial and allowing for the segregation of related people into separate domains. The further intent of the early sociologists was to describe these separate social worlds in the city; according to Park, it was possible for an urbanite to move freely from one small domain to another without any contact between the domains (Park 1952:47). Finally, it has been noted that locality, as linked to social life, does not thrive under conditions of modernism (see Appadurai 1996:179). In this case, locality refers to the concept of the local in opposition to either the nation-state or the rest of the world.

In one of the most important and widely read works to deal with urbanism outside of the United States and Europe, "Urbanism as a Way of Life" (Wirth 1938), Louis Wirth discussed the influence of urban life on the inhabitants of cities and also described the lure of the city to those who live on the outside:

> The influences which cities exert upon the social life of man are greater than the ratio of the urban population would indicate, for the city is not only in ever larger degrees the dwelling-place and the workshop of modern man, but it is the initiating and controlling center of economic, political, and cultural life that has drawn the most remote parts of the world into its orbit and woven diverse areas, peoples, and activities into a cosmos. (Wirth 1938:2)

Wirth's description of the city as a "a relatively large, dense, and permanent settlement of socially heterogeneous individuals" (Wirth 1938:1) was intended to apply to all cities and defined the polar opposite of the idealized folk society as described by Robert Redfield. Redfield was also a product of the Chicago school, and his concept of a typical folk society was that of a nonliterate, self-sufficient, homogeneous group of people existing in almost total isolation from outside influences (Redfield 1947:294). Louis Wirth saw rural and urban societies as representative of a polar relationship between two societal types. Anthropologists have since treated this rural/urban model as a continuum into which human societies may be placed, recognizing the fact that neither extreme actually corresponds to reality (Hannerz 1980:64).

In the years since Wirth and Redfield, anthropologists have worked to create models for many different cities, developing certain urban types to reflect the unique features of particular cultural traditions. For example, Hannerz describes the development of typologies for the "Latin American city" or the "Muslim city," corresponding to features that should be present in a city to which that typology is assigned (Hannerz 1980:75). The acknowledgment and description of the existence of certain types of urban centers has allowed for a more accurate assessment of the position of each city in relation to the others that was unaccounted for by Wirth. Some of Wirth's ideas may still, however, be applied to the modern phenomenon of tembang Sunda in the city. In spite of his assertion that urbanism causes the relative superficiality of personal relationships, he also indicated that certain behavioral patterns of rural society may carry over into urban life (Wirth 1938:3). Behavioral patterns in music-making that have continued in the face of urbanization form a major focus of the present study.

In marked contrast to Wirth's concept of the superficial nature of personal relationships in the city, work in urban anthropology has recognized the existence of urban networks (Hannerz 1980:102), which may replace or supplement kinship systems. In these networks, particular domains in the lives of urban inhabitants enable each individual to maintain strong ties—through family, neighbors, coworkers, friends, and other acquaintances—that support the individual. The introduction to Part II of this book includes a discussion of these domains in urban Sundanese musical society, as a function of sorting out the network system of tembang Sunda musicians. In many ways, the ties between urban tembang Sunda musicians are far stronger and more clearly defined than those between musicians in the areas surrounding Bandung.

Another important concept in urban anthropology is the notion that cities may be classified by their primary and secondary functions, for example, commerce, regional administration, spiritual and intellectual pursuits, or as a stopping place on a route to another city.

> As a "central business district," the city is obviously a market-place, a place to buy and sell, "to do business"—to truck, barter and exchange with people who may be complete strangers and of different races, religions and creeds. As a religious and intellectual center, on the other hand, the city is a beacon for the faithful, a center for the learning and perhaps doctrine that transforms the im-

plicit "little traditions" of the local non-urban cultures into an explicit and systematic "great tradition." (Redfield and Singer 1954:55–56)

Tembang Sunda represents the latter phenomenon, in which the local tradition of Cianjuran was transformed as a result of urbanization into a standardized, regionwide genre. Although the term tembang Sunda may refer in a general sense to all Sundanese song, it is used throughout this book to describe what was once known as Cianjuran. Referring to tembang Sunda as a "great tradition" does not necessarily imply that it is universally beloved and performed by all Sundanese. Rather, it is a Great Tradition because it is an idealized music of aristocratic Sundanese society (see also Nettl 1978b:128). The perpetuation of traditions such as tembang Sunda has enabled the modern Sundanese to cope with issues such as the aftereffects of Indonesian Independence, and the economic crisis of the late 1990s. Tembang Sunda has become a Great Tradition in Bandung, with all the influential power that its status implies, and has systematically overshadowed the more rural performance practice as it has been performed in the regency of Cianjur.

Although the institutions and networks that support the tembang Sunda community in Bandung seem relatively inflexible and static (for example, the teaching of outmoded music theories), certain performers in the community have introduced major changes in performance practice. Because these innovators work actively to make changes in tembang Sunda performance practice, a description of "standard" performance practices should only be taken as a basic direction for analysis. The consideration of urban institutions, together with the innovators who operate within their domains, should provide a stronger, less restricted analysis (Hannerz 1980:173).

One of the most important features of urban areas is that they become a focus of certain activities, organized "socially, politically, and economically, through the agency of urban institutions which extend their influences outward and bind the surrounding regions to the central city" (Friedmann 1961:92). This phenomenon is manifested in the arena of tembang Sunda, because much of the current musical activity of this type is now focused in the urban area of Bandung. Many musical styles have been altered as result of urban migration, and the subsequent reorganization of musical culture based on social, political, and economic factors has been an important field of study in the anthropological literature (recent writings include Turino 1987 and Waterman 1990).

Although the literature on urban anthropology has increased steadily since World War II, urban ethnomusicology only developed as a subfield of ethnomusicology in the late 1960s. The first work to collect urban ethnomusicological studies was Bruno Nettl's *Eight Urban Musical Cultures* (1978a). According to Nettl, urban ethnomusicology arose from urban cultural studies in anthropology as well as in musicology (Nettl 1978a:3). These studies, however, concentrated primarily on Western European cities. The urban ethnomusicologist faces such issues as continuity and change within the urban setting, technological innovation and its adoption by a particular musical community, the relationship between modernization and urbanization, and contact between urban and rural musical communities.

> The problems of urban ethnomusicology have long been recognized, implicitly and sometimes explicitly . . . there is a need for scholars to view the world's musics in their proper context, and today this is substantially an urban context in which the characteristics of the twentieth century city, its rapid growth, its cultural diversity, and its inevitable conglomeration of social and musical interactions are given proper attention. (Nettl 1978a:15)

The study of a genre such as tembang Sunda in its urban setting also requires an understanding of the processes of musical culture change. For example, the recording industry has had a significant impact on the music of Indonesia (Gronow 1981:275); it is essential to assess how performers have adapted music to reflect this impact. The adaptation of tembang Sunda to the primarily urban conditions under which it thrives has been determined primarily by the response of musicians to changes in Sundanese social and cultural conditions.

This adaptation is not a one-way reaction to external conditions; instead, musical adaptation functions as a way to reshape the external conditions affecting the music and to establish a new position for music in society (Coplan 1982:114). In addition, changes in music can reflect changes in the identity of certain musicians among others, highlight particular status divisions within society, and ground the music in its new environment. Musical change also may reflect adaptations in the society to which the music belongs, or changes in the multiple social networks in the urban context. These networks ultimately affect performance practice as the musicians react to change. In his article "Towards an Ethnomusicology of Culture Change in Asia," Daniel Neuman explains that music may constitute a commentary on or interpretation of a culture (Neuman 1976:2). In the observation of change in musical behavior, it is possible that the larger picture of societal change may be observed as well.

> The process of urban social change is not a simple one. It involves a complex articulation between kinship, ethnic-regional, residential and class ties as people's position in the emerging status system becomes increasingly important in determining their cultural behavior. Performance expression thus results not only from the nature of specific cultural influences or occasions of performance, but also from the institutional complexes within which music is produced. (Coplan 1982:115)

The urbanization of tembang Sunda is only one of the musical results of the gradual development of Bandung as a major Indonesian city of over three million people. Many other types of Sundanese music have been altered, developed, or abandoned, partly as a result of urbanization. An example of a dramatic alteration to an existing genre has been the development of *jaipongan*, a very popular form of urban social dance derived from the village genres of *penca silat* and *ketuk tilu*. Jaipongan dancing was popular in Sunda in the late 1970s and early 1980s, reaching its peak in approximately 1984. It is still popular, and in each of the larger Sundanese cities—but especially in Bandung—jaipongan classes of several hundred students are taught nearly every day of the week in large halls. Some of the dance institutions that were formed in response to the tremendous demand for jaipongan lessons provide certificates to the students on completion of each new dance.

Other Sundanese musical genres, however, have not experienced the same extraordinary efflorescence in the urban environment. The classical *gamelan degung* ensemble, which once performed for the entertainment of the Sundanese aristocracy and welcomed important visitors, now performs only rarely. Formerly an all-male instrumental group performing songs of the classical Sundanese repertoire, the original ensemble (now known as *degung klasik*) shifted in emphasis to include vocalists, female musicians, and songs that were easier to learn and perform (see also Heins 1977:67–70 and Williams 1990:105–136). The classical repertoire has been almost abandoned by the new urban performers. This new style of gamelan degung is known as *degung kawih*, to reflect the addition of *kawih* or fixed-meter songs. Variations on the original ensemble, such as the use of a flat board zither (*kacapi siter*), back-up vocals, rhythmic influences from other styles, and studio-enhanced special effects have contributed to cassette sales. In turn, sales have contributed to the popularity of degung kawih as opposed to degung klasik (instrumental gamelan degung), which has fallen almost completely out of prominence. The genre of tembang Sunda, however, has continued to thrive in its new setting, and the more the music is supported by urban institutions, the more dependent it becomes on these institutions for its continued existence.

As more researchers develop their work on the urbanization of Indonesian genres in other regional cities such as Jakarta, Den Pasar, Medan, Surakarta, and Kupang, the research should yield useful results. Each one of these large cities maintains active recording studios and figures prominently in the promotion of regional Indonesian music. As the music scene in Bandung is largely determined by networks among Sundanese performing musicians and their sponsors, other regional groups (for example, the Balinese) have developed a complicated system of individual musical domains that work to support the music industry through cassettes, performances for tourists, and sponsored touring groups. The systems at work in and between these larger Indonesian cities deserve closer scrutiny.

Arjun Appadurai uses the term *neighborhood* to discuss "life-worlds constituted by relatively stable associations, by relatively known and shared histories, and by collectively traversed and legible spaces and places" (1996: 191). Such a description is appropriate for the practitioners of tembang Sunda, whose worlds coincide with each other many times a year at performances, gatherings, and social events. Even in the heart of a city with several million inhabitants, the artists' network that links these tembang Sunda performers, sponsors, and audience members is engaged in such a way that the processes of creating locality and reaffirming identity are constantly in motion.

The Sundanese area of West Java boasts over two hundred musical genres, of which only a few have been explored by scholars (Indonesian or otherwise). The scope of literature in English that deals exclusively with tembang Sunda is quite limited. Many works on Indonesian music have concentrated primarily on the music of Central Java and Bali, and have either ignored Sunda altogether or treated it only peripherally. One of the earliest and most widely used of these works is *Music in Java* (Kunst 1973); it includes a large section on Sundanese music, focusing on the description of instruments, ensembles, and the measurement of tones and scales. An essential work for the study of the poetry in Javanese and Sundanese songs is *Matjapat Songs in Central and West Java* (Kartomi 1973a), which includes song transcriptions and a discussion of the setting and performance practice of the songs.

The most recent publication on tembang Sunda is *Sundanese Music in the Cianjuran Style: Anthropological and Musicological Aspects of Tembang Sunda*, by Wim van Zanten, published in 1989. Van Zanten's book is a revised edition of his doctoral dissertation, "Tembang Sunda: An Ethnomusicological Study of the Cianjuran Music in West Java" (van Zanten 1987). Because both works are not only recent but also directly relevant to the present study, they are cited frequently throughout the book, and I highlight points that either support or conflict with my information. Van Zanten has also published several articles that highlight data from his further research (van Zanten 1984, 1985, 1986, 1993, 1994, 1995a and b, 1997).

I review several Indonesian and Sundanese sources in Chapter 6 ("Learning the Craft"), because of their use in the music schools. In general, however, those works tend to describe the mechanical features and notation of the music, and in most cases do not discuss nonmusical features. Sources in Indonesian and Sundanese that deal exclusively or at least partly with tembang Sunda and related genres are included in the bibliography for reference.[1]

Western anthropologists have largely overlooked Sunda as a research location; therefore, the background material in English for this work is limited primarily to Wessing's articles and dissertation, together with anthropological materials in ethnomusicological works by Western scholars. Indonesian and Dutch scholars, by contrast, have been quite active in publishing works about Sundanese history and culture. Among those works relating directly to tembang Sunda are Saleh and Atja Danasasmita's 1981 work, *Sanghyang Siksakandang ng Karesian*; Endang S's *Pangajaran Tembang Sunda* (1979); Satjadibrata's *Rasiah Tembang Sunda* (1953); Somawidjaja's *Nyukcruk Galur Nu Kapungkur* (1982); Enip Sukanda's *Pangeuyeub Ngeuyeub Kareueus kana Dunya Seni Mamaos* (1978) and *Tembang Sunda Cian-*

juran (1983); Viviane Sukanda's *Sekelumit tentang Tembang Sunda* (1978); Atik Supandi's article "Penyelidikan Secara Musikologis dan Kemungkinan Standardisasi Lagu-Lagu Tembang Sunda" (1976b), and Apung Wiratmadja's two books *Sumbangan Asih kana Tembang Sunda* (1964) and *Mengenal Seni Tembang Sunda* (1996).

Hannerz's *Exploring the City* (1980) has been quite useful in providing an overview of late-twentieth-century developments in urban anthropology, as have several influential articles (particularly "The Urbanization of African Music: Some Theoretical Observations," by David Coplan [1982]). Lastly, the theoretical focus of this work has been influenced by the writings of Benedict Anderson, Clifford Geertz, and many other Indonesianists. The names of these and others appear frequently throughout this book; however, the absence of direct citation does not indicate the absence of influence.

RESEARCH METHODOLOGY

I conducted fieldwork in the Sundanese city of Bandung on three separate occasions: from 1987 to 1989, and again in 1991 and 1996. I have had frequent contact with some of my primary teachers since then, thanks to the telecommunications industry. I also worked in several cities outside of Bandung (still within the Priangan or highland area) to achieve an understanding of tembang Sunda as it is performed, rehearsed, and taught outside a major urban center. For most of the time, I was a participant observer. In the process of trying to understand the operative codes of behavior in Sunda, I attempted to act in a manner appropriate to my gender and position in Sundanese society. I spent much of my time with singers and instrumentalists, I ate Sundanese food, and I rode on public transportation (with the exception of the ten-month period in which I owned a small motorcycle). I wore modest American-style skirts and dresses, because they are standard wear for middle- to upper-class female Sundanese urbanites.

In the time I spent researching this music and its lifestyle, I attempted to study the vocal tradition as would a fledgling Sundanese singer.[2] I also studied kacapi and suling privately, not in a traditional Sundanese manner but, rather, similar to the way an American would study a Western classical instrument: with a tape recorder and plenty of questions. I chose not to study *rebab* or rincik (two other tembang Sunda instruments) in an in-depth manner. Few students take formal lessons on the rincik; they claim to simply "follow along," according to nearly everyone with whom I spoke (but this claim is not entirely true; see Chapter 8 for more information about the rincik). The rebab is extremely difficult to play and is not nearly as essential to tembang Sunda as the others. My reason for studying kacapi and suling privately and in an accelerated manner had to do with the fact that learning to play by sitting and listening for years was simply too slow, because I only had a few years to work with instead of twenty.

For my vocal lessons I attended the twice-weekly *latihan* (rehearsal or, more accurately, jam session) at the home of Euis Komariah, an outstanding singer and recording artist. Together with several other female Sundanese students mostly within my age group, I studied the art of singing tembang Sunda. During the latihan, Euis gave us all one or more songs to learn from the free-rhythm mamaos style of *tembang*, and one panambih or fixed-rhythm "addition" song to conclude the lesson. We were each encouraged to develop our own style of notation to use as a visual aid during our practice time at home, and my sing-by-the-numbers method was accepted although it varied markedly from that of the other students. I performed regularly, although my performances were regarded locally as a novelty act to lighten things up rather than as genuine tembang Sunda performances.

In research directly relating to urbanization, I frequented recording studios and made inquiries about the cassette, radio, and television industries and their effect on tembang Sunda performance. I subscribed to the local newspapers to follow the articles and letters to the editor concerning Sundanese music and dance. I also interviewed people responsible for sponsoring performances of tembang Sunda in Bandung. During my trips outside of Bandung, I tried to note the differences not only in performance practice but also in extramusical behavior associated with the performance context.

The language used for most of my research was *Bahasa Indonesia*, the Indonesian national language. I also improved my Sundanese language skills, and eventually was able to follow any discussion about music in addition to understanding all social conversations in Sundanese. On occasion, I used halting Dutch to communicate with some older people who generally assumed that I was Dutch. (Prior to Indonesian Independence in 1945, any young person from a good family would have had adequate knowledge of Dutch, and some of the older people spoke with me as if I was a young Dutch girl from that era.)[3] In the present text, all instrumental and vocal terms are Sundanese. Some of the quotes and expressions are in Indonesian, however, and are identified as such.

The way my research was conducted was affected by local concepts about American women and foreign researchers in general. During the time I spent researching tembang Sunda, I made constant corrections and adjustments to my behavior so that I could either confirm or deny expectations of me. I had already been married for four years by the time I began my research, so my childless condition was a constant source of consternation and discussion. Because my husband was in Indonesia for only five months during the two years of my research (and half of that time was spent out of town), I was often treated like a single woman, or a divorcée. During a recent visit I was at last able to show at least two-dimensional proof of motherhood (and, evidently, prove my legitimacy as a grown woman) by passing around photographs of my daughter.

The examples of American women shown on Sundanese television ("Dynasty" and "Hunter" were quite popular in the 1980s, "L.A. Law" and

"Baywatch" in the 1990s) frequently portrayed inappropriate behavior, according to Sundanese standards. In order to counter the resulting assumptions about American women, my conversations and behavior were tailored to give the impression that I was far more oriented to home and family than the American women portrayed daily on television. I lived in a small home in the lower-middle-class southern part of Bandung and was closely supervised by my female servant. The employment of a servant was essential in the preservation of my reputation among the Sundanese. Because I was alone for most of my research time, my servant's real job was to act as a chaperone and to send home (at the appropriate hour) the male musicians who came to visit at my house. The inappropriateness of the musicians' visits to my house—had a servant not been there—would have prevented them from visiting altogether.

With female singers and the wives of instrumentalists, discussions often focused on children, gender issues, shopping, cosmetics, and fashion (standard topics of conversation among Sundanese women) long before coming around to the topic of tembang Sunda. Conversations with men, by contrast, often were more directed toward tembang Sunda and away from matters of home and family, primarily because men rarely seem to discuss these issues when women are not present. Male instrumentalists spend hours discussing every aspect of tembang Sunda, going over the meaning of songs or discussing various performers, both past and present. These discussions and debates (*polemik*) are interspersed with jokes and unrelated conversations, but are a daily occurrence and are crucial to the continuing development of the genre. Frequently a younger musician may turn to an older one and ask to have the meaning of a particular song explained. This question then provides an opportunity for the community's collective knowledge to be passed on to the younger generation, and it is also a respectful way of inviting one's elder to take the lead in the conversation. Such rich conversations build strong bonds between musicians, and are mutually beneficial to the participants.

It quickly became clear to me that humor is an essential feature of the Sundanese performing arts.[4] Being creative with puns and other wordplay and telling funny stories the way many Sundanese love to do brought me closer to the inner circle of tembang Sunda musicians. I also tried to react to difficult and potentially dangerous situations as would a normal, well-brought-up Sundanese woman. Most of the people with whom I worked kindly overlooked my behavioral anomalies such as driving a motorcycle by myself at night, typing for several hours at a time, and needing occasional privacy. Although looking rather obviously foreign (with all the difficulties and occasional hilarious moments that looking different engenders), I did my best to fit in.

In addition to studying tembang Sunda, attending performances, and participating in the everyday lives of musicians, I interviewed members of the tembang Sunda ensemble at the Bandung branch of Radio Republik Indonesia and occasionally attended broadcasts when it was appropriate. To discover more information about the inner workings of the Sundanese recording industry, I interviewed owners of cassette stores, recording engineers, producers, and recording artists, and I attended studio sessions at the Jugala recording studio. My little black-and-white television provided opportunities to watch tembang Sunda performances being broadcast, and I attended several tembang Sunda recording sessions for TVRI (TeleVisi Republik Indonesia) to better understand the process of filming and promotion of regional artists and their work.

In this introduction, I have attempted to summarize the theoretical concepts of urbanism and urbanization, and have given a brief introduction to Sunda and the Sundanese, whose musical genre of tembang Sunda is firmly placed in an urban environment. The description of the literature and methods used to arrive at my conclusions about tembang Sunda gives only a partial picture of Sundanese participation in the arena of tembang Sunda. Many people devote a large part of their lives to the performance and perpetuation of the genre, and do not spend their time visiting cassette stores and recording studios or interviewing various musicians. Instead, these people go from one practice session to another, blocking out many hours of each day just to talk, play, and sing tembang Sunda. The commitment of these true devotees is a major factor in the continuation of the genre.

I

THE TRANSFORMATION OF THE PAST IN POLITICS AND MUSIC

Tembang Sunda is an aristocratic Sundanese chamber music sung to the accompaniment of zithers (kacapi) and bamboo flute (suling). Its origins date to the mid–nineteenth century, when it emerged in the region of Cianjur, one of the Sundanese regencies or administrative districts. Due to a combination of historical factors affecting music patronage, many tembang Sunda musicians left Cianjur for the regional administrative capital of Bandung in the early part of the twentieth century, causing the cultural milieu surrounding tembang Sunda to relocate in a large urban center instead of remaining in a traditional setting. Modern tembang Sunda is directly related to the history, development, and gradual urbanization of West Java. Tembang Sunda is also associated with traditional Sundanese cosmology. The performance of tembang Sunda has continued to develop in its urban location, and the changes in performance practice that have occurred as a result of this relocation have served at least partly to contribute to its continuing vitality.

More than thirty-five million Sundanese live in West Java, and only a relatively small number are able to perform tembang Sunda themselves. Most singers are either descendants of the old Sundanese aristocracy or connected to aristocratic families through marriage or through participation in musical performing groups supported by the modern aristocracy. The metropolitan superculture (see Hildred Geertz 1963:35) in Bandung has created a very strong sphere of influence through the use of media and other urban institutions that pervade the smallest Sundanese villages. Although tembang Sunda is only one aspect of the Bandung music scene in comparison to the many other performing arts genres, those who perform it outside of Bandung look continually to the urban center for new developments in performance practice. Most Sundanese are unfamiliar with (or even resistant to) tembang Sunda, because of its association with the upper and upper-middle classes. Those who are familiar with it tend to ignore it in favor of more popular genres such as jaipongan (social dance) and *pop Sunda* (a blend of local tunings, compositions, and instruments with international pop music). Among the several thousand Sundanese practitioners and audience members of tembang Sunda, however, the music is treated with reverence.

1

Sundanese Culture in Transition

The historical and cultural developments that have dramatically shaped the nature of Sundanese identity in the past century and a half illustrate the reasons for the shift of tembang Sunda musicians from a semirural area to the city of Bandung. Through the establishment of tembang Sunda in Bandung, musicians who performed the genre were able to take advantage of new venues offered by the urban environment, and the genre experienced a revival following the move to the city. This shift of the musicians to Bandung occurred largely as a result of gradual urbanization combined with other social and economic factors directly tied to the position of Bandung in relation to smaller, outlying cities. Although this chapter covers certain historical events, it is not intended to be a comprehensive history of West Java or of Sundanese culture. The reader is directed to Kern (1898), de Graaf (1949), Hidding (1935), and de Haan (1910–12) for more complete historical information.

SUNDA AND THE SUNDANESE

The Sundanese region, known officially as Jawa Barat or West Java (and unofficially as Sunda), is located in the western third of Java. Although

Jakarta, the capital city of Indonesia, is also located on the western part of the island, it is not part of the province of West Java and is treated by the Indonesian government as a special district. The region is separated from the rest of Java by a border extending from the west of the city of Cirebon to the southern coast of the island. The subdistrict of West Java known as Priangan, where the primary research for this study took place, is located primarily in the mountainous highlands.[1] The five regencies of Bandung, Cianjur, Tasikmalaya, Sumedang, and Garut belong to the Priangan region and are considered the home of tembang Sunda. Figure 1.1 indicates some of the major Sundanese cities, most of which are mentioned in this book. Bandung is the largest city of the area, followed by Cirebon. Cianjur (where tembang Sunda originated) is approximately an hour away from Bandung by car. Roads connect all of these cities, and some are also connected by rail. The city of Bandung is situated in a former lake basin, surrounded by active volcanoes. Some of the most prominent volcanoes in the area (including Galunggung, Pangrango, and Tangkuban Prahu) are mentioned in tembang Sunda texts, and are an important aspect of Sundanese cosmology.

The Sundanese are ethnically of Malay origin and speak a language they call *Basa Sunda* (in English: Sundanese). The language, which bears some influence from Javanese due to frequent contact between the neighboring ethnic groups, uses five different levels of speech (cf. Wessing 1974). Many Sundanese people also use words that have become a part of Bahasa Indonesia, the national language of Indonesia. In addition to the five language levels of Sundanese, many Sundanese use words borrowed from Dutch, English, Javanese, and Betawi, the *patois* unique to Jakarta. Compared with Basa Sunda, Bahasa Indonesia is relatively easy to learn (it has no language levels). Some Sundanese children—particularly in the regional capital city of Bandung—are more comfortable speaking Indonesian than Sundanese, because Indonesian usually is the language of instruction in the schools and is always used on national television. Bahasa Indonesia has become a unifying force only since the 1950s (Anderson 1983:122), and this shift toward using Indonesian came about during the second half of the twentieth century. Urban Sundanese parents express concern about their children facing increasing direction (from politicians, schools, and the media) toward a national rather than regional identity.

Outside the city, many Sundanese subsist on rice farming (Wessing 1984b:729). Rice is unquestionably the most important food for the Sundanese; other foods are considered a side dish. As a result of the importance of rice to the Sundanese, rituals and musical genres performed in honor of the rice goddess, Nyi Pohaci Sanghyang Sri (also known as Déwi Sri) also are used to promote fertility and protection (Baier 1986:52). Among these musical genres are *angklung*, a processional outdoor ensemble that uses shaken bamboo rattles played in interlocking patterns. This and other musical genres associated with rice cultivation are far more common in the rural areas of Sunda (and are not limited to the highland areas) than in Bandung, which has its own outlets for musical expression.

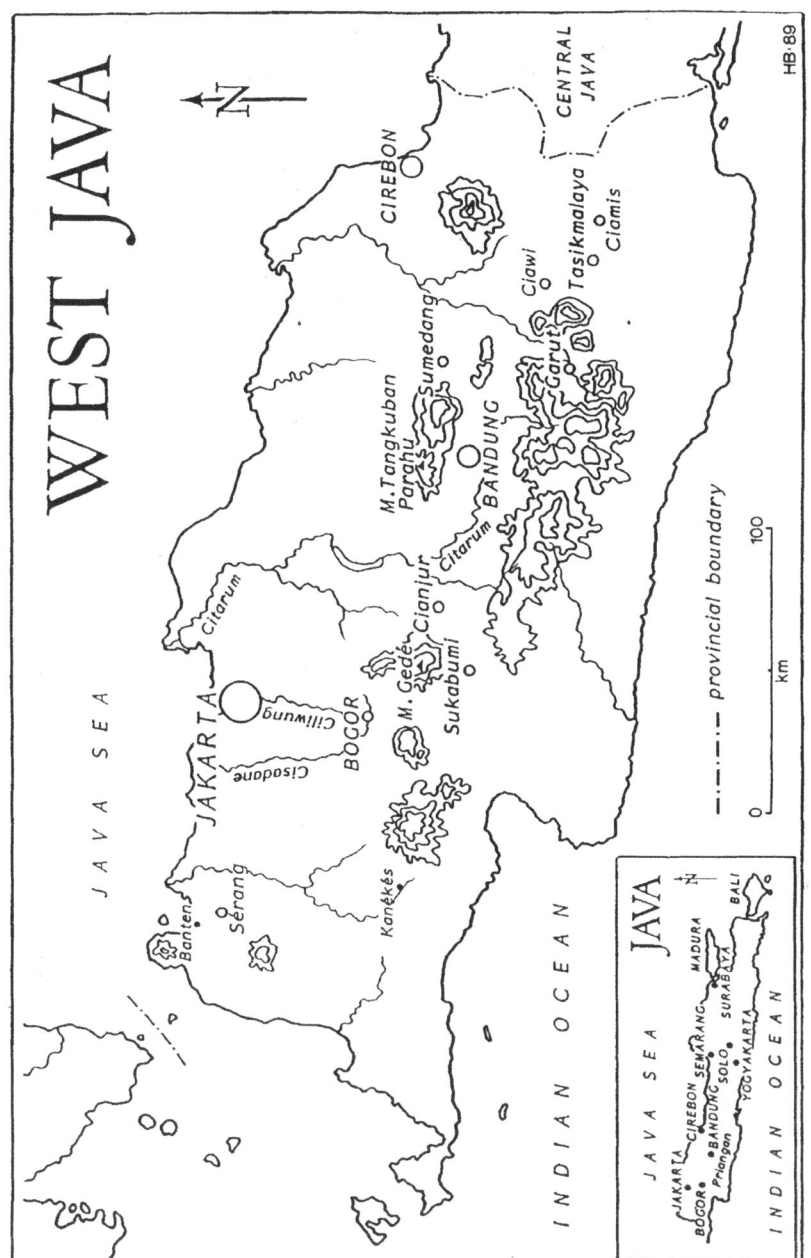

FIGURE 1.1 Map of West Java, Indonesia (courtesy of Dr. Hans Borkent)

Bandung is divided by railroad tracks that run close to the center of the commercial district. On the north side of the tracks are the homes of many of Bandung's wealthiest people (including almost all foreigners) and most of the schools and municipal administrative buildings. On the south side of the tracks are the homes of most of the rest of Bandung's inhabitants: many belong to the lower and middle classes, often settled in housing projects, which consist of small neighborhoods of nearly identical houses that may be leased from the government for a small monthly fee. Streets within the projects are often named so that they are similar in association. For example, one entire project has streets named for Sundanese musical instruments and tuning systems (*Jalan Saléndro, Jalan Suling, Jalan Go'ong, Jalan Kacapi*, etc.). Other sections of Bandung are organized like small villages within the confines of the city; one may find even a small rice field within a crowded neighborhood. Like every other city in Indonesia, Bandung is divided into small administrative districts and subdistricts, and the residents of each district are regulated by minor officials and guarded by neighborhood watchmen.

Bandung has a thriving array of musical genres that coexist not only in the various musical networks that function across the city, but onstage as well. A performance of tembang Sunda may be preceded by a *sisingaan* (lion-dance procession) and followed by a performance of gamelan with vocalists, staged social dancing, or rock and roll. Some of the people who perform tembang Sunda may also perform other musical genres professionally, but most practitioners of tembang Sunda claim primary allegiance to it. The complicated networks connecting tembang Sunda performers with one another and with other musicians are explored further in Part II.

URBANIZATION IN THE SUNDANESE REGION

McTaggart has identified three phases of urban development in Indonesia: the precolonial era (prior to 1600 A.D.), the colonial era (1600 to 1950), and the postcolonial era (1950 to the present; McTaggart 1982:296). The beginnings of tembang Sunda date from the latter part of the colonial era in Sundanese history (approximately the middle of the nineteenth century), at which time there were very few noncolonial cities in West Java. Because of a very low population density, most Sundanese people lived in scattered settlements. The development of Bandung as a colonial administrative city began in earnest after the middle of the nineteenth century, and the relocation of tembang Sunda activity to Bandung occurred in the first several decades of the twentieth century.

Most Sundanese have come through the Indonesian elementary and high school systems with very little understanding of Sundanese history. The reason for this lack of knowledge is that only one curriculum for teaching history is allowed in the primary schools, and national policy emphasizes national (as opposed to local) history at the elementary school level.

Therefore, Sundanese schoolchildren are *not* taught about the Sundanese "golden-era" kingdom of Pajajaran (1333–1579), or the importance of the Tangkuban Prahu volcano to Sundanese mythology, or about any of the deities with whom most rural Sundanese ritual events are associated. According to one prominent historian who asked to remain anonymous, only one version of Indonesian history is allowed to be taught in the schools: the history of the Central Javanese. The statement of this historian, however, is not entirely true; children are also required to learn about Dutch history as it pertains to Indonesian history, about the invasion of the Japanese, and particularly about the struggle for Indonesian Independence.

Many Sundanese recognize and resent the lack of formal education about local history. "The Dutch stole our history, of course," said one musician. "It's all locked up in Holland and now we'll never know what really happened to us." What he was referring to is that much of the local historical research conducted by foreign researchers is not published in Bahasa Indonesia; the relative inaccessibility of these materials to Indonesians interested in their own history is a sore point. Others have invested certain historical figures and events with mythical status, asserting that no historical records concerning these people or places exist (even if they have already been published). This deliberate obscuring of historical facts is particularly true of the time of Pajajaran, which is considered by many Sundanese to be the one time in Indonesian history that Sunda was strong and independent. The kingdom of Pajajaran is explored further in this book not only because of its important historical position but also particularly for what it represents to the Sundanese.

The gap in understanding local historical events is often filled by certain types of expressive culture. For example, the tradition of epic recital (known in Sunda as *pantun*) has a long history in Sunda, and many Sundanese musical traditions play a strong role in the continuing cultural education of Sundanese people, young and old. Part IV, "The Meaning of Tembang Sunda," demonstrates how tembang Sunda performance fills in some of these gaps and provides the Sundanese with a story about themselves and their history.

The Precolonial Era

Wessing points out that one of the difficulties in writing about Sundanese history is that very few historians have paid attention to the area because of its small population and insignificance in relation to the other centers of power (Wessing 1978:8). The Sundanese are currently the second most numerous ethnic group in the country, but their population experienced significant expansion only in the twentieth century. The area now containing the city of Bandung was once a lake surrounded by neolithic settlements (Heins 1977:2). Most Sundanese prior to the early fourteenth century primarily engaged in slash-and-burn or swidden agriculture, which later changed to wet-rice cultivation (Peacock 1973:8). The preference for swidden agriculture, however, persisted into the early twentieth century. A series of small kingdoms rose and fell in the first millennium A.D., but few rose to any prominence or had a strong political impact outside of the area.

One of the exceptions to the relative obscurity of the early Sundanese rulers is the kingdom of Sunda (eleventh–twelfth centuries). This kingdom is believed to have acted partly as a buffer zone between the warring East Javanese kingdom of Singhasari and the Sumatran kingdom of Srivijaya (Wessing 1978:9). Neither of the two Hindu kingdoms (Singhasari or Srivijaya) appears to have laid any extensive claim to the uplands of West Java at that time. The kingdom of Srivijaya, however, which derived most of its power and influence from trade, maintained ports in West Java in the area of Banten (Wessing 1978:9). Srivijaya was later defeated by Kertanegara, the king of Singhasari, who was in turn supplanted by his own son-in-law. Kertanegara's son-in-law, Wijaya, founded the kingdom of Majapahit at the end of the thirteenth century (Peacock 1973:14). The fourteenth century was an important time for artistic achievement among the East and Central Javanese; Majapahit is believed to represent the height of Hindu-Javanese culture (Noorduyn 1978:207). During the fourteenth century, the Sundanese also experienced a measure of power and control that has not occurred since then; it continues to be celebrated in story and song throughout Sunda.

After the fall of Srivijaya, a new kingdom arose that was to become the most important in Sundanese cultural history. Pajajaran was founded in 1333 at Pakuan, near what is now the city of Bogor. The importance of historical Majapahit to the Sundanese of today is that a humiliating blow was delivered to the Sundanese by the king of Majapahit, Hayam Wuruk. According to legend, Hayam Wuruk wanted to marry the daughter of the king of Pajajaran in 1357, probably as a means to bring Pajajaran under his control (Wessing 1978:10). The Sundanese bridal delegation that came to the wedding, however—staying at Bubat, to the north of Majapahit—was not treated with respect by the hosts; instead, they were treated as servants. The Majapahit prime minister, Gajah Mada, felt that the bride was merely brought in tribute (Coedès 1968:239). This resulted in a loss of face for the bride, and the wedding never occurred because the ensuing violence resulted in the death of the king of Pajajaran and his followers. This event and the violent reprisals have remained in the memory of the Sundanese as the beginning of their difficulties with Central Java. Since that time, relations between Sunda and Java have been civil, but strained.

Pajajaran had become powerful partly through trade, which it began to develop after the fall of the Sumatran kingdom of Srivijaya. It remained Hindu, however, while many of the coastal cities had become Islamized by the early sixteenth century, and its inland location prevented it from fully controlling the port towns. By 1525, the newly Islamic port area of Banten had cut off Pajajaran's revenues from trade (Wessing 1978:11). In 1579, Prabu Siliwangi, the last king of Pajajaran, is said to have disappeared without a trace when the Sultan of Banten killed the royal family at Pakuan (Stapel 1930:28). The disappearance of King Prabu Siliwangi led to the belief that he was not actually killed; it is believed that he will eventually return to restore the kingdom of Pajajaran to its former glory. Some Sundanese also feel that the other noblemen of Pajajaran disappeared from Pakuan as well, and that Pajajaran still exists.

Pajajaran was typical of the pre-Islamic Indonesian kingdoms in that its power was defined by its center, not by its periphery (see Anderson 1972: 28). Modern Sundanese never try to define the limits of Pajajaran's rule; rather, they concentrate on discussions of what constituted the center. Similarly, modern Sunda is not defined by its borders but, rather, by its center in the Priangan highlands. Clifford Geertz describes the vanished classical precolonial Indonesian states as the primary shaping factors of modern Indonesian life (Geertz 1980:3). Pajajaran was one such classical state, described in Sundanese songs and stories as *nagara Pajajaran*.

> Negara (*nagara, nagari, negeri*), a Sanskrit loanword originally meaning "town," is used in Indonesian languages to mean, more or less simultaneously and interchangeably, "palace," "capital," "state," "realm," and again "town." It is, in its broadest sense, the word for (classical) civilization, for the world of the traditional city, the high culture that city supported, and the system of superordinate political authority centered there. Its opposite is *desa*—also a Sanskrit loanword—meaning, with a similar flexibility of reference, "countryside," "region," "village," "place," and sometimes even "dependency" or "governed area." Between these two poles, *negara* and *desa*, each defined in contrast to the other, the classical polity developed and, within the general context of a transplanted Indic cosmology, took its distinctive, not to say peculiar, form. (Geertz 1980: 4)

The degree of understanding with which the Sundanese view the events surrounding the rise and fall of Pajajaran is difficult to assess. However, in the minds of the Sundanese, Pajajaran is more an image than a historical kingdom. The connection between Pajajaran and the modern Sundanese is discussed further in Part IV, because the existence of the kingdom of Pajajaran is an important validating feature of Sundanese history celebrated in modern Sundanese urban culture.

The fall of Pajajaran in 1579 roughly coincides with the penetration of Islam into the Sundanese uplands. The officials who were not killed at Pakuan had fallen under the domination of the Sultanate of Banten (Wessing 1993:1–17), located in the northwest end of West Java. The Islamic Central Javanese kingdom of Mataram (which had replaced fallen Majapahit as the center of Javanese power by the late sixteenth century) was then in a position to take over the Sundanese region from the East (Heins 1977:12). Following their annexation by the kingdom of Mataram, the highlands of Sunda were divided by the Central Javanese into four regencies: Bandung, Sumedang, Parakanmuncang and Sukapura (Wessing 1978:11). At this time (mid–seventeenth century), Javanese became the language of politics and commerce in the area (van Zanten 1987:18).

In 1656, all of West Java was divided by Sultan Amangkurat I into twelve regencies, which were administrated by Javanese regents (Heins 1977:14). The regency of Cianjur, which would later see the rise of tembang Sunda, was created later than most of the other regencies, at the end of the seventeenth century (van Zanten 1987:19). The Sundanese area was controlled by the Javanese partly as a measure to prevent the development of another strong and independent Sundanese kingdom but also to supply their own armies with Sundanese men (Heins 1977:14). It was during the middle and latter parts of the seventeenth century that the influence of Central Javanese culture on Sunda was felt most strongly. Heins mentions among these cultural influences the entry of *batik*, *gamelan*, dance, *macapat* (sung poetry), *wayang* puppet theater, and other arts from Central Java (Heins 1977:15; van Zanten 1987:18). The influences of Central Javanese culture on the Sundanese, however, were felt primarily at the upper levels of society (Rosidi 1984:4). The effect of the Javanese on the lower classes was more a process of filtration and selection than change resulting from direct contact. One of the reasons for this dispersed influence is the small numbers and wide distribution of the Sundanese population during the time of Central Javanese influence.

Urbanism in Central Java predates Dutch colonialism. The Sundanese region differed from that of Central Java in that the latter had a much larger, more diverse population than that of Sunda. Inland cities and coastal cities were the main types of Javanese cities. Sometimes referred to as the "court city," the inland Javanese city before 1600 comprised several basic zones: the palace (Indo.: *kraton*), the town square (Indo.: *alun-alun*), the market place (Indo.: *pasar*) near the square, the houses of nobles, and the outer regions where peddlers and poorer people lived (Kroef 1953:563; O'Connor 1983:62; Wertheim 1956:168). The commercial district varied in size and internal organization depending on the proximity of the city to the sea. Whereas inland city dwellers were supported primarily by a rice-based economy supplied by surrounding farmers, the inhabitants of the coastal cities were supplied with goods from India and China (Keyfitz 1976:349).

Early Javanese coastal cities were far more cosmopolitan than inland cities, attracting foreign merchants and artisans (Wertheim 1956:168). The variety of inhabitants and musical tastes in the coastal cities supported entertainment as varied as the number of ethnic groups (cf. Kornhauser 1978: 122). Coastal cities were often organized around particular wealthy businessmen and their families, who became patrons of music. Inland cities tended to be organized around the service of the ruler, and performers often lived within his property (Kroef 1953:566). Thus, by the time the Dutch had become established in Java, these two types of urban areas had already developed distinct musical subcultures based on their respective systems of patronage.

At this time, there were few urban enclaves in the Sundanese highlands, and the population was spread out over large tracts of land. Colonial and regency administrative cities eventually developed in the area. The regency had already been in existence in West Java before the Dutch takeover, because of the placement of Javanese regents as administrators in various parts of Sunda following the annexation of Sunda by Central Java (Heins 1977: 14).

Islam in Sundanese Culture

The majority of ethnic Sundanese are followers of Islam. Even a cursory glance through any neighborhood or village will reveal a mosque (or several), and the calls to prayer are clearly announced through dozens of loudspeakers from dozens of mosques in all directions. Bandung, in particular, is the home of many Islamic schools (from elementary schools through colleges), and some women cover their hair, arms, and legs entirely, in a style that any Muslim would recognize. The fasting month of Ramadan is strictly observed by most Muslims of Bandung; even those with a more casual approach to Islam work hard to keep the fast. Local speech is peppered with Arabic comments, from blessings to curses.

Part of Indonesia's national policy of religious tolerance requires that everyone must declare a religion, indicated on national identity cards. The officially recognized religions in Indonesia are Islam, Christianity, Traditional Belief, Hinduism, and Buddhism. Clifford Geertz has described the inhabitants of Java as dividing into categories of devout Muslim (Indo.: *santri*), hereditary aristocracy (Indo.: *priyayi*), and animist peasant (Indo.: *abangan*) (Geertz 1960b:5). The categories, however, are not as neatly divided as Geertz would have us believe. Many Sundanese shift the degree to which they emphasize their relative "Islamism" depending on the situation; furthermore, multiple levels of spirituality occur in the lives of each individual. It is very common for Sundanese Muslims to hold certain animist beliefs and engage in animist practices on occasion, while at the same time practicing and believing in Islam (see also Wessing 1978:20 about the near-universal claim of "being a good Muslim"). Thomas Gibson correctly points out that local autonomy in Indonesia is quite strong in the face of extensive exposure to what he calls "world systems" of religion, including Islam (2000:45). The complicated layers of belief at work in Sunda do not lend themselves to easy categorization, and Sundanese Islam is often highly individualized.

The rural mountain dwellers of Sunda experienced relatively little influence from the early Hindu-Javanese practices prior to the entry of Islam (Wessing 1984b:728). They were more concerned with their daily lives than with outside political intrigue. Furthermore, although a large area of Indonesia was Hindu-Buddhist during the pre-Islamic period, not all of the Hindu-Buddhist practitioners were members of a single, specific religion. Compared to the relatively unifying characteristics of Islam, the belief systems adhered to by many Indonesians were largely individual combinations of very local animist beliefs and polytheistic Hindu beliefs, depending on the area. The Sundanese were no exception, maintaining a combination of

Hindu and animist beliefs, many of which still have their place in modern Sunda.

> Spirits and ancestors continue to play an important role and are often seen as intermediaries between a person and Allah. Practices such as visits to ancestral and other venerated graves, which survive from pre-Islamic and probably pre-Indianized times, are integrated in such Islamic festivals as Maulud, as are the ritual cleanings of weapons and amulets. The non-Islamic spirit world is either partially Islamized or otherwise integrated into popular belief. (Wessing 1984b: 730)

The first Muslims to arrive in Indonesia were Sufi traders from South Asia—in particular, from the region of Gujarat (Drewes 1968:457; Pacholczyk 1986:4; Robson 1981:272). Were it not for the passage of Islam through India before its entry, the religion might not have gained such strength in Indonesia (Benda 1963:128). Because most of the first Muslims to reach Indonesia were Sufis (Legge 1965:48; Peacock 1973:24), the eventual spread of Islam into the Sundanese region was gradual. The coastal rulers had already welcomed the Sufis, seeing an alignment with Sufis as a means for gaining personal prestige. Furthermore, the cash that began to flow into the hands of the Sundanese élite from agricultural profits enabled these people to be by far the largest group of Indonesians to travel to Mecca in the mid-nineteenth century. At this time, travel increased to and from Europe as a result of the improvement of ship building techniques coinciding with the 1869 opening of the Suez Canal (Peacock 1979:245).

At the local level, the religious teacher was considered a link between local inhabitants and the coastal areas, and in some ways with the rest of the world (Geertz 1960a:230). As a result, Sundanese Islam is quite diverse; on a single street in Bandung or any of the outlying cities, a visitor might encounter anyone from a fundamentalist to someone whose identity card reads "Muslim," but who does not actively practice Islam.

Although Islamic diversity is currently the norm, the Sundanese region has in the past been known as a strongly Islamic area within Indonesia. Furthermore, one of the largest pro-Islam rebellions that ever took place in Indonesia occurred in Sunda. The Dar'ul Islam Rebellion advocated an Islamic State that was to have an *imam* as its religious and political authority (Jackson 1973:14). The rebellion began in 1948 under the leadership of Kartosuwirjo, a Western-educated man who never had any real understanding of either Arabic or Islamic law (Boland 1971:54). The problems inherent in the rebellion were that its members came from widely divergent backgrounds, and that they were drawn to the movement by the charismatic qualities of its leader (Jackson 1973:52). As a result, the group splintered constantly, and most of the rebels were unclear as to the actual direction of the movement.[2]

Since the 1962 execution of the Dar'ul Islam leader Kartosuwirjo, the Sundanese region has not been unified by a single ideology. The lack of communication between Sundanese villages and the corresponding lack of access to printed literature (in part because of an illiteracy rate of 70 percent at least until the mid-1970s) has led to problems in transmission of innovative ideas or expectations through printed means (Jackson 1980:50). Although oral transmission of ideas (through, for example, *wayang golék* puppet theater or pantun epic performance) is common, the messages conveyed during these performances are not always directly connected with Islam. Approximately half of all Sundanese Muslims regularly go to the mosques (Wessing 1984b:730). Among middle-class urbanites, the tendency is to go to the mosques only during Islamic holidays or if the person wants to pray for something. For example, frequency and length of daily prayers (beyond the standard prayers five times a day) increase when someone hopes to win the (now outlawed but still practiced) lottery. This phenomenon is not necessarily a feature of the lives of musicians, but rather an aspect of the lives of many Sundanese.

In the way that Sundanese practitioners of Islam respond to trends in other Islamic areas, Sundanese women generally do not wear veils or cover their hair. In the 1980s, most women were comfortable wearing Western street clothes instead of Islamic leggings and long flowing blouse, or traditional Sundanese dress of long straight skirt and tightly fitting blouse. By the late 1990s, however, a trend developed among the upper-middle classes that linked wearing modified Muslim fashions with being refined.[3] Although Islamic schools abound in Sunda, most children attend regular public schools with other Sundanese children, Chinese-Indonesians, foreigners, and other non-Sundanese Indonesians, particularly in the largest cities. In addition to projecting the call to prayer five times daily, every Sundanese mosque also broadcasts prayers all night during Islamic holy days and offers lectures to the neighborhood on (for example) the importance of bearing and raising children properly. In a sense, the proper behavior of a Muslim is also considered the proper behavior of a Sundanese person; this belief ties in with the belief that being Sundanese means being a Muslim.

Most tembang Sunda performers feel no conflict between descriptions of mythological beings in a song text and their own interpretation of Islam. These performers, however, are generally comfortable with the dichotomy between Hindu and Muslim beliefs in performance. On occasion, a devoutly Muslim woman from the audience might consent to sing at a tembang Sunda performance; however, the text in such a case is carefully selected to reflect Muslim values. The song "Hamdan" is a kawih or fixed-meter vocal piece from outside the tembang Sunda repertoire composed by Mang Koko Koswara. It contains many Arabic words and is semidevotional. "Hamdan" is very often the song of choice for overtly devout women who wish to participate without compromising their Islamic beliefs.[4] For the typical tembang Sunda performer, however, this distinction is irrelevant and "Hamdan" may be performed together with songs about Pajajaran.

Whether Qur'anic chant has influenced tembang Sunda is a subject of debate. Euis Komariah has studied both Qur'anic chant (*pangajian al Qur'an*) and the traditional Sundanese genres of tembang Sunda and kawih. She notes that Qur'anic chant uses completely different parts of the mouth, tongue, and throat, and asserts that vocal production in Qur'anic chant has no influence on vocal production in tembang Sunda. She demonstrated various vowels, consonants, ornaments, and melodic figures to illustrate her point. Ms. Komariah added that chanting the Qur'an is a distinctly foreign style that has nothing to do with Sunda or Sundanese music. In Kartomi's *Matjapat Songs in Central and West Java*, the influence of Islam on Javanese music is discussed: "Qur'an recitations and Islamic incantations remained the property of orthodox religion, having no apparent influence on classical Javanese song apart from the texts, some of which incorporated Islamic religious and moral concepts and Arabic words in the general vocabulary." (Kartomi 1973a:25). These statements about classical singing differ from the opinions of some of the people with whom van Zanten spoke, who "pointed out that to a large extent this singing of Qur'an texts undoubtedly influenced the singing of tembang Sunda" (van Zanten 1987:43). Jaap Kunst also felt that "Sundanese singing seems to have been subject to a fairly strong influence from both Arabian and European singing" (Kunst 1973:357).

Clearly, there is no unified assumption of influence among performers of tembang Sunda. Like most of the minutiae around which musicians engage in daily debates, however, problematizing an issue like the relationship between Qur'anic chant and tembang Sunda highlights a larger issue. In this case, the situation is a microcosmic representation of the position of Islam vis-à-vis the hereditary aristocracy. If all aristocratic roads lead to the Hindu kingdom of Pajajaran, where does Islam fit in? It is possible that as the Sundanese middle class pulls further away from its localized syncretic past and closer to a more nationalized version of Islam, class divisions will begin to more closely reflect differences in religious ideology. Stylistic clues that might link Qur'anic chant and tembang Sunda may be only the beginning of a fruitful study.

The Colonial Era

During the early part of the period in which the Dutch began to colonize Indonesia, only certain parts of the archipelago officially came under Dutch control. The Priangan highlands of Sunda were officially ceded to the Dutch East India Company (Verenigde Oost-Indische Compagnie, or VOC) in 1677 by the ruler of Mataram, who owed the Dutch a favor for their support in putting down a revolt. The trade connections between the VOC and the Sundanese regents were extremely important to the Dutch because of the profits to be obtained from the cultivation of cash crops such as coffee, tea, and indigo.

Dutch power gradually increased during the seventeenth and eighteenth centuries, and urban development in the areas under its control began to accelerate. As cities on the island of Java began to expand in response to increased population and the need for more services, the Dutch sought to design them along European lines (Keyfitz 1976:350). A prime example of a former Dutch colonial city in Indonesia is Batavia, now known as Jakarta. It was established as a trade center on an isolated piece of land in the area of Jacatra, and was modeled after Amsterdam: "It featured the small cobbled streets, the closely built houses, the narrow, stagnant canals with their drawbridges and other features of urban life in seventeenth-century Holland, out of place in a tropical environment." (Kroef 1953:567).

The Dutch idea of a city was unworkable for the swampy coastal areas of Indonesia because of heat, humidity, and inadequate construction techniques. Poor drainage of the canals (still a problem) caused disease and death, and many Dutch eventually had to move from their canalside residences to spacious villas in the countryside, designed after local upper-class Javanese homes (Keyfitz 1976:350). Following the migration of the Dutch to the outer areas of Batavia, many of the poorer Indonesians and Chinese immigrants moved into the deserted homes. This arrangement created the classic colonial city (Kroef 1953:567; Wertheim 1956:171). To the rural population, Batavia was only another place to which to pay taxes, in the form of rice; its impact on the peasants was minimal (Cobban 1974:109). During the nineteenth century, however, enough roads were constructed for European vehicles to connect Batavia with most of the other urban areas in West and Central Java (McTaggart 1982:297) and resort areas for the wealthy (Cobban 1974:137).

One of the most important factors contributing to the ethnic composition of the early colonial cities was the large number of Chinese immigrants from the three southernmost provinces of China: Kwangtung, Fukien, and Kwangsi (Koentjaraningrat 1978:363). The Chinese immigrants formed Chinese neighborhoods within the colonial cities, most frequently in the commercial districts (McTaggart 1982:307). The Dutch favored Chinese nationals (and their descendents) over native Indonesians, in that they were accorded special privileges in the colonial environment enabling them to find adequate housing, develop successful businesses, and obtain a Western-style education (Koentjaraningrat 1978:365). Indonesian cities of the present still include commercial districts run primarily by Chinese-Indonesians (McTaggart 1982:307). Chinese-Indonesians still constitute the majority of the Indonesian merchant class.

The Dutch colonial city developed in Indonesia—distinct from the inland court city—at least partly because of migrants who gathered in specific areas but also because, as the cities grew, they began to absorb some of the surrounding villages (Cobban 1974:405). As village members sold off parts of their land, the city grew around the houses until nothing was left of the original village except its houses in the center. This process gave rise to the inner-city urban village (Indo.: *kampung*).

> One of the characteristics of colonial cities on Java which came to the fore during the last 35 years of Dutch rule was the presence within the boundaries of the urban municipalities of indigenous villages which existed as independent

entities, self-regulating in their internal affairs and whose autonomy was guaranteed by the Dutch East Indian Constitution of 1854. The inclusion of extensive and often populous villages within the boundaries of the cities led to differences in physical attractiveness, population densities, hygienic conditions and standards of living, as well as to variations in the effectiveness of governing authority. (Cobban 1974:403)

The very existence of the kampung is one of the main features of Indonesian cities that contradicts Wirth's hypothesis about the superficial nature of relationships within the city (see Introduction). The kampung is by nature a fictive kinship system (O'Connor 1983:5); relationships developed in the kampung essentially take the place of the village kinship system. In a city with a widely divergent population, such a system is important for survival. In the early eighteenth century, the population of Batavia consisted of Dutch, slaves, Mardijkers, prisoners of war, English, Middle Easterners, South Asians, East Asians, and people from all over the local islands (Cobban 1974:122). Within such a diverse group, each subgroup developed its own enclave within Batavia to cope with the urban lifestyle on its own terms.

As Dutch hegemony over parts of Indonesia was extended, a series of treaties with the rulers of Mataram resulted in the expulsion of the Javanese regents from Sunda in 1705; their replacement by Sundanese hereditary nobility led to a hiatus of direct cultural influences from Central Java (Heins 1977:15). The Dutch presence on Java led to a certain amount of wealth entering the economy, and the immigration of many Chinese resulted in the development of a large merchant class. This merchant class had greater economic advantages, and traditional authority relationships became disrupted, allowing economic centers to develop without the presence of a local Indonesian ruler (O'Connor 1983:68). One such center was the colonial city of Bandung. The city's cool climate and strong economic development led to its Dutch nickname of "Parijs van Java" (the Paris of Java), reflecting its somewhat European colonial atmosphere, particularly among the very wealthy colonial inhabitants and their homes.

Although West Java had many administrative districts previously owing allegiance to Central Java, the colonial administration of the province was primarily centered in Bandung after 1864. Prior to that, it had been in Cianjur, a Sundanese city situated much closer to what is now Jakarta than Bandung. During the colonial period, a Sundanese nobleman who answered to the Dutch administrator in Bandung governed each Sundanese regency. This system corresponds to the precolonial practice common in Southeast Asia of a central administrator wielding power over a number of semi-independent areas (Wessing 1978:11). The Dutch had very little direct contact with the people under their control outside of the administrative representatives. In other words, the regents themselves, rather than the Dutch, wielded the most symbolic power, and were able to maintain all the symbolic vestiges of power, even as the Dutch gained further control over the area.

Regents did well under the Dutch in much of West Java because the areas under their control provided large profits from agricultural production. As a result, these Sundanese noblemen were comparatively wealthy during the nineteenth century and had the time and money to patronize various traditional art forms (Heins 1977:36). This patronage and the desire for a particularly Sundanese form of aristocratic musical expression led to the development of the two main genres of what is now seen as Sundanese classical music, gamelan degung and tembang Sunda (van Zanten 1987:20). Although the direct line to Central Javanese and even European influence had been broken by the Dutch in the treaty of 1705, Javanese influence continued to be felt in the Sundanese regencies where such Javanese trappings as gamelan ensembles, state umbrellas, and carriages became indispensable symbols of power (Heins 1977:35). The Sundanese regencies supported a musical patronage system similar to that of Javanese court cities, in that the musical entertainers were often closely connected to the families of certain noblemen (Heins 1977:58 also mentions the absorption of Central Javanese court behavior by the Sundanese).

The Postcolonial Era

Indonesia declared its independence on August 17, 1945, and won it after a revolution in late 1949, when the Dutch agreed to transfer sovereignty. Indonesian Independence dramatically altered the existing economic system and affected music patronage. The relocation of tembang Sunda to the urban center of Bandung took place gradually before and after independence, and was caused at least partially by the loss of power and wealth of the Sundanese regents. One of the major changes following Indonesian Independence was that the position of Sundanese regent was no longer hereditary but was instead appointed by the new government. Existing patronage systems were disrupted by this change, causing musicians to seek employment elsewhere. Although many performers chose to remain in the outlying areas, others moved to Bandung in search of greater financial opportunities.

Many Sundanese musicians believe that the shift of the center of tembang Sunda to Bandung from Cianjur began some time before independence, in the first few decades of the twentieth century. Several spoke of the need for local officials in the colonial administration to travel frequently to Bandung to take care of business concerning the area under their control. On occasion, small groups of musicians accompanied these officials. It is believed that some of these musicians were engaged to teach tembang Sunda in Bandung and that its establishment there evolved gradually as the city became more important as an economic and cultural center. Bandung was a center for the development of other Sundanese arts in the nineteenth century, and tembang Sunda evenings were held there as well, setting the stage for further development after independence.

The mountainous district of Sunda known as the Priangan has several administrative regencies. Currently the most populous of these regencies, Bandung has over three million inhabitants and has been the administrative center of the province of West Java for over one hundred years. During the growth and gradual modernization of Bandung over that time, the city has developed into a composite of small homogeneous villages, similar to the kampungs of Jakarta. Whereas Jakarta has attracted people from all over Indonesia and around the world, Bandung has primarily attracted people throughout West Java. Bandung's various kampung populations include people come from the smaller regional Sundanese cities of Garut, Subang, or Ciamis—just as in Jakarta there are Chinese, Ambonese, and even wealthy European and American kampungs. Similarly, though everything in Bandung is on a smaller scale than Jakarta, economic opportunities for migrants from outside Bandung are just as attractive to the Sundanese as those in Jakarta are to people from the outer islands or from outside the country.

When a Sundanese villager moves to Bandung, he is able to take advantage of the prior establishment of these ethnic enclaves in the city, and can work his way into a series of networks in Bandung based on whom he knows from the village. The new migrants who take advantage of existing urban networks enhance the strength of these social ties in the city.

> Kinsmen became important contacts from whom the migrant can expect limited hospitality when he first arrives and with whom he may continue a relationship if interaction is rewarding. This element of greater choice is critical in urban kinship. With alternate means of making a living, finding housing or a spouse, and creating friendships, kin relationships are not as obligatory in the city as in the village. They are, however, an important social and economic resource to the migrant or the city dweller. (Friedl and Chrisman 1975:15)

The musicians who moved to Bandung after their sponsors were no longer able to support them took advantage of those social and kin ties to resettle themselves and their families. Through social connections and other networks available to musicians, these players and singers worked their way into employment as musicians in Bandung. The addition of more singers and instrumentalists to the musical pool has acted as a centripetal force, so much so that most promising young tembang Sunda musicians have migrated to Bandung to further their musical experience either formally or informally. The historical events that shaped the region created in Bandung a colonial administrative city that is now under the administration of the Sundanese and, peripherally, the Indonesian national government.

Certain features are essential to the function of Bandung and other major Sundanese cities as the centers of Sundanese activities. The fact that each center has its own large market or markets, commercial districts, and government buildings indicates a measure of independence for each place. Bandung, although it takes its national direction from Jakarta, is fairly independent from the nation's capital and is known for occasionally being ahead of Jakarta in fashion and in modern developments. For example, for a period of approximately eight years between the mid-1980s and 1990s, Bandung boasted what was reputedly the best disco in all of Southeast Asia, complete with laser shows, brilliant spinning lights, and fancy mirrors. Dozens of people in Jakarta made the six-hour drive to Bandung every weekend, just to experience its disco. Much of the capital for this development came from Jakarta-based firms, and also from a few multinational corporations. The factors (such as local economic strength) that shaped Bandung's post-independence development have continued to draw new residents and new musicians as well.

Krismon: The Economic Crisis of the 1990s

Indonesia was being hailed as one of Asia's economic "tigers" by the early 1990s. With unemployment figures declining, major foreign investment from such multinational companies as Nike, Shell, and others, and a relative degree of prosperity echoed by increasing levels of education, Indonesia seemed ripe for economic expansion. But, in 1997, what began as an economic meltdown in Thailand gradually spread to other nations, including Japan and Indonesia, where the rupiah collapsed in a matter of months. Then-President Suharto, long suspected of filling the deep pockets of his children and close allies in the government, in early 1998 became the target of student protesters who demanded his resignation over issues of corruption and the falling value of the rupiah. Although most of the protesting took place in Jakarta and Surabaya, Bandung (as an important university town) was also the site of massive demonstrations by students and, in some cases, their professors as well. In a stunning series of events that took some of the outside media by surprise, Suharto was ousted after over three decades of power, and was replaced in May 1998 by B. J. Habibie, a former protégé.

The dramatic fall of the rupiah and the economic crisis of 1998 led to food shortages, violence in the streets,[5] extraordinary price hikes, and the collapse of the once-healthy urban patronage system for music. The prices for rice and cooking oil, the two most important staples, soared to over ten times their previous rate. Young couples postponed weddings (a major source of employment for musicians), and legions of private employees lost their jobs nearly overnight. The neologism *krismon*—a truncated version of the Indonesian words *krisis moneter* or monetary crisis—became the watchword for anyone invited to contribute money or do something interesting: *Saya lagi monitor* (Indo.: "I'm monitoring [my finances]"). The phrase was also used to justify not hiring musicians for events large and small, public and private.

The crisis sharply revealed one of the undercurrents of the Sundanese economic system, in which one wealthy patron might take care of dozens, sometimes hundreds, of dependents. Many Sundanese are beholden to one or more wealthy person(s), meaning that they have a service-exchange relationship. If, for example, the son of a family friend or distant relative shows up at the door, offering to be of service (and then performing useful tasks for the patron), that person has the right to expect health care for himself and his family. Similarly, musicians who all operate under the umbrella of a single musical patron expect to be at least partly taken care of when a crisis strikes. The crisis of the late 1990s struck so hard, however, that many of the musical patrons themselves discovered their assets frozen at the bank and their ability to receive credit severely diminished.

The former President Habibie, once a government minister who reportedly had twice turned down offers to be vice president, had a good reputation among some Sundanese aristocratic musicians because of his apparent deep enjoyment of and appreciation for Sundanese music. The sympathy he received from some of the wealthier Sundanese showed promise of trickling down to the middle and lower classes, but his time in office was limited because of his promise to hold democratic elections before the year 2000. The current president, Abdurrahman Wahid, is an intellectual who oversaw the difficult transition to the twenty-first century, a period marked with violence, increasingly vocal political debates and a spate of local independence movements. Indonesians now speak more comfortably about the climate of reformation (Indo.: *reformasi*) and look forward to more stability, not only of the rupiah and of marketplace prices, but of their daily lives.[6]

The economic havoc at the end of the twentieth century and beginning of the twenty-first made life difficult for professional Sundanese musicians, and for those whose music work supplements their day jobs. In tembang Sunda circles, musicians still came to rehearsals and singers still practiced the usual repertoire, but a distinct atmosphere of hiatus prevailed. It was hoped that the economic crisis would end soon, and that weddings and other employment opportunities would reappear quickly. It took the staging of a major tembang Sunda competition in 1999, however, for confidence to return to the performers of the genre. After that major event and the simultaneous lightening of the monetary crisis, performance life began to return to normal, with tembang Sunda musicians being hired once more to perform at weddings and other life-cycle events. The economic crisis left many musicians—especially instrumentalists—with very little in the way of financial resources to support themselves or their families.

2

The Antecedents of Tembang Sunda

This chapter includes a discussion of the processes that led to the development of tembang Sunda as it is performed today and a description of its original performance setting. The end of the chapter also offers a brief overview of some related vocal styles to distinguish tembang Sunda from the rest of Sundanese vocal music. In attempting to reconstruct how the music was performed in the late nineteenth and early twentieth centuries, I draw on early recordings, verbal accounts from older performers, and aspects of rural performance practice. We cannot, assume an exact recreation of the genre based on what it is like now in Cianjur however. Researchers on urban music deal with this issue in many areas of the world (see, for example, Coplan 1982:117). In attempting to understand the earliest forms of tembang Sunda, we may better understand its urban offspring.

The earliest name for the genre was *Cianjuran*—something that comes from Cianjur. As a result of the formal acknowledgment of this genre as regional—and no longer local—during a conference held in 1962 (Wiratmadja 1964:107), its name was changed from Cianjuran to tembang Sunda. A name change needs years to take hold, however, and many of the older people who practice the genre—especially those who live outside of Bandung—still use the term *Cianjuran*. Others use the term *mamaos* ("reading"), a refined Sundanese word originally applied only to the free-rhythm songs within tembang Sunda. Some of the older performers combine the terms, calling the genre *tembang Sunda Cianjuran*.

EARLY MUSICAL DEVELOPMENT

The exact origin of tembang Sunda is unclear. It appears to have been influenced by several other Sundanese genres, among them pantun, *beluk*, and gamelan (Sukanda 1983:8). What is clear, however, is the influence of Mataram culture on the Sundanese poetic meters known as *pupuh*. These meters are thoroughly discussed by the Sundanese, not only in the literature but also among the practitioners, and nearly every performer recognizes the Javanese legacy. It is generally acknowledged that tembang Sunda was developed at the home of the regent (*bupati*) of Cianjur. Furthermore, the peak of its development occurred during the time that the bupati Raden A. A. Kusumaningrat of Cianjur was in charge of that regency or *kabupaten*. Kusumaningrat, who is more commonly known as Dalem Pancaniti, was the regent from 1834 through 1864 (Sukanda 1983:17). A member of the Javanese aristocracy (Raden Mas Natayuda) taught Kusumaningrat's daughters to dance in Solonese style and to sing Javanese *tembang macapat*. He is also said to have contributed several poems to the repertoire (Ernst Heins, as quoted by van Zanten 1989:22).

At the time of the early development of tembang Sunda, Javanese was the language in use among the aristocracy in Sunda. Even though the Javanese had been expelled as regents by the Dutch treaty of 1705, the Javanese had been considered more cultured and of a higher status than the Sundanese—even by the Sundanese aristocracy themselves. The use of Javanese sung poetic meters at the aristocratic level was, therefore, appropriate. By the time tembang Sunda had become established during the era of Dalem Pancaniti in the mid–nineteenth century, however, the Dutch treaty with Mataram had already ensured that Sundanese political connections with Central Java were severed. This breaking off of connections between the Sundanese and the Javanese was an effective means of ensuring that the two groups did not unite against the Dutch. The use of the Sundanese language and the assertion of local (as opposed to Javanese) culture among the Sundanese aristocracy were just becoming important issues in the mid–nineteenth century, and tembang Sunda was one of the most important tools among the aristocracy for strengthening a sense of Sundanese identity. Some songs in the tembang Sunda repertoire still show Javanese influence (*kajawénan*); among them are songs using Javanese words and ornamentation, such as "Bergola," "Langendria," and "Cirebonan."

The Sundanese scholar Enip Sukanda, who interviewed many of the older people of Cianjur, believes that both tembang Sunda and pantun were known in Cianjur well before the middle of the nineteenth century, and that the roots of tembang Sunda were already in place as early as the end of the seventeenth century (Sukanda 1983:19). Van Zanten places its beginnings at the end of the eighteenth century or beginning of the nineteenth (van Zanten 1987:20). Even if the genre had already begun to develop before 1850, however, Dalem Pancaniti is believed to have been the preeminent sponsor of tembang Sunda, because, through his own energy, interest, and wealth, he directly encouraged the musicians under his employ to devote time to developing the genre and composing new songs (Sukanda 1983:20).

The musical influence of the Dutch on the early development of tembang Sunda was practically nil; however, they drew up the 1705 treaty expelling the Javanese regents from Sunda and established Sundanese hereditary aristocracy in place of the Javanese, thereby setting the stage for the development of aristocratic Sundanese arts. The Dutch also were responsible for the large profits accorded to Sundanese regents from the Cultivation System (Dutch: *Cultuurstelsel*) in place in the nineteenth century.[1] Because of these two important aspects of Sundanese history, the Dutch were responsible for establishing the original context of the Sundanese regents and making them wealthy, leading to the development of tembang Sunda and its subsequent patronage by the regents.[2]

Dalem Pancaniti's appreciation for music led to the active sponsorship and further development of many musical forms. In his fostering of tembang Sunda, he is said to have brought together mostly the educated members of the aristocracy (including his immediate family members) at a special place in his home, creating new songs (Sukanda 1983:22). As these members of the aristocracy spent night after night working on songs, singing to the accompaniment of local instrumentalists, the basic structure—both musical and social—of tembang Sunda fell into place. That is, the composers and singers themselves belonged to the aristocracy, and the supporting instrumentalists did not. The historical emphasis on the aristocratic element in the singing of tembang Sunda is one of the factors that separates those who sing the music and those who play it today, and it is an issue that causes ongoing tension and debate among singers and instrumentalists.

PANTUN EPIC NARRATIVE PERFORMANCE

The nineteenth-century musicians used for the instrumental support of tembang Sunda were performers of pantun, a Sundanese narrative form interspersed with songs and accompanied by plucked zither (kacapi). The earliest written reference to pantun dates from the early sixteenth-century work *Sanghyang Siksakandang ng Karesian* (Danasasmita 1981:14); however, it was probably performed much earlier. Pantun texts center on events in the fourteenth-century Sundanese kingdom of Pajajaran, and also on stories of Sundanese ancestral deities. In its most traditional form of performance, a blind man accompanies himself on the kacapi in the *pélog* tuning. The *saléndro* tuning on the kacapi in pantun accompaniment also has been in use at least since the early 1940s (Weintraub 1990:66). On occasion, a second performer may accompany the recitation on the *tarawangsa*, a bowed lute

on in the area of Sumedang. Pantun is primarily associated with
nt of rituals, such as circumcisions, festivities to celebrate a
rvest, a baby's first haircut, or a *selamaton* (ritual feasting cel-
...un).[3]

The influence of pantun on the development of tembang Sunda was very strong, not only because both pantun and tembang Sunda use the instrument most closely associated with Sundanese musical history. Songs of the *papantunan* ("similar to pantun") style within tembang Sunda are believed to be the earliest songs of the genre, so much so that—according to Enip Sukanda (1983:22)—they used to be referred to in Cianjur as *lagu-lagu Pajajaran* ("songs of Pajajaran"). Both the pantun playing style on the kacapi and pantun songs are used in papantunan performance (see Chapter 8 for examples of kacapi playing style). Papantunan lyrics and several song titles are in many cases derived directly from songs interspersed with pantun narratives (Wibisana et al. 1976:737; van Zanten 1987:33–34; van Zanten 1993). For example, the pantun songs "Mupu Kembang," "Pangapungan," and "Kulu-Kulu" are standards in the current repertoire. The pantun song "Jemplang" is a possible origin for the entire *jejemplangan* ("like jemplang") style.

Rosidi's 1973 article ("My Experiences in Recording Pantun Sunda") includes an outline of the difficulties of trying to make good, transcribable recordings of pantun. Rosidi also warns of the rapid disappearance of pantun due to "bad influences" from the city, such as transistor radios, which are believed to corrupt traditional epic narration because pantun performers imitate the performance style heard on the radio (Rosidi 1973b:106). Pantun is also said to be too slow to keep up with the rhythms of urban life.

> Even as a form of recreation, the pantun is not tuned to the times; it is not lively and dynamic enough, it is too serene. The audience has to listen quietly and attentively to the story and the melody as chanted by the bard; these have come to be seen as monotonous and even boring. The only pantun-lovers are the older people who still feel a certain emotional attachment to ancient stories or perhaps just to the past. (Rosidi 1973b:106)

According to current research on pantun, however, the genre has subdivided into a multiplicity of styles (Weintraub 1990:108). Principal among these is the style developed by Mang Beton, an innovator who has shortened the time required for pantun performances, and has made other changes in performance practice. Pantun may still be heard all over Sunda, more frequently in the villages than in the urban environment. The performers who play *pantun beton* (after Mang Beton) are not representative of everything going on in pantun today but of only one of many pantun styles. Pantun beton is the style that most clearly demonstrates the impact of urban influences.

In the process of pantun urbanization, the epic narration is shortened, more songs are inserted, and the entire performance may last only a few hours instead of from the early evening until dawn. Some urban performers of pantun now use a female *pasindén* (vocalist), or even perform with a gamelan ensemble. Traditional pantun is still quite common in village areas outside of Bandung, and—according to Weintraub—the genre appears to be experiencing continual change and development (Weintraub 1990:107–113).

TEMBANG SUNDA BEFORE INDONESIAN INDEPENDENCE

After the initial flourishing of tembang Sunda under the patronage of Dalem Pancaniti in the mid–nineteenth century, the regents following him continued his tradition of patronage. Performances took place in a small building set slightly apart from the home of the regent. The earliest practitioners of tembang Sunda performed short suites of free-rhythm (mamaos) songs, most often of the papantunan and jejemplangan style (see Chapter 7 for an explanation of the stylistic divisions), and song topics were usually historic and spiritual. Very brief instrumental postludes played on the kacapi and suling followed these groups of songs. Performers added texts to these brief closing pieces toward the end of the nineteenth century and the beginning of the twentieth century, leading to the development of the *panambih* ("additional") songs that close tembang sets today.

At approximately the same time, other members of the Sundanese aristocracy were introduced to tembang Sunda through visits to or from Cianjur and through the efforts of Raden Étjé Madjid Natawiredja (d. 1928),[4] who is believed to have frequently left Cianjur to visit the other regents at the request of these regents (Sukanda 1983:34), but against the wishes of his patron, Raden Prawira Diredja II (1864–1910). In addition to teaching the other regents' families to perform tembang Sunda, Raden Étjé Madjid also taught dance and gamelan degung. He seems to be the one musician from that period within living memory of many of the oldest performers, and the one to whom most musicians accord responsibility for the spread of tembang Sunda throughout the Priangan (highland) area of Sunda. He brought tembang Sunda to the regencies of Tasikmalaya, Garut, Sumedang, and Ciamis, and particularly to Bandung (Sukanda 1983:34). Raden Étjé Madjid's students carried on his attempts to spread tembang Sunda across the rest of the Priangan.

Most of the first singers of tembang Sunda were male, and all instrumentalists were male. Women also sang tembang Sunda, however, even from the earliest days of the genre. The first important female vocalist of tembang Sunda was Raden Siti Sarah of Cianjur (Sukanda 1983:31), who worked with a small group of specialists at the home of Raden Prawira Diredja II in the latter part of the nineteenth century. The number of women performing tembang Sunda increased significantly after the 1950s. Some musicians point to the mass media as the reason for the eventual shift in the vocal performance of the genre from men to women, because cassettes sell more effectively if women are featured on the covers. Cassettes did not really become popular, however, until the 1960s and 1970s. Women rarely play the instruments associated with tembang Sunda professionally, although exceptions include the late Ibu Haji Siti Rokhayah (1915–1981), and Rina Oesman, who has performed kacapi and tembang professionally since the 1980s.

In the early twentieth century, the activities and difficulties related to the Indonesian War of Independence significantly curtailed tembang Sunda activity. Because Indonesian Independence brought about major financial changes in the lives of the aristocracy, tembang Sunda musicians associated with these aristocratic families suddenly found themselves without any means of support. In the 1950s, the genre went through a significant period of regrouping. The Daya Mahasiswa Sunda (an organization of Sundanese students) held one of the first official tembang Sunda competitions in the 1950s (see Chapter 3, "Contexts for Performance"). With the resettlement of tembang Sunda musicians and the general shift in tembang Sunda activity to the city of Bandung, the genre underwent more changes as a result of urbanization (which will be discussed more thoroughly in Part II).

EVIDENCE FROM EARLY RECORDINGS

The old recordings on which these conclusions are based date mostly from the 1920s and 1930s. Many of the first singers recorded by Odeon and other companies were the students of Raden Étjé Madjid. One preliminary conclusion about early tembang Sunda performance practice is that the pitch level of song performance was considerably higher than it is today. Van Zanten has measured many of the old recordings and found that the relative pitch is between 300 and 500 cents higher (approximately between a minor third and a perfect fifth) than most modern tembang Sunda performances. This overall lowering of pitch during the twentieth century has caused some significant changes within vocal ornamentation, instrumental performance practice, and song composition. Some of these changes also correspond to certain features of modernization and urbanization, such as the use of sound systems, which have enabled those singers with even the quietest voices to be heard over long distances.

One of the most striking changes in vocal ornamentation that stands out clearly in the old recordings is the use of the technique known as *jenghak*. The jenghak technique (see Chapter 8) is a manipulation of the break between chest voice and falsetto. During a melodic line, the voice breaks upward into falsetto very briefly, as high as a major third above the sung pitch but usually just one step or a half step higher. In the oldest recordings of tembang Sunda, the jenghak technique occurs quite frequently. Furthermore, the falsetto pitch to which the singers jump during the jenghak is not strongly controlled or even necessarily within the tuning system. It is not a question of whether the singers in these recording were good vocalists or not; the ones used for this study were acknowledged as being among the best and studied directly with Raden Étjé Madjid. If the overall pitch level was once considerably higher, singers would have to go into falsetto to produce some of the highest notes. Using jenghak is one way in which a singer can reach high pitches without forcing the chest voice. In modern tembang Sunda performance practice, the overall pitch is low enough so that the highest pitches in a song are not only easily accessible but can be emphasized with a strong, short vibrato known as *beubeutan* (see Chapter 8).

Another vocal ornament that seems to be used much more liberally in older recordings is the slide or *lengkung* ornament. Overemphatic use of the lengkung in modern tembang Sunda performance practice results in a laughing accusation of singing in kawih style. The lengkung occurs in many, if not most of the older songs, however. The old performance of lengkung is long and drawn out, sliding very slowly down to the next pitch. In modern performance practice, the lengkung is quite brief.

The famous tembang vocalist Euis Komariah began studying in 1987 with a very elderly Cianjur man named Cucu, whose style of tembang Sunda is called *Bojong Herang* (named for a district in Cianjur) and includes only thirty songs of the papantunan and jejemplangan styles. Bojong Herang style and its more modern counterpart, *Pasar Baru* ("New Market"), are derivatives of the old style of singing in Cianjur. Cucu first began studying in the 1920s, and his style reflects many of the qualities found on the old recordings. Some features no longer belonging to modern tembang Sunda performance practice were once considered important. Cucu was very firm about the type and amount of dynamic pressure to use in the songs. He also would emphatically speak the word "geus!" ("done!") at the ends of phrases. In modern performances, no singer speaks during the course of a song, and performers try to incorporate more subtle shifts in dynamics than one hears in older recordings. One other change that Cucu has noted is that singers were not in the habit of using notebooks with lyrics the way they do now, because "so few songs were used at the time" (Cucu, personal communication, 1987).

The general timbre of the voices on older recordings is more shrill (*lengking*) than is acceptable in modern performance practice.[5] It is possible, however, that the shrill timbre of the old style of singing is a feature of the higher pitch orientation. Until early in the twentieth century, many aristocratic Sundanese still regarded the Central Javanese way of doing things as the best—from dress to language to musical performance practice—and the Javanese way of singing for court music is indeed very high-pitched. It is also possible that a deliberate change in vocal timbre was made sometime during the twentieth century as part of an overall move away from Javanese culture toward an assertion of Sundanese identity.

Some musicians concluded that the high pitch of former tembang Sunda performance practice was due to the lack of microphones and sound systems. Without microphones, people had to sing at a high pitch and volume in order to be heard. If the original setting of tembang Sunda was a fairly small room, however, the use of high-pitched singing purely for the purposes of sound transmission would be unnecessary. It is possible that people have begun to select lower-pitched songs more frequently (to avoid sounding "noisy," in the words of several singers) since the advent of sound systems; however, this idea does not necessarily point to an overall lowering of pitch.

The very fine tembang Sunda vocalist Yayah Rochaeti Dachlan is known for her high-pitched range, and says that the lowering of pitch has caused her to be at a distinct disadvantage. She has difficulty reaching most of the low notes, and states that one of the biggest problems with microphones is that a singer's inability to reach low pitches is just as clearly revealed as if he or she had made a mistake. Fortunately, a singer can use a microphone to cheat on the low pitches by simply singing a low breathy note not necessarily on the accurate pitch.

One of the most important aspects of low-pitched singing throughout Sunda is that it is associated with relatively high status (Kusumadinata 1969: 18–19). That is, the songs that include low pitches are considered deeper in musical "weight" (*beubeut*). The Sundanese have in some ways experienced a conscious rejection of certain musical features considered Javanese, such as high-pitched singing, particular types of vibrato, and what they refer to as lengking vocal timbre.[6] By rejecting those features felt to be associated with the Javanese, Sundanese performers of tembang Sunda assert their cultural identity through musical performance practice.

A striking difference in kacapi playing between the older and newer recordings of tembang Sunda is that the low strings on the kacapi are rarely played in the older style. The kacapi's three lowest strings are emphasized as grounding elements in today's performance practice; in the old style of playing, the pitches on the upper strings guided the singer. It is possible that the use of low-pitched strings simply represents the full use of technological changes in kacapi construction, or that the use of low-pitched strings is a response to the overall lowering of the pitch during the twentieth century. Furthermore, when the kacapi is played in *tandak* (fixed-rhythm) style in the accompaniment of a free-rhythm vocal line, the stability of the tempo varies considerably in the older recordings. In modern kacapi playing, the player must keep a steady tempo during the tandak ostinato patterns, even though the vocalist is singing in free rhythm. The kacapi player who does not keep a steady tempo is ridiculed and replaced by one who can.

According to Burhan Sukarma, suling (bamboo flute) playing in the old recordings includes more melodic improvisation than would currently be acceptable in tembang Sunda (Sukarma, personal communication, 1990). It is probable that the greater freedom for improvisation in the early days of tembang Sunda stems from the fact that there was very little musical communication between the different regencies except at the beginning of the century through the teachings of Raden Étjé Madjid. Until tembang Sunda was performed on the radio and cassettes and became available to any suling player, many suling performers were freer to accompany a singer in whatever manner they liked. The codification of suling performance practice has really occurred only since the 1970s, when cassette production and access provided a standard against which other players would be judged.

RELATED VOCAL GENRES

In addition to tembang Sunda, musicians and vocalists perform several other types of music that bear some relevance to the study of tembang Sunda. But none of them is used to express Sundanese cultural identity in exactly the way tembang Sunda is used. Among these related vocal genres are *Cigawiran*, beluk, kawih, and *kliningan*. Only the latter two have been extensively recorded by Bandung's cassette industry. Although many Sundanese musicians support the documentation of disappearing genres, few are willing to seek out the older village musicians or to attempt the documentation process themselves.[7]

Cigawiran is sometimes included in the category of tembang Sunda because of similarities in the singing style (Supandi 1976a:33). It is sung unaccompanied and, therefore, does not correspond to one of the most basic and important features of modern tembang Sunda—that it must be accompanied at least by a kacapi, even if the other instruments are absent. Cigawiran is the vocal performance of primarily religious pupuh (Javanese-derived poetic meters), although the lyrics may also contain governmental material, such as lectures on family planning. The most important function of Cigawiran, however, is to spread the message of Islam (Supandi 1976: 33). The only known recording of Cigawiran is on the cassette tape available with Wim van Zanten's book *Sundanese Music in the Cianjuran Style* (1989). Most Cigawiran songs are found in villages, sung in saléndro tuning, and appear to reflect some influence from Qur'anic recital (pangajian al Qur'an) in the vocal ornamentation. Supandi (1976a:34) provides an example of Cigawiran lyrics in the following song in Sundanese, which includes an Arabic phrase in the first line.

Lailahailalahu	There is no God but God
Teu aya sembaheun abdi	There is no veneration from me
Iwal mung ti ka Pangeran	Except only to the Prince
Ka Gusti nu ngan sahiji	To the One and Only God
Jeung Kangjeng Nabi Muhammad	And Kangjeng Nabi Muhammad
Utusan Gusti Illahing.	Envoy of the God Almighty.

The unaccompanied Sundanese village vocal form known as beluk is read and sung by groups of men (and occasionally women), who take turns performing *wawacan* or long stories written in Javanese macapat poetic meters (Sukanda 1983:10). Texts used for performances of beluk are written in the old Sundanese script or, occasionally, in Arabic (Sukanda 1978:1). Its range is high for men and it is sung in a loud manner, using vocal slides and glottal stops. The purpose given for the high vocal range and loud dynamics is that beluk was originally intended to frighten away wild animals who could come out of the forest to steal children (Mitra Sunda 1988:1). Early beluk performers were dry rice cultivators, practicing slash-and-burn agriculture near forests (Sukanda 1983:10).

Beluk is primarily performed at night in connection with birth and the first several months of life as the people guarding the first forty days of the baby's life keep themselves awake (Supandi 1985:23; Mitra Sunda 1988:2). It is difficult to assess the influence of beluk upon the early development of tembang Sunda, although Atik Supandi notes the roots of tembang in beluk (Supandi 1976:2). Although Sukanda describes it as one of the vocal styles forming the basis of tembang Sunda (1983:11), he does not describe exactly how it influenced the genre. It is believed, however, that the relatively few people who worked close to the regent's home entertained themselves by singing beluk (Sukanda 1983:19). Beluk was performed by at least one member of the aristocracy, Raden Wasitareja (younger brother of then regent, Bupati Enoh Wiratanu VI [1776–1813], and influential grandfather of Dalem Pancaniti), which indicates that it was not restricted to the lower classes (Sukanda 1983:19).

According to Sukanda, the term *kawih* is an originally Sundanese word (Sukanda 1983). In the early-sixteenth-century Sundanese palm-leaf manuscript *Sanghyang Siksakandang ng Karesian*, the word *kawih* appears several times as a generic term for vocal music, followed by identifying words that distinguish the various subgenres (Danasasmita 1981:14). Several sources indicate that the Baduy people of West Java (the most strictly traditional and isolationist of all the Sundanese) use the term kawih to describe pantun recital (van Zanten 1989:15).

Kawih describes not only a type of accompanied vocal music in fixed rhythm, but also the style of kacapi playing that accompanies it. Kawih songs generally contain much less ornamentation than mamaos (free-rhythm) songs, are not composed using strict poetic forms, and are considered much easier to sing than mamaos. They may be used after the mamaos section of a tembang Sunda set to conclude it. Indeed, many panambih songs are also called kawih, and the precise distinction between the two is not always clear. When a gamelan degung or kacapian ensemble accompanies kawih songs, the songs are pitched much higher than when they are accompanied by a tembang Sunda ensemble. Although men are restricted by standard performance practice from singing panambih in performances of tembang Sunda, they may sing kawih in other contexts. For example, men sing kawih when accompanied by instruments other than those used in the tembang Sunda ensemble. Kawih is also used to describe songs of the pop Sunda repertoire when gamelan degung or other pélog ensembles accompany them.

For kacapi accompaniment of kawih, the players grow their nails long on both hands so that they can produce a metallic sound when striking the strings of the kacapi. The instrument is usually a kacapi siter, or flat-board zither with two extra (lower-pitched) strings. Playing in kawih style requires much more melodic activity by the left hand of the player than kacapi tembang. The left hand performs countermelodies without being restricted to the lower strings, or to a purely supportive function as in the free-meter style frequently used on the kacapi tembang. This more elaborate style of kacapi playing was popularized—though not invented—by kawih-style composer Mang Koko Koswara, who developed it as a means for attracting the attention of the rapidly urbanizing Sundanese youth. Mang Koko's kawih compositions are heavily arranged and sometimes include changes in tempo and texture; therefore, not all kawih songs may be used as panambih in tembang Sunda performances. Since the death of Mang Koko, many new composers of kawih and kacapian have risen in prominence, and one segment of the population listens almost exclusively to kawih rather than to tembang.

Kliningan is usually accompanied by gamelan saléndro, which is also used in wayang golék and dance. Kliningan (sometimes called *sindénan*) uses a different vocal style from that of tembang Sunda, in that it has a more strident, nasal tone. It is also generally sung at a higher pitch. The status of kliningan singers was historically somewhat lower than that of tembang Sunda or degung kawih singers. Urban singers who alternate kliningan with other styles—or who perform with dance groups at government functions—have had a role in the upward shift of their status to a level on a par with gamelan degung and tembang Sunda vocalists. Songs from the wayang golék repertoire (known as *kakawén*) may be found in saléndro performances of tembang Sunda. Most urbanites do not distinguish between the vocal genres, calling them all kawih, sindénan, or kliningan.

Throughout the historical development of tembang Sunda, one can observe the interest its practitioners had in distancing themselves not only from their neighbors the Javanese but also from their own village roots. The interesting shift in pitch level during the middle of the twentieth century, which seems to have occurred *after* the musicians left the rural areas for Bandung, reflects a focus on the idea of preserving a musical style for the aristocracy in a climate where the previously existing hierarchies were being undermined. In the chaos following Indonesian Independence, as new alliances were formed and new networks were established in Bandung, members of the aristocracy found new ways to express their perceived connection to the old ways and the ancestors; this connection was expressed primarily through the medium of tembang Sunda. The following chapters set the stage for the various urban performance contexts encountered by tembang Sunda musicians, and explain the urban institutions that have come to support and be supported by the musicians.

II

TEMBANG SUNDA IN THE URBAN ENVIRONMENT

This section places the genre of tembang Sunda in the urban milieu of Bandung. The following chapters describe the way tembang Sunda is supported and performed in the city, the issues surrounding tensions between male and female performers as their roles become redefined, the effects of the mass media on the music, and the transmission of tembang Sunda through urban institutions such as the Sekolah Menengah Karawitan Indonesia, Bandung's music high school. One essential feature of this section is that its ideas should apply to music from other urban areas of the world that have experienced a similar recent history. In many ways, this music has an effect on its listeners similar to that of urbanized music in other major postcolonial cities, including highland panpipe music in Lima, old-style Irish singing in Dublin, and rural banjo and fiddle music in Nashville. The effect of the music is, most commonly, to create a reaction of positive longing and nostalgia among certain listeners, and a reaction of scorn among others for whom the music has a particular set of negative associations.

Although Bandung is ethnically diverse, the original ethnic group of Sundanese still comprises most of the city's inhabitants. The city still attracts more emigrants from its outlying areas than from other parts of the country. Many of the features of this urban center that were established during the colonial days, such as the radio stations, schools, and commercial centers, are still in place and flourishing. Such a setting also may be found in other colonial administrative cities—such as Hong Kong—created during the colonial period but later abandoned by the colonists.

Because Bandung is a large, sprawling city with a population of more than three million inhabitants, the city provides the setting for thousands of small social networks that weave through each other in a complicated tangle. Musicians and nonmusicians alike not only maintain intricate social networks within the city but also try to uphold their ties to places outside of Bandung, either to a particular village or to one of the smaller Sundanese cities. The maintenance of these ties is mostly verbal and spiritual, in that a musician will claim to be of a certain village but rarely actually go there except during Lebaran, the Islamic holiday to celebrate the end of the fasting month of Ramadan. At Lebaran, many people leave the city for at least one day and return to the village or to the place of their birth to renew their ties and honor their ancestors, especially their mothers. Even as they go through this process, however, many urbanites complain about the difficulty of going "home" during the rush, and are happiest when it is all over and they can return to their normal lives in the city.

3

Contexts for Performance

In David Coplan's article on urbanization in African music, he discusses the availability of choice as part of the process of urbanization (Coplan 1982: 114). When a musician chooses to perform in a certain style for a particular occasion, he acknowledges the diversity of his potential listening audience. "Such judgements of appropriateness are based upon the capacity of specific styles to embody or express the social position of particular communities or categories of listeners" (Coplan 1982:114). Because tembang Sunda is a very strong symbol of only one sector of society, the urban tembang Sunda musician is required to make many choices regarding not only the appropriate style but also the tuning system, the use of primarily free-rhythm songs or fixed-rhythm songs, and the appropriate song lyrics. Some of these choices are outlined in this discussion of the various performance settings for tembang Sunda.

The musical networks through which Bandung musicians circulate add new dimensions to their myriad connections of family, neighborhood, and friends. Many are tied closely through relatives or by marriage to one of the smaller Sundanese "satellite" cities such as Garut, Sumedang, or Sukabumi. For various reasons, however, these musicians either moved to Bandung when they were fairly young, or were actually born in Bandung but maintain ties with their nonurban roots. The urban network arrangement of these musicians may be seen as a dichotomy between insiders (the musicians) and outsiders (the rest of the world). Tembang Sunda musicians are tied inextricably to these outsiders because of their multiple positions as parent, neighbor, spouse, employee, friend, and fellow musician. The insiders' position and status further differentiate the classification of each one of these domains (higher or lower) relative to that of the others (Wessing 1978:165).

Each musician in a network functions as a member of several peripheral domains (such as an office or a family) and may enter and leave them as he wishes or is obligated. The members of those domains, however, may not enter the inner circle of musicians. If they do (for example, by attending a jam session simply for the social reason of being in a group of people), they are politely received but privately seen as a disruptive element. Intense discussions of the inner workings of tembang Sunda dissolve when an outsider (such as a minor government official, a neighbor, or one of the musicians' spouses) appears, and the conversation immediately becomes bland and general, usually stemming from polite attempts to include the newcomer. It is probable that such a transformation would take place when an outsider to any network attempts to participate in that network. The very occurrence of this transformation, however, helps to establish the tembang Sunda circle as a domain all its own.

Tembang Sunda musicians place themselves "inside the world of tembang Sunda" (Indo.: *dalam dunia tembang Sunda*), and some describe themselves as insiders in this world, compared to their families, neighbors, coworkers, and nonmusician friends (who are the outsiders). It is generally agreed that an outsider has no credence within tembang Sunda circles, and it is sometimes said of the outsider who ventures an opinion about some aspect of the music that he is *sanes urang tembang* ("not a tembang person"). This characterization of attitudes about insiders and outsiders extends to non-tembang Sunda musicians as well. Although relations between other musicians and tembang musicians are usually quite friendly, status and occupational lines are often drawn when a performance (for a governmental function, for example) involves the music of several different genres. In most of these situations, tembang Sunda musicians generally keep to themselves, are treated better by the hosts because of the élite standing accorded to tembang Sunda, and may be said to be *sombong* (arrogant) or *ménak* (aristocratic) by the other musicians. This behavior occurs even though the instrumentalists themselves are not of the élite.

On a deeper level (within tembang Sunda circles only), a further classification system may be developed that illustrates the relative positions of instrumentalists, singers, the informed versus the uninformed audience, student musicians, student singers, and sponsors. In tembang Sunda circles, vocalists are always said to hold a higher position than instrumentalists do. Furthermore, older singers, musicians, and composers (and also dead singers, musicians, and composers) are held with higher respect than currently active vocalists and some living composers. The oldest and best instrumentalists may be viewed, however, with deeper respect than the student vo-

```
older singers        ⎫     ⎧ dead singers
older composers      ⎬  =  ⎨ dead composers
older instrumentalists ⎭   ⎩ dead instrumentalists
```

famous singers
famous composers

sponsors   = famous instrumentalists   = average singers
informed audience   = average instrumentalists = student singers

student instrumentalists
uninformed audience

FIGURE 3.1 Hierarchies within the community of tembang Sunda participants

calists. The uninformed audience is placed in the lowest position in its relationship to the musicians, and in fact may conceivably include all of those people named as outsiders. The hierarchy within tembang Sunda circles is illustrated according to the way singers, instrumentalists, politicians, and audience members discussed these issues with me. The highest levels of relative status are at the top of Figure 3.1, and groups of a relatively equal status are indicated as such by an equals (=) sign.

In this figure, I have placed the sponsors in a position similar to that of an average singer. The reason for this placement is that many sponsors are very interested in tembang Sunda themselves, and may practice it themselves in a nonprofessional context; that is, at a tembang Sunda evening but not at a paid performance. This places them above the level of an informed audience because of their actual participation in musical activity; furthermore, the relative power and money held by many sponsors commands respect among the less-wealthy practitioners of the music. Similarly, although composers of tembang Sunda songs are rarely performers themselves, most are of a very high status because of their perceived position of authority vis-à-vis the musicians. Furthermore, sponsors who express a genuine interest in tembang Sunda are viewed kindly by the musicians, and are treated as latter-day aristocratic hosts. All of these networks form an integral part of Bandung musical life.

LINGKUNG SENI, BANDUNG'S PERFORMING ARTS GROUPS

Tembang Sunda in Bandung has as one of its primary stabilizing elements the *lingkung seni* ("arts circle") or musical group. Lingkung seni are an informal urban institution and usually are the province of singers and their sponsors. Although there are hundreds of lingkung seni in Sunda, only a handful are large, diverse, well established, and have a name that extends outside of the province.[1] Lingkung seni are not exclusively associated with tembang Sunda, but instead tend to include tembang Sunda as one of the types of Sundanese music that the group is capable of performing or contracting.

These groups are especially evident in Bandung, although any singer with a name in one of Sunda's smaller towns like Garut, Sumedang, or Sukabumi forms a lingkung seni of his or her own. As is frequently the case in tembang Sunda, some of these singers have actually lived and studied tembang Sunda in Bandung for years but claim for their groups, their style, and themselves a non-Bandung identity. It is standard practice to assert and discuss the maintenance of one's personal ties to the non-urban environment in tembang Sunda. In the case of musical groups, this is demonstrated by the identification of a group name with a specific place. Villages do not usually have formal lingkung seni, and in fact very few villages even own *kacapi indung*, the boat-shaped kacapi.

Each musical group has its own name and is strongly associated with at least one singer (male or female, although usually female) and with the style of Sundanese music considered to be the specialty of that group. Some groups use only one name and are associated with one singer or team of singers but may be capable of providing several different styles of music. An example of this is the group Sasaka Domas, with a husband-and-wife team (Didin Badjuri and Mamah Dasimah) as its primary singers. Didin Badjuri was a winner of the prestigious All-Sunda tembang Sunda competition (*pasanggiri DAMAS* [Daya Mahasiswa Sunda, the organization of Sundanese students]) in 1969, and his wife, Mamah Dasimah, has performed tembang for years. This couple may simply hire the three or four good musicians necessary to fill out a tembang Sunda ensemble, and give an excellent performance. As the leaders of Sasaka Domas, however, they have at their disposal the musicians and dancers for complete performances of jaipongan or gamelan degung, the ensembles most frequently in demand for weddings and circumcisions. If necessary, the leaders of a musical group should be able to locate and hire performers of any type of Sundanese music or dance, even if they have to search outside of Bandung for the appropriate people. Therefore, the leaders of some of these groups act as entertainment brokers as well as musicians themselves.

Other groups specialize in a single style, and their primary singers are famous exclusively for that style. For example, the group called Simpay Tresna is a lingkung seni specifically dedicated to tembang Sunda, and has as its primary singer Yayah Rochaeti Dachlan, although there have been many secondary singers, both male and female, who have acted as her singing partner. When singers make a cassette recording, the name of their lingkung seni is noted either on the cassette cover or somewhere on the insert. A typical cover will have the title of the cassette followed by the name of the female singer and the name of the group using the initials "L. S." (lingkung seni) followed by the name in quotation marks, as in L. S "Simpay Tresna."

The instrumentalists for Simpay Tresna, Déwi Pramanik, Sasaka Domas, and other lingkung seni change constantly depending on the availability and willingness of the musicians to rehearse with little or no pay, or to associate themselves with a particular singer. Some musicians may simply be contracted for a single performance. Other musicians may involve themselves with a single group for several years at a time before moving on to other groups. Still others do not claim allegiance to any particular group but, rather, prefer to think of themselves as freelance musicians who are available for all tembang Sunda rehearsals, performances, and recordings. In any of these cases, there is a sense of pride, either of being involved with a particularly prestigious group, or of avoiding the whole complicated scene and just concentrating on producing good music. One musician, a young Bandung man tied to a famous group that occasionally travels abroad, said, "I want people to look at me when I walk down the street and say, 'There goes one of the players for group A.' I am proud to be a part of this group." Another player, a young Bandung man as well, said, "I would much rather have people say 'He plays well,' than to stoop to become a flatterer of powerful sponsors."

SPONSORSHIP AND REMUNERATION OF TEMBANG SUNDA MUSICIANS

Tembang Sunda groups in Bandung are generally connected to a particular sponsor. He (it is almost always a man) handles the contracts for the group, arranges for payment of the musicians and singers (usually through the lead female singer), and is financially responsible for instrument maintenance, costumes, and transportation to performance sites. Group sponsors are often nonmusicians who enjoy the sound of tembang Sunda, believe in the importance of maintaining the genre, or are married to tembang Sunda singers. In many cases, these sponsors are involved in one way or another with the government or with the military, or both. Many sponsors believe that the support of a music group is a good public relations move as well as a means for publicly emphasizing one's own ethnic background in the face of increasing ethnic diversity in the upper ranks of the government.

Sponsorship of tembang Sunda in Bandung is one way in which the traditional authority systems of the regents have been replaced with a similar patron-client system based on the principles of power and influence but now determined by a cash-based economy (Jackson 1978:389; Scott 1972: 105). The audience, however, almost never pays cash for music. Sundanese audiences are always accustomed to hearing traditional music for free, and are sometimes shocked to hear that Americans, Europeans, and Japanese spend money to hear music.[2] Therefore, the cash-based economy refers to the economic relationship between the sponsor and the host of the event; the audience has little to do with it except influence the decision of the host and the sponsor on who will be hired for the performance. These modern patrons have ultimate control over hiring and firing of musicians, and are frequently responsible for determining which songs the singer will record. Some sponsors are also composers themselves, and use the tembang Sunda ensemble under their control as a means for the dissemination of their latest compositions.

A vital aspect of the Bandung music scene is intergroup politics, each group vying for an ongoing relationship with particular politicians, corporations, or foreign tour sponsors. Relationships between group sponsors are civil but strained as a result of competition for the best jobs; musicians are lured from one group to another with promises of better pay, a recording contract, or the possibility of an international tour. In most of the larger groups, the sponsor is able to speak at least a little English, an essential skill for getting a tour outside of the country or a performance contract for a foreign group of tourists.

To conduct research on remuneration in Indonesia is not to simply discuss money. Instead, it requires the acknowledgment of a variety of favors and spheres of influence as subsets of payment. As I mentioned in other sections of this book, finding out the actual sums of money paid to musicians is a very difficult venture as it changes from one week to the next, depending on how the musician wishes himself or herself to be viewed by the researcher or the researcher's potential readership. For example, I was quoted three different sums alleged to have been paid to one musician at one performance. The sums differed from each other by almost $50. Therefore, any time that a fee is quoted here, this number should only be taken as a broad approximation of the actual amount.

When money is actually the form in which the remunerative transaction occurs, it is always cash. Checking accounts are virtually unknown in most parts of Indonesia; although these accounts occasionally are used in some of the bigger cities (usually only for very large transactions between banks, or among Chinese-Indonesians, between the largest department stores and their smaller branch stores). Cash is used for daily transactions at stores, and also for almost all large expenditures such as yearly rent money, the purchase of a car or a gamelan, and monthly payment of employees. In the music business, musicians and dancers are usually paid immediately after the performance, unless it is understood that the money will arrive in a few days. Payment is placed in a small white envelope and handed to the payee just as he or she is leaving the home of the group's female leader.

The association of musicians with a particular group and its sponsor establishes an atmosphere of mutual dependency between these musicians and the sponsor. This type of relationship has been described as an ideal distributor-dependent relationship, in which "honor and respect along with intermittent economic benefits flow toward the center while a service or scarce commodity flows back" (Wessing 1984a:30). On the surface, each tries to help the other out of difficulty, and to acquire the best and most lucrative jobs for the group. For example, a musician whose child is ill may ask for money for the medicine from the group sponsor, even if the sponsor does not know the child. In some cases, the child may not even be ill, but the musician simply needs the money. It is the responsibility of the sponsor, therefore, to provide this kind of money (if he has it on hand) to the members of his group. Musicians are, for the most part, careful not to abuse this privilege, and some never ask for anything at all in an attempt to strengthen their credibility with their sponsor.

Money for performances is generally not agreed on beforehand between the sponsor and the musicians, so it is up to the individual musician to trust the sponsor enough to assume that the money will appear after the job has been completed. Similarly, the sponsor must trust the musicians to arrive on time for a performance. Tembang Sunda musicians usually gather at the home of the female singer (if she is not married to the sponsor), and all of them are picked up in a group from there and brought to the performance site. The performers usually return to the home of the singer or the sponsor once the performance has ended. If they are lucky, a late-night dinner is provided for everyone, usually comprising either rice and chicken wrapped in banana leaves or *bakso* (a kind of meat soup). It is common for some members of the performing group to stay overnight at the home of either the singer or the sponsor. If the sponsor has a car, then all female performers are brought home after the evening is over and the men are left to fend for themselves on public transportation.

When cash is not provided as part of the remuneration expected for the performance, the musician has a right to expect some other kind of compensation for his efforts. For example, he may be rewarded with a recording contract or the chance to perform for a particularly well-paying job, or may perform "for free" in exchange for being included in an international tour. I attended one performance in which the musicians were paid with three bars of imported soap each. The soap was brought from outside of Indonesia by the host, and although it was also widely available within Indonesia for approximately 20 cents a bar, it was welcomed by most of the performers. Many Indonesians automatically distrust domestic products, labeling them as poor imitations of foreign goods. The host and at least some of the musicians felt that the foreign soap would be of far better quality than the same, but less expensive, brand already available within Indonesia.

Some musicians perform in a partial exchange for the prestige that the association with a certain group gives them. In some cases, the pay is no better in one group than in another, but one group may have a larger name or a more prestigious reputation than others may. It is standard behavior among tembang Sunda instrumentalists to discuss the various merits of the groups, and the advantages and disadvantages of working with one group over another. Because of the diversity of forms of payment, these advantages can never be measured in monetary terms; rather, they are measured more in general attitude (both of the sponsor and the singers), in the possibility of going on tour or getting prestigious gigs, and in the treatment of musicians. For example, a group might not command a high fee for its performances, but the sponsor may take a much smaller percentage of the gross profit for himself. In another case, the job might not be very prestigious, but the singer may be a very enjoyable person to work for; someone who makes sure that the musicians are fed well and treated with respect.

Performers outside of Bandung experience quite a different situation from that enjoyed by those in the city. Although many lingkung seni operate in the former regencies of Garut, Tasikmalaya, and Sumedang, they do not have the same type of performing opportunities as those in Bandung and in many cases lack the financial support (for instruments, transportation, etc.) as well. For example, in the smaller cities outside of Bandung, only one or two lingkung seni in each place ever achieve the kind of status that enables them to be invited to Bandung or perform for visitors. If they get that far, it is usually only because the group's lead female singer will have studied in Bandung and built a name for herself back home through her big-city associations. She also may have made a successful recording or won a tembang Sunda contest. In some cases, she may bypass local musicians in favor of those from Bandung. Enah Sukaenah, for example, is one of the very finest tembang Sunda singers. She lives in Sumedang, a small city about an hour from Bandung. She has made many successful recordings and won the pasanggiri DAMAS contest twice; therefore, no question is ever raised as to her position among the highest ranks of tembang Sunda singers. She relies primarily on Bandung musicians for her most important performances and recordings, however, and has considerable difficulty in finding professional-quality musicians for her performances in Sumedang.

THE SPECTRUM OF PERFORMANCE SETTINGS

This section of Chapter 3 presents most of the various live performance settings for tembang Sunda, excluding live broadcasts and cassette recordings (dealt with in Chapter 5). I have not included a discussion of the *latihan* or jam session/lesson phenomenon here, because it is better suited to Chapter 6, in which the transmission of tembang Sunda is the main focus, not its performance. Each performance setting requires a unique selection of songs and tunings deemed appropriate to the situation, a varying amount of interaction with the audience, and a specific function assigned to music and musicians. These functions may range from musical and visual wallpaper to the uncontested center of attention. The outward architecture of a tembang Sunda performance, however, varies only slightly from one performance to another.

In many urban performances, the audience has not the slightest concept of what comprises tembang Sunda, and is happy to loudly assert their misunderstandings of the genre and of Sundanese music in general. At one wedding in which I had to sit with members of the host family and chat politely instead of listening to the musicians, a well-meaning woman indicated the tembang Sunda musicians performing over the din of the eating, talking guests, and asked "Soni sudah bisa main angklung?" ("Can Sean already play angklung?")[3] Since the rural fertility-oriented bamboo rattle music of angklung is almost as far from tembang Sunda as it is possible to go, I said no; I only play kacapi and sing a little bit in the style of tembang Sunda. She replied that that was what she meant: angklung. Because I was annoyed by my position as the token white woman in the proceedings, I made some comment about the deep division between the two styles. The woman insisted that the tembang Sunda ensemble was exactly the same (including the instruments, the repertoire, and the performers themselves) as the angklung ensemble. She invited me to "ask the mayor of Bandung!" if I didn't believe her. I smiled politely and changed the subject.

The point is that many urban Sundanese simply do not understand either the smaller or greater differences between various Sundanese ensembles, between the Western and traditional Sundanese tuning systems, or between Western and Sundanese ensembles. I have been commanded by urban Sundanese people on several different occasions to perform Madonna's "Like a Prayer" on the kacapi, Bruce Springsteen's "Born in the U.S.A." on the suling, and to breakdance (American-style) to jaipongan accompaniment because it was "all the same music" to the spectators. Fortunately for my potential audience and for the sake of Sundanese music in general, I didn't know how the American songs went and couldn't breakdance either. Therefore, in the following descriptions of when and where tembang Sunda appears in performance, the audience must be taken into consideration. The knowledge gap between the tembang Sunda insiders and the average uninformed audience of their performances is one more feature that serves to separate them and invent new uses for the old aristocratic divisions, even in the modern Bandung at the beginning of the twenty-first century.

One performance context for tembang Sunda not summarized in the following categories is a type of tembang Sunda opera known as *gending karesmen*. I discuss it here briefly, because it is only rarely performed and is usually considered a separate genre. Gending karesmen was already being performed in the 1920s as a type of opera to accompany actors (van Zanten 1989:36). By the 1990s, it was described as a modern phenomenon, in that it sometimes uses prerecorded music to which the members of the show's cast lip-sync. It also still may be performed live. Typical plots for gending karesmen are based on Sundanese mythology; for example, the tale "Lutung Kasarung" was made into a gending karesmen and recorded commercially. It included some of the top tembang Sunda instrumentalists and vocalists, took a long time to make, and was released in an elaborately decorated boxed set.

As with every kind of innovation in tembang Sunda, putting "Lutung Kasarung" into this context led to heated debate and strong disagreement that still persists. Many Bandung musicians feel that using tembang Sunda in gending karesmen is inappropriate, for reasons including the fact that tembang should not be performed in a large concert hall, that the music should be heard and not watched, and that the audience would have no other interest in the music (Gelanggang Mahasiswa Sastra Indonesia 1975: 16). Others who are more interested in the further development and promotion of the genre feel that it is exactly through performance contexts such as gending karesmen that tembang Sunda will become more familiar to the average Sundanese person (*memasyarakat*), instead of remaining accessible only to the upper classes.

The Ideal Performance: *Malam Tembang Sunda*

A concept of what the most ideal performance of the music should be exists in the minds of many tembang Sunda practitioners. It is called *malam tembang Sunda*, or tembang Sunda evening. In this type of performance, there is no official sponsor of the event, no invitations or speeches, and no audience. The "performers" in this case are simply vocalists and instrumentalists who have gathered together to create music, and in their gathering together are able to reinforce their ties to each other and to their common Sundanese heritage. A malam tembang Sunda is for the enjoyment and benefit of the musicians only, and is a very personal and spiritual event for the people involved. I was fortunate to enjoy many of these malam tembang Sunda in various forms; my own going-away party (hosted by Euis Komariah) was a malam tembang Sunda par excellence, attended almost exclusively by tembang Sunda people and lasting until 7:00 A.M. the next day.

At a malam tembang Sunda, the instruments are tuned to pélog[4] and the musicians play a bubuka or instrumental opening song. The evening officially begins with a *lagu rajah* (see Chapter 7 on the stylistic divisions of tembang Sunda) to invoke the presence of the gods and to provide a type of benediction on the proceedings. The most experienced male singer is given the honor of singing the lagu rajah, and either a male or a female may sing "Papatet." After several sets of papantunan songs have been sung, one or more singers may perform a single set of jejemplangan songs. It is normal for three or four singers to trade off verses and individual songs during the course of a single set, and in some cases a married couple may trade verses. If one of the female singers is known for her particularly high vocal range, she may sing a set *of dedegungan* songs, closing with a panambih appropriate for dedegungan (such as "Degung Panggung").

During this progression through several different styles, the less experienced singers present will usually hang back until a set of *rarancagan* songs is reached. The apparent reluctance of the younger singers is due to respect for the greatness and "weight" (*bobot*) of the older songs, as well as out of respect for the more experienced singers. At this point in the evening (the first several hours), all of the songs are still in pélog because most of the stylistic divisions of the genre are in pélog. Between sets, the musicians take a short break to talk, smoke, eat snacks (such as boiled peanuts, bananas, or cookies), drink tea or coffee, and discuss the next set of songs. After several more sets of rarancagan songs have been performed in pélog, the instruments are retuned to *sorog* and all the following songs will be of the rarancagan style. After a few more hours of songs in sorog, the instruments will be retuned to saléndro, the rebab player sets up and tunes his instrument, and the last sets of songs will be drawn from rarancagan and, occasionally, kakawén (wayang golék) repertoires. The saléndro section of the evening may last until dawn.

During the course of the evening, the most experienced of the singers may perform any song they wish, but most of them select the songs with which they have made successful recordings, songs that they perform the best, or new compositions that were written especially for them. Although there is no official ownership of songs, it is at least considered unfair for a singer to perform a song that has been recorded more successfully by (or belongs to the repertoire of) another singer. The vocal students are allowed and expected to sing, but in general only during the rarancagan sets. In saléndro tuning, the students often sing far less than the experienced vocalists, and only actively participate in the songs that use a chorus.

No matter how many experienced singers are present, they all act as if they are unwilling to sing, and refuse (even to point of acting offended) when the current singer calls on them to do the next verse or song. Apung Wiratmadja described the musicianship of an older kacapi player (Mang Tarya, the teacher of the now-famous kacapi player Uking Sukri) as being so good that he himself was unable to resist singing. Turning down requests to sing is the polite way of behaving in a tembang Sunda evening; however, in this situation, Pa Apung said that he asked if he could sing first. If a younger singer is told to sing during a time considered inappropriate, he or she must refuse out of deference to an older singer. The game of invitation and refusal is played out in many aspects of Sundanese upper-class society; for example, a guest is obligated to refuse an offer of food or drink at least twice before accepting. In a malam tembang Sunda, this game is extended to include invitations to sing and play one of the instruments.

This ideal performance of tembang Sunda is fairly rare except among the more experienced singers who are very serious about tembang Sunda (for example, Euis Komariah, Apung Wiratmadja, and Yayah Rochaeti Dachlan). The reason for its rarity is the constant intrusion of work, children, and household management into the daily lives of the singers and instrumentalists. It is also difficult to get people together, and the likelihood that people involved in politics will find out about gatherings of this kind and make an appearance is great (Wiratmadja, personal communication, 1989). Once the atmosphere has been changed through the presence of an outsider or other disturbance, the warmth, seriousness, and concentration of the event is dispersed and people who would have been eager to stay all night singing and playing music end up going home early.

Panglawungan or Small Formal Gatherings

The advantages of participating in a malam tembang Sunda include the fact that it is a good opportunity to meet and get to know other tembang Sunda people, and that one can increase one's own repertoire and understanding of the genre by listening closely. In an attempt to duplicate this event on a formal scale, several organizations in Bandung sponsor *panglawungan* or formalized tembang Sunda evenings. One of these organizations, the Yayasan Pancaniti, sends out invitations approximately once a month to selected singers, and holds formal meetings at the homes of local politicians or at government buildings or hotels. The sponsoring organization pays a very small stipend to a set of instrumentalists, and transports them to the event. The audience present at a panglawungan consists primarily of male members of the Sundanese upper class and government officials (who in earlier times would have been singers themselves), and tembang Sunda musicians. Members of the local press come to these events and list the names of the political participants and, on occasion, who performed what songs.

Because of the presence of the political element at these gatherings, the music performed is, in many ways, merely secondary to the networking and intrigue going on among the politicians. The appearance of a politician at a panglawungan is considered an important means of increasing his relative status; the association of the genre with the aristocracy is attractive to politicians who want to look good and associate themselves with the aristocracy. During all the panglawungan events at which I was present, a large group of men in batik shirts (standard Indonesian dress for political and formal events) spoke together during the entire evening, and everything I heard them speak of was directly related to politics. They sat separated from the musicians and paid no attention to the music. All participants at these events sit on a carpeted floor, and the female singers sit separated from the male singers (who often sit fairly close to the musicians).

Depending on the type of panglawungan—but particularly if the gathering is held at the home of a politician—the instrumentalists generally come from a lower class and sit grouped together, separated from the élite. This grouping represents a holdover from an earlier era, in which the classes of aristocracy and common people were more clearly defined and maintained, and it is felt to be offensive to some of the better urban musicians. Many of these urban instrumentalists have worked to dispel the practice of separation according to status, either by boycotting this type of gathering or only accepting jobs that do not reflect these divisions. As a result, the instrumentalists to be found at a panglawungan do not necessarily belong among the best players. By the action of boycotting a panglawungan, an instrumentalist may be consciously rejecting his subordinate status vis-à-vis the vocalists, while simultaneously protesting the interference in the music by the politicians (Rukmana, personal communication, 1988; Subari, personal communication, 1989).

James Scott points out the revealing nature of a "dissonant subculture of a subordinate group and its relationship to dominant elite values" (Scott 1976:233). The reader will have noted the discrepancy between tembang Sunda instrumentalists and their élite patrons. To what extent, however, are any of the instrumentalists going along with élite requests and/or values? If they do, is it because they believe passionately in these values? The kacapi or suling player who boycotts a panglawungan may not be any more obvious in his disdain for the system of patronage than the one who appears, performs, and is deferential—but who inwardly mocks the entire proceedings. Resistance to the status quo takes many forms: "By easily showing a regard that he does not have, the actor can feel that he is preserving a kind of inner autonomy, holding off the ceremonial order by the very act of upholding it. And of course in scrupulously observing the proper forms he may find that he is free to insinuate all kinds of disregard by carefully modifying intonation, pronunciation, pacing, and so forth" (Goffman 1956:478).

A panglawungan may only last several hours; it is not a full-scale malam tembang Sunda. As is usually the case with formal Sundanese events, a master of ceremonies makes brief speeches, announces late arrivals, and lists the songs that are about to be performed. Buffet-style food is usually a feature of every panglawungan, because the singers are not paid to attend. At one panglawungan I attended, the singers were all requested to write down the song(s) they planned to perform, and the master of ceremonies planned to arrange the evening according to the appropriate order of the songs. Because the master of ceremonies was not a tembang Sunda person, however, utter confusion ensued. The order and tuning systems were mixed together and sorog songs were scheduled before pélog songs, and inexperienced singers were placed before senior singers. Furthermore, many songs were duplicated, a practice that rarely happens in a true malam tembang Sunda. The intent of these organizations, therefore, may be to promote and foster the further development of tembang Sunda, but the results are sometimes far from what was expected.

Tembang Sunda Competitions

In the past several decades there have been a number of small tembang Sunda competitions, known by the Sundanese term *pasanggiri*. Among these are the now-defunct competition for the Saodah Cup (named in honor of the late Saodah Harnadi Natakusuma [1922–1981], one of the most important female performers of tembang Sunda in recent memory), competitions held by the Bandung branch of Radio Republik Indonesia or the Mimitran [friends of] Tembang Sunda, and the most important and long-lasting competition, the pasanggiri DAMAS. The initials DAMAS stand for Daya Mahasiswa Sunda, the organization of Sundanese students. DAMAS is responsible, among other things, for sponsoring activities related to the Sundanese performing arts. The pasanggiri DAMAS is the one competition occurring with regularity (approximately every two years), and the location of the competition usually changes each time, as one aspect of the competition is the general DAMAS support for and inclusion of each region of Sunda within its purview.

Preparation for a pasanggiri begins several months before the actual event. Many of the more advanced vocalists experience a sudden increase in the number of students attending their latihan sessions, and tembang Sunda activity both in Bandung and in the outlying areas increases exponentially once the list of songs has been released by DAMAS. The standard practice at a pasanggiri DAMAS is for a list of songs to be released, most of which must be prepared by the contestant. The contestant has a choice of certain songs; the required songs are called *lagu wajib*, and the optional songs are called *lagu pilihan*. The required songs may be different between men and women, and usually the three main tuning systems are represented. Before the mid-1970s, evidently, the saléndro tuning system was not used in the pasanggiri DAMAS (Rukmana, personal communication, 1987). Each contestant (*peserta*) must perform a tembang Sunda set, as in normal performance practice. Although a contest among instrumentalists may be held on very rare occasions, it is the vocal competitions that generate the most excitement in the tembang Sunda community.

A committee (usually consisting of former *pasanggiri* winners, DAMAS members and a few politicians) chooses the list of songs; however, it is important for contestants to ask permission of the singers who made the songs famous before competing with those particular songs. Similarly, contestants must pay close attention to the selection of the instrumentalists for the competition. According to over a dozen musicians I queried about this matter, it is common practice for the instrumentalists to be treated with small gifts and honored very well by contestants for several weeks before a pasanggiri. The hope is that the instrumentalist will not "accidentally" cause the contestant to make a mistake during the competition. The causing of an accident may be due to several different factors, but it is usually done in such a subtle manner that the instrumentalist is able to protest his lack of ill intent toward the contestant.

The presence of one's own teacher on the jury for the competition poses advantages and difficulties for a contestant, because the other members of the jury are likely to weigh more heavily against that contestant to balance the positive judgment of the contestant's teacher. In the past, contestants' teachers were not allowed to act as members of the jury because of potential conflicts of interest; however, this is no longer the case, because the teachers themselves know the tradition better than anyone else. In the 1990s, it became standard practice to issue a cassette of the required songs prior to a competition. In addition to opening up more opportunities of access for hopeful contestants, such cassettes further standardized the songs. In preparing for a competition, it is generally not a good idea for a contestant to try out a new interpretation of a song, including even the slightest deviation from established norms of vocal ornamentation. As Yano notes in her discussion of Japanese *enka* singing, "What the audience wants to see in a singer is not something new, as much as something old, familiar, and thereby comforting in a world which has changed rapidly and exponentially" (1997: 119).

I conducted a long interview with Apung Wiratmadja, one of the most famous practitioners of tembang Sunda and one of the first winners of the pasanggiri DAMAS in the late 1950s. He shared his opinions of thirty-five years of watching and judging pasanggiri competitions, listing the positive and negative aspects of competition in tembang Sunda. On the positive side, it forces people to be brave in singing before a crowd; it is educative in that people learn from their mistakes; and it increases the repertoire among the contestants. Negative aspects of tembang Sunda competitions are that there is no follow-up, so the contestants cannot learn to improve; no one pays attention to the instrumentalists; people have to learn more songs than they can remember; and there is only one winner, because the runners-up disappear.[5] Pa Apung also acknowledged that in the juries for the competitions, the final selection is completely subjective, because each person has his favorite style of singing and also may be influenced by favors and gifts.

In spite of the negative aspects of the pasanggiri DAMAS, however, it is the one tembang Sunda competition that can make or break the career of a singer. The Hidayat recording company almost always records the entire event, releasing a cassette afterward of the three top finalists (the woman are on Side 1, and the men are on Side 2). For the top winner, it is likely that recording contracts will follow, as will requests for well-paid performances. In addition, the male and female winners (*juara*) are usually presented with a small gold replica of a kacapi each in honor of their musical achievement. After the pasanggiri is over, tembang Sunda activity tends to drop off significantly as people take a break from the pressure of the event (lasting from one to three days) and spend more time talking about the event itself than resuming playing. In most cases, the mistakes of the contestants are the most heatedly discussed aspect of the competition, and the reasons for the selection of certain singers over others are debated. Mistakes and other events that happen at a pasanggiri tembang Sunda can provide the fuel for discussions for several years. The preparation, gossip, rewards, and cassette releases all point to the pasanggiri DAMAS as being the most significant public event in the life of tembang Sunda.

In 1988, I attended a *pasanggiri pupuh* (competition in the performance of poetic meters) sponsored by the Departemen Pendidikan dan Kebudayaan (Department of Education and Culture). From each of the sixteen different areas within Bandung, a male and a female schoolteacher were selected to compete against other teachers, with the expressed aim of firing up enthusiasm (*membakar semangat*) among the students to become interested in pupuh meters. The contestants had a choice of meters in the three tunings of pélog, sorog, and saléndro, and all were accompanied by some type of kacapi (usually the flat kacapi siter, performed in kawih style). Contestants were judged on three points: voice (volume and timbre), technique (tempo and expression), and appearance (behavior and fashion). During this competition, held at one of the schools in Bandung and including officials from the Kantor Pendidikan dan Kebudayaan (Education and Culture Office), all students were barred from attending or entering the room where the competition was being held. The discrepancy between the expressed goals of the competition and the actual results is symptomatic of the difficulties experienced by the Sundanese whenever the issue of cultural preservation or promotion comes up.

In 1996, I observed the feverish preparations for that year's pasanggiri DAMAS. The event had been scheduled for earlier in the year, but the unexpected death of Ibu Tien Suharto, the then-president's wife, led to the postponement of the pasanggiri until late June, once the thirty-day period of national mourning had ended. Teachers who were going to sit on the jury were swamped with students eager to develop their voices in just a few weeks. Euis Komariah had recorded a preparation cassette, and it was made available to prospective contestants for study purposes. Because it contained songs that Euis Komariah had never formally recorded, the cassette itself was being treated as an important new "bootleg" release, and students were quite excited to have access to the new recording. The female winner of the pasanggiri was the late kacapi player Uking Sukri's teenage daughter Fitri, who had been the early favorite.[6] The singer Ajat Sudrajat—associated with the "Simpay Tresna" lingkung seni primarily as a kacapi player—was the male winner. The next pasanggiri, scheduled for mid-1998, was planned well in advance, but had to be postponed due to the economic crisis and riots that surged southward from Jakarta and briefly took over Bandung in the spring of 1998. At the time, it was believed to be prudent that the upper classes (associated with tembang Sunda) not make too obvious a show of their position in society.

Based on my observations of the enthusiastic preparation and implementation of musical (tembang Sunda, kawih, *kroncong*, jaipongan dance, pupuh meters, and pop Sunda) and other competitions (fashion and beauty), there is no question that competitions stimulate performance (see Williams 1999, for more detailed information on Sundanese performing arts competitions). The current high status and popularity of a performer may be based solely on his or her becoming a winner or, at least, a finalist in a competition. Because of this, many performers compete only once so that they do not lose their position to a newcomer. The Sundanese feel that "once a winner, always a winner," which means that a winner has only to prove him/herself once. The musical genres in which these contestants compete, however, must be "proven" to be legitimate again and again (through competitions), because of the concern on the part of the Sundanese that certain musical genres are in danger of dying out. There is a genuine concern that with the loss of a musical genre, the whole culture of Sunda will have lost part of what makes it Sundanese.

Sundanese Weddings

In addition to the above-mentioned settings for tembang Sunda performances, many middle-class urban Sundanese now utilize groups of this type as background music or when a large ensemble such as a jaipongan dance troupe is prohibitively expensive. Weddings and circumcisions, in which either the groom or the young newly circumcised boy is dressed like a Sundanese nobleman, are a common setting for tembang Sunda. In these situations, guests at the reception use the music as background accompaniment to the consumption of food. The audience for performances of this type can number up to one or two thousand people, depending on how wealthy the families are and in front of how many people they need to express their power and influence. Among the hundreds of guests, only a few pay attention to the music. Most of the guests pay closer attention to the rules of studied detachment; trying, as it were, not to listen to the music (Pemberton 1987:20).[7]

In a performance for a wedding reception, the tembang Sunda musicians are restricted to the performance of certain styles because of the situation. The background of the audience is usually middle and upper class, but many members of the audience do not belong to the aristocracy and resent hearing those styles that are considered too closely associated with the feudal times. Hosts and attendees of weddings and other ritual events far prefer to hear love songs rather than "serious" songs with historical and/or spiritual content. During one wedding in which I shared the microphone with only one other singer for five hours of nothing but panambih songs, the other singer (Ibu Tintin Suparyani) explained the situation as follows:

> Audience itu kan terdiri dari dua macam. Satu, kita itu harus nembang kalau di dalam riung yang—kalau seperti panglawungan—lingkungan yang fanatik. Itu kan mereka dengaaaaaar, gitu. Kalau di sini itu, kalau ada yang memperhatikan syukur. Kan kita hanya sekadar mengiringi makanan, ya. Jadi harus bisa menyesuai dengan suasana. Kan ini waktu untuk yang ringan, ya? Kan ini adalah waktu yang tidak terlalu . . . berat.
>
> [There are two types of audiences. One, we have to perform tembang in a room which is—like at a panglawungan—a fanatical environment. That's because they're *really* listening, like that. But as for here, if anyone pays attention then just be thankful. You know that we're really only accompanying eating, yeah? So we have to be able to adjust to the atmosphere. This is a time for lightheartedness, you know? This is a time which is not too . . . heavy.] (Suparyani, personal communication, 1989)

When the tembang Sunda musicians comply with the request of the host or submit to the need to "keep it light" (by playing panambih songs and the occasional rarancagan song), the audience is satisfied that the musical wallpaper will remain undisturbed. As in a Javanese wedding, the entire social order of a Sundanese wedding reception is based on the need that nothing be unusual, low class, or out of place (Pemberton 1987:20). A tembang Sunda ensemble fulfills that need by providing first a visual symbol of high status and power (the image of the ensemble is equated with the prestige of the aristocracy). Second, it provides a soft, refined-sounding music with a beat to which the audience can, and often does, absentmindedly tap its collective feet. Although audience members may occasionally focus on the music, the point of the experience is to feel a sense of "rightness" when everything is in place and is proceeding according to plan: "For the Sundanese, proper listening to music also includes hearing the 'inner voices.' These voices tell about the shared tradition and in particular about the human struggle for harmony. It is not just the music, but also human life, with all its sorrows and happiness and with its relation to the cosmic and social order, that is experienced" (van Zanten 1997:42).

At some weddings and many circumcisions, depending on the number of guests and their entertainment needs, a tembang Sunda ensemble may be the first of a whole series of musical events that span several days. In some cases, the hosts try to provide a broad spectrum of entertainment, from tembang Sunda to jaipongan to gamelan degung kawih to *musik bén* (Western-style pop music). In cases such as this, the host may simply hire an entire lingkung seni (such as Jugala or Sasaka Domas) that will provide all the musical entertainment for the event, and draw on its own members to perform in various capacities all day or several days in a row. The leader of the lingkung seni hangs a banner across the back of the stage, proclaiming the name of the group (and sometimes the name of its leader), and he provides a master of ceremonies for the entire event. His financial reward is also far greater if he is hired as the entertainment broker for the event instead of just the broker for the tembang Sunda portion.

Because the sound of tembang Sunda relative to the other ensembles is much quieter and less *ramai* (fun, active, busy-sounding), the tembang Sunda ensemble is usually onstage first. After only one hour, the performance may be over and the next ensemble may be ready to move onstage. The narrow time allotted to tembang Sunda only allows for one tuning system, and at least half the time the chosen tuning system is sorog, because it has a larger proportional repertoire of rarancagan and appropriate panambih songs than pélog. Saléndro is almost never performed by a tembang Sunda ensemble at Sundanese weddings or circumcisions.

When the pélog tuning is used at a wedding, however, the songs may not even belong to the tembang Sunda repertoire. Instead, they may be kawih songs, or part of the repertoire of pop Sunda songs (always composed in pélog) performed by a tembang Sunda ensemble instead of a band. In the wedding or other ritual reception context, it is appropriate for members of the audience to come onstage and *kaul*, or participate, by singing or playing one of the instruments. The songs most frequently chosen by members of the audience are kawih and pop Sunda songs, leading to the inclusion of the most popular of these songs in the wedding repertoire. In a brief perusal of another singer's songbook (Yayah Rochaeti Dachlan), I found a section of pop Sunda songs in the back of her book, unmarked. When I commented on my discovery, she said "Ya, kalau ada pernikahan atau sunatan, banyak yang minta lagu-lagu pop dan kita harus siap dulu" ("Yes, if there's a wedding or circumcision, many people ask for pop songs and we have to be prepared in advance").[8]

The addition of these songs to the repertoire for wedding and circumcision performances has not yet seemed to affect the repertoire used for tembang Sunda evenings or panglawungan gatherings. It has contributed, however, to the belief among members of the uninformed audience that all of those songs belong within the tembang Sunda repertoire. Indeed, the songs *do* belong in the repertoire if they are performed at tembang Sunda events, but their comparatively brief "shelf life" relegates them to secondary status.

Military and Governmental Performances

The Indonesian government and members of the military have replaced the hereditary Sundanese aristocracy as the most visible powerholders in Sunda. Until the 1980s, tembang Sunda groups enjoyed frequent patronage from many different levels of the government. Sundanese officials (often descended from the aristocracy) have been proud to sponsor performances at their homes and at government buildings. In 1989, the Sundanese officials were rumored to have been told by the national government that hiring Sundanese musicians was a waste of the government's financial resources (*penghamburan*), and that such practices had to stop. Many Sundanese (musicians and nonmusicians alike) took offense at this perceived belittling of their culture in light of the fact that much larger (and more expensive) Javanese ensembles were still regularly used at national functions. After some negotiation, the local hiring of musicians was reduced but kept for special occasions (such as visits from foreign prime ministers, kings, and presidents). The eventual result of this alleged prohibition[9] has been a diminishing presence of Sundanese culture at government events, replaced by those types of performances that correspond more closely to a national, popularized style (such as *pop Indonesia*, which uses diatonic tuning and a keyboard-based band). In the late 1990s, the economic crisis demanded even stricter curtailment of government-subsidized performances, to the point that lingkung seni were requested to bring the bare minimum number of performers who could easily cross stylistic boundaries.

The few available contracts for military and government performances are actively sought after by the sponsors of tembang Sunda (and other) groups, because they still pay well and increase the prestige of the group. When an ensemble is able to acquire the position of being the favored group of a particular government minister, for example, it is more or less guaranteed a performance contract every time the minister visits Bandung or any other area in West Java. When a tembang Sunda ensemble performs for an important government official, the relative prestige of the group climbs in relation to the position of the official. For example, any group that has performed at the Istana Negara (the Indonesian equivalent of the U.S. White House) is considered by many to be at the top of the tembang Sunda ladder, perhaps even more so than a group that has participated in an international tour. Therefore, it is to the advantage of these groups to gain access to government and military performance contracts, and to maintain good relations with everyone involved in the contracting process. Some of this networking occurs during events such as panglawungan gatherings, where minor officials, sponsors, and other entertainment brokers look for an opportunity to establish contact with the politicians.

Several of the highest members of the Sundanese government are members of DAMAS. Because of their educated background in Sundanese culture, these officials are able to select the musicians known for the quality of their performances. Not all members of the Sundanese regional government are Sundanese or understand Sundanese culture, however, and in some cases the members of performing groups have to rely more heavily on their connections and personal networks to get jobs than on their reputation alone.

The types of jobs for which tembang Sunda musicians are called are usually to accompany eating, or when a going-away party is held to honor a local official getting promoted to Jakarta, or when an official from Jakarta is in Bandung or some other Sundanese region on business. In these cases, a Bandung ensemble is almost always selected for the job over an ensemble from one of the outlying areas, and the performance usually stays within one tuning system. When asked why military and government performances use only one tuning, one of the musicians replied that "the audience doesn't understand about retuning, and will only think that we are wasting time onstage."

These performances occur in many variations. In some cases, the musicians are treated with deep respect and are fed very good food and even paid attention to for the duration of the performance. In other cases, the audience pays no attention at all except to make comments about the singers or to play-act with the microphones. In the last performance I attended before returning to the United States, every mayor (and his spouse) in West Java was assembled for an event at a large government building in Bandung. In this performance, the guests were quiet and polite and they appeared to genuinely appreciate the music. A situation such as that one is the best that musicians can hope for when they perform; doubly so when the audience represents the holders of power for the entire region.

Some performances for which the musicians are hired by the government are for foreign heads of state. Newspaper articles almost always mention the next day that the foreigners were "awestruck" by the sound of the ensemble, simply because they sat quietly during the performance. Most Indonesians are unaware of the fact that most educated foreigners sit quietly during a music performance out of custom and politeness, whether they enjoy the music or not. Nonetheless, many tembang Sunda performers are hired to entertain foreign visitors through the government, and these performances may be tailored to the audience just as much as a wedding performance conforms to the situation. For example, a large contingent of Thai officials came through Bandung in 1989, and it was agreed by the performers of the lingkung seni that the most important event of the evening should be that Sundanese female dancers pull Thai men onstage to dance with them. I was commanded to be the master of ceremonies for the evening, and also to dance with the Thai officials. In one performance for the president of a strongly Islamic country, the singers searched through their songbooks to find all the lyrics with Arabic words in them so that the rather un-Islamic tembang Sunda performance would sound more Islamic. Heads of state and businessmen from Holland and Japan are treated to verses with Dutch and Japanese words. The use of foreign words and the general lyric content of tembang Sunda will be discussed in greater depth in Chapter 10.

Hotels and Restaurants

The image of tembang Sunda ensembles (and especially the image of the kacapi) as most representative of Sunda has led to the hiring of groups to perform in the lobbies of large Sundanese hotels and in outdoor pavilions at some of the fancier European-style restaurants in Bandung. These hotels and restaurants are most often frequented by foreign tourists and businessmen, who claim to enjoy the quiet sound of the tembang Sunda ensemble rather more than that of the gamelan. "I hate those gongs," said one English businessman who spends several months out of every year in Indonesia. "They sound just like pots and pans." I interviewed the manager of one of Bandung's largest hotels, who said that since he hired the tembang Sunda group to perform in the lobby, he has been deluged with requests from foreigners to purchase not only cassettes but even the instruments themselves. The musicians are paid by the month for their services, approximately as much as they would receive if they worked in an office, and some very good musicians hold these hotel and restaurant jobs as performers.

I took several opportunities to observe tembang Sunda performances at several hotels and restaurants and noticed that most of the pieces performed in these situations are either panambih songs or just one mamaos song followed by a long panambih. During one performance in which I observed from the lobby of a hotel, a Texan businessman wearing a large cowboy hat requested "The Yaller Rose of Texas." When the musicians simply smiled and continued playing, he stood up and began singing the song over the sound of the instruments and the female singer. She (the tembang singer) stopped singing but continued smiling politely, and the musicians continued until the end of the panambih cycle and finished the song. Without the kacapi and suling accompaniment, the lobby became rather quiet except for the sound of "The Yaller Rose of Texas" being sung at full volume. As soon as the music had stopped, the Texan quickly became embarrassed and sat down, and the musicians instantly began playing again to cover his embarrassment. According to the manager, that sort of scene happens fairly regularly, and he feels that it is because the guests are "inspired" by the sound of the music.

Performances at European-style restaurants in Bandung are often contracted for a single event, such as a party for foreigners. If the performance is not for a specific event, sometimes an ensemble may only be hired for Friday and Saturday night, when the restaurant expects to do most of its business for the week. I observed, however, that although a full tembang Sunda ensemble is often hired for hotel lobby performances, the groups hired by restaurants are usually instrumental only; that is, a singer is not hired. As the manager of one restaurant explained, if he hired a singer he would have to pay much more than if he simply hired a kacapi-suling instrumental ensemble; hiring a singer would significantly cut into his profits for the evening. Furthermore, none of the restaurant patrons pay attention to the music and would not even be aware if a singer was present (see Chapter 8 for more information about kacapi-suling). By hiring an instrumental ensemble, the restaurant manager gets the same musical background at approximately half the price, and is able to advertise "live music" at his restaurant even if the group only performs once a week. Finally, because almost all kacapi-suling music is based on panambih song structure, it is guaranteed that the performance will be lighter in character than that of a tembang Sunda performance.

Outside the City of Bandung

It should be mentioned that many tembang Sunda performances still occur in smaller, less densely crowded cities, most notably in Sumedang, Garut, Sukabumi, Tasikmalaya, and Cianjur. The national capital city (Jakarta) supports tembang Sunda musicians but not on the same scale as in Bandung. Because most of the better quality musicians live in Bandung, it is often very difficult to find a good kacapi player in one of the outlying cities, let alone the full complement of tembang Sunda musicians. Tembang Sunda performances in the outlying cities are still quite often performed in the old style (rather like the malam tembang Sunda), in which many members of the small audience actively participate by singing. Because of the lack of professional-quality performers, however, formalized or sponsored tembang Sunda evenings (such as panglawungan) are rare.

Other common performance contexts in the outlying areas are cultural "revues," in which all performers in the area are expected to perform a type of variety show for visiting politicians or dignitaries. In this type of performance situation, the time allotted to tembang Sunda is quite brief—usually not more than ten minutes. The primary singers of these small cities, however, most often are people who have gone to Bandung to study and who have brought the "Bandung style" back home with them. In some cases, their only musical affiliation with their home area is that during the pasanggiri DAMAS (the biannual competition), they are registered as representatives of Garut, Sukabumi, or Sumedang, even if they learned everything they know from Bandung teachers and recordings.

Although these performances outside of Bandung may be seen as holdovers from some of the earliest performances of tembang Sunda, many musicians in the outlying areas are so strongly influenced by the power and prestige of Bandung style that most regional styles have been obliterated. Although this topic is hotly debated, I was only rarely able to observe specific examples of regional style. Whereas once there actually was a Garut style, a Sukabumi style, a Bogor style, a Tasik style, and so on, many musicians both in Bandung and outside of Bandung claim that these stylistic differences no longer really exist. Some songs within the tembang Sunda repertoire use place names for their titles (such as "Garutan," "Sumedangan," and others), but, according to the musicians and some of the composers, no real musical traits separate these songs from the rest of the repertoire.

Several musicians mentioned a Cirebon style, and pointed in particular to songs which either use Javanese words or use Javanese-sounding ornaments in the melody. Cirebon is on the border between Sunda and Java, and is not considered a part of the Priangan or inner boundary of Sunda. Very few Bandung musicians are aware of musical events going on in Cirebon outside of masked dance and wayang performances.[10] A small group of musicians agreed that Cirebon-style tembang Sunda sounds like *tarling*, a suling and guitar ensemble from Cirebon that plays popular melodies. None of these musicians, however, was able to actually describe the musical features common to both tarling and tembang Sunda of the Cirebon style.

The one main exception to the apparent dearth of regional styles is Cianjur style, which has held onto particular stylistic traits such as the vehement rejection of songs in saléndro, and the selection of higher-pitched ornaments and melodic lines for performances in Cianjur. It was privately admitted by tembang musicians in Cianjur (and eagerly echoed by Bandung musicians!) that the tembang Sunda scene in Cianjur is no longer very active because almost all tembang Sunda activity is centered in Bandung. Cianjur musicians are described, however, as being the most dedicated and traditional in their study of the genre, and musicians from Cianjur are still held in admiration by Bandung musicians. It is the pangjiwaan or inner soul of the music that is still held the strongest by the musicians of Cianjur.

TRENDS IN CLOTHING AND STAGE DEMEANOR

Stage clothing—both for men and women but especially women—is a constant topic of discussion. Although the basic requirements for stage clothing are partially determined by standard Sundanese formal dress, clothing for performances of tembang Sunda must conform to certain ideal specifications. These specifications are closely tied to the urban setting of tembang Sunda, and reflect new requirements placed on female singers in particular by the demands of urban society. For example, the presence of strong lighting onstage requires very bright, striking makeup, and the shoulder-length hair favored by urban Sundanese women—as opposed to the hip-length hair of village women—has given rise to an entire industry in wig construction and maintenance.

Performances require that male instrumentalists and vocalists dress like Sundanese male colonial aristocracy, and female vocalist(s) look physically—but regally—appealing to the primarily male audience (cf. Pemberton's 1994 discussion of nineteenth-century Javanese costuming in the establishment of a Javanese colonial identity distinct from that of the Dutch). Men occasionally wear basic formal clothing such as the batik shirt and pants required at all nonmusical Indonesian formal or government occasions, but it is generally preferred that they wear the clothing associated with the Sundanese aristocracy. Women almost never stray outside the prescribed boundaries of stage wear. If they do, for example by wearing a skirt and blouse or dress (never long pants), the audience will recognize the inappropriateness of the situation and laugh at or talk badly about the singers. Because clothing for men is far less important either to them or to the audience, more attention and detail is given to women's performance wear.

The standard articles of women's formal clothing are the *kain* and *kabaya*. A kain is a long length of batik into which seven one-and-a-half-inch pleats have been ironed or pressed by hand. The pleats are then fixed with bobby pins until just before the performer goes onstage, when they are removed. Many singers forget to remove the bobby pins themselves, or tease others who have forgotten. The kain, after it has been pleated appropriately, is then wrapped very tightly around the legs of the singer, who then crosses her legs at the ankles to achieve maximum tightness. The final effect is that of an upside-down pyramid, and permits the possibility of demurely sitting only on neatly folded legs. The upper folds of the kain are loosely gathered around the waist, and are cinched with a very thin belt or shoelace. A corset is used to hold the kain in place. Some modern kain are sewn into the pyramid shape with sewn pleats and a zipper in the back. This presewn method, however, is sometimes considered "cheating" and a wrapped kain is preferred.

The kabaya is the other standard feature of women's performance clothing. It is an extremely close-fitting blouse with a front closure and wrist-length sleeves. Although two main styles prevail (an open front with a matching panel across the chest area or a completely closed front with no panel at all), the closed-front style is considered more Sundanese and is, coincidentally, capable of being worn much more tightly than the other (Javanese) style. The bottom edge of the kabaya flares slightly outward at the hips. Stylistic variation in kabaya detailing, such as puffiness of sleeves, depth of décolletage, presence or absence of embroidery, and length or line of the bottom edge is an essential means of individual creativity and style and is also the main feature that separates *kabaya tradisionil* from *kabaya modern*. The kabaya and kain should be in related colors such as pink kabaya and pink and white kain, although they aren't always. Sometimes a long, narrow length of matching batik or appropriately colored polyester chiffon, called a *selendang*, is draped over the singer's right shoulder.

Underneath the very tight kabaya must be worn a waist-length or "push-up" brassiere (called a *long torso*), with or without straps, and a corset for the lower abdomen. These two articles of underwear are frequently visible through the kabaya, which is often constructed of a lacy see-through material or net with flowery designs. The purpose of mentioning these articles of clothing is to point out their function: the brassiere provides the singer with substantially uplifted breast cleavage, and the corset forces the singer's body into an hourglass shape. Both of these features were repeatedly described to me as essentials for tembang Sunda performance, "so that she [the singer] will have a more interesting body" (*Supaya badannya akan lebih menarik*). Strapless high-heeled sandals called *selop* are worn with the ensemble, deliberately chosen so that the singer may gracefully step out of them without bending down to unfasten them when she gets onstage.

A final essential in the performing outfit of a tembang Sunda singer is the hairpiece, or *sanggul*. The sanggul varies between two essential styles: the traditional style consisting of a large, smooth wig in the shape of a bun, and the modern style using the singer's own hair. The sanggul is a phenomenon that has developed in response to a uniquely urban demand: women in Bandung and other large Sundanese urban centers wear their hair short. In Sundanese villages, women almost always wear their hair very long, wrapping and twisting it up for formal occasions. Sanggul makers from Bandung approach village girls and purchase their hair from them for a small sum. This hair is used to supply the large demand from urban women for sanggul of different shapes and sizes, all for use in formal occasions or, in the case of tembang Sunda singers, performances. Once constructed, these sanggul sell for approximately U.S.$10).[11] The same women who construct sanggul also visit the homes of performers and conduct simple maintenance on the performers' sanggul collection, combing them into order and respraying them with "serious-hold" hairspray.

To prepare the singer's existing hair, it is first thoroughly sprayed with hairspray until it is damp, then the hair is ratted (brushed backward). The outermost hairs (at the hairline) are then combed straight on top of the ratted hair to gather it together in a large puff, and are then gathered into a small bun or ponytail at the back of the head. The effect, before the sanggul is placed on top of the small bun, is of smooth-looking but extremely thick hair, so full that it rises several inches above the head. The sanggul is then pinned close to the head by using very long (three-inch) bobby pins. The desirable effect is to have no gap showing between the sanggul and the head. The traditional style of sanggul is constructed from human hair, wrapped around a convex wire shell, and looks like a fist-sized lock of hair completely encircled by a very wide twist of thick hair. The actual size of the sanggul varies from year to year.

Between the sanggul and the singer's real hair is a ten-inch strand of very densely threaded fresh jasmine flowerbuds that lies crosswise on top the head, from ear to ear. The flowers hide the gap between the sanggul and the real hair, and are very fragrant. It takes several hours to create one of these garlands. Some singers use a semicircular piece of balsa wood, carved and painted to look like jasmine flowers, but many prefer to use the real thing if they have the time to purchase and thread them. The use of wooden flowers instead of real jasmine is considered a disagreeable but often necessary concession to the demands of time placed on the urban woman. People speak with approval, however, of women who wear genuine flowers. There is an association of gentility and free time with the threading of the flowers, carrying a further implication of high status and wealth. All of these qualities are desirable among Sundanese women, but particularly for tembang Sunda singers who are constantly trying to guard and improve their aristocratic reputation among competing groups and potential clients.

The modern style of sanggul—worn primarily in the cities—does not use a wire shell, although wire is often used to stabilize the final result. The ponytail is sprayed again and combed out so that the hair may be separated into straight, wire-like sections. These sections are then fashioned like flower petals, holding their shape through repeated applications of hairspray and bobby pins. The final result of a modern sanggul is the appearance of flower-like wide black ribbons, adding volume to the back of the singer's head without the use of a wig. Other styles such as extra-thick braids, highly piled curls, and even an enormous puff of hair behind the head may be used as well, provided that the hair underneath has been ratted and piled so that it rises well over the forehead. The front is often cut into short bangs, from which a single section is combed down, in conscious imitation of Michael Jackson's mid-1980s hairstyle. Undoing one's hair from this complicated series of steps is called *buka* ("opening"), and results in significant hair loss from pulling out the ratted tangles.

Both styles of sanggul are a direct result of urbanization. Styles move much more slowly through the villages and there is far less impetus to be modern and wear one's hair in the latest fashion. Although all Sundanese men are said to prefer long hair on women (according to both the men and women with whom I spoke), only the urban women seem to have favored fashion over traditional attractiveness.

In both traditional and modern styles of dress, large pieces of glittering jewelry are essential. The most important pieces of jewelry are earrings and a necklace or brooch, fastened at the top closure of the kabaya. Rings, although desirable, are not as essential as earrings—except on the right hand, which holds the microphone. Heavy makeup is another requirement, beginning with a shade of foundation that makes the singer look very pale. Paleness and white skin in general is a mark of high status and desirability, particularly among women.[12] Cherry-red lipstick and brilliant eyeshadow in shades of blue, purple, and green are deliberately used, so that the face of the singer does not wash out under strong stage lighting.

As standardized as women's clothing is, it at least is open to individual variation and subject to minor changes in fashion. Men's clothing, by contrast, changes very little and few men seem to care whether it does or not. Most male instrumentalists do not own their own set of performing clothes; the sponsor of the musical group (who is sometimes the husband of the lead female singer) supplies these. Cut in sizes designed to fit generic Sundanese body types, outfits (particularly the coats) for male instrumentalists rarely fit very well. If a man is associated with one group for a long time, an outfit may be made to fit him and it will be set aside as his. Male vocalists occasionally own and use their own performance clothing, but they sometimes borrow from the female vocalist's selection of clothing used by the instrumentalists.

The standard outfit for performances, whether the man is a singer or an instrumentalist, is the ensemble of *sarung, takwah*, and *bendo*. The sarung is a length of batik similar to a woman's kain, except that the pleats are much wider (approximately three inches across) and there are usually fewer pleats (four or five). Many sarung are sewn into a tube so that they are easy for the man to step in and out of, and do not require complex wrapping procedures. Because playing music requires the men to sit cross-legged on the floor or stage, sarung are never wrapped tightly but instead allow plenty of legroom. Men are always fully dressed under their performing outfits, unlike the women. Men simply roll up their pants legs a few inches and wrap the sarung over them. The batik patterns on men's sarung are often larger than those of kain, and the pattern for both frequently slopes downward in a diagonal from right to left. The sarung is held in place at the top by a belt, and is sometimes held in place by a *stagen* or thick piece of wrapping cloth, six inches in diameter that is wrapped repeatedly around the man's waist and fastened with safety pins.

The takwah is a type of morning coat, made out of thick double-knit polyester in a neutral color such as brown or gray. In some styles, it buttons directly up the front, and in others, it overlaps across the man's chest so that the lapel of the coat falls in a diagonal from the shoulder to the waist. The takwah fits down over the top of the sarung and is never unbuttoned during a performance, even though it is extremely warm, often ill fitting, and uncomfortable to wear. The bendo or small cap is worn over the head, placed directly on top of the head so that it partly covers the upper forehead. The bendo is made of folded batik, so many sarung and bendo are made of the same material. To complete the outfit, men wear shiny flat black leather sandals with covered toes. These sandals, like the takwah, rarely fit properly and are difficult to walk in, so the musicians have to shuffle their feet as they walk. Like the shoes for women, men's performing shoes are strapless and therefore very easy to remove. Men like to wear rings with very large stones set in them, and they enjoy comparing stones and discussing rings when passing the time.

Although men do not spend as much time on their clothing as women do, the set standard for male performance wear reflects an essential feature of tembang Sunda: Men who perform tembang Sunda are responsible for representing the aristocracy from the time of the kingdom of Pajajaran.

When a man chooses to wear a batik shirt with pants, he runs the risk of associating himself with the current Indonesian government that requires batik at all formal occasions and on national holidays. To wear a batik shirt while performing tembang Sunda is to make a potential statement of allegiance to the government and with the modern world. Tembang Sunda is so strongly associated with Pajajaran and with the Sundanese precolonial times that every aspect of appropriate tembang Sunda performance, such as wearing the proper clothing, is an affirmation of what it means to be Sundanese and to share that heritage. As Christine Yano notes, singers of Japanese enka are so clearly linked to the genre that even their clothing, hair, and makeup serve to embody the values of the *furusato* or hometown (Yano 1997:123). Association with the rural past thus becomes the key to success. Markedly, the rules of tembang Sunda stage clothing are paid attention to far more closely inside the city of Bandung, however, than outside.

Once the performers have completely dressed themselves and done their hair and makeup (a process that may take several hours for women), they are ready to perform. Depending on the performance setting, the vocalists may mix with the audience or are expected to wait until they are signaled to begin. Male instrumentalists are expected to wait and, because of their lower status in relation to the singers, do not mix with the audience. The instrumentalists are responsible for carrying and placing the instruments onstage and setting them up appropriately in relation to the microphones. Although most formal performances have soundmen who set up the microphones, it is still the instrumentalists who are primarily responsible for making the sound system appropriate for tembang Sunda. After the setting up of the instruments, microphones for the instruments, and vocal microphones is complete, the instrumentalists simply remove their shoes and climb onstage at the appropriate time, and begin playing with no introduction at all. They generally lower their heads as they are in the process of getting onstage, but they do not alter the way they walk for the benefit of the audience, as do the female singers. Instrumentalists do not smile or even look at the audience, and are not expected to have any connection to them. Male vocalists climb onstage at the same time as the female vocalists.

Female singers carry thick songbooks with them to performances, and these books are carried onstage in large purses or may be carried by hand. Because of the extreme tightness of the kain and kabaya, fully dressed tembang Sunda singers are forced to mince slowly in very small steps when they walk, causing their hips to sway. Their hands are generally at their sides, even if they carry their songbooks, and they lower their heads to appear elegant, modest, and aristocratic. Because many performances of tembang Sunda are preceded by at least one instrumental piece played by the kacapi, suling, and rincik, the instrumentalists are generally already present and in place when the singers arrive.

Female singers take off their shoes before they climb onstage and usually get on their knees almost immediately, before they are actually in position. They push themselves forward on their hands and knees until they are in front of the instruments, then sit back on their knees and carefully rearrange their clothing so that the pleats in the kain are in order, the kabaya is straight, and the selendang, if there is one, is draped gracefully across the right arm. During the performance, the singer's legs usually fall asleep (*singsireumeun,* "bitten by ants"), so it is normal after about ten minutes for the singer to shift onto one hip, often supported by one of the thick songbooks or a small pillow. The singer may then shift back and forth from one hip to another and up onto the knees again, but once their feet are asleep they try to wake them up by hitting them with their fists between songs or when another singer is taking her turn. They also complain to each other and to the musicians about their feet. At the end of a performance, the singers close their songbooks, lean forward, and, supporting themselves with their hands, push themselves onto their feet and stand still until they regain the feeling in their feet. To get off the stage, singers often request the help of the instrumentalists.

After the performance or during the middle if the performance is long enough to warrant taking a short break, it is customary for the performers to eat something. If the event is a wedding or other ritual for which a large catered buffet is provided, the musicians are expected to help themselves after the guests have been served. When the musicians eat in the middle of a performance, they are expected to get onstage immediately afterward and continue performing, even if they are full. Singers usually take advantage of being too full to sing by sending the instrumentalists back onstage first for instrumental kacapi-suling. The excuse given is that the rice hasn't "gone down" yet (Indo.: *Nasinya belum turun*). By avoiding going back onstage themselves, the singers sometimes gamble on the fact that most of the guests will leave as soon as the food is gone, so that their part of the performance will already be finished.

If the event is a government function or part of a series of other performances, the musicians are given a small portable snack (*sanak*), provided for them by the host. The snack comes in a small white box and almost always contains rice, chicken, a very small banana, a plastic bag with hot sauce or peppers, and a piece of cake or hard sweet gelatin. The snack may be eaten immediately or taken home as a gift for those who did not come along to the performance. The instrumentalists always eat after the vocalist, because they are responsible for carrying the instruments off the stage and back to the car or bus that transported them to the performance. Only after the stage is cleared do the instrumentalists eat.

ACKNOWLEDGING CHANGE

In both 1964 and 1976, one-day seminars were held in Bandung about the history and current conditions of tembang Sunda. Although extremely rare, the very existence of such a seminar indicates the seriousness with which tembang Sunda is taken by its participants (see also Sutton 1984:238–241, about music seminars held in Yogyakarta). In each case, the attendees were prominent musicians, vocalists, historians, and composers from many different places both inside and beyond the borders of the Priangan area, each of whom was interested in the promotion and dissemination of knowledge about tembang Sunda. Participants took notes at each seminar, and some were published afterward. At the 1964 seminar (notes of which were obtained from Dr. Ernst Heins), participants discussed the origins of the genre, the stylistic features, related genres (among which were listed Ciawian, Bantenan, Sumedangan, Cirebonan, and others), and the names of the main proponents.

At the 1976 seminar, the results of which were published in the *Buletin Kebudayaan Jawa Barat* (Panitia Seminar Tembang Sunda 1976), participants agreed on several points. Among these were that tembang Sunda should be studied comparatively with other Sundanese musical genres; that the terminology should be standardized; that related genres such as Cigawiran, Garutan, and others should also be studied; that the term tembang Sunda is still the most appropriate term for the genre; and that tembang Sunda in general requires further study (Panitia Seminar Tembang Sunda 1976:4). Long-range goals cited in the seminar proceedings include a restructuring of the notation system, the establishment of a curriculum to teach both tembang Sunda and the Sundanese language in the schools, and the establishment of a "Creativity Board" to protect copyright laws and to support composers.

These two seminars (and other smaller, less formal seminars) are an important forum for the discussion of change and the future direction of tembang Sunda. So far, none of the long-range goals has been realized; however, the fact that they were brought up and discussed at the 1976 seminar indicates that the people involved in tembang Sunda had different issues on their minds from those who attended the one in 1964. As is the case with tembang Sunda competitions, discussions such as these are remembered and brought up repeatedly for years afterward. Several musicians in the 1990s continued to speak about the 1964 and 1976 seminars, comparing the issues discussed then with what is being discussed now. The wide variety of opportunities available for live performances of tembang Sunda in the city is one of the most important features of urban living contributing to the stabilization and maintenance of the genre. These opportunities for performance, combined with the support of tembang Sunda by the mass media, have enabled it to survive in the face of other, more popular genres.

4

Musical Interactions between Men and Women

I have stated previously that most tembang Sunda vocalists are women. This dates from the genre's earliest development, and women have dominated since the 1970s. Although several famous female instrumentalists in the past (especially Ibu Saodah Harnadi Natakusumah and Ibu Haji Siti Rokhayah) have achieved some degree of fame, almost all instrumentalists now are men. The relationship between the primarily female vocalists and primarily male instrumentalists is a topic of frequent conversations, not just among the musicians but among the sponsors and potential clients of the sponsors. Not only do women "sell" an urban performance better than men (by providing the appropriate decoration of the stage merely with their physical appearance), but they also have the exclusive privilege of performing panambih songs. The performance of panambih has grown increasingly popular in urban performance practice.

Panambih songs, of all the styles belonging to tembang Sunda, have the fewest associations with the old aristocracy. They are considered easy to sing because of their fixed meters, are easy to accompany on the kacapi, and most panambih lyrics deal with various aspects of love instead of history or spiritual topics. Because of this, they are easily accessible to a larger population not only of singers but also of middle-class audiences who have no ancestral connection to the aristocracy. Therefore, the average middle-class urban audience may derive considerable enjoyment from their idea of a tembang Sunda performance simply by seeing the visual trappings of the genre (the instruments and the beautiful singer) and hearing lyrics dealing mainly with love. The presence of a male vocalist onstage in an urban tembang Sunda performance often indicates to this type of audience that the songs will be of a more serious, historical, or spiritual nature. Although this type of song will not be rejected outright, it is not as preferable in an urban setting as lighter love songs performed by a pretty singer. As always, exceptions abound. For example, the presence of a male singer onstage may indicate to some members of the audience that the singer will perform kawih songs, or even songs of the pop Sunda repertoire. Considering Bandung's size and increasing heterogeneity, some audience members may not even be aware of what is onstage, and may simply categorize it all as background music for the main event, which is people-watching.

SELLING A PERFORMANCE

Women performers are very important contributors to the overall success of a tembang Sunda performance. As the primary singers of the genre, female vocalists are expected to lead performances. Cassettes almost invariably feature a photograph of the female vocalist on the cover; men rarely appear photographed solo or sing solo on recordings (cf. Sutton 1987:120). In addition, a performance may be announced and attended solely on the basis of the name of the primary female performer.

It is, therefore, in the interest of the group sponsor and the hiring client to combine the visual impact of the female singer(s) with the aural impact of love songs (as opposed to historical or other songs), strengthened with the high status of Sunda's most élite musical genre. An urban client may receive the best of both worlds, and a successful performance for his own guests, if he hires the outer shell of a tembang Sunda group—the ensemble—leaving out the historical and spiritual depth of some of the older songs that could displease some of the guests. These statements are not intended to imply that male vocalists do not sing love songs; on the contrary, they perform and enjoy them as much as the women. The urban setting of modern tembang Sunda has contributed to a stronger division of gender roles in performance practice, however, resulting in the prevalence of female vocalists and male instrumentalists.

The sexual dynamics at work in the world of tembang Sunda comprise one of the favorite topics among vocalists and instrumentalists. The historical status differences between vocalists and instrumentalists persist today, so that there are very few physical relationships or marriages between these groups. However, the relationship between the female vocalist and the male instrumentalist is quite strong, and both sides tell stories of love relationships *anu teu janten*, "that never happened." Sometimes it is felt that the performance of tembang Sunda represents the consummation not only of those relationships but also all other potential relationships that have been thwarted by status or societal boundaries. Some men also include the connection between a man and his musical instrument in their discussions of the various relationships of tembang Sunda (see also Chapter 10 on the relationship between male musicians and their instruments). It is said that the appropriate attitude of a woman should be that of someone who waits for her man to lead her; in tembang Sunda performance practice, this attitude is illustrated through the musical roles played out by the vocalist and the instrumentalist.

The female vocalist depends on her accompanists to provide her with the appropriate pitches at the expected time, and their job is to lead or "bribe" her through the song and the entire performance (Rukmana, personal communication, 1988). She also has an unfair advantage over them in that they are required to know the entire repertoire as part of their job, whereas she herself may only need to know thirty songs well enough to perform. She receives better treatment from the hosts, often lives in a nicer home than her accompanists, is paid more, and is much more of a "star" performer than her accompanists. The accompanists often feel very close to their singer and can feel protective of her or defensive in a fatherly or brotherly fashion. Backstage clowning between male instrumentalists and female vocalists reinforces this connection. Some instrumentalists claim that one of the greatest joys of performing with a good female singer is in knowing her and her repertoire well. Both artists may then participate in the type of nonverbal communication that leads to unspoken song selection, greater improvisational freedom for the instrumentalists, and the private sharing of their mutual love for tembang Sunda in a public forum.

While very few of these male instrumentalists will actually speak openly about their own experiences (out of concern for disrupting their social and professional connections), many short stories and anecdotes of other peoples' experiences are brought into discussions. Most of these anecdotes deal with how certain vocalists or musicians were able to communicate their feelings (or lack thereof) through tembang Sunda. During long conversations in which male musicians are working through the smallest details of tembang Sunda performance practice and telling stories about performers, some musicians like to describe certain lyrics and explain the circumstances under which they should be performed. In a particularly moving rendition of certain songs, some performers or audience members may be moved to tears. Moving someone to tears is believed to deepen the person's *pangjiwaan* or deep-level understanding of the music.[1] Songs that move people to tears are not always love songs; some of the deepest of the spiritual songs also may have this effect.

FEMALE PERFORMERS AND THE
POLITICS OF SEXUALITY

The dynamics of gender politics here make it seem to the outsider that women are placed at a disadvantage. For various reasons (including limited performance options, or the demands of home and family), some women musicians are considered to be among those marginalized performers in the Sundanese music scene. Yet, as bearers of a musical culture that at least partly revolves around the primacy of the female voice, they tend also to be recognized as crucial participants in any performance. Indeed, the undercurrent of Sundanese matrilineality and matrifocality in Sundanese culture permeates even the urban setting (see Williams 1998b). Musicians in Bandung operate in multiple social networks, and many middle- and upper-middle-class women musicians find themselves intersecting with (and sometimes at odds with) the social and political networks of their husbands. Because so much musical work in Bandung requires the straddling of boundaries in communicating with all kinds of people outside of one's own immediate social sphere, many performers find themselves shifting back and forth between public and private, respectability and disrespectability, and even male and female roles.

The people of West Java are known for their adherence to Islam and for the less-obvious presence of Hinduism in their lives than in the lives of their Javanese neighbors.[2] Issues of music and respectability come up in conversations and affect their beliefs (as Muslims) about whether or not women should perform. Because of traditional links between the voice of a singer and the voice of God, and between song lyrics and the verses of the Qur'an, the Sundanese tend to accept singers as performing their art within the traditional boundaries of respectability. Instrumentalists fall into the more problematic position of having to do without the links to God and the Qur'an, but because almost all Sundanese instrumental music is used to accompany vocalists, instrumentalists can still walk the line of respectability.

Due at least in part to these important ideas about what is respectable, the female performer tends to fall (or be pushed) into the role of vocalist or dancer rather than instrumentalist. Although some women do become instrumentalists, they only do so in certain contexts; for example, when the musical pieces are considered unchallenging. The woman who dashes off a virtuoso instrumental piece on the kacapi at a public performance not only threatens the masculinity of every male performer in the place but also jeopardizes the public perception of her own femininity. Women speak rather carefully about their own musical abilities; anyone who has won a competition has the right to be slightly more revealing about her musical skills. The open secret among Sundanese musicians is that women can be (and sometimes are) excellent instrumentalists, but only in the private sphere, where—in a temporary suspension of their Muslim identities—they also smoke heavily, tell off-color jokes, and occasionally drink alcohol. As

Suzanne Brenner points out in her discussion of Solonese women of Central Java, "To the extent that their comportment and speech are accorded less weight than men's, women have the freedom to engage with relative impunity in behavior that would be compromising to men's status" (Brenner 1998:142).

The female performer also may hold the position of group leader for lingkung seni. In some cases, acquiring the position of female leader stems from being married to a powerful man who owns instruments and has connections; still, a female performer does not usually rise in stature through her husband's fame and fortune but more often from gathering her own. From this central position, the female leaders of these groups exercise power and influence over dozens of other performers, including male instrumentalists.

Almost all of the roles that women take on in becoming the leader of a performing group revolve in one way or another around activities of mothering. In taking on the responsibilities of group manager, they are usually responsible for the arrangement of performances, disbursement of money (cf. Brenner 1998:144), the hiring of performers, and making certain that everyone arrives together and on time for those performances. Once at the performance, the female leader makes sure that all of the other performers are dressed properly, and assists each one (including the men) in straightening sarongs, keeping street clothes hidden underneath costumes, and arranging hair. Performers are scolded if the pleats in their sarongs are not straight, or if they are sloppily tied. After the performance is over, all costumes except for female wigs are stored at the female leader's house, in the "private space" away from where guests are received.

Women tread the fine line between public and private space in their ability to move between the back parts of the house and the front receiving area. Music is performed in the semiprivate interior living room, beyond the area where guests are received. Musicians usually enter a house through the back door, where the servants enter; indeed, musicians themselves also tread the fine line between public and private, because they can more easily pass beyond the public area to the semiprivate area than even close friends of the owners. Some male musicians can even visit the women's areas of homes without causing an uproar (see Koskoff 1987:7). Nonmusicians generally do not have this freedom.[3]

The fact that performers can easily pass through the boundaries of public/private, respectability/disrespectability, and male/female adds to the outside perception of their power and influence. It is those people who exist in the marginal regions of unsettled boundaries who often engender the most power (see also de Lauretis 1990:116). Women, in particular, can perform in the most public place, controlling the stage, and yet they also rule the back of the house, the most private area. As they age, they become even more powerful and more respected,[4] especially as they pass out of childbearing age and enter the period in which sex ceases to have a reproductive function.

Suzanne Brenner brings up an interesting paradox of men's and women's desire, potency, and spirituality. The standard model for Central Javanese behavior, according to the prevailing literature, is that men are well in control of their desires, while women are not. Yet, Brenner points out that women are often the ones deemed to be more in control (1998:149). Indeed, my Sundanese host summed up the whole contradictory idea for me by saying "A man will do whatever a woman wants because men are cheap to buy."

> When a man controls his desires, it is commonly believed, he makes himself potent. When he lets his self-control lapse, he is a danger to the family, but his sexual potency may also be linked to a more spiritual kind of potency. When a woman controls *her* desire, she accumulates economic and spiritual value for the family, more than personal potency. But a woman with too much control over her own person, it appears, is considered a threat to society. (Brenner 1998: 166)

The context, finally, is crucial: in the public sphere, the male-dominant model holds sway. In the private sphere (within the inner sanctum of the home), the woman is the powerful one. It is worth pointing out that in the chaotic atmosphere of the market, as well as on the performance stage, women are also "at home" (see Williams 1998b, for more about the concept of gender and home).

In West Java, as in Central Java, certain attributes determine personal power (see Anderson 1972), and certain features, such as the gathering of a large number of followers, are reflective of that personal potency (Errington 1990:43). In his discussion of the Central Javanese *pesindhèn*, Sutton has noted that certain women performers may be believed to have supernatural powers (Sutton 1987:119). Among female vocalists, supernatural and sexual powers are deeply linked, and both inform the character of their musical expression. Among female performers who have garnered a great deal of public recognition and a reputation for scandal, even the possibility of sexual potency is enough to make their currency rise in local opinion. Koskoff has written that "one of the most common associations between women and music links women's primary sexual identity and role with musical performance" (Koskoff 1987:6). The influence that comes with fame, followers, and fortune because of musical activity is compounded by public perception of a heightened sexuality. As Suzanne Brenner says, "The more money a woman controls, the more autonomous she is, and an autonomous woman is always somewhat suspect" (1998:162).

As a contrast to the overt refinement of the female tembang Sunda vocalist, the female performer of the Sundanese village comedic team is generally renowned for her sexual appetite and energy. Rumors abound about how the female member of the team has to have good sex with her husband before she agrees to get onstage. This speculation is fueled by the stage appearance of the two: She is strong and brassy, while her husband looks weak and exhausted. The sum of their two performances creates a type of funny and appalling cautionary tale for the Sundanese. Her public sexuality is unquestioned and welcomed as part of the performance; his is treated as the obvious and comedic/tragic result of what happens when women's sexuality is loosed on the world. Although the comedic team may appear remote from the aristocratic arena of tembang Sunda, the two genres may appear on the same stage in succession. Through her ubiquitous presence, the female comedic artist's overt sexuality ends up affecting the reputation of every female performer.

Male Transvestites as Female Performing Artists

Another type of person who tends to easily cross boundaries is the transvestite prostitute, the *banci*. Male Sundanese transvestites tend to dress like female performers—especially tembang Sunda singers—in tight outfits, corsets, and stage makeup. Bancis sometimes perform by the side of the road or in certain nightclubs that cater to gender-bending entertainment, in which a banci may sing or dance with a male customer for a fee and with the possibility of later sexual employment. Because of his position as someone who walks the line between male and female, the banci is considered to have a great deal of personal power, but little or no influence either socially or politically.

Brenner brings up the notion of the banci as putative female in his/her ability to control money and resist its temptation in the marketplace. Using an example of specific banci, Brenner notes, "His femaleness suggested trustworthiness, a self-control of which an unambiguously gendered male would probably not have been assumed capable. By taking on the mannerisms and clothing of a woman, [he/she] also acquired the reputation women have for being able to control their desires" (Brenner 1998:161).

In his act of taking on the identity of a female performer, the banci tries to capture the heart and soul of female sexuality in his creation of a performance. Because most bancis are clearly identifiable as male transvestites, part of their unique attraction stems from what de Lauretis calls "a disidentification with femininity that does not necessarily revert or result in an identification with masculinity" (de Lauretis 1990:126). The banci, although male, is included in this discussion of female sexuality because the social construction of femaleness here is not limited to biological determinants (Errington 1990:58); rather, it is more an issue surrounding the creation and assertion of sexual power through the adoption of those traits considered most intensely female:

> Older listeners look to the *enka* stage for affirmations of maleness and femaleness past: men in control of lives, situations, people; women reacting to men's actions. Here is hierarchy and dominance, to be sure, but also place and comfort in the restrictiveness of the roles. These listeners find solace in the unchanging world of these songs and the gendered images of their singers. (Yano 1997:125)

Keeler points out that the way one behaves (in comportment and vocal tone) leads to assumptions about moral character (Keeler 1987). While treading the fine line between physically behaving properly and visually enhancing audience perceptions of their potency, tembang singers tend to choose performing outfits that accentuate their sexual attributes. While the standard performance clothing of front-closing blouse and wrapped batik is common to all of Java and Bali, only the Sundanese performers wear clothing this tight.

Female Circumcision among the Sundanese

The heightened sexuality of female performers, from comedy teams to aristocratic singers to its representation by transvestites, leads to questions of regulation and control. Urban Sundanese women sometimes drive; they may go out alone or without the company of men; and they are often educated to at least the high school level and beyond. Yet the practice of female circumcision is common. Concerns about women's sexual potency—especially for those women who spend their lives crossing the boundaries of respectability—lead to local comments such as, "Not every woman is unclean, but some performers need circumcision," and "We don't ever know how women are going to turn out when they grow up; that's why we do this ritual when they're only ten days old."

What actually takes place during circumcision varies from family to family; in general, however, the baby girl has the operation performed at ten days. A group of older women (generally past menopause) gather at the home in Muslim dress, and after washing the genital area, a small incision is made at the lower base of the clitoris. The clitoris is not removed, although often a small piece of flesh is cut out from the incision site ("the dirtiest part," said a young woman who had witnessed several operations of this kind). After the operation, the girl is then decreed to be "clean" (bersih). No men are present at this operation. Every woman with whom I spoke about this matter had had the operation done, and each one mentioned that she had no memory of the operation.[5] In response to questions about the long-term results of the operation, most of the adult urban women who spoke about the practice indicated that sex was "difficult to enjoy," "took too long," and was "too much trouble to bother with."

As a religious practice, ritual purification (making one's village, oneself or someone else "clean") is quite common, accepted, and enjoyed among Muslims, Hindus, and the members of other mainstream religions. Many Indonesians bathe twice a day in frigid water, welcoming the sensation of cleanliness. In fact, after a woman's monthly menstruation has ended, she is free to engage in sexual relations, again under the terms of being "clean."

While spoken of matter-of-factly by both men and women as a regular practice of making women "clean" and "less interested in other men," female circumcision has been denied, or discounted as "rare" in the Western anthropological literature (see, e.g., Wessing 1978 and Geertz 1960b:51). The

Sundanese use of circumcision among women goes beyond the fact that there is a fundamental difference between the image and the physical enactment of sexuality. The tight performance clothing, song lyrics trading heavily on missed opportunities for intimacy, and the tremendous gossip and intrigue surrounding performers belies the fact that—as a result of female circumcision—many women have some difficulty being physically intimate. Furthermore, the silence in academic circles about the prevalence of female circumcision raises the possibility that deeper issues are at stake than male circumcision—for example, because performance is used at male but not female circumcision rituals.[6]

Cultural Politics and Gender Divisions

Each area within Indonesia is represented within the state discourse on multiculturalism by that which makes its culture unique. For example, one of the many maps issued by the government shows the various parts of Indonesia depicted by pictures of a man and a woman in their *pakaian adat* or traditional clothing. Those groups whose traditional clothing is minimal are often represented in grass skirts and t-shirts. Other maps show cultural artifacts such as unique hat styles, foods, architecture, or musical instruments (see Pemberton 1994).

In a musical map of Indonesia, each area is characterized by a certain feature of its music that indicates its home area. For example, Indonesians will talk about Balinese music as being intensely rhythmic, or Javanese music being stratified. In a similar vein, that which is considered most characteristically Sundanese (*kasundaan*) is the sound of the voice, especially when performed by a female singer or when played on the suling. Locally, the suling is itself considered a "female" instrument (van Zanten 1989:105), appropriate to be played only by men. The female voice or its bamboo representative is depicted as performing a sad song that invokes feelings of nostalgia or lost love. In the national process of mapping out a region and locating a group of people (Anderson 1983:175), Sundanese diversity becomes reduced to female singers as signifiers of culture.

The gradual reduction of the Sundanese—a diverse, fragmented, transitory group of over thirty million people spread over all of West Java—to representation by the image of the female singer has been a slow process of local invention of tradition. From a map with a kacapi and suling behind a female singer to the televised depiction of a *ronggeng* (female singer/dancer accompanied by gamelan or *ketuk tilu*), women appear constantly as stand-ins for Sundanese culture in the national dialogue. As Sundanese officials have struggled to create a regional sense of separateness, outsiders have pegged the Sundanese as being more unified than they actually are (see Appadurai 1988:16). Appadurai notes that "one man's imagined community is another man's political prison" (1996:32). The representation of Sunda in the body of a female tembang Sunda singer results in the commodification and feminization of the Sundanese image.[7]

In the Sundanese music scene, certain social mechanisms have developed that allow for a locus of power in the person of the female vocalist; for example, the placement of female singers at the most visible place onstage, or the prominence of women as leaders of performing arts groups. At the national level, singers such as Elvy Sukaesih have attained considerable power—but not because of their local identity. Differences in identity, sexuality, and the interpretation of these two concepts lead ultimately to these differences being reflected in political power (see Solie 1993:6). If, as Susan McClary states, "music helps shape our internalized ideas about feelings, the self, gender, the body, pleasure, and even models of social organization" (McClary 1993:419), then it certainly has the potential to shape and distort political identities as well. The representation of the Sundanese by the image of the female singer[8] may more or less render an entire ethnic group mute (see Modleski 1991:52), in that in its feminization it remains outside the national political discourse and must develop and sustain its own networks of power and influence. For example, a common practice includes the promotion of Sundanese officials to positions of power in Bandung offices, rather than outsiders (including Javanese) who happen to live in Bandung.

"SHOOTING" A SONG AND AIMING TO KILL

In many urban performances of tembang Sunda, a balance is struck between the old setting and the new; in other words, some portion of the audience may belong to the circle of tembang Sunda performers, while the rest will be oblivious. It is in situations such as weddings (or other gatherings that contain both informed and uninformed members of the audience) that songs may be deliberately used to communicate something to someone. The Indonesian verb used is *menembak* ("to shoot"), as in the shooting of songs at a person in such a way that he is struck and, in some cases, seduced by them. In some cases, the intended victim does not even have to be present at the event; he may hear about it from others, or anyone who is paying attention may be made aware of the current status of the relationship. If the song reaches its mark and the person struck by it becomes obviously and abruptly enamored of the singer, he may be jokingly referred to as *ditembak mati* (Indo.: "shot dead").

The use of tembang Sunda songs as a form of ammunition has its antecedents in older, nonurban performances, because the genre has long been used as a medium for the communication of feelings. The modern settings of tembang Sunda, however, create a far greater field for this kind of communication. Because the audience is no longer limited to practitioners of the genre, and because dozens of people can be present at these performances, the vocalist has a wider range of potential victims and a more varied network through which to communicate. The fact that a victim may not realize that he is a "mark" leads to general gossip and enjoyment among insiders. Some of the newer songs of the repertoire contribute to this phenomenon, and some are composed specifically for this kind of situation. Although I describe the poetry and the meaning of the lyrics to selected tembang Sunda songs in greater depth in Part IV, I mention this point here because songs are specifically selected in order to cause a reaction in a member of the audience.

It is common for a female vocalist to choose a song with particularly eloquent lyrics and then act as if the intended listener is not there. Such actions are one aspect of the more subtle game-playing that goes on between the singers, the instrumentalists, and members of the audience. Therefore, it is not just the lyrics themselves that cause this reaction among the active participants of a tembang Sunda performance but, in fact, the situation itself that sets up certain members of the audience and other performers to react to the lyrics. In a case such as a wedding performance, the active participants need to be alert for the use of emotionally charged songs as a type of artillery by the singers. In some cases, as was proved by my occasionally mistaken selection of songs in my own performances, some members of the audience may in fact be far more alert than the singer to possible underlying meanings and the establishment of one's emotional status as happy, sad, hurt, available, complaining, loyal, longing, or depressed.

At an all-night tembang Sunda gathering, nearly all the men were on one side of the room and the women were on the other, as usual. At one point in the evening, a young and pretty singer was performing a historical song, which caused another woman to lean over to me and whisper, "The men can't wait for her to do a love song! She has no idea." Later that night, several men (in low voices) discussed the lyrics being sung at the moment, the singer performing them, and which one of the men she was aiming at. While they jokingly speculated at first that the target must be one of them, they eventually decided that it was a young man on the other side of the men's group, who was studiously avoiding the glances of the singer.

Although the most overt use of special lyrics to convey an emotional state is done by the performers themselves, some well-informed patrons take advantage of their prestige and power (as the client of the performing group) to request special songs for the singer(s) to perform. For example, a client or host may ask the singer to choose special lyrics that use the old aristocratic terms of *Raden* and *Juragan*, or a song composed from the viewpoint of a lower-status person toward a higher-status person, and request that the song be performed especially for him.[9] The use of these songs that contain aristocratic terms may function as a way of establishing her relative inferiority to him and his power over her. Because singers work very hard to present themselves in a sexually appealing manner, it is not surprising that some patrons actually respond to the sex appeal of the singer and attempt to exercise some measure of control over her.

In some cases, a tembang Sunda vocalist may be so attractive to her patrons that her husband may forbid her from singing in public. Bandung has several excellent singers who do not perform very often because their husbands no longer allow them to appear publicly. Making a cassette recording seems to be acceptable for some of these women because of the money they produce; however, public appearances may suddenly be strictly curtailed when a patron shows more than a casual interest or begins to act like an informed member of the audience. By contrast, a happily married singer who has one or more children may be allowed by her husband to sing, because the setting for tembang Sunda is generally quite safe in its impact on her reputation. That is, it is far better—for a singer's reputation—to be seen performing in front of a known and limited audience that deeply appreciates the music (as in a malam tembang Sunda), or a well-lit government building, than to be outside all night, accompanying a wayang performance until dawn.

A singer who is considered too overt in her sexual attractiveness is generally designated as *bahaya* ("dangerous"), not only in that she could be a threat to the marriages of the other women, but as dangerous competition for high-paying performance jobs.[10] Other singers are then outwardly friendly but verbally destructive behind the person's back. The general instability of Sundanese marriages, resulting in a divorce rate of over 50 percent (Peacock 1973:97, 100), contributes to the distrust and anxiety occurring not only between husbands and their frequently attractive vocalist wives but also among singers themselves.

Tembang Sunda can be used to communicate emotions and gender-laden messages, all within the framework of standard performance practice. Tembang Sunda also may ensure not just the hiring of one group over another (if the vocalist is more attractive and the client cares only about the outward appearance of the group), but also the relative success of an event, based on the uninformed urban audience's expectations of what they will *see*, not hear. In wielding powerful songs at performances, both men and women have the option of marking a hapless audience member for (at least temporary) ruin, particularly if the effects of the song become publicly known.[11] In the arena of politicized sexuality, women inhabit the border region between respectability and disrespectability, making their performances simultaneously irresistible and dangerous.

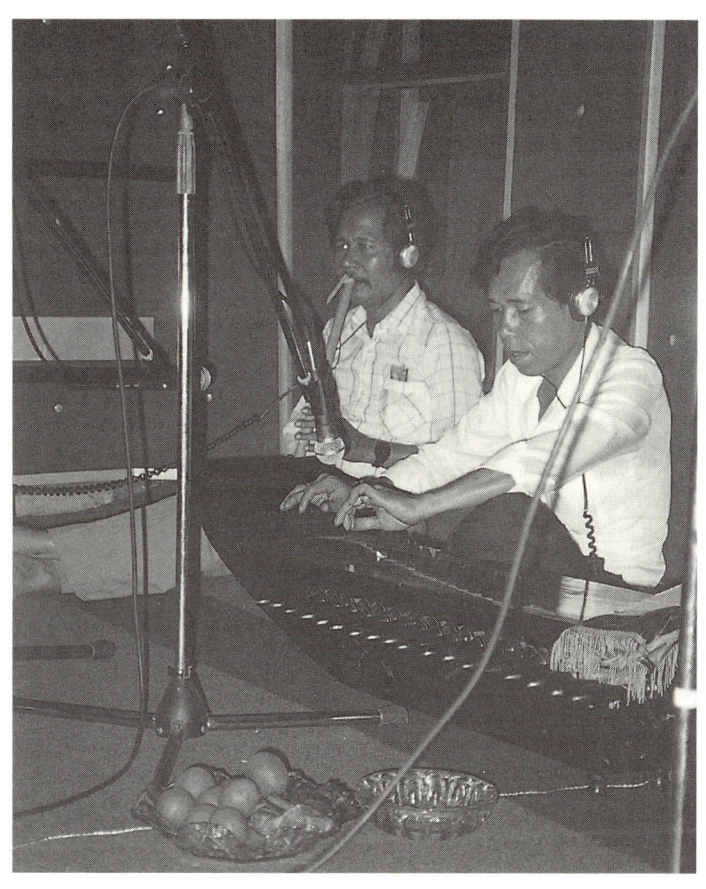

PLATE 1 ABOVE Burhan Sukarma (*left*) and Rukruk Rukmana (*right*) play suling and kacapi, respectively, during a studio session.

PLATE 2 BELOW Tembang Sunda musicians (*left to right*) Nana Suhana (rincik), Iwan S. (suling), and Gan-Gan Garmana (kacapi) during a malam tembang Sunda

PLATE 3 ABOVE The late Dacép Eddy plays rebab (*left*) at a malam tembang Sunda, accompanied by Nana Suhana (rincik) and Tatang Subari (kacapi).

PLATE 4 RIGHT Kacapi player Rukruk Rukmana demonstrates the pasieup technique.

PLATE 5 BELOW The members of the lingkung seni Simpay Tresna pose in front of their trophies after a 1991 Festival Tembang Sunda victory.

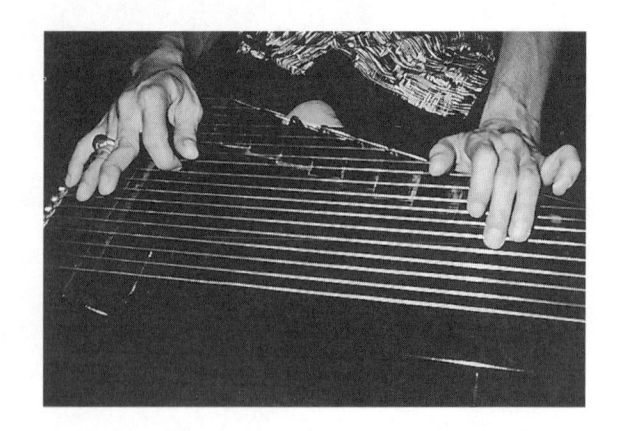

PLATE 6 Euis Komariah and Neneng Dinar Suminar perform tembang Sunda at a performance for the Gambian head of state in 1987, accompanied by Gan-Gan Garmana (kacapi), Iwan S. (suling), and Cucu S. (rincik).

PLATE 7 Traditional suling construction method

PLATE 8 Rukruk Rukmana plays the kacapi, the ancestral ship of the book's title.

PLATE 9 The men's side of the room at a malam tembang Sunda. Note the sound system in the foreground.

PLATE 10 The women's side of the room at a malam tembang Sunda

PLATE 11 An idealized vision of the Sundanese village

PLATE 12 A more dramatic view of the forest (*leuweung*). Note the distant volcano floating above the clouds.

PLATE 13 Vocalist Euis Komariah in full performance wear of *kain*, *kabaya*, *selendang*, *selop*, and *sanggul*

PLATE 14 BELOW Vocalists (*from left to right*) Teti Affienti, Mamah Dasimah, and Tintin Suparyani in matching pink *kain* and *kabaya*, accompanied by Rukruk Rukmana on kacapi and Burhan Sukarma on suling

PLATE 15 Vocalists Teti Affienti and Tintin Suparyani at an outdoor performance, accompanied by Gan-Gan Garmana (kacapi), Iwan S. (suling), and Cucu S. (rincik). Note the drum set and synthesizer in the background.

PLATE 16 Vocalist Yayah Rochaeti Dachlan at an outdoor performance for the sister of the three instrumentalists: Rukruk Rukmana (kacapi), Tatang Subari (suling), and Pepen Subari (rincik)

5

The Mediation of Sound

The industry of communication has had a profound impact on the development of current Indonesian culture. Indeed, modernization is closely linked with media, including by members of the media-related workforce themselves. The Indonesian mass media, which developed strongly during the last few decades of the twentieth century, has become at least as important a means for entertainment as live performance (Susanto 1978:229). Indonesia has particularly been affected by the cassette industry since the development and mass production of cassettes began in the 1970s (Manuel and Baier 1986:99). This chapter discusses the recording and radio industries, television, and printed media such as newspapers and magazines. Each of these media has had some impact on Sundanese music in general, and tembang Sunda in particular, either through a direct influence of style or in the creation of new outlets for the transmission and dissemination of the genre.

Modern tembang Sunda musicians depend on patronage from certain urban institutions for the continuation and support of tembang Sunda. Among these institutions are sponsored performing groups, the cassette industry through which the sounds of new songs and singers are disseminated, and the schools that teach tembang Sunda theory and practice to younger generations. Economically, factors such as the centralized management of prices, goods, and services have furthered the growth of urbanism in Sunda, and this growth has led to further influences on tembang Sunda via the mass media. Because of this relationship between modern tembang Sunda and the mass media, this chapter focuses on the details involving each of these industries and how they relate to tembang Sunda.

Current performance practice reflects changes in the use of tuning systems, brought about by the shift of tembang Sunda to an urban setting. Although two of the three main tuning systems are used in almost all live performances of tembang Sunda, the advent of the cassette industry has led to ventures into rare tuning systems. The radio industry, by contrast, tends to reinforce the primacy of the three main systems. A considerable amount of statistical data concerning the Sundanese tuning systems has already been collected and explored by van Zanten (1986), and his work need not be duplicated here. His excellent discussion of Sundanese tuning models should be referred to particularly for more information on written Sundanese theory compared with actual performance practice, in which he demonstrates the marked difference between the two (see also Weintraub 1993b).

RECORDING STUDIOS AND THE CASSETTE INDUSTRY

An entire job market has been built around the Indonesian cassette industry, originally based in Surabaya and Jakarta but now highly developed in other large Indonesian cities such as Bali's Denpasar and West Java's Bandung. In addition to sponsors, cassette producers, retail and wholesale outlets, recording technicians, and various middlemen, singers and instrumentalists can make a considerable profit from cassette recordings. Many of these people depend almost entirely on the cassette industry to support themselves and their families, and certain producers and sponsors have become quite wealthy from cassette production. The cassette industry also has produced a form of cooperation between two groups of people that normally make a point of keeping themselves separate: the Chinese-Indonesians, who run the cassette retail and wholesale outlets, and the Sundanese, who make and purchase the music.[1]

The data used for this section on the basic workings of the Sundanese recording scene were derived primarily from my experiences at the Jugala Studio, owned by Gugum Gumbira Tirasonjaya. Jugala is the largest and most completely equipped of the Bandung recording studios, and is very much in demand by groups from all over Bandung, various small towns in other parts of Sunda, and even Jakarta. The studio is in use at least four or five days out of every week. My almost daily visits to Jugala for vocal lessons and performances allowed me the opportunity to witness the recording of many different types of music, including *seriosa* (Indonesian Lieder-type singing), tembang Sunda, kroncong (early-twentieth-century pop), and musik bén (rock). I also interviewed musicians and producers from other recording companies, and was able to interview several owners of cassette stores not only in Bandung but also in several of the outlying Sundanese towns.

The first recordings of Indonesian music were by foreign companies such as Odeon. These recordings were produced on 78 rpm discs for sale within Indonesia and, occasionally, in Europe. Lokananta, Indonesia's national recording company, did not begin production until the 1950s. Private companies produced the first Indonesian commercial cassettes in the late 1960s, pirated from preexisting recordings (Yampolsky 1987:2). By the mid-1970s, disc manufacturing was no longer a part of the Indonesian recording industry, and private companies had emerged in many parts of Indonesia to cope with the demand for cassettes, that were neither as expensive nor as easily damaged by heat as records. Most regional recording companies specialize in recordings of the music of that area (Yampolsky 1987:22); in other words, the recording companies in Medan specialize in North Sumatran music, companies in Surabaya specialize in East Javanese music, and companies in Bandung specialize in Sundanese music.

Making a Recording of Tembang Sunda

In Bandung, many different recording companies utilize the facilities of several recording studios. For example, although recording studio A produces its own cassettes and sells them under the name of A, companies B, C, and D also may hire out this same recording studio and its technicians. It is not necessary for these other companies to use the name of studio A anywhere on the cassette jacket, although they might for status reasons. Recording companies that do not have their own recording facilities would pay studio A the equivalent of several hundred U.S. dollars for the privilege of using the facilities. In the 1980s, they would also pay for the audio tape used to create the two-inch master tape. Now that most of the studios use digital technology, companies bring their own CDs. Included in this fee is not only the time used to make the original recording, but also the postproduction time spent after the recording process is finished, in which the producer and the recording technician adjust the balance of the different instruments and voices. This process is known by the English term *mixing*.

Much of the recording process uses English terminology, from the word *teprecorder* (tape recorder), through other terms such as *miking, booking, mixing, didubbing* (overdubbing: making a second recording over an already existing one), *tes* or *cek* (for testing the microphones), *son sistem* (sound system), *spiker* (speaker), and *polume* (volume). One of the recording engineers with whom I had very frequent contact (Basuki Leksobowo) had a good command of the English language, which may have influenced the use of English by his coworkers. I often heard those terms used in nonrecording situations, however, spoken by people who had no contact with this particular recording engineer, in which the speakers were discussing past or future recording sessions. The term *dapur rekaman* ("recording kitchen") is often used instead of the English term *studio*. "Entering the kitchen" (*masuk ke dapur*) is a way of describing the process of recording.

Equipment for Indonesian recording studios is usually imported from Singapore or Japan, but it also is occasionally imported from America or Germany. Current Indonesian tax laws add a luxury tax of 200 percent onto the purchase price of any electronic equipment from outside the country. As a result, recording equipment is very expensive and few people can afford to create an entire studio set-up themselves. The economic complications presented by the government's taxation laws result in the forced cooperation of many competing recording companies that otherwise might not be in such frequent communication with one another. When a small company tries to pay the required fees to the studio, musicians, composers, designer, photographer, cover duplicator, marketing middlemen, and government officials, it may have to go in with another company to try to combine services.

There are few rules for booking the studio; in other words, anyone (regardless of the style of music or ethnic background) may reserve immediately or weeks in advance if the facilities and the technicians are available. In a standard recording session, the studio is booked for either a half-day or a whole day. The half-day booking may begin either in the afternoon or the evening. An evening booking usually ensures the use of the studio almost all night, so many people take advantage of this opportunity to get in more studio time. The vocalist(s) usually arrive later than the instrumentalists, because the instrumental tracks are always recorded first. Most songs are run through at least once before the first tracks are made, and, in some cases, this preliminary run-through is the only rehearsal many of the musicians have before the recording is made. Depending on how much money the sponsor has provided for the recording or whether the studio is vacant, long rehearsals may be conducted in the studio prior to the actual recording time.

As in many American recording studios, a good Indonesian recording studio has several soundproof rooms attached to the main recording room, in which the louder instruments are isolated to prevent their bleeding onto other tracks. In the case of a tembang Sunda recording, the isolated instrument is usually the suling. If overdubbing is necessary—for example, if one of the musicians coughs or makes a mistake—it is comparatively easy to have the musician repeat his section without the original mistake appearing in the background of the kacapi track. Professional tembang Sunda recording artists are quite familiar with the processes involved in making a recording and maintain that the facilities for overdubbing have simplified the recording process considerably. A distinct disadvantage seems to be the lack of visual contact between the kacapi and suling players due to the isolation of the suling player; such visual contact (usually through peripheral vision) is an essential aspect of performances.

In setting down the instrumental tracks, the instrumentalists are provided with headphones that completely cover the ears. These headphones enable the listener to hear not only the tracks of all the instrumentalists but also the sound of the vocalist and the speaking voice of the engineer, neither of which are recorded at this time. The vocalist sits in the sound room with his or her own microphone, together with the recording engineer, his assistants, the producer, and the sponsor. Spectators and hangers-on double as assistants if their help is needed to move instruments or locate cigarettes, food, or drink. The kacapi is often placed on the floor near a wall so that the player can lean against the wall and so that the microphones and headphones can be plugged into outlets positioned along the wall, approximately two feet off the floor. The rincik and rebab, if used, are also on the floor, either against an adjoining wall or at right angles to the kacapi player to provide more visual contact.

The overall structure of tembang Sunda performance practice has *not* changed as a result of cassette recordings, because it happens to be particularly suited to cassette production. Three tembang sets can fit on one side of a cassette tape. During the recording of tembang Sunda, a single set of two to four songs is recorded from beginning to end without stopping. These songs must be recorded in this manner because each song is directly connected by a section of rapid, free-rhythm runs performed on the kacapi. If the kacapi player makes a mistake, the whole process needs to be repeated, because the momentum of the set depends almost completely on the kacapi player. Overdubbing of the kacapi tracks usually occurs only during the panambih, because the playing is far more standardized, less improvisational, and in a fixed meter. During the mamaos section of a recording, the tempo of the kacapi varies constantly and it is far more difficult to do the kind of standard overdubbing techniques that require stopping and starting the tape at certain points.

In the recording of the instrumental tracks, the instrumentalists play as if they were performing with the vocalist. The vocalist watches the instrumentalists (particularly the kacapi player) closely, entering the vocal part as he or she normally would, and the players can hear these vocal lines through their headphones. After all of the instrumental tracks have been completed for a single set, there is usually a break. The instrumentalists come into the soundroom to talk, smoke, drink tea or coffee, and eat snacks, while they listen to the results of their efforts. The cigarettes and snacks are usually provided by the sponsor. The recording studio generally provides tea and/or coffee.[2] After the break, the vocalist may record her vocal tracks, but it is more likely that the instrumentalists will proceed to the next set of songs. Sometimes the first side of the cassette is recorded during the afternoon, and the second side (often in a different tuning system) recorded at night. When the vocalist finally records her tracks, the instrumentalists often stay around the studio in case they are needed, or simply to kibbitz.

Many recordings are completed in one or two days, and the process of mixing may take several more days. If the person in charge of making the recording owns the studio, however, the entire process may take weeks. I witnessed the recording process of one cassette that took over three weeks to complete, because the songs were altered and recorded several different ways before the final versions were chosen. One possible reason for the extended length of that particular project may have been that the recording took place during the fasting month of Ramadan; because of the prohibitions of Islam, all the recording activity took place only at night. On the opposite end of the spectrum, I also witnessed the recording of a kacapi-suling cassette that took approximately four hours from start to finish. When I asked why these particular musicians were able to complete their recording in such a brief amount of time, they answered, "Because we spent a few hours last night rehearsing, so now all we need to do is play."

The mixing process is conducted after the instrumentalists (and vocalists, usually) have gone home, and is usually considered a matter between the recording engineer and the sponsor or producer. Although these mixing sessions are fairly private in comparison to the actual recording session, two or three spectators are inevitable. In some cases, musicians try to add their input to the mixing session, although the sponsor usually has the last word about whether something is used or not in the final mix. Musicians have occasionally been surprised to hear the results of the final mix of a cassette, discovering that particularly interesting instrumental ornaments are left out or obscured by another instrument or vocal part, or even that mistakes that were thought to have been covered up are suddenly quite audible.[3] Once the cassette has appeared on the market, however, nothing can be done to change the mistakes made during mixing. The musicians are generally held blameless, however, for the end result.

Cassette Covers and Inserts

After the recording has been made, the photographs for the cassette cover are taken and the basic design is created. Most recent cassette covers use photographs rather than paintings or drawings. With the notable exception of Hidayat studios (with its rural outdoor photographs), these cassette covers usually include the female vocalist in traditional Sundanese dress against a blank background, frequently facing forward or off to one side with a solemn expression. Indonesians generally do not smile when their picture is taken. Male vocalists are rarely included in these photographs, unless they have achieved the status of juara or winner of the pasanggiri DAMAS competition. Some male vocalists may be pictured with a female vocalist if they (the men) are frequently pictured on other cassettes as performers of pop Sunda, or if the tembang Sunda cassette actually includes selections of songs from the pop Sunda genre. Male instrumentalists are almost never pictured on cassette covers (cf. van Zanten 1989:49). "No one wants to see men on cassette covers," said one male recording professional. "Men are ugly and don't sell cassettes" (Rukmana, personal communication, 1988). In 1996, Neneng Dinar Suminar broke with tradition and featured a clear photograph of all three of her accompanying musicians in the background on her first recording.

The Hidayat recording company is probably the most responsible for the continued recording and promotion, not only of tembang Sunda cassettes but also of instrumental kacapi-suling. The naturalistic photographs on the covers of Hidayat's cassettes reinforce the already strong association of tembang Sunda with a more rural, calmer past, represented by the Sundanese term *wa'as*. Wa'as, which is described more completely in Chapter 10 ("Connecting with the Ancestors"), is used to describe a feeling of nostalgia and longing for the old, pre-Independence days, when things were more stable. Wa'as is also strongly associated with tembang Sunda, because of the association of the sound of tembang Sunda with the feudal times.

The insides of cassette covers contain a varying amount of information. On the most complete cassette inserts, not only the song titles, complete names of all musicians, recording date and place, composers, and tuning systems are included but also the lyrics to the songs. Other cassettes simply have the song titles and do not include the name of the vocalist. Some cassettes do not even list the song titles. If the vocalist is a recent winner or finalist from the pasanggiri DAMAS, this is specified after the vocalist's name. Singers of considerable fame, such as Euis Komariah or the late Dadang Sulaeman, do not include the dates of their victories in these competitions. It is believed that an informed public is already aware of that particular singer's previous accomplishments. Actual cassettes themselves, separate from the box they are sold in, are rarely identified at all, except with the name of the recording company and, in the case of Hidayat, the identifying number of the cassette. As one recording company owner told me, "The important thing is that they know which company made the recording. It doesn't matter which singer is on the cassette as long as my company is the one from which they buy their cassettes" (Gumbira, personal communication, 1989).

Recording Contracts

Because there are far more vocalists than musicians, good players are very much in demand by singers, and competition is strong between singers to acquire the best musicians for their performances and recordings. Although musicians may be tied to a particular singer for their performances, they may also be bound by an exclusive written contract with a particular recording company. A contract may be skirted, however, if the musician uses a different name, or plays a different instrument than that which is specified in the original contract, or is simply not listed on the cassette.[4] Van Zanten also mentions the prohibitions against outside recordings that were placed on musicians from Radio Republik Indonesia as a reason for not being listed on the cassettes (van Zanten 1989:41). It is usually clear to other musicians and singers who the unnamed instrumentalist is, because of distinctive differences in playing style or selection of ornamentation.

Instrumentalists are generally paid a set fee for their services if the recording they do is part of a freelance arrangement. That is, although some musicians are paid in advance as part of a contractual agreement to make a certain number of recordings with a particular singer, others are offered cash for a single day of recording. According to several players in the 1980s, the standard pay for top-quality kacapi and suling players for a single cassette was 100,000 rupiah (U.S.$55.55 in 1989). Although the number of rupiah has increased, the essential value of the payment in U.S. dollars remains approximately the same. Rincik players, because of their limited duties, frequently receive approximately half of the kacapi player's fee or less. Rebab players receive approximately the same as players of rincik. Because a second rincik is occasionally added to the ensemble, those musicians may receive almost as much as the first rincik player or slightly less. The second rincik, or *rincik dua*, position is not considered to belong to specialists of rincik, but rather one that can be filled by anyone.

It is extremely difficult to verify these figures, because money is a difficult subject to broach with the Sundanese in general and musicians in particular. A musician may choose to inflate the amount of his own salary to make himself look more professional or in demand in the eyes of a foreign researcher, or may lower it to look more humble. The information for this discussion of remuneration was obtained from some of the musicians of five different groups. A frequent answer given to the question of payment is "Just barely enough to support my family's daily needs," or "Not as much as I used to receive from so-and-so." Similarly, when discussing the amounts that other musicians receive, an amount may be adjusted to raise or lower the status of the other instrumentalists or vocalists in relation to himself. Similarly, sponsors pay fees to their musicians according to their own financial standards, and what is true within one group may have no bearing on another group. Actual recording contracts, however, are a far more public subject, because they are openly discussed among the musicians. The issue at hand is that a recording contract accepted by one musician has an affect on future recording contracts for other musicians. Musicians try among themselves to maintain certain standards of pay for recording contracts; for example, a particular fee for five recordings over a two year period.

Singers, too, are bound by recording contracts when the recording company is not owned either by the singer or the spouse of the singer. Most recording companies have either a one- or two-year contract, stipulating that the singer must produce a certain number of recordings within that period, for a flat fee to be provided at the beginning of the contractual period. Many singers are willing to accept the contract offered, because the fee is often more than the average Sundanese yearly income. Under a contract of this type, the singer does not usually have the choice of which vocalist he or she may be paired with, which musicians are used, which songs are recorded, or how the cassette is marketed if, indeed, it reaches that stage.

The unfortunate result of some of these contracts is that the singer may be poorly recorded, or paired with bad musicians, or the recordings made but not released. The cassette market may be flooded with too many recordings of one singer and the good name of that singer goes down. Because the recording company usually has ultimate control over when the cassettes are released, it may be years before the recordings made within that contractual period reach the market. Sometimes promising young students of established singers are approached by the owners of recording companies, who offer a lucrative contract to the usually low-income student before that person is actually ready—in the opinion of his or her teacher—to record. Driven by difficult financial circumstances, the young singer can be lured away from the better advice of the teacher and make the recording(s), that might only be released after the student has become well-known or won a prize at a tembang Sunda competition.

The recording of singers before they have established a name for themselves or won a competition is a clever marketing technique that may save a considerable amount of money for the recording company. Once the singer has become established, his or her recording fees can go much higher. The company is at less of a financial disadvantage if it makes recordings for low fees when the singer is still underprepared than if it waits until the singer is fully developed and ready to command higher fees. By releasing the recording as soon as the singer becomes successful, the recording company is able to capitalize on its position as the first one to discover the singer's talent. If the singer is not a success, the company's loss is minimal, because it doesn't automatically reproduce and market every cassette it has recorded. I spoke at length with one promising young singer who had turned down several offers of recording contracts, even though the money would have been very useful, because the singer felt that maintaining a good relationship with one's teacher was far more important than trying to make some quick money.

It should be made clear that many excellent musicians and singers regularly perform tembang Sunda in a variety of settings but have not been recorded and have no intention to be recorded. Some musicians simply prefer all of their performances to be live; others feel that "the essence of tembang Sunda [is] the inner feelings, and not their expression in the singing" (van Zanten 1989:42). Still other musicians would like to be recorded but do not have a sponsor or are not in the right financial situation to produce their own recording. I interviewed several young singers who would like to make a recording "someday," but were afraid of being considered too brave or brazen (*berani*) if they tried to do it on their own. Therefore, the key to making a recording for some of these young singers is usually to have a wealthy patron arrange the entire recording session for them, hire the musicians, and finance the deal.

Cassette Marketing

Each cassette is expected to have at least one musical feature that separates it from any other previous cassette. This is not only a good marketing technique, but it is also spoken of as an important means for the continuing development of tembang Sunda. Cassettes are expected to have a mixture of tembang Sunda standards with newer compositions. The very first cassettes of tembang Sunda (in the early 1970s) featured almost all older songs from the papantunan style on the first side, then rarancagan in pélog or sorog on Side 2. Each set concluded with a panambih, but there was little focus on having each cassette differ from the others because there simply were not very many cassettes with which to be compared. Since the 1980s, however, most new cassettes feature at least one new song.

Of the many Sundanese composers who are currently active, several are considered to have an important enough name in tembang Sunda circles to lend prestige to the new cassette by having one of their new compositions featured on the cassette. Among the important or well-known composers are Bakang Abubakar, Engkos, Idi Rosidi, Suarna, and Rachmat. A composer may be approached by singers or their sponsors for new tembang Sunda compositions, with the understanding that if a song is composed specifically at the request of a singer or her sponsor, a fee will be paid. That fee may be enough to support that composer for several months, and the name of the composer is specified on the inside of the cassette cover. Again, these facts vary according to what is claimed by the individuals involved. Sometimes the agreement may include the title of the new song being used as the title of the cassette, or at least the new song title being featured in capital or boldface letters in the list of songs.

If a composer has agreed to create something new for the cassette, the song is generally paired with one or more of his other compositions as a set. For example, the cassette recorded by Yayah Rochaeti Dachlan called "Simpay Tresna" features three compositions in a single set on side two, all by the composer R. Achmad: "Kinayungan," "Kalalen," and "Simpay Tresna." The last, a panambih, is not only the only new song on the cassette but is also the title song. By becoming the first singer to record a new song, the singer is allowed a nominal claim to the song, and it is unlikely that other singers will perform that song when the original recording artist is present.

Another feature of new songs affected by the recording industry is that the first recording of a new song is taken as a standard for how it should be performed, and other singers are more likely to study from the original recording instead of asking the composer himself. It is believed that composers change songs constantly, especially as they teach them to singers, so it is a safer bet to rely on a prerecorded version than on the current version of the composer, who may have completely altered the song by the time he has finished teaching it. I witnessed a composer change a song around six times during a single evening when one young student asked him to teach it to her directly. The original recording artist, who was present at the time, became confused as well and the matter was settled by all of them listening to her recording of his song.

The presence of a new song on a cassette allows the cassette producer or group sponsor to convince cassette wholesalers that they have a potentially money-making cassette on their hands. After selling a certain number of cassettes to a wholesaler such as Toko Kaset Tropic (the "Tropic" cassette store: the largest wholesaler of traditional Sundanese cassettes in Bandung), the producer waits to see how the market will react. Because owners of cassette stores are usually Chinese Indonesians, release of a cassette depends very much on whether the day is auspicious or spiritually appropriate. One record company owner in 1989 complained bitterly that none of the store-owners wanted to release cassettes unless they had just won a large amount of money through the then-legal Chinese-run lottery. The same owner also expressed his opinion that the lottery was responsible for a decline in cassette sales, because there was no financial return from a cassette purchase, whereas for the same amount of money one could receive "millions in cash."

The original release of a cassette is rarely more than five hundred copies. A second release follows only if the original is a wide success or has an unusual feature such as an entire cassette side in a rare tuning system, or the addition of an unusual instrument or particularly catchy tune that becomes a hit song in tembang Sunda circles. Prices for cassettes generally vary, depending on the quality of the cassette used for the recording, the name of the recording company, and the name of the singer. Cassettes of musical styles other than tembang Sunda vary even more widely in price, particularly unlicensed cassettes of the type sold on the street corner. Many of these cassettes sell for very few rupiah, and often are of such poor quality that the cassette does not play in a machine, is seriously distorted, or may even be blank.

Purchasing a cassette from a well-known company or large store is no guarantee of good quality, however. Cassettes are generally not checked to insure against distortion before they are wrapped and sold, and because the amount of tape on a cassette may vary, the last several minutes of a cassette may be missing because the duplicate cassette ended before the master copy was finished. Other problems include blank spaces, wild variations in cassette speed, or extraneous noise such as clicks on the cassette itself. Most reputable storeowners will allow a direct exchange for the same cassette if the problem is obvious and the cassette producer is a local one with whom the company does frequent business. These reject cassettes are returned to the recording company, which has the choice of recording them over again, reselling them to the same store in a different batch, or selling them to another buyer.

As an attempt to make up for the problem of unevenly timed sides on a cassette, many cassettes end with a *panutup*, or closing song, designed to use up the extra space at the end of the cassette. The panutup is a fixed-meter, up-tempo instrumental panambih that begins immediately after the final vocal panambih on each side of the cassette. In a rough estimate of where the end of the cassette will be, the recording engineer fades the panutup out so that the two sides of the cassette approximately will match. The panutup is almost never listed on the cassette insert, except occasionally as "Panutup," which, like "Bubuka," may be mistaken by nonmusicians for the title of a song. Sometimes even the best intentions fall short, and the song is still mercilessly cut off near the end because the cassette runs out. Another technique used to even out the timing in cassettes is rerecording of the first or title song at the end of the cassette, with a fade-out at the appropriate time. Although the second playing of this song on a single side is not listed on the cassette insert, it serves to cement the melody of that song into the head of the listener, increasing the chances that the new song will become popular. This technique is used most frequently in the pop Sunda genre, where songs depend more heavily on radio and television airplay than on frequency of performance to sell or become hits.

Tuning Systems and the Cassette Industry

The use of particular tunings in the cassette industry partly reflects standard performance practice, and partly augments it. Most of the cassettes on the market today are in one or two of the primary three Sundanese tuning systems. Because the standard progression of tuning systems in a tembang Sunda performance is from pélog tuning to sorog and then (if time allows) to saléndro, the first side of the cassette is often in pélog and the second in sorog. Sometimes this order may be varied, for example by having sorog on Side 1 and saléndro on Side 2, or an entire cassette may be in a single tuning system. In general, producers and performers try to confirm the expectations of their audiences. This system of cassette production according to audience expectation sells cassettes; however, musical experimentation also may sell cassettes if the idea is particularly creative or interesting. The recording industry therefore augments the selection of tunings used in standard performance practice by opening an arena for experimentation with unusual or rare tuning systems.

In addition to pélog, sorog, and saléndro, several other tuning systems are given attention in recordings and, on rare occasions, in the context of a latihan. These tunings are *mandalungan, pélog wisaya,* and *sorog-saléndro*. Van Zanten mentions several others, including *sorog singgul* and *mataraman* (which my teachers called *mandalungan*) (van Zanten 1989:118). Although two performers mentioned that mandalungan was also called mataraman, they both (separately) said that they used the term mandalungan because mataraman refers to the Central Javanese kingdom of Mataram, an unpopular reference from the Sundanese point of view. Aside from the three primary tunings, practitioners of tembang Sunda frequently confuse the terms of these secondary tunings and spend hours discussing the various merits, tone material, and appropriateness of each one.

Pélog wisaya differs from pélog in that its fourth pitch is raised by a half-step. It has so far appeared on a single cassette of instrumental kacapi-suling, but seems to have had no impact on composing or tembang Sunda performance practice. Similarly, sorog-saléndro (which derives its name from using a kacapi in saléndro and a suling in sorog) has been worked on by one or two latihan groups, but so far has only been recorded as a kacapi-suling instrumental cassette.[5] The use of unusual or nonstandard tunings seems to have occurred on occasion long before the cassette industry appeared in Indonesia; recordings of rare tunings only recently have taken place. One such cassette, called "Sumanding Asih" and recorded by Euis Komariah, is entirely in the mandalungan tuning on the first side. The word mandalungan is clearly specified both on the cassette cover and the cassette insert, and, although the second side is in saléndro, no mention of this is made anywhere on the cassette.

In some cases, the production of a new cassette in a rarely used tuning is a deliberate attempt to financially exploit the Sundanese penchant for musical experimentation. Sometimes a composer wants to try out some new compositions and convinces a musical group that one side of a cassette should be devoted to an unusual tuning. A singer may want to expand his or her recorded repertoire or simply do something new on a recording. Financial considerations are, however, usually the most important reason for experimenting with a new tuning. I describe one of these rarely used tunings below in an attempt to demonstrate that the use of an unusual scale may be considered creative and interesting, and not only cause considerable comment, but in the opinion of certain persons involved in the cassette industry may cause people to buy new cassettes.

Mandalungan, the most commercially successful of the unusual scales, is said to have been in fairly common use earlier in the twentieth century (van Zanten 1989:118). Its popularity waned, however, and in the living memory of tembang Sunda community it only recently became popular due to the success of the "Sumanding Asih" cassette with Euis Komariah as vocalist. I concentrate briefly on mandalungan here because of its relationship to the cassette industry and because of the effect that the success of a single cassette had on the life of this tuning.

Mandalungan has the same internal relationship of pitches that the pélog tuning has; however, it is transposed, so that the scale begins at the interval of a fourth higher than pélog. This transposition causes a shift in the orientation of pitches, because if one attempted to perform pélog songs in mandalungan tuning, the pitch would simply be too high. Of the small handful of kacapi players who know how to tune and perform in mandalungan, most agree that both the *rofel* (double density) and *takol balik* techniques of playing are appropriate for every panambih. The reason given for this is the bright sound of songs in mandalungan; using the rofel and takol balik techniques helps to make the songs even more lively, and gives enthusiasm (*kasi semangat*) to the vocalists.

Rukruk Rukmana, the kacapi player on the first mandalungan recording, mentioned that it would be appropriate to add a nineteenth string to the kacapi for it to be truly a kacapi mandalungan. A nineteenth string could incorporate the lowest pitch necessary for the kacapi to play in mandalungan as it does in the other tunings. Furthermore, the continuing development of mandalungan has caused many suling players to add a special suling to their collection of instruments that they sometimes bring to latihans: the suling mandalungan. This special suling is much shorter than the normal suling (seventeen-and-one-half inches as opposed to twenty-three-and-three-quarters inches) and plays at the pitch required for mandalungan songs.

The first recording of mandalungan included a special bubuka, unique to mandalungan, that has helped in the establishment of the tuning system. Like the bubuka for the other tuning systems, this one is not listed on the cassette insert and appears as both a bubuka and a panutup on side one of the cassette. It is usually the first mandalungan song that kacapi players attempt to master, because it incorporates several rather difficult kacapi techniques in which the technique of string dampening is used by both hands simultaneously. The use of a special kacapi technique has also been important in the establishment of mandalungan as an addition to pélog, sorog, and saléndro.

Vocalists describe mandalungan compositions as having several special *senggól*, or ornaments, exclusive to the tuning system. These vocal ornaments, however, have become the domain of mandalungan more because they were a feature of the original mandalungan recording, not because they belonged in common performance practice. Because there was no mandalungan performance practice to speak of, the "Sumanding Asih" cassette was adopted as a standard from which the vocal ornamentation and other musical features from the new compositions could be studied and copied. This, therefore, is a case in which a single cassette spawned the growth and development of a tuning system, and provided the standard against which other mandalungan recordings and performances could be judged.

In spite of the apparent evidence of activity, few outside of the inner circle of tembang Sunda practitioners have heard of this tuning, and fewer still would be able to tell the difference between mandalungan and pélog because of the similarity of internal pitch relationships. Similarly, performances of tembang Sunda tend to be within the usual repertoire of pélog, sorog, and occasionally saléndro. Because of factors that both encourage and mitigate its popularity among tembang Sunda musicians, mandalungan is in an unstable position in relation to the three main tunings. It is possible that the popularity of mandalungan outside the tembang Sunda community may grow stronger as more successful recordings are made. Until that time, the one recording has spurred activity only on an internal level (latihans, compositions, and discussions), and has not yet caused mandalungan to reach the performing stage.

Stylistic Changes as a Result of the Cassette Industry

The recording industry has had a profound impact on contemporary tembang Sunda style. The development of the "star system" of recording professionals and the partial homogenization of vocal style are two of the major results of the cassette industry's proliferation in Sunda. In the development of the star system, certain performers connected to particularly wealthy or prestigious sponsors may be featured quite frequently on cassettes, or at prestigious performances (for example, performing for heads of state). The appeal of the fame and status of these performers causes some singers and instrumentalists to emulate that particular style, whether vocal or instrumental. Although most professional tembang Sunda singers like to be known for their individual vocal style, it is sometimes considered a compliment to them if their students and other people imitate their style exactly. I listened to the commentary of several singers at one latihan, at which they were critiquing the performance of another singer's student. "She sounds exactly like her teacher!" they said. The pleasure of having students imitate one's style weighs against the necessity to cultivate an individual recording style. The result is the development of particular schools of style evolving from the individual styles of the teachers.

Cassettes produced in Bandung are marketed all over West Java, which further spreads the influence of "Bandung style." When people from the outlying areas buy cassettes, they most often select a famous Bandung singer accompanied by Bandung musicians. Thus, a symbolic cluster arises, equating urbanism with wealth, power, fame, and good musicianship. Indonesian performers (beyond Sunda) are constantly facing the demand to imitate or somehow orient their performances toward a center of musical activity believed to be culturally superior. In the case of tembang Sunda, the perceived superior center of activity is in Bandung. As the following quote about a town in Sulawesi reveals, the centralization of power and authority often comes at the behest not only of urbanites, but also of rural officials (Wessing notes that this situation is similar to Dutch policy for West Java [personal communication, 2000]): "Villagers were admonished to live in compact villages rather than dispersed field huts so that everyone could go to school and church and assemble for group labour oriented to development. Over and over the *camat* [administrator] emphasized the need to learn dances so as to be in tune with the culture of Palu [the local administrative city]" (Acciaioli 1985:149).

In the last thirty years, cassettes of tembang Sunda have continued to be produced and marketed, even though they are rarely bestsellers. Cassette store owners do a small business in tembang Sunda cassettes because musicians purchase these cassettes to study with the great singers and musicians in the privacy of their own homes. Others purchase cassettes of tembang Sunda or its instrumental offshoot, kacapi-suling, to use as background music or as a symbol of élite status. With Bandung as the center for recordings, radio, and musical instruction in tembang Sunda style, cassette-buying musicians and singers imitate directly what they hear on the tape, sometimes duplicating exactly the errors made on the recordings. Among the top musicians, however, everyone knows where the mistakes have been made and cautions are given to beginning players or singers about which recordings to avoid or which ones to listen to for the "real" version. Few nonmusicians actually listen closely to tembang Sunda.[6]

THE IMPACT OF RADIO ON TEMBANG SUNDA

Bandung is home to many radio stations, most of them private. While the cassette industry has had an important role in the last twenty years, radios are owned by far more people and have gained more ground in rural areas than has the cassette industry. The data for this section of my research was obtained during interviews with past and present staff musicians from the Bandung branch of Radio Republik Indonesia (the national radio network known henceforth as RRI). These staff include not only those hired directly by the station as contracted *pegawai negeri* (civil servants) but also those invited by the station to perform as guests. I also attended broadcasts at RRI, consulted monthly schedules to determine the amount of airplay allocated for tembang Sunda and kacapi-suling, and was able to obtain copies of several recordings of broadcasts made in the 1960s with the assistance of Ade Suandi (staff suling player for broadcasts of tembang Sunda). Finally, I listened to broadcasts of tembang Sunda not only on RRI but also on private stations, enabling me to gauge roughly proportions of time devoted to tembang Sunda on different stations. Almost all of my research on the radio and its effect on tembang Sunda, however, concentrated around the activities of RRI Bandung.

It was, in fact, RRI that played a role in the initial dissemination and popularization of tembang Sunda. The first singers to be broadcast on the radio before Indonesian Independence were Raden Emung Purawinata, together with Nyi Mas Saodah, Nyi Raden Imong and Nyi Emeh Salamah (Sukanda 1983:40). In the beginning of Sundanese radio broadcasts, the only people who owned radios were the élite. During the 1960s and 1970s, RRI Bandung frequently broadcast live performances of tembang Sunda that could be heard over a large area because there was little interference by smaller, private stations. Some of the very finest singers and musicians have been employed by RRI, and, according to many musicians, listening to or attending RRI broadcasts of tembang Sunda was once a very important social and musical event. Moreover, tembang Sunda broadcasts became a normative standard for performances of tembang Sunda.

During the last decade of the twentieth century, however, the criteria for selection of radio musicians have changed. Officials at RRI now select musicians based on their status (i.e., connections) within the community, their education, and their musical ability—not necessarily in that order (Suratno, personal communication, 1985). A diploma is said to have become more important than musical skill; as a result, musical standards have fallen in the opinion of some musicians. The radio station expects that these radio musicians will remain within a certain stylistic sphere (for example, performing all light-hearted songs) in their performances, rather than performing what might be more musically appropriate. The result is that certain styles of music may be highlighted on the radio and others are ignored altogether. Sutton describes the politics of repertoire selection at RRI Yogyakarta, which has begun to promote styles exclusively in Yogya style at the expense of everything else (Sutton 1984:236); this trend appears to be happening in Bandung as well. With the increase in the number of private radio stations, transmission has become so poor that RRI is often very difficult to receive within the city of Bandung. Transmissions are still clear, however, *outside* the city, so the radio still has some influence in areas outside of Bandung.

RRI Bandung includes in its programming regular evening broadcasts of tembang Sunda and kacapi-suling. Kacapi-suling is now most frequently heard, however, as background music to short story readings (*dongeng*) during daytime RRI Bandung broadcasts. In August of 1988, daytime broadcasts of kacapi-suling (without the story reading going on in the foreground) became a feature every Wednesday from 2:15 to 3:00 P.M. Tembang Sunda is still broadcast only at night, in accordance with the widely held belief that night is the only appropriate time for its performance. The maintaining of audience expectations of appropriateness is a very important service that RRI has provided for the tembang Sunda community. Some musicians complain that the use of prerecorded instrumental kacapi-suling as background music on RRI has cheapened it considerably, but the continued nighttime-only broadcasts of tembang Sunda help to reinforce the appropriate performance setting for it in the minds of its listeners.

I obtained monthly schedules from 1987 through 1989 for rehearsals and broadcasts of the RRI tembang Sunda group and other musical ensembles broadcasting out of RRI Bandung. In an average month, the tembang Sunda group at the radio station broadcasts three times a week, usually for one or two hours at a time. Broadcasts almost always begin at 9:15 P.M., after the national news broadcast from RRI Jakarta. A break of ten or fifteen minutes occurs at 10:00 P.M. for the hourly news, during the middle of the broadcast, and then the music sometimes continues until 11:00 P.M. Unless one of the performers is ill, almost all broadcasts are live. Some broadcasts are recorded so that they may be aired in the event of an illness or absence, and occasional recordings are made during the daytime rehearsals for this same purpose.

The schedule of broadcasts at RRI Bandung reflects several changes that have taken place in the last thirty years. Copies of programming schedules from 1968 (obtained from Dr. Ernst Heins) indicate that in the late 1960s, tembang Sunda was broadcast almost every evening from 10:15 P.M. until 11:00 P.M. Other genres, such as Indonesian popular music and *orkes melayu*, also were broadcast frequently; however, RRI Bandung seems to have included much more news and information at that time than it does now. Copies of programming schedules from 1981 (obtained from Wim van Zanten) indicate that the radio station had already begun to include much more musical entertainment in its weekly schedule but had scaled down the number of tembang Sunda broadcasts to only twice a week. Evidently, since the early 1980s, the number of broadcasts has increased slightly, perhaps as a result of a stronger emphasis on musical entertainment at the station.

An average monthly schedule for RRI Bandung reflects its support of traditional Sundanese musical arts. These broadcasts are interspersed with news (local, national, and international) in both Indonesian and Sundanese, editorial commentary about political events, children and teenage programs, story readings, pop music, the Islamic *azan* or call to prayer, development programs (on subjects such as childrearing and good nutrition), comedy programs, and some advertisements. Musical features from other RRI stations are occasionally aired, such as gamelan broadcasts from Central Java or Bali. Most traditional Sundanese music programming occurs at night.

In the monthly schedule for June of 1988 (Table 5.1), for example, kroncong (referred to as *orkes kroncong*) and tembang Sunda are performed quite frequently, and other ensembles such as gamelan degung, ketuk tilu, and gamelan Sunda rather less so. The term *orkes* also seems to refer to broadcasts of seriosa, the Indonesian version of diatonic accompanied song, similar to German Lieder. The feature "Assorted Sundanese musics" refers to a grab bag of styles, depending on who is available at the time of the broadcast. The feature titled "Tembang Sunda Guest Night" (Mitra Tamu Tembang Sunda) is the occurrence, at least once a month, of a broadcast by a tembang Sunda singer who is not regularly on the RRI staff. Guest singers usually bring their own musicians, although it is not unusual for the regular staff musicians to attend these guest broadcasts and sometimes join in playing.

Broadcasts seem to take place in a rather informal atmosphere. At the tembang Sunda broadcasts that I attended, there were always many more spectators present than musicians. People whisper quietly in the background, smoking cigarettes and making noise. Broadcasts take place in a large studio (approximately fifty feet long by thirty feet wide) that contains other instruments (several complete Sundanese gamelan ensembles, for example) used and owned by RRI. A large chalkboard is set up close to the group that lists the songs to be performed on that particular broadcast. The song list changes during the course of the broadcast depending on the time available and the choices of the singers and instrumentalists. Singers stand next to a microphone, and individual microphones are placed close to the instruments. A television is set up in an adjoining room, visible to the musicians, and when I attended a kacapi-suling broadcast on one occasion, all the musicians were watching the ordinary commercial broadcast in the next room even as they were playing and being broadcast themselves live.

RRI Bandung reinforces the tendency to use pélog more than sorog or saléndro. In its broadcasts, it includes performances in saléndro only about once a month; the bulk of airplay is given to performances of pélog and, secondarily, sorog. Therefore, audiences come to expect only pélog and sorog in performances. Because the selection of songs in pélog and sorog is far more broad, several singers can provide a different selection of songs between them for each broadcast. During guest performances at RRI (that occur approximately once or twice a month), a three-hour performance is usually broadcast in one-hour increments: an hour of each of these three

TABLE 5.1 Scheduled broadcasts at Radio Republik Indonesia, Bandung, June 1988

Date	Day	Time	Type of Music
1	Wednesday	21:15–22:00	Orkes Kroncong
2	Thursday	14:15–15:00	Orkes Kroncong
		21:15–22:00	Tembang Sunda
3	Friday	22:15–23:00	Kacapi-suling
4	Saturday	10:15–11:00	Celempungan
5	Sunday	prerecorded broadcasts	
6	Monday	08:05–09:00	Gamelan Degung
		21:15–22:00	Tembang Sunda
7	Tuesday	11:15–12:00	Orkes Kroncong
		21:15–23:00	Assorted Sundanese Musics
8	Wednesday	13:25–14:00	Orkes Kroncong
9	Thursday	14:15–15:00	Orkes Kroncong
10	Friday	22:15–23:00	Tembang Sunda
11	Saturday	21:15–22:00	Gamelan Sunda
12	Sunday	prerecorded broadcasts	
13	Monday	14:15–15:00	Ketuk Tilu
14	Tuesday	11:15–12:00	Orkes Kroncong
		13:25–14:00	Gamelan Sunda
		21:15–22:00	Tembang Sunda Guest Night
15	Wednesday	13:25–14:00	Orkes Kroncong
16	Thursday	14:15–15:00	Orkes Kroncong
		21:15–22:00	Tembang Sunda
17	Friday	22:15–23:00	Kacapi-suling
18	Saturday	10:15–11:00	Réog
19	Sunday	prerecorded broadcasts	
20	Monday	08:05–09:00	Kacapi Kawih
		21:15–22:00	Tembang Sunda
21	Tuesday	11:15–12:00	Orkes Kroncong
		13:25–14:00	Gamelan Sunda
22	Wednesday	13:25–14:00	Orkes Kroncong
23	Thursday	14:15–15:00	Orkes Kroncong
24	Friday	22:15–23:00	Tembang Sunda
25	Saturday	21:15–22:00	Gamelan Sunda
26	Sunday	prerecorded broadcasts	
27	Monday	14:15–15:00	Ketuk Tilu
		21:15–22:00	Tembang Sunda
28	Tuesday	11:15–12:00	Orkes Kroncong
		21:30–24:00	Wayang Catur
29	Wednesday	13:25–14:00	Orkes Kroncong
30	Thursday	14:15–15:00	Orkes Kroncong
		21:15–22:00	Tembang Sunda

main tunings, with a break on the hour for news and advertisements. The break then allows the kacapi player just enough time to change the tuning of the instrument and for the other musicians to switch places if necessary.

The support of RRI Bandung for tembang Sunda and other traditional Sundanese arts is one of the most important features lacking in private radio stations. I asked employees and general managers of private stations about their programming of traditional music, and searched my radio dial constantly for other broadcasts of tembang Sunda. Most private stations in Bandung include no programming of tembang Sunda at all but, rather, adhere closely to American, English, and Australian popular music. Those private stations that do not play foreign pop music concentrate instead on various Indonesian popular musics such as *dangdut*, pop Sunda, and pop Indonesia. Private stations are heavily subsidized by advertising, particularly from Indonesian cigarette companies that target the national teenage market with cigarettes such as Remaja ("teenage") brand. Cigarette companies and radio stations are also frequent cosponsors of various musical contests (Williams 1999).

Because private stations rarely feature tembang Sunda broadcasts, RRI Bandung remains one of the sole supporters of the genre by the radio industry. RRI's close historical connections with tembang Sunda (as one of its original proponents) gives it the unique feature of being a "father" of modern, urban tembang Sunda. Musicians, particularly former RRI staff musicians from the 1960s and 1970s, still retain a positive feeling for the station, even if fewer people are able to receive it within Bandung and in spite of the fact that musical standards are said to have fallen. In particular, the way in which attending broadcasts was once popular appears to be a primary factor for the fondness directed toward RRI in the old days. In a sense, RRI served as a setting for malam tembang Sunda; it was a place with no speeches, just good music played for musicians. To many musicians, RRI is seen as one more provider of jobs for selected tembang Sunda musicians, together with the cassette industry, academic institutions, and various sponsors. In the 1960s and 1970s, many of the tembang Sunda broadcasts were recorded on reel-to-reel tape and stored in the RRI archives. Because of complicated political factors such as the unregulated borrowing of these recordings by government officials, however, the sum total of the RRI tembang Sunda archives now consists of three tembang Sunda tapes and one kacapi-suling tape.

RRI Bandung attempted in 1989 to sponsor a pasanggiri tembang Sunda in honor of its own fortieth anniversary. A list of chosen songs was published and many new ones were created by one of the staff singers. All of these songs were in one of the four main poetic meters most commonly used in tembang Sunda (*kinanti, sinom, dangdanggula,* and *asmarandana*). At that time, I regularly attended the latihan sessions of four separate performing groups, at which the main singer of each group went through the list of songs provided by RRI, selecting appropriate lyrics from the choices provided, and drilling their students in the performance of the songs. Unfortunately, the pasanggiri tembang Sunda at RRI never materialized due to lack of necessary funding from outside sources. The enthusiasm with which the project was greeted, however, reflects not only a strong interest in tembang Sunda contests but also the strength of ties between the Bandung tembang Sunda community and RRI.

THE ROLE OF TELEVISION

The television is a fairly recent entry into the Indonesian mass media. As part of a national development plan to facilitate the dissemination of information throughout the country, former President Suharto stepped up operations to bring electricity into each village as quickly as possible in the 1980s. In addition to the national television station in Jakarta, there are branches on most major islands and television receiving towers on many of the other inhabited islands. Indonesian national television (TVRI) is a mix of domestically produced programs designed to aid in national development programs, with international imports, primarily from English-speaking nations. Almost all middle- and upper-class homes have a prominently displayed television. The television is always turned on as soon as the broadcasts begin, and its ubiquitous presence in the homes of tembang Sunda musicians should not be underestimated.

In the early 1990s, Indonesia opened up its television arena to private stations. For many years prior, then-President Suharto and his cabinet stated that allowing privatization of television would lead to a sharp escalation in the expectations of the poor, particularly once they began viewing advertisements and shows depicting the very wealthy. This statement came, paradoxically, during a time when the United States television show "Dynasty" (portraying lifestyles of the extraordinarily wealthy) was heating up the airwaves. In spite of Suharto's dire predictions, Bandung residents now have the option of viewing multiple private and internationally broadcast stations (including, for example, CNN and MTV Asia) in addition to the national television station.

TVRI broadcast days generally begin with foreign cartoons for children (usually Japanese, dubbed into English with subtitles in Indonesian), followed by regional entertainment such as traditional music and dance videos recorded and provided by the local station, followed by government development programs during the dinner hour and early evening. Later in the evening, the stations usually switch to light entertainment such as sports or nature programs, Indonesian soap operas, lessons in English, or more regional entertainment such as the "From Village to Village" program that broadcasts songs, dances, and customs from Aceh (for example) to villages in Flores. Late at night, the programming switches to American drama or adventure series, or one-hour movie-of-the-week films from English-speaking countries such as America, England, and Australia. These late-night shows are subtitled in Indonesian. Thus, the primary support for traditional music and dance on TVRI occurs before the dinner shows, on weekends, and before the foreign film series begin late at night.

In 1989, only two television stations were accessible in Bandung, both of them government stations (because private stations have until recently been outlawed in Indonesia). One was the TVRI station from Jakarta, which at the time only reached certain areas in Bandung, and the other was the Bandung branch of TVRI, which reaches all over Sunda. In the current privatized climate, multiple stations (public and private) compete for airspace, some broadcasting late into the night and all of them broadcasting all day long. In the 1980s, most rehearsals ground to a halt as soon as the television came on in the late afternoon. By the closing years of the twentieth century, television had become a serious competitor for rehearsal time at any time of the day or night.

The specialization of regional programming seems to have been left entirely up to the regional branches of TVRI. Music videos are frequently used to fill the space between shows on TVRI that, in the United States for example, would be filled by advertisements. The use of traditional music videos, based loosely on music video formats from India, England, and America, is not just an in-between program filler but also includes entire programs devoted exclusively to the promotion and dissemination of traditional regional music. TVRI Bandung fulfills the role of promoter of regional music and dance most frequently in the late afternoon and on weekends, when music videos are broadcast more frequently than at other times. Live or prerecorded performances of wayang golék, for example, are broadcast relatively frequently (every few weeks).

TVRI attempts to educate as well as entertain, so its music videos occasionally include interviews with composers, choreographers, singers, musicians, and dancers, who discuss their art and the factors that influence it. Following the interview, which has been interspersed in the manner of "Lifestyles of the Rich and Famous" with carefully choreographed glimpses into the daily life of the featured artist, the television audience is treated to a music video featuring his or her art. For example, an interview with a famous dancer is followed by a performance of one of his or her dances. At the beginning and end of each music video, the name of the song and the female singer are subtitled below; the names of the male vocalist (if there is one) and the composer are usually left out, unless the composer is famous. It is normal for music videos to be cut off toward the end of each performance, sometimes for announcements, other times to fit in the next video. This cutting usually results in shouts of dismay from the viewers, but it seems to be an accepted aspect of musical life as portrayed by TVRI.

Performers—or, at least, their sponsors—pay for the privilege of being filmed by TVRI. As a result, it is taken for granted by artists but not by the average television audience that those whose performances were filmed by TVRI were chosen primarily because they could afford to pay the price; the quality of the performance is not guaranteed. The quality of the filming varies as well; TVRI cameramen (usually accused of being "Javanese," whether they are or not) tend to focus on the face, breasts, or hips of the prettiest dancer, ignoring the difficult arm and hand movements that characterize much of Sundanese dance.

In tembang Sunda, two types of filming (known by the English term *shooting*) prevail. The first type, favored by most tembang Sunda musicians and singers, portrays a performance of tembang Sunda in an indoor setting. The camera not only focuses on the singers (male and female) but also even strays to the instrumentalists. Occasionally, although it is unnecessary because the sound has already been recorded, the singers carry microphones as if it were a live performance. The second type, which is far more common, entails the female singer walking around in an outdoor setting, gesturing dramatically as she lip-synchs the lyrics. This style of shooting, which is standard practice in most music videos, especially those of the kroncong and Hindi-film-music-influenced dangdut genres, is the style most strongly influenced by Indian music videos. Male instrumentalists are rarely visible in televised performances of tembang Sunda.

The difference between the two types of tembang Sunda video shooting reflects the value systems of the musicians. Those who are willing to go along with the outdoor setting are often believed to have "sold out" or to have acquiesced to the demands of Jakarta-based producers, who are uniformly believed to be Javanese. Those musicians who insist on indoor shooting feel very strongly that they can coerce the Jakartan producers to conform to Sundanese ideals, and that tembang Sunda will remain exclusively Sundanese without being corrupted by Jakartan influences.

I attended a TVRI recording session of the second type in 1987. A single set of tembang Sunda was scheduled for Ciwidey, a quiet rural area about an hour from Bandung. After everyone (musicians, camera crews, engineers, and spectators) had arrived in Ciwidey, the location was changed to Lembang, a semirural area very close to Bandung. After arriving in Lembang, it began to rain very heavily, so everyone waited inside and got dressed up, while most of the musicians complained about the television engineers. According to the musicians, the engineers had no idea about the inappropriateness of shooting tembang Sunda outdoors. The preferred location would have been indoors, and some of the musicians began to get angry.

When it finally stopped raining, the musicians went on strike and refused even to act as if they were performing tembang Sunda outside (the music had been recorded the week previously). Several of the singers decided to follow the example of the musicians, and loud arguments ensued. Finally one of the female singers who didn't go on strike went ahead with her performance, without the instrumentalists. The planned setting for the shooting was on the lawn of a large government building. The singer was dressed up in modern performance wear, fully made up for television, and there were about a hundred locals hanging around. Just as she was about to begin, the rain started again, causing the spectators to discuss the wisdom of God for showing his disapproval of tembang Sunda being performed outside. As the singer performed, people mimicked the way she walked slowly across the grass, gesturing the way singers do for performances of pop Sunda. It turns out that the one singer who wouldn't go on strike was a singer of kawih, and everyone spoke of how appropriate it was that none of the "real" singers had lowered their integrity to the level desired by the television officials.

The next day, everyone went to the RRI studio to find an appropriate room, and the result was far more satisfying to the musicians. The setting was the usual for tembang Sunda: female singer in front on her knees, male singer sitting cross-legged next to her, kacapi player behind in the middle, two rincik players (one on each side) also toward the back, and the suling player off to the side. The musicians in the television broadcast were different from those on the recording, but according to musicians watching the broadcast, the discrepancy did not matter because they were all professionals. Among the tembang Sunda musicians I spoke to following this event, all were proud of the musicians who went on strike and felt that it was an appropriate way of maintaining the high standard of tembang Sunda performance. They also felt vindicated because the television officials had given in to the demand of the Sundanese musicians to be filmed in what they believed to be a more appropriate situation. More than one musician referred to Sunda, representing all that is good and traditional and pleasant, winning against Java, representing power and the modern world; it was one small way in which the Sundanese attempted to maintain their resistance against cultural dominance by the Javanese.

The paradox of choosing to film indoors (allegedly more traditional) rather than outdoors (more modern) is that if the musicians wanted to represent tembang Sunda as being closer to the conceptual cluster of rural/historical/ancestral, presumably they would want to be outdoors. The Priangan (highland) area is known for its natural beauty, so it is a logical setting for a performance in which regional songs mention the outdoors and the rural past. Such a "traditional" setting would at least bear some relationship to the outdoors (for example, if it had been shot in the planned setting at Ciwidey), but this indoor urban performance was held up as best representing tembang Sunda. In the negotiations between the performers and the TVRI executives, what was being played out was precisely the representation of rural and urban according to different sets of expectations. In this particular battle, the modern, urban location won. Whether this is yet another example of Bandung's artistic hegemony over the outlying areas or whether it was simply a power struggle, the urban musicians felt vindicated.

Although television is ubiquitous in Bandung homes, until the 1990s it did not interfere too much with tembang Sunda latihan or jam sessions. These latihan only broke up to watch television if there was a particularly compelling adventure or disaster movie being broadcast, or if traditional Sundanese music or dance was being performed. Sundanese musicians pay particularly close attention to televised music and dance, offering critiques of everything from how much the dancer should be swinging her hips to whether the vocal ornaments performed by the singer are appropriate or not, whatever style is being performed. If no traditional music or dance is being broadcast, and it is not yet time for the real entertainment of the evening (the late-night shows), the television simply blares loudly in the background. If the television happens to be in the same room as the latihan, most of the musicians tend to keep one eye on it and the other on the musical situation at hand.

The effect of television and televised performances of tembang Sunda on the genre itself appears to be the forced integration of tembang Sunda into the medium favored by most music video producers: the outdoor setting. Although on certain occasions it is performed outside, tembang Sunda is generally considered to be an indoor ensemble. In outdoor performances of tembang Sunda, the musicians are always on a covered platform or on the porch of a house. There is almost never any direct contact of the instruments or singers with the earth or any actual "nature" setting. Television, however, favors a different visual setting. The image of a woman strolling around outside and singing is one found in almost all nondance music videos.[7]

THE PRINTED MEDIA

Although newspapers and magazines (as media incapable of transmitting music) would seem to function with little impact on the world of tembang Sunda, it happens that they serve a very important role in the social life of the genre. Bandung's largest daily newspaper is called *Pikiran Rakyat* (Indo.: "Thoughts of the People") and competes with other local papers, including those in Sundanese. The eighteen-page *Pikiran Rakyat*, or "PR" (the nickname includes a pun: PR = *pekerjaan rumah*, homework), frequently features articles about prominent singers of tembang Sunda. These articles are most often published on Sundays when two entire pages are devoted especially to articles about music, dance, theater, and literature. Although some international gossip is always included, the PR usually features Sundanese artists.

Before telephones became more commonplace (in the late 1990s), newspaper articles were a good way for artists to find out about the activities of their colleagues. Reports and photographs from Sundanese performing groups traveling abroad continue to be scrutinized and discussed at length, as are all articles featuring individual artists. Editorials discussing the merits of certain musical genres or even specific songs are taken up as a part of general discussions about tembang Sunda, in some cases spurring letters to the editor and long debates. Deaths of prominent musicians warrant extensive articles, as do awards and competitions. At least one newspaper makes a point of listing the attendees at each month's panglawungan or tembang Sunda gathering, so that those who did not attend could find out exactly who did attend, who the sponsor was, where the panglawungan was held, and what songs were performed.

The Sundanese-language magazine, *Manglé*, is responsible more than any other magazine for the promotion of tembang Sunda and especially the polemik surrounding the genre. Even more so than the newspapers, which have international news to report as well, *Manglé* focuses and even directs some of the debate about tembang Sunda, drawing heated discussions from its readers. Some tembang Sunda practitioners are regular contributors to *Manglé*, in fact, which is generally not the case with the newspapers. *Manglé* is far more interactive with its readers than any other magazine. It takes issues such as the banning of sad songs (*lagu cengeng*) in 1988 by Harmoko, the then-Minister of Information, and outlines the pros and cons of each issue with contributions from many sides.

Because the magazine pays close attention to issues that affect Sundanese artists, *Manglé* is often at the center of arguments among tembang Sunda musicians. For example, a scandal involving one of the top female teachers and suspicions of jury rigging at a pasanggiri received extensive coverage, fueling tremendous debate and outrage among the community of practitioners. Musicians and audience members fell into different camps, some siding with the teacher, others calling into question the larger issue of juries at competitions.[8] "If someone is problematizing tembang Sunda," said one musician, "you can be certain that *Manglé* is at the center of it."

Another journal is the *Buletin Kebudayaan Jawa Barat* (the West Java Bulletin of Culture), which during the 1970s and early 1980s published many articles about tembang Sunda and other Sundanese musical genres. This bulletin, also known as *KAWIT*, published articles about the inner meaning (pangjiwaan) of tembang Sunda (Somawidjaja 1983), and summarized and commented on a seminar held about tembang Sunda (Panitia Seminar Tembang Sunda 1976). It also included descriptions of many related genres such as pantun, Ciawian, and Cigawiran (Danasasmita 1979, Supandi 1976b, and Suryana 1978), and was for at least a decade a very active contributor to the debate about tembang Sunda. By publishing photographs of Sundanese musical arts in the United States, Europe, and Japan, the publishers of this bulletin also hoped to instill a sense of pride in Sundanese culture among its readers.

The extent to which publications such as books and pamphlets influence tembang Sunda is debatable. The Sundanese carry a significant amount of respect for the written word, which may be an influence from Islam. Several musicians spoke with reverence about books that had as their topics tembang Sunda and related Sundanese musical genres, yet, when questioned further, none of these same people had actually read the books in question, nor did they know how to obtain them. This appears to be symptomatic of a greater tendency to appreciate books, or sometimes to collect books, but not to actually read them. In most of the homes of Sundanese musicians with whom I visited, rarely were any books actually visible, even in the inner living rooms where most Sundanese actually spend their time. Assuming that at least some people might have books in some kind of inner sanctum (a private study, perhaps), I occasionally asked about them, and the answer was that books were at bookstores, not in people's homes (Indo.: *Di toko buku mah banyak; di sini mah nggak ada*). The answers may have been calculated to ward off the overinquisitive researcher, of course, but it seems likely that there really were no books. The exceptions to this general rule were at the homes of musicians who had attended universities, usually not in music but in unrelated fields. Some of the elderly master musicians such as Apung Wiratmadja and Bakang Abubakar also had books about tembang Sunda in their homes and referred to them in conversation.

The lack of books in the homes of most practicing musicians does not indicate that musicians are unaware of books about music, or unaware of their contents. Rather, many musicians seem to form opinions about books based on their knowledge of the author. For example, every musician knows Apung Wiratmadja as a famous singer and author of an important early work on tembang Sunda (Wiratmadja 1964). They were all aware of his book, and because Pa Apung is loved and highly respected as a proponent of tembang Sunda, his book is believed to be of excellent quality. Many claimed to have it at their homes. On no occasion, however, could the book ever be found when I asked the person at his home. A book may be respected and discussed based on the musicians' sense of respect for the author (due to status differences, experience, education, wealth, or other factors), but I rarely heard of music books used as a reference or active sourcebook outside of Bandung's schools. It is a testament to the lively debate surrounding tembang Sunda that the ideas in relevant books end up in wide oral circulation even if the books stay on the shelves of only a handful of people.

One important exception to this general rule is the use of printed books containing the lyrics of songs. These lyric books are ubiquitous at performances and latihans. Some singers carry their own hand-printed books to these performances, while others rely on a set of four small books (published in the mid-1980s).[9] The set comprises book for mamaos songs in pélog, one for panambihs in pélog, another for mamaos in sorog and saléndro, and the last for panambihs in sorog and saléndro (Sobirin 1987). The songs are listed under specific titles, but a singer can choose lyrics from another song if that song conforms to the same poetic meter as the tune she wants to sing. It is not unusual for singers to borrow each other's songbooks, and when singers forget to bring songbooks, they simply sing the first verses of whatever songs they can remember. At one performance, two singers alternated the same first verse of "Kembang Bungur" for ten minutes because they had both neglected to bring their songbooks. One later laughed about it to me, explaining that the audience wasn't listening anyway, so it didn't matter. The use of songbooks, however, seems to be an essential fixture of modern tembang Sunda performances, as important as microphones and sound systems.

The printed media seems to have had multifaceted impacts on the world of tembang Sunda. Newspapers inform musicians and singers about current social and musical events that affect them, such as the scheduling of panglawungan gatherings, or the latest performances of their colleagues. Magazines—*Manglé*, in particular—have the function of carrying on a printed debate about tembang Sunda, thereby extending the debate process. Books about Sundanese musical arts, by contrast, appear to be strongly revered but rarely consulted. Most musicians would rather actively discuss the issues at hand with other musicians than refer to a book. Given that most Sundanese (including the highly literate ones) live more in an oral traditional world than one dominated by print media, such a statement is no surprise.

The link between all these media and modernization has been in the ways that people have become able to gain access to a formerly restricted genre. Anyone may listen to or study tembang Sunda, including people from well outside the aristocracy. The appearance of compact disc recordings of tembang Sunda (with complete translations of the lyrics) has led to the genre's mediated spread to Australia, Japan, Europe, and the United States. Appadurai points out that "Globalization has shrunk the distance between elites, shifted key relations between producers and consumers, broken many links between labor and family life, obscured the lines between temporary locales and imaginary national attachments" (Appadurai 1996:10). Members of Bandung's aristocracy who participate in tembang Sunda performances may be surprised some day to find Americans, Europeans, and Australians performing (and even teaching) tembang Sunda without ever having visited Indonesia.

This chapter has outlined the mass media that not only influence and inform the people who perform tembang Sunda but also provide an important means of transmission (through the radio and television) and dissemination (through the cassette industry) of the genre. The printed media (particularly serial publications) are a locus for debate and gossip, which themselves are a major fuel for the continuation of the genre. Tembang Sunda is dependent on these industries for the livelihood of its practitioners and, by extension, its own continued existence. The cassette and radio industries are in turn dependent on tembang Sunda and other musical genres for their continuing patronage. Television and the printed media, although far less tied to the arts community than other media, have a stake in the arts as a means of entertainment for their consumers. The commercial relationship that binds tembang Sunda to these media appears to be mutually beneficial, for without the mass media it is likely that tembang Sunda would not be nearly as highly developed and widespread as it is today.

plicated for many singers because almost every singer (male or female) is also a chain smoker.[1]

The levels of difficulty for vocal students are in some ways different from those of the instrumentalists. Kacapi students, for example, find the techniques necessary for the production of jejemplangan songs prohibitively difficult, whereas the heterophonic accompaniment of a rarancagan song or the fixed-rhythm ostinato patterns of a papantunan song are quite simple on the kacapi if the player knows the vocal part. Panambih songs are easiest of all for kacapi players, whereas for suling players, the long instrumental passages or *gelenyu* in the songs force the suling player to improvise. In many of the other styles of tembang Sunda, the primary function of the suling player is to follow and occasionally lead the singer. Each type of student reaches and surpasses different levels or plateaus of difficulty, and every plateau has its own challenges for the student.

The Sundanese use three systems of nomenclature to describe and teach the pitches of the Sundanese tuning systems: a cipher system (1-2-3-4-5), a type of Sundanese solfège (da–mi–na–ti–la), and a system of kacapi string names (*barang—kenong—panelu—bem—galimer*). Musicians do not use an absolute tuning reference, but the Sundanese nomenclature remains stable from tuning to tuning. In other words, although the actual pitch value of barang is variable, it always occurs as the first pitch in a descending scale.[2] The Sundanese number and conceptualize their musical scales from the pitch with the highest frequency (1) to the one with the lowest (5), exactly the opposite of the Javanese numbering system (and the Western, for that matter). Van Zanten attributes this reversal to an accentuation of the difference in culture between the Sundanese and the Javanese (van Zanten 1989:113). Although I agree with him, I also feel that this distinction is not always clear in the minds of the people who follow this style of notation. Although at first I thought that only those musicians influenced directly by one of the music institutions in Bandung were subject to this system, I soon discovered evidence of actual conceptualization of it in the notation of singers and in the gestures used by musicians to describe changes in pitch. A raised hand, for example, means a lowered pitch; a dip in an otherwise straight line over the lyrics of a song means an upward shift in pitch.

The way the Sundanese use the nomenclature reflects to some extent the degree to which they have been influenced by Sundanese methods of learning. Each arena of learning (group rehearsals, private lessons, books, and institutions) has its own preferred system. Most of the instrumentalists I dealt with on a regular basis used the cipher system when they referred to specific pitches. Older kacapi players like to use the string names barang, bem, and so on, but younger players simply use the numbers. The three or four suling players that I worked with also frequently used the cipher system. People who have attended one or more of the Sundanese music schools such as Sekolah Menengah Karawitan Indonesia (SMKI) or Sekolah Tinggi Seni Indonesia (STSI) tend to use the da–mi–na–ti–la system.

USES OF HUMOR IN THE LEARNING PROCESS

One of the most important factors to be taken into consideration in the study of learning processes in tembang Sunda is how humor is used by the Sundanese to train performers. One of the quickest and most effective ways to cause a student to learn quickly is to make him so embarrassed by his mistakes that he never repeats them. Laughter is used as a method of social and musical control, particularly in the latihan or public lesson/jam session. In my following discussion of the latihan, I mention that the situation is never private. Frequently, large groups will spend hours watching, laughing, and criticizing. Although such boisterous behavior is more prevalent in a dance latihan, for example, humor is still an essential teaching tool in every genre of Sundanese music.[3] Many say that a latihan is more fun if there are more people present, and claim that they attend to give *semangat*, or enthusiasm, to the proceedings.

When anyone makes a mistake, the entire group dissolves into laughter. The singer always laughs, too, and such laughter works as an incentive to avoid future mistakes. Almost no one actually becomes angry at being laughed at—although it is indeed an embarrassing experience—because to do so would be bad form. Although I do not discuss the uses of humor in each of the following methods of study, the reader should be aware that humor in Sundanese musical situations can be very persuasive in correcting mistakes and in controlling musical behavior. Musical creativity is certainly acceptable, particularly among the top-ranking performers, but it must be within certain stylistic limits. This principle applies as well to performers who attempt to sing, play, or dance something different from what is expected of them, such as unusual ornamentation, or switching instruments unexpectedly.[4]

The methods of learning available to a potential student of tembang Sunda are not mutually exclusive; however, most students choose a certain way of studying the music and generally remain with that method as long as they remain active in tembang Sunda circles. Some students combine several different ways of studying in order to gain the fullest comprehension of tembang Sunda possible. These methods include frequent attendance at one or more latihans, private study with a teacher, enrollment at one of Bandung's music schools, independent study methods (books and cassettes), and simply spending a lot of time with musicians, picking up information from them.

While researching tembang Sunda in Bandung, I used all of the above methods, with the exception of enrolling in a music institution. Because attending a music institution would have required me to spend far less time on my own research and with my own teachers, I chose instead to interview teachers and students at these institutions to ascertain the amount of time spent on tembang Sunda and the content and quality of the material provided to the students. This work also included obtaining copies of books, and going through some of the notation provided to the students. Of all these methods, the single most effective method for studying tembang Sunda is participation in the latihan.

THE LATIHAN

The term *latihan* refers to a musical event, which may last all afternoon and evening, or may only last an hour. Loosely defined, it is an informal study session for any type of music or dance. Each latihan is unique, not only between genres but also (within the arena of tembang Sunda) from teacher to teacher. These latihan are usually held at the home of the main singer in a group. On rare occasions, they may be held at the home of an outside sponsor or a prominent musician, but generally the singer is the latihan host because of his or her role in the training of other singers. A latihan tembang Sunda is almost always held primarily for the benefit of the singing members of tembang Sunda practitioners; the presence of instrumentalists (especially a kacapi player) is considered very beneficial to an effective latihan, but is not essential unless the main singer herself works on songs as well.

A latihan may involve very intensive working through of the finest details of tembang Sunda performance practice, or the participants may sit around eating, laughing, and talking all afternoon, and never sing or play a note.[5] During the fasting month of Ramadan, few people have the energy to attend latihan, and when someone is making a recording or has a large project to complete, latihan activity is curtailed. If a performance has been scheduled for that evening, the latihan will be canceled altogether. This extra time gives the singers' voices a chance to rest, and gives them the opportunity to do their hair, put on makeup, and get dressed; the process of physical preparation takes (at least) several hours. Furthermore, the presence or absence of guests in the home will affect whether or not a latihan will be held that week. In preparation for any kind of tembang Sunda competition, latihan activity is doubled or tripled in Bandung, and the aforementioned all-night sessions take place.

Money is almost never exchanged for lessons in latihan sessions, even if active teaching is taking place. The whole concept of the latihan is that all attendees benefit from the experience, including the teacher or primary singer. Because a latihan is more than just an extended lesson, people other than students appear each week. Among potential latihan attendees are the regular students, prospective students, composers, and family members or neighbors of the singer who have nothing else to do. Others appear periodically, including servants who keep an eye on the supply of tea and snacks, one-time-only students (who talk at length about their desire to study the music but never come back), house guests, and local politicians. Each of these attendees participates to some degree in the relative success or failure of a latihan, and it is usually the responsibility of the singer to act as the informal master of ceremonies. Although some latihan are larger than others (particularly Euis Komariah's latihan), all are characterized by an atmosphere of interest and dedication.[6]

At the home of Euis Komariah, a latihan was held, on average, every few days—usually on Tuesdays and Fridays. Some singers will only hold a latihan once a week—for example, every Wednesday night, all night. It is normal for singers who frequently perform together to have a joint latihan, with the senior singer acting as host. Other singers do not participate in the latihan scene at all, and—in many cases because of this seeming unwillingness to improve or even maintain their own vocal ability—they are considered less serious and unprofessional. It is considered prestigious to host a latihan, and even more prestigious to have students. For this reason, some vocalists try to arrange for certain instrumentalists to attend latihans and on occasion pay them *uang rokok*, or "cigarette money," to attend. The money is only the equivalent of one or two dollars, but pays for their transportation and cigarettes, and is casually handed to them just as they leave at the end of the latihan.

Because I did not have the opportunity to attend every latihan in Sunda but, rather, only a few each week over a period of months, I cannot give a clear picture of what the true "average" latihan is like. Furthermore, the following description of a latihan may not apply to more than a few singers. At most of the latihans I attended, however, the procedure is to sit around and talk for at least an hour (sometimes up to four hours) until the regulars have all arrived. Everyone sits in a circle, usually at the same height so that no one is sitting on the ground when others are on a couch or in chairs. Most latihan hosts have a special area set aside for tembang Sunda practice. The area is either a raised platform to separate the tembang Sunda place from the rest of the room, an interior living room in which the instruments are kept, or simply a section of the floor that has been covered with rugs or rattan mats.

After the instruments have been tuned and the opening instrumental bubuka has been played, the songs from the previous session are run through. The regular students (usually only four or five people) sit in a line or a circle, and each one has an individual lesson on each song in front of up to thirty people. One at a time, the student and the singer go through the song over and over. The other students listen closely and often sing along very softly under their breath, checking with each other as they wait their turn. At this point in the latihan, the main singer acts as an instructor, listening with great care to the vocal ornaments of the students and correcting the smallest details. The teacher's singing is limited to correcting the errors of the students, and the instrumentalists do not necessarily follow along except to provide the student with the basic lead-in to the first line of the song. Sometimes the instrumentalists or other attendees will also correct the student, which is usually not regarded as an intrusion by the main singer. In some cases, the instrumentalists know the song better than the singer does, so both the singer and the students usually welcome their participation in the teaching process.

After the first student has gotten the song right, the singer moves on to the next student, who has been paying close attention to the lesson of the first student. Each subsequent student is therefore in a better position to get the song right on the first or second try, because the lesson taught to the first student applies to all of them. This review is often accompanied by discussion of the pangjiwaan, or inner soul of the song. Everyone participates in this aspect of the latihan, because it allows each individual to interpret the song individually. As part of the ways in which people discuss all the inner workings of tembang Sunda culture, this interpretive discussion allows for variation, debate, transmission of historical facts or beliefs, and a much more profound awareness of the depth of the song. The discussion may be quite brief, or may extend well into the evening. When the review of the previous session's songs is completed, the participants normally take a break to eat, smoke more cigarettes, talk about other things, tell jokes, and relax. Children—who run around and make noise regardless of latihan activity—usually choose the break time to ply their parents with requests.

If the latihan takes place in the afternoon, the break roughly coincides with the late afternoon call to prayer. Because there are loudspeakers on every mosque, and several mosques in each neighborhood, the call to prayer is a loud and unavoidable disruption of all activity. Although almost all tembang Sunda practitioners are followers of Islam, many of them are relatively secular in their practice and simply ignore the call to prayer. The actual aural interruption of the call to prayer only lasts a few minutes, but the ensuing break in vocal activity during a latihan can last for more than an hour. General musical activity will only resume after the early evening call to prayer, which is the last one of the day.

The second part of the latihan involves working on new material. The main singer (usually a woman) looks through her songbook, or entertains requests from students for specific songs, or discusses her choices with the instrumentalists. Because the order of a tembang Sunda set is to begin with one or more mamaos or free-rhythm songs and to end with a panambih or fixed-rhythm song, she selects a mamaos song first. After she has selected a new song, she usually sings it once or twice with the accompaniment of all the instrumentalists, refreshing her own memory and making sure she remembers all of it. The musicians usually help remind her with comments and musical cues, and when she feels that she remembers it well enough, she gives the lyrics to the students by speaking them out loud or having them copy it directly from her own songbook. If the selected lyrics are in a standard poetic meter and the set of lyrics are frequently used in other songs, she may simply recite the first line of the verse: "Abdi mah sok sesah deui" ("I am in great difficulty again") and the students can then fill in the rest of the lines from memory. Sometimes the singer substitutes a different set of lyrics in the same poetic meter and works through the new lyrics with the musicians before giving them to the students.

After the students have the lyrics written down, the singer runs through the song one or more times to give the students a chance to become familiar with the song and to do a bare-bones transcription of it, if they use that method. I have never seen students carrying tape recorders, though I often brought one myself. In spite of the availability of cassette machines, blank tapes are not as accessible as prerecorded tapes, and students either cannot afford the machines or do not believe in the learning method of recording the teacher.[7] Once the basic outline of the song has been learned, the students have the same type of lesson as in the review of the previous session: Each student has an opportunity to work through the song individually with the teacher, while everyone else concentrates and follows along. If the first song was learned quickly and easily, and everyone has enough energy, a second mamaos song (or even a third) is learned in the same manner.

The active learning section of the latihan is closed off with a panambih selected by the singer according to its appropriateness to the previous songs. In other words, it should have some correspondence to the other songs of the set either in lyrical content (for example, "Budak Leungit" or "Lost Child" should be followed by the panambih "Budak Ceurik" or "Crying Child"), or in tonal material. The appropriate tonal material required to pair a mamaos (free-rhythm song) with a panambih (fixed-rhythm song) is most evident when the final tone of the mamaos corresponds with the gong tone or closing tone of the panambih. When all of the songs have been learned and sung by each student, the latihan may either come to a close or, as is more likely, may break for more snacks, cigarettes, and gossip.

The third section of the latihan is usually reserved for the main singer herself to work on her own material. It is in this section that the singer derives the most useful musical benefit, because it is usually the only chance she has to rehearse with her accompanists for performances. It is often the most enjoyable time for her students, who can now relax and watch their teacher in action without having to interact socially themselves with non–tembang Sunda people. The socialization required at actual performances of tembang Sunda is distracting to students because most of the people who attend performances are not involved in the music and see it as background accompaniment to the more important activity of talking. At a latihan, therefore, a student can closely study the technique of the singer, pick up ideas to improve her own performance, and almost completely devote her attention to the music. Socializing and eating is kept to a minimum during this last section of the latihan, unless a food vendor comes by with a particularly appetizing type of food such as *sekoteng* (sweet hot ginger soup) or *pisang goreng* (banana fritters), which happens frequently. In such an event, everyone takes another break and the latihan ends there about half the time.

Some people (particularly composers and older people who love, but do not practice, tembang Sunda) come to this section of the latihan only to listen to the singer work through parts of her repertoire undisturbed. By the time the second section of the latihan has finished, many of the casual hangers-on have typically gone home or are watching television. After the second break and well into the third section of the latihan, the children go to bed and outside sounds (of traffic, animals, and other people) fade into the night. Until the end of the latihan, which may be as late as three in the morning, the main singer and her accompanists are the only focus of attention. They may use this opportunity to go into a rare tuning system, or to experiment with rarely performed songs, or work exclusively on the repertoire of one of the older tembang Sunda composers. If the latihan reaches the saléndro tuning (which does not happen very often), the singer may add a few gamelan saléndro songs or try singing sorog songs in saléndro. The presence of a rebab player, although enjoyable, is not necessary for the performance of songs in saléndro. If a rebab player comes to a latihan, however, the kacapi may be retuned to saléndro immediately to take advantage of the rebab player's presence. During a very long tembang Sunda evening, beginning singers rarely perform during the saléndro section.

Toward the end of the evening, well-known songs using a *rampak* (chorus) are used to close off the latihan and to bring all the participants back into the circle. When all the songs are finished, the instruments are covered up with cloth and placed in their usual places, and everyone goes home. Although it may seem strange that the Sundanese who attend these events have enough time and energy to devote up to fifteen hours to the study of this music in one day, it should be kept in mind that many female singers neither work nor go to school, and in fact have very few cares outside of their own households. If they are unmarried, their situation is even easier. It is quite common, in fact, for various unmarried girls to show up once or twice at a latihan, not because they are interested in becoming a performer of tembang Sunda but simply because they have nothing better to do.

The picture that I have presented of the latihan is in many ways an ideal one and generally describes events as they took place at the home of Ibu Euis. Not all latihan are that constructive, and not all are that casual. I have attended latihan sessions at the homes of singers in which the students cried in frustration at the difficulty of learning the songs; at other homes, the students claim never to work on new songs but simply to review old songs for months at a time. Sometimes a new student is accepted unconditionally, and other times he or she must go through a trial period of watching and listening. Anger is a rare emotion at a latihan; more frequently, laughter is heard more often than music. In spite of the talk and all the distracting elements such as children and animals, the latihan is still the strongest medium for the continuation of tembang Sunda in the city, and is said to be the equivalent of the "heart and soul" of learning tembang Sunda.

FORMAL AND INFORMAL LESSONS

The phenomenon of private, formal lessons in tembang Sunda is rare and very recent in Bandung. Because of its rarity, few musicians are aware of it and those who do it are often believed to be in it just for the money (*cari uang saja*). The association of a formal lesson with money is so strong, in fact, that tembang Sunda musicians who give private, paid lessons are often looked down on and sometimes accused of prostituting their art. Lessons to foreigners are a different situation, however, because many tembang Sunda musicians understand how foreigners study at home and are willing to conform to the foreigners' need for privacy and individual instruction. Some of the more experienced teachers willingly accept a foreigner as a private student not just for the money but, more important, for the prestige that having a foreign student brings to the teacher.[8]

The brief time allotted to private lessons is in marked contrast to the four or five hours accorded to students in latihan sessions. Furthermore, the teachers who told stories of private students who paid cash for their lessons usually mentioned that the student never came back after two or three lessons, or wasn't serious, or ran out of money. During my stay in Bandung, I never saw anyone give private, paid lessons except to foreigners. The arrangement of those lessons was often by a third party. Because of the rarity of these lessons and the comparative availability of latihan sessions both inside Bandung and, less frequently, outside of Bandung, the private lesson seems untenable in Bandung's musical environment.

Tembang Sunda instrumentalists rarely have individual latihan sessions in the manner of the vocalists, nor does their practice of learning vary from kacapi to suling to rebab. Instead, the most common practice is for an interested student to request a specific ornament or technique from a more experienced player. In some cases, this small request may occur during a break in a vocalist's latihan session. At this time, the instrumentalists may take advantage of the situation to hold a very small latihan of their own, in which the inexperienced players have a chance to ask questions politely or request the demonstration of a particular technique on one of the instruments from the older players. The experienced players do not discourage short questions in this informal setting, and a single technical question from a young player is enough to establish a teacher-student relationship with an older musician.

Another type of informal lesson occurs when a student comes to the home of a player. The gesture of approaching a player at his own home is considered very polite, and an experienced player is quite likely to receive the student and show him what he wishes when the trip to his home is made. After a brief period of socializing, the student may then briefly ask about the ornament. After he has been shown the ornament and a few more minutes of socializing has taken place, the student politely takes his leave. Although students rarely pay for the few minutes of the teacher's time, they often bring cigarettes or a small gift or token of appreciation. Most instrumental study takes place in the context of these informal lessons.

MUSIC INSTITUTIONS

The scope of formal musical instruction through institutions in Bandung ranges from being drilled in the performance of patriotic songs in elementary school, to the achievement of advanced degrees in music. As already mentioned, I did not actually enroll formally in any of the music institutions in Bandung, but rather conducted interviews with teachers and students about these and other institutions. Opinions among musicians, teachers, and students about the relative advantages and disadvantages of attending one of these schools vary widely. Among the musicians who perform regularly and have a working relationship with lingkung seni, sponsors, recording studios, and maintain a regular schedule of performances, attendance at an institution is simply a waste of time and money. For a good student who attaches himself to a single teacher at one of the institutions, however, attendance may be profitable because most teachers promote their own students and create lingkung seni with membership selected from their best students from school.

Music education at the elementary school and junior high school level in Sunda is usually limited to instruction in the diatonic system and an introduction to some of the traditional Sundanese and Javanese instruments. Dance classes are sometimes held after school in special workshops for the children. Although few schools actually have a teacher whose domain is exclusively music, many musicians function as part-time guest instructors and are able to add to their meager incomes by visiting various schools once a week or once every two weeks. The situation is different in high school, where more musical instruction is allowed and students are encouraged to participate in music groups such as diatonic angklung ensembles. It is unusual, however, for musical instruction to proceed beyond this basic level except at institutions specializing in *karawitan* or traditional music.

Sunda's most important music high school is the Sekolah Menengah Karawitan Indonesia (SMKI), a rapidly expanding group of new buildings set in the middle of a group of kampung (semi-urban villages) surrounded by rice fields on the outskirts of Bandung. At this institution, many Sundanese and some non-Sundanese musicians who have acquired degrees themselves teach and attend planning meetings for most of each day. Musicians who may be better qualified as performers are barred from teaching at SMKI and any other institution if they lack the necessary degree, which apparently may be in any subject. Students are given basic instruction in Sundanese theory and notation, based on theories developed by Machyar Kusumadinata who worked with Jaap Kunst in the 1920s and 1930s. As van Zanten has shown, these theoretical premises are ineffective in describing current performance practice (van Zanten 1989:124–126; 1995:219). SMKI and other institutions persist in teaching these theories, however, primarily (as one teacher put it, who wished to remain anonymous) "because we need to hang onto our jobs and cannot afford to make trouble." Andrew Weintraub (1993b) also writes about the dichotomy between theory and practice, pointing out the difficulty in reconciling older theory to newer practice when so many aspects of teaching and learning are based on older models.

At SMKI there are four levels of coursework, and in the senior class there are two groups of thirty-five to forty students each. Students spend two hours a week on kacapi kawih for class levels 1, 2, and 3, and then class levels 3 and 4 spend two hours a week on kacapi tembang. Therefore, instruction in tembang-style kacapi only begins in the last two years of instruction, and only two hours a week. Of those two hours, the first hour is spent reviewing the material of the previous week, and the second begins on new material. The kacapi tembang teacher is unable to check on individual students because of the large class size and the lack of time available for the lesson, so no corrections are made to the students' playing.

The teaching of vocal technique in tembang Sunda at SMKI occurs once every two weeks only, for a period of two hours each time. The tembang teacher alternates teaching with another (kawih) teacher each week. The students are all used to Sundanese cipher notation, but the tembang teacher uses only notation in gamelan and kacapi classes, not in the tembang Sunda singing class. Instead, the whole class of forty is given the words, and the song is gone through one line at a time. The students are free to create their own notation. Most students, however, use cipher notation, which they know best. At the most, the students leave SMKI with no more than five songs, either on the kacapi or singing. These five songs are usually only in pélog and include "Papatet" and other papantunan songs. The students usually receive only one panambih from their teacher, because kawih songs may also be used as panambih and it is felt that panambih songs are far easier to learn than mamaos songs.

Classes on other tembang Sunda instruments are mixed into the general curriculum and are not exclusive, as are the classes on vocal style and kacapi. For example, students who study rincik are taught only how to play in the *carukan* style, which is imitative of *saron* playing and is used only during the bubuka in tembang Sunda. One of the most obvious signs of a graduate from one of the institutes is that he can only play rincik in carukan style. The lack of specialization among the teachers at these institutions is a reflection (in most cases) of their own experience and education. Most of the teachers are graduates of those exact institutions, and may never have had experience as a working musician in competition with other musicians.

The situation for tembang Sunda at Bandung's academy of music and dance, Sekolah Tinggi Seni Indonesia (STSI; formerly Akademi Seni Tari Indonesia (ASTI), is slightly different from that at SMKI. Kacapi lessons at STSI are evidently not differentiated between kawih-style kacapi and tembang-style kacapi or, at least if they are differentiated, the students coming out of STSI do not seem to know the difference. Most students of kacapi at STSI learn kawih-style kacapi, which enables them to play all the latest songs of the pop Sunda genre and show off their dexterity.

According to the tembang Sunda voice teacher at STSI, when he teaches tembang singing, he spends several weeks on *olah vokal* (vocal technique), without the words at all, just working through the song using the syllable "ah." His intention is to just get the students to sing vowels properly, before he goes into the songs themselves. Following the olah vokal, the students are taught all the different kinds of ornaments; for example, the slow vibrato but on each pitch of each scale. When the song is finally given to them, the teacher simply tells them where to place the vocal ornaments. At STSI there are thirty-two students to a class, so—similar to the situation at SMKI—there can be very little individualized training because there are too many students. In the student's final semester at STSI, the tembang Sunda teacher tries to work on polishing the individual technique of each student but is unable to do more than walk them through each song.

The teaching of tembang Sunda at SMKI and STSI is only of the most basic type and, in addition to being fraught with difficulty due to the large class sizes, shows strong influences from gamelan terminology, which is not the terminology used by tembang Sunda musicians themselves. For example, musicians who graduate from music institutions tend to use the gamelan terms degung for pélog and madenda for sorog, even though most tembang Sunda musicians differentiate between pélog tembang and pélog degung because of slight tonal differences. Furthermore, in one of the study books published at SMKI, it is claimed that tembang Sunda is "extremely popular among all people of Sunda" (Sekolah Menengah Karawitan Indonesia 1981: 12). The association of tembang Sunda with the aristocracy and the extreme dislike with which many nonaristocratic Sundanese view tembang Sunda would seem to discount this claim of popularity. These errors are only a few of those perpetuated by the literature used for teaching tembang Sunda.

In addition to SMKI and STSI, several other institutions of higher education offer musical instruction. Among these are IKIP Bandung, which offers a music degree, and Universitas Padjadjaran. Some music students choose to attend these universities because of the broader training they offer, and because a degree from IKIP or one of the other prominent Sundanese universities offers greater employment potential in a nonmusical field. Most musicians not already employed by SMKI, STSI, or RRI have to work at some kind of day job, either at a government office or in some other nonmusical capacity.[9] A diploma in Sunda is still one of the main stepping stones to a high-paying job. Since the required job (and subsequent income) is generally not in the music business, a degree from a prestigious, non-music-oriented university is considered a safer bet than an SMKI or STSI degree. The exception to this, of course, is if the student intends to get a job teaching at a music institution. In such a case, the student does well to cultivate the good wishes of his teachers and to remain well within the boundaries of the institution in his musical creativity and thought. The politics of getting a paying job as a music teacher would probably fill several volumes, but my observations led me to believe that at the very least, personal connections (in addition to a music degree) are extremely important in getting a job at SMKI or STSI.

In all of these institutions for training musicians, one of the most common deficiencies seems to be the lack of specialization in one or two genres. In other words, a graduate with a music degree seems to be able to perform many types of Sundanese, Javanese, and Balinese music at varying levels of competence, but rarely excels in any single genre or dance style. The music institutions of Bandung are perceived to be a good way for a promising musician to get out of the village and into the lucrative urban music scene. The general musical education offered by SMKI and STSI is important for providing a broad background in Indonesian (not just Sundanese) music. The student should not expect to leave the school with a specialized knowledge of any type of music, let alone the playing skills necessary to make it in one of the highly competitive music professions of Bandung.

INDEPENDENT STUDY METHODS

Students of tembang Sunda choose certain methods of study based on the avenues open to them. Some students come naturally out of music playing families, as is the case with Fitri, winner of the 1999 pasanggiri DAMAS and daughter of the late kacapi master Uking Sukri. In a case such as that, studying tembang can be as natural as visiting a relative. Many students are, in fact, remotely related to their teachers. Other students find themselves drawn to the sound of a particular instrument, like the suling, or are fortunate enough to know someone who owns a kacapi. In some cases, a student may begin his musical career as a gamelan player, but branch out into tembang Sunda through contact at SMKI or STSI, or through friends who take him to a latihan. Several of my musician friends became tembang Sunda musicians because their mothers enjoyed singing the music so much that they themselves became interested in it as well.

Many people, however, do not have the advantage of being raised in a tembang Sunda environment, or to have contacts with musicians, or the right social status or skills to become involved at the bottom level of tembang Sunda study. These musicians must, therefore, choose another method or methods in order to approach tembang Sunda and learn about it without the benefit of a teacher. Among these methods are the use of instruction books, cassettes, and radio broadcasts. Although these independent methods of study are possibly a good way to increase one's general understanding of tembang Sunda, some of the sourcebooks are full of errors, and there is little critical discussion of the literature among musicians. As a result, a potential student is likely to come into contact with (and uncritically believe) the wrong information. Cassettes and radio broadcasts are not error-free either, because many recording professionals do not take the time to record over mistakes that they have made on cassettes before the cassette is marketed. Similarly, a live radio broadcast allows no room for overdubbing. Therefore, these methods of independent study are only useful in the presence of critical discussion and in combination with other methods such as attendance at a latihan session.

Instruction books about tembang Sunda and other forms of Sundanese music vary in quality. Most of these books supply the lyrics and occasionally the cipher notation for the vocal part of selected songs, without any indication of the ornaments or of accompaniment. Examples of this type of book are *Nyukcruk Galur Nu Kapungkur* (Somawidjaja 1982) and *Pangajaran Tembang Sunda* (Endang S. 1979), which list song texts only. Very little detailed analysis of the music accompanies these books; instead, tembang Sunda is divided into fixed- and free-rhythm sections, and the stylistic divisions and poetic meters are listed with a few examples.

Several works provide a more thorough background to tembang Sunda than just a list of songs. Among them are the very useful *Tembang Sunda Cianjuran* (Sukanda 1983), *Rasiah Tembang Sunda* (Satjadibrata 1953), *Sumbangan Asih kana Tembang Sunda* and *Mengenal Seni Tembang Sunda* (Wiratmadja 1964 and 1998, respectively), and several small pamphlets published by the Mimitran Tembang Sunda, a Bandung organization dedicated to the promotion of tembang Sunda. The one book devoted solely to kacapi instruction that I could find was *Pelajaran Kacapi* (Koswara 1973), which unfortunately for students of tembang Sunda is only about kawih style. Other than the above-mentioned books, there are several general surveys on Sundanese music which are of limited usefulness to potential students specifically interested in tembang Sunda.

Several problems arise with the study of tembang Sunda from books only. One fundamental issue is the understanding and good production of vocal ornamentation that can be gained only through periods of close listening. Although some claim to know about tembang Sunda simply through the collection of books and pamphlets, their lack of knowledge is evident as soon as they speak about it. A commonly heard phrase is "Just ask *me* about tembang Sunda; I have plenty of books at home" (Indo.: *Tanya saja pada saya mengenai tembang Sunda; buku saya banyak sekali di rumah*). Some of these same people will claim to have "all the cassettes" or to have studied "in detail" (*diditél*) the kacapi style of one or more performers. The sparest investigation, however, indicates that many people would like to be considered knowledgeable about tembang Sunda, but are content with the claimed presence of printed material and cassettes.

The use of cassettes provides a chance for people outside the urban centers to enjoy and familiarize themselves with the tembang Sunda repertoire and, if they desire, to "study" privately with some of the finest singers and instrumentalists. If a student is acquainted with a recording professional, he may choose a single instrumental ornament from a recording and try to learn it himself first, then approach the player quietly at home or during a break at a latihan and ask to be trained on the ornament in person.

Vocal students must face a different situation if they wish to study from a cassette. Although it is common now for a student to approach a singer and ask if he or she may participate in a latihan, the initial study of songs from cassettes may result in mistaken lyrics, duplication of errors on the cassettes, and the perceived theft of songs that may be the possession of only one singer. For this reason, it is far more beneficial to the student to participate in a latihan and not to risk the possible wrath of a teacher and exclusion by the other students for making the mistake of "stealing" songs from cassettes. Although the concept of thievery (of melodic ornaments in particular) is common in Sundanese music, almost all suspicion is assuaged if the potential thief simply approaches the artist politely and requests to be taught the ornament in question.

This chapter has covered most of the ways in which a student of tembang Sunda can gain knowledge of the genre, from attendance at a latihan to the "stealing" of songs from cassettes. Depending on the origins of the student (aristocratic or lower-class village) and his or her intentions (to become a kacapi player or a vocalist), one or more methods of study may be selected. As was mentioned earlier, most serious students use a combination of several different methods to provide themselves with the most comprehensive education in tembang Sunda specialization. Because of the greater opportunities available in the city for potential students to succeed in tembang Sunda, most young village players and singers make a pilgrimage to the city to seek out the people who they believe are the best musicians. This migration to the city for tembang Sunda lessons has its antecedents in some of the very finest of the singers, such as Ida Widawati, Yayah Rochaeti Dachlan, and Enah Sukaenah, all of whom were from outside of Bandung (Garut, Tasikmalaya, and Sumedang, respectively), but studied in Bandung and became very famous singers. Although latihan sessions and other types of training occur in the smaller cities, the draw of Bandung is so strong that, in the minds of the village Sundanese, Bandung may be one of the only places to go to study tembang Sunda.

In Part II of this book, I have discussed many of the urban institutions that support and underwrite the performance and continuation of tembang Sunda in the city of Bandung. It is clear that tembang Sunda enjoys a broad base of urban patronage at several different levels. In spite of this support, however, tembang Sunda is still regarded as the exclusive provenance of the wealthy, landed aristocracy. The descendants of the aristocracy encourage this belief, because it reinforces their own higher position. Furthermore, the aristocracy is not exclusively urban, and outside the city the distinctions in wealth between aristocratic families and the villagers living near them are even broader.

The people who hire tembang Sunda ensembles desire the element of élite status that the ensemble brings to any occasion, and the regional government itself is a frequent client of certain lingkung seni. According to many of the Sundanese with whom I discussed this issue, the military and government are now the élite, because they hold all the power. No matter what the official word is on social stratification, it is quite appropriate for tembang Sunda to be performed for the people in power. The power segue from early performances for the regional aristocracy to modern performances for members of the national government and military would be a fairly simple transition, were it not for the fact that anyone can hire an ensemble if they can afford to pay for it. In other words, because the current people in power do not have an exclusive claim to performances of tembang Sunda (as did the late-nineteenth- and early-twentieth-century aristocracy), the ensemble and its élite associations with the aristocracy may simply be paid for and shaped to fit any situation.

III

THE MUSIC OF TEMBANG SUNDA

This section of the book provides the reader with an outline of some of the musical elements that constitute tembang Sunda. Beginning with the stylistic divisions of the genre and proceeding through a discussion of the instrumental and vocal components of the music, this information will clarify the discussion of urban settings, institutions, and general meaning of the genre to the people who produce and listen to tembang Sunda. Most of the following information is common knowledge to tembang Sunda musicians and scholars. This section does not duplicate the extensive information on instrument construction, tone measurement, or other information presented by van Zanten (1987:85–193 and 1989:80–190). Basic information is essential for clarification, however, and some of the following information differs from that presented by van Zanten simply because it came from different local sources. Tembang Sunda is continually debated and problematized not only by its practitioners but also by its audience members (and foreign scholars). Differing opinions abound, and it is precisely these differences in opinion that lead to some of the most interesting debates.

The discussion of this music is central to the issue of urbanization, because in many cases the performance practice of the music has been strongly affected by its presence in the city. In the following chapters, I present the musical features in a manner relevant to the discussion: What happened to the music when it came to the city, and how does the current state of the music reflect urban attitudes and support systems? The clarification of stylistic divisions within tembang Sunda demonstrates that certain styles are not commonly used in the city because of their association with colonial times. Similarly, an outline of the instrumental and vocal techniques illustrates the new developments occurring partially as a result of urbanization.

The selection of particular styles or tuning systems for performances and recordings may be seen as a reflection of the degree to which an urban setting supports experimentation and creativity. Certain playing techniques on tembang Sunda instruments are more strongly associated with particular styles or tunings, and serve as signifiers of context and message to the informed audience. The following chapters clarify the relationships between appropriate styles and instruments, and go into a deeper explanation of symbolism of the primary instruments.

7

The Parameters of Style

This chapter not only makes distinctions between the five primary stylistic divisions of tembang Sunda but also illustrates the performers' stylistic choices. Except in cases where the general lyrical content is tied to a particular style, the focus here is more on the music than the lyrics. The reason for this focus is that tembang Sunda singers may use many different texts for the same song, provided that the syllabic count of the selection is appropriate. Part of the individual creativity and mastery expected of good singers is the selection of texts appropriate to the situation. Although the focus of this section is on those five main styles, I also discuss musical features that are not a part of those styles. For example, the chapter includes instrumental music used to open and close performances and cassette recordings of tembang Sunda, and the invocational song (lagu rajah) that precedes traditional performances.

The choices made in each situation reflect the performers' awareness of the relative status of their sponsor, host, audience, and themselves in relation to the other participants of the event. Before selecting a song, the singer and accompanists must assess the potential audience reaction. Most of the audience may be oblivious to the political positioning of the music occurring onstage and offstage but, to the musicians, the sponsor, and the host, an attempt must be made to fit the music to the situation. In selecting a particular style to perform, a singer (because the song selections are usually made by singers in tembang Sunda) defines both the audience and the entire performance context: "The concept of styles as normative structures realized in performance practice and subject to multiple, context-sensitive interpretations and evaluations provides an analytical link between musical processes and products, on the one hand, and patterns of urban cultural identity and social organization, on the other" (Waterman 1990:24).

The selection of one style over another by a tembang Sunda singer indicates that certain styles are appropriate for performance at weddings, for example, while others are not. The social codes interpreted by the singer are generally the same as those interpreted by the audience; that is, a singer chooses a style because he/she knows from experience that it is the most appropriate style for that type of audience.[1]

The five main styles of tembang Sunda are papantunan, jejemplangan, rarancagan, dedegungan, and panambih. With the exception of the last style (panambih), the names of each of these terms duplicate the first syllable and use the syllable -an as a suffix. The use of these prefixes and suffixes in the Sundanese language is intended to convey the meaning of "in the style of . . ." and indicates also the general feeling associated with each style. One of my teachers, Tatang Subari, discussed the matter at length, using the words *kuda* and *kukudaan* for comparison. *Kuda* is the word for horse, and *kukudaan* is the word for child's horse toy. Although there is no question in anyone's mind that kukudaan is not actually a horse, it is similar to a horse and is, in fact, derived directly from real horses and their actions (Subari, personal communication, 1988).[2] In the same sense, the musical style papantunan is derived from or based strongly on the genre of pantun. Each of the four styles using this configuration in their terminology bears some resemblance to the style or character after which they are named. The term *panambih* is an exception, because songs of that style are in a fixed meter and will be dealt with separately.

In the following discussion of tembang Sunda styles, each style is treated as a unit of analysis. As such, a style may form part of the vocabulary with which social and cultural processes may be described (Coplan 1982:124). Because the performance of certain styles in particular situations is fairly predictable, the selection of a particular style by the musicians (or sponsor, or host) can indicate specific nonmusical standards to which the music must adhere. For example, the selection of a papantunan-style song at a wedding of middle-class urbanites is deemed inappropriate on many different levels; the following pages give an idea of why and how styles are appropriate in some situations and inappropriate in others.

Table 7.1 provides an outline of the placement of stylistic divisions within the context of performance. All of these styles may be performed in the pélog tuning system, but only rarancagan and panambih songs also may be performed in sorog or saléndro. The majority of songs fall within the rarancagan category. Panambih songs comprise the second most numerous stylistic division. One reason for this disparity in numbers between styles is

THE PARAMETERS OF STYLE 143

TABLE 7.1 The five styles of tembang Sunda

Style	Tuning System	Repertoire	Rhythm
papantunan	pélog	closed	free
jejemplangan	pélog	closed	free
dedegungan	pélog	closed	free
rarancagan	pélog, sorog, saléndro	open	free
panambih	pélog, sorog, saléndro	open	fixed

that papantunan, jejemplangan, and dedegungan are believed to have a closed repertoire. The categories of rarancagan and panambih are still considered open for new compositions and, therefore, the songs belonging to those stylistic categories continue to grow in number.

TUNING SYSTEMS IN TEMBANG SUNDA

Tembang Sunda evenings are organized according to a particular hierarchy of tuning systems.[3] The Sundanese rank the three primary tunings of pélog, sorog and saléndro in order of their importance to the genre. Pélog is a category to which the largest number of tembang Sunda songs belong, and usually appears first in a performance. Once the kacapi has been tuned to sorog after pélog, it will not be retuned to pélog until the next day. Similarly, once the kacapi has been tuned from sorog to saléndro, it will not be retuned to sorog until some other time. The kacapi is usually left in the pélog tuning when it is not in use. Although a suling player may easily convert to sorog, he must adjust his fingers to achieve the changes in pitch and scale orientation. All of my teachers agreed that the oldest, most important, and most characteristic tembang Sunda songs are those of the papantunan and jejemplangan categories, found only in pélog.

The sorog scale is used after at least one hour of pélog has preceded it. The only times I ever heard sorog performed without first hearing songs in pélog was in performances where the audience was uninformed about tembang Sunda—in particular, performances for members of the military or government, for foreign dignitaries or businessmen, and for Javanese visitors. I questioned performers about the decision to play exclusively in sorog for these audiences, and the responses varied according to the type of audience. In the case of the military or government, the answer was "They don't care what we do. They're not even listening." For the foreigners, the response was, "Sorog sounds more exotic and interesting to them, like Japanese music, and they don't understand about papantunan songs anyway." For the Javanese, it was emphatically stated that "we have sorog and they don't." In emphasizing the sorog tuning in performances for Javanese people, the Sundanese express in a musical way their difference from the Javanese and, according to at least one musician, their musical superiority for having the capability to use more than just two tunings.

Many kacapi players, even the most competent professionals, experience difficulty in tuning the kacapi to saléndro. A frequent complaint heard during the tuning process is that the results "smell Chinese" (*bau Cina*) and there is usually discussion among the players and vocalists about which pitches to adjust to get rid of the "smell."[4] In spite of the fine distinctions perceived between Sundanese and "Chinese" saléndro, some singers are unable to perceive the narrow difference in pitch relationships if a song begins on one pitch as opposed to a neighboring pitch.[5]

Saléndro is usually reserved for the rare occasions when the players and audience are willing to stay up quite late at night.[6] Several people closely involved in tembang Sunda mentioned that saléndro should really only be performed after midnight, when all of the hangers-on, jokers, children, talkers, politicians, and bored or boring nonmusicians have left. The Jakarta and Bandung television stations used to go off the air at close to midnight in the 1980s, sending most peripherally involved people to bed. Even with late-night television, Bandung is at its most peaceful after midnight, and because street noise is a fact of life during both latihan and performances, people are far more comfortable concentrating on music when all distractions have quieted down.

One of the reasons that saléndro is rarely performed is that paid performances of tembang Sunda usually do not last more than a few hours. This limitation does not give the ensemble enough time to switch from one tuning to another. In addition, many performances are now held during the day. A daytime performance is already believed inappropriate for tembang Sunda, but particularly so for saléndro performances. A third reason is that pélog is considered the most characteristic tuning for tembang Sunda, and saléndro the least of the three. When only pélog and sorog songs are gone over during a latihan, then it is likely that those will be the best-prepared songs when the ensemble is hired for a performance.

THE *LAGU RAJAH*

In the most traditional performances of tembang Sunda, the evening begins with a song known as *lagu rajah*, or invocational song. It has a primarily spiritual role in tembang Sunda performance, and is rarely used at commercial gigs. The rajah is derived from pantun performance practice (Danasasmita 1979:7). It asks permission for the performance that is about to

EXAMPLE 7.1 Pantun style on the kacapi

EXAMPLE 7.2 Kacapi accompaniment for the lagu rajah

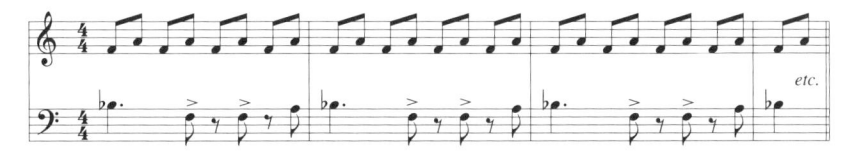

begin, apologizing to God and to the spirits of the "old people" (Indo.: *orang tua*—in this case, the ancestors) for any mistakes that may be made, invoking the presence of the good spirits and asking for a blessing on the evening's musical activities. Furthermore, the song is performed so that the spirits do not disturb whatever is about to take place (Sukanda 1978:1). The use of a rajah is not exclusive to performances of tembang Sunda; rather, gamelan saléndro groups may use the song "Kidung" or "Kembang Gadung" as their rajah. In tembang Sunda, the song of choice is usually "Kuna Sari." The kacapi accompaniment for "Kuna Sari" is nearly the same as that used by performers of pantun. The association of pantun and its musical accompaniment with the feudal days and the perceived supernatural power of people who lived during that time is a frequent topic among performers. Using a pantun pattern on the kacapi as the accompaniment for an invocational song is considered very appropriate for a successful evening.

Examples 7.1 and 7.2 demonstrate the differences between the kacapi style of playing as it is used to accompany a recital of pantun, followed by an example of kacapi accompaniment to the invocational song or lagu rajah, "Kuna Sari." Example 7.3 is of kacapi playing in a papantunan song. Whereas pantun recital is half-spoken and half-sung, "Kuna Sari" is only sung. Many of the vocal pitches in "Kuna Sari," however, correspond with the pitches of the sung performance of pantun. The style of kacapi playing remains within the sphere of ostinato-type accompaniment as seen in Examples 7.1 and 7.2.

Although the lagu rajah may be classified as a papantunan song (because of its similarity to those songs within papantunan style), it actually belongs in a class by itself because it is only performed under certain circumstances and may not be substituted for another song. Even if most of the singers at a tembang Sunda evening are women, it is usually a man who performs the rajah. This feature of gender limitation in the performance of the rajah is another link to pantun, because blind males were the usual performers—

EXAMPLE 7.3 Papantunan style on the kacapi ("Pangapungan" group)

simultaneously reciting and playing kacapi—in traditional contexts for pantun.

PAPANTUNAN

Papantunan is generally believed to be the oldest of the tembang Sunda styles (van Zanten 1987:35).[7] Papantunan songs usually begin with an opening phrase called a *narangtang*, which serves primarily to introduce the sound of the tuning system and prepare the singer to begin. Chapter 9 ("A Name Is All That Remains") includes explanations of sample phrases used as narangtang for papantunan style songs. The word *narangtang* (bridge) carries the implication that singers, instrumentalists, and audience members all experience a type of journey during a performance of papantunan, in which they leave the current setting (whatever it may be) and cross over to a different time and place.

Papantunan songs should be sung in a rather declamatory style, because they are believed to carry the history not only of tembang Sunda, but also of Sunda itself (Wiratmadja, personal communication, 1988). In many cases, the lyrics are very quickly run through and the intent of the singer is to tell a story rather than to display technical dexterity through long melismatic ornaments. Within this style, the only ornaments are quick upturns at the ends of phrases or other brief decorations. Melismas are never a feature of papantunan. It is said of Bandung people, however, that they perform papantunan songs in a manner too slow to be appropriate for the style, and that they deliberately put in more ornaments to try to make the songs sound like those of rarancagan style (Wiratmadja, personal communication, 1989; Sukanda 1983:48).

Songs in papantunan style usually use historical, spiritual, or descriptive lyrics, which distinguish these songs from the more romantic topics of some rarancagan and panambih songs. Some songs carry two or more titles (such as "Sampiung" and "Pangapungan"). Musically, it is believed that papantunan contain the essential vocal elements of tembang Sunda performance practice, and singers are often judged solely on the rendition of a single papantunan song (as opposed to jejemplangan, rarancagan, or dedegungan). These songs are taken quite seriously by the older and more dedicated practitioners of tembang Sunda, who regard papantunan as the basis from which all the other styles are derived (see Chapter 9).

The deep respect accorded songs of this style, however, does not mean that they are frequently performed. The strong association of papantunan songs with Sundanese history and with feudal times leads some people, especially middle-class urbanites, to dislike them. This dislike is expressed not so much in explicit terms as in a general dismissal of older-style tembang Sunda songs simply with the word *féodal*, meaning feudal. The feudal times were, for many people, an extremely difficult period in which the aristocracy were believed to have all the benefits of Dutch domination and none of the pain. Singing about the good times to be had in the pre-Independence days merely serves to emphasize the differences between the modern descendants of the aristocracy and everyone else. In the early twenty-first century, the Sundanese upper-middle class is in many cases descended from those who were in the oppressed groups, and tends to believe more strongly in equality with the aristocracy than in separation from them. In addition, the members of the former aristocracy are not necessarily the wealthiest members of Sundanese society. Songs that discuss the lives of the aristocracy or use aristocratic language reinforce these disparities, and are not nearly as popular in performances for weddings or other life-cycle events (attended by hundreds of middle-class people) as are songs dealing with romance.

Therefore, in paid performances for a generally uninformed urban audience, song selection tends toward those in rarancagan and panambih style. Generally, any song that sounds like papantunan is dismissed outright by the audience as féodal, whether it is or not. At performances, instrumentalists and singers discuss song selection in occasionally tense whispers: "Don't sing those feudal songs! Sing *sad* songs!" "They *are* sad songs!" The power struggle between the singer and the musicians is often mitigated by the circumstances. If the performance is a malam tembang Sunda in which everyone present is either a singer or musician, papantunan songs can be performed for hours. Otherwise, the trend in paid performances is toward love songs.

An essential feature of papantunan style is that it is believed that no new songs can be added to the existing group of songs (see also van Zanten 1987:35). Although several songs that belong in the papantunan style have been composed in the last twenty years (for example, "Salaka Domas" by Bakang Abubakar was added to the repertoire in 1975), there is virtually no new composing activity occurring in this style anymore. According to several composers with whom I discussed this issue, it is believed that attempting to compose a song in papantunan style is like placing oneself on the same level as the great composers of the old days, and composers today feel that the older composers were in a different (higher) league altogether. One composer explained that he wanted his songs to be different from other songs, and that many papantunan songs are very similar to each other, lacking a quality that made each one unique (Suarna, personal communication, 1989).

The musical similarities between certain selections of the twenty-odd songs belonging to papantunan style lead to the grouping of these songs during performances into sets, followed by a *panambih*, or "addition," at the end of the set. For example, the songs "Pangapungan," "Goyong," "Salaka Domas," "Banjar Karang," "Balagenyat," and "Tejamantri" are melodically similar, and the style of kacapi accompaniment is almost the same for each. These songs, as well as many other songs in papantunan style, are accompanied in a style deliberately reminiscent of pantun-style kacapi playing. Therefore, two or three of them are performed in a row with only a slight change in the tempo or the ostinato pattern played by the kacapi. In general,

EXAMPLE 7.4 Gelenyu for a papantunan song

the kacapi plays an ostinato pattern during the course of almost the entire song, and the vocalist is free to perform the song as quickly or as slowly as is desired. The suling player is much more restricted in papantunan songs as well, and tends to make his playing conform very closely to the melody.

During sections in which the singer is not performing, the kacapi player sometimes plays an instrumental section or gelenyu. The gelenyu is a feature of many papantunan and jejemplangan songs, as well as most panambih and some rarancagan and dedegungan. It usually consists of a melody in fixed rhythm that does not necessarily have a melodic connection to the melody performed by the singer. Each song that contains one of these instrumental passages has a unique melody associated with the gelenyu (van Zanten 1987: 138), so that the gelenyu for "Mupu Kembang," for example, will vary from the gelenyu for "Rajamantri." The one exception to this rule is that dedegungan songs use the same gelenyu.[8]

A gelenyu for a papantunan song ("Mupu Kembang,") is transcribed in Example 7.4, and includes an ostinato pattern in the first four measures, followed by the gelenyu. The ostinato pattern is normally played to accompany the singing portion of "Mupu Kembang," and in this context it is used to set up the entrance to the gelenyu. The gelenyu has no relation to the vocal melody, but is exclusively associated with "Mupu Kembang" in the minds of the audience.

The song called "Papatet" is unique among songs of papantunan style, because the kacapi plays in a manner usually reserved for songs in the rarancagan and dedegungan styles. That is, rather than playing an ostinato pattern that provides an almost static background accompaniment to what the singer is doing (as in most papantunan songs), the kacapi player performs in a manner closer to free-rhythm heterophony with the singer. This technique of kacapi playing is known as *pasieup*. Another essential feature of "Papatet" is that it is frequently described as the most important song in the repertoire, not only for singers, but also for kacapi players and suling players as well. Its unique position is explored further in Chapter 9, "A Name Is All That Remains."

Papantunan lyrics in general emphasize historical and cultural themes essential in understanding what it means to be Sundanese. Although the vocalist may select one set of lyrics over another, many of the lyrics used for papantunan belong to the historical type. As a result of the narrowness of the lyric content, the musical rendition of these lyrics causes the listeners to automatically associate the sound of papantunan melodies with the past, the aristocracy, and an older lifestyle. The use of pantun-style ostinato patterns on the kacapi (a feature of many papantunan songs) is also an aural link between the pantun performers of the village and the descendants of the aristocracy who live in Bandung today. Therefore, songs in papantunan style are not only the most strongly favored for their connection to the rural past but also are (paradoxically) the most strongly disliked by listeners and practitioners on each side of the aristocratic fence.

JEJEMPLANGAN

Songs of the jejemplangan style are similar in some ways to those of the papantunan style. They are always in the pélog tuning and are believed to be almost as old as papantunan songs. Jejemplangan songs are also believed to be part of a closed repertoire, for many of the same reasons as described above in the papantunan section. Texts of jejemplangan are not always historical, however, but also may concern romance or other topics. Furthermore, certain musical characteristics present in these songs mark them as quite different from those of papantunan songs, even though "Papatet" is said to contain all essential musical elements found in tembang Sunda. These musical characteristics manifest themselves not only in the vocalist's ornamentation but also (and especially) in the patterns played on the kacapi. Jejemplangan songs almost always include the word "Jemplang" in the title, as in "Jemplang Panganten," "Jemplang Pamirig," "Jemplang Ceurik," and others.

Songs in the jejemplangan style generally begin with a narangtang or bridge, as do those in papantunan style. The narangtang for jejemplangan songs differs from that of papantunan style, however, in that it does not have interchangeable lyrics. Instead, it always uses the words "Nyukcruk parung beulah bantar, birit leuwi peupeuntasan." Wim van Zanten translates this narangtang as, "I wade through the shallows of the river, in between the deeper parts. Downstream from the deeper part is a place to cross" (van Zanten 1987:84). In the same way that "Papatet" provides a type of musical

EXAMPLE 7.5 Narangtang for songs in jejemplangan style

Nyuk - cruk pa - rung   beu - lah ban - tar

Bi - rit leu - wi   peu - peun - ta - san

Bi - rit leu - wi mah   geu - ning;

Peu -   peun - ta -   san

blueprint for vocal ornamentation in all papantunan songs (and, by extension, all tembang Sunda songs), the narangtang used for almost all jejemplangan songs (Example 7.5) outlines the vocal ornaments unique to jejemplangan.

Vocal ornaments provide an important aural indication of the type of song being performed. In addition, the kacapi accompaniment functions as a style marker, particularly in jejemplangan songs. Most jejemplangan songs are considered incomplete without a gelenyu or instrumental section. As in papantunan songs, the gelenyu of jejemplangan are unique to each song and do not have a particular melodic relationship to the vocal line although they identify the song before the vocalist begins.

The style of playing kacapi for jejemplangan songs differs markedly from that of papantunan. Although both styles frequently utilize ostinato patterns, the kacapi pitches most strongly emphasized in papantunan are e and a in Western notation, or 2 and 5 on the kacapi. The opening pitch of the vocalist is usually e. Jejemplangan songs, on the other hand, emphasize pitches f and b-flat or 1 and 4 on the kacapi. According to van Zanten's study of pitch structure in these two styles of tembang Sunda songs, however, the opening and closing vocal pitches of both styles are essentially the same (van Zanten 1987:140). The entire pitch relationship between the kacapi and the singer is altered downward by a half-step, which makes the vocalist's opening pitch (still on e) a major seventh above the lowest pitch on the kacapi, instead of an octave, as in papantunan.

It is this intervallic relationship between the kacapi and the voice that, in addition to the lyrics themselves, gives jejemplangan songs their particular quality known as keueung (Rukmana, personal communication, 1988). The word *keueung* is always used to describe jejemplangan songs, and is used as a criterion in judging the quality of the performance. Keueung means fear, worry, and uneasiness, and several musicians spent a long (and rather stormy) afternoon in the midst of the rainy season providing examples of situations in which one would experience keueung. Among these situations are the feeling of walking alone in a forest at night, worrying about someone who is far away and might never come home, being all alone and hearing someone crying, or being hurt with no one to turn to (Rukmana, personal communication, 1988).

The word *jemplang-jempling*, meaning absolutely and eerily silent, is the root of the word *jejemplangan*. During a lesson in which several of us were producing unsatisfactory versions of "Jemplang Leumpang," the leader of the lesson sighed, shook his hand and said "Kudu ka leuweung wae" ("You'll just have to go spend some time in the forest"). Therefore, songs in jejemplangan style should convey the feelings associated with all of the above-mentioned situations. As the kacapi player Tatang Subari put it, the tonal instability caused by the intervallic relationship between the vocal line and the kacapi part, combined with the also unstable-sounding *suara spiral* ornament transcribed in Figure 7.5 (on the words *bantar* and *leuwi*), are two of the features responsible for creating that unique feeling (Subari, personal communication, 1989). A soft, whispering style of singing is also considered an important feature of this song category (van Zanten 1987:181), as is a breathy style of suling playing (Suandi, personal communication, 1988).

Jejemplangan songs are considered extremely difficult to perform not only by kacapi players but also and especially by singers. Younger urban singers complain about having to work on them for competitions, and talk about not really being able to convey the feeling of keueung. Wim van Zanten has pointed out that the number of recorded jejemplangan songs is far below that of papantunan and rarancagan songs (van Zanten 1987:139). The kacapi player Rukruk Rukmana indicated that a beginning singer might not want to record one of the most difficult tembang Sunda songs but, rather, ones more appropriate to her age and status relative to some of the more experienced singers (Rukmana, personal communication, 1988).

Whereas the negative associations of papantunan songs with feudal times have led some singers to reduce performances of papantunan in paid jobs for urban audiences, the association of jejemplangan songs with worry, uncertainty, and fear also may have led to the decline of these songs in urban performances. According to two performers (Apung Wiratmadja and Euis Komariah), these feelings are not appropriate for a modern urban setting, where it is never quiet and where those feelings associated with being alone in a forest are no longer supposed to occur. Another man (a politician) added that citizens of the "new Indonesia" should not express "primitive" feelings in their music. My own observations also indicate that the sheer difficulty of performing jejemplangan songs is one of the main reasons singers and kacapi players do not choose these songs anymore.

RARANCAGAN

Most tembang Sunda songs belong to the rarancagan category. These songs may occur in any of the three main tuning systems (pélog, sorog, and saléndro), and in the infrequently used tunings as well (such as mandalungan, a type of high-pitched pélog), whereas songs in papantunan, jejemplangan, and dedegungan styles are restricted to pélog. Not only is the repertoire considered open and available for additional pieces, but also the style of rarancagan is considered one of only two main styles for new tembang Sunda compositions (together with panambih, or fixed-meter songs). Topics of these songs are not nearly as restricted as are those of papantunan and jejemplangan, and most are concerned with various aspects of love, sadness, nostalgia, and the beauty of nature.

Within the rarancagan category, most songs are accompanied using the kacapi technique of pasieup or fast melodic runs in free rhythm that outline the major melodic points of the song. Although some of the songs in rarancagan use a type of fixed-rhythm kacapi accompaniment (for example, "Liwung Jaya" in pélog, "Asmarandana Ros" in sorog, and "Pamuragan" in saléndro), most rarancagan are performed in heterophony by the singer, kacapi and suling (or rebab, if the song is in saléndro) players. Therefore, it is this heterophonic style that is generally the most characteristic musical feature of rarancagan songs.

Songs in rarancagan style are known for their use of the Sundanese poetic forms known as pupuh. On occasion, the title of a song will reflect the appropriate pupuh form to go with it, such as "Asmarandana Rancag," "Sinom Madenda," or "Dangdanggula Pancaniti." In each of these three songs, one of the four main pupuh forms used in tembang (*asmarandana, dangdanggula, kinanti,* or *sinom*) is named before the actual song. Song titles are occasionally altered slightly, and, although it causes great consternation among foreign researchers, to the Sundanese musicians themselves the mere altering of a title is not a cause for concern.

Another distinguishing characteristic of rarancagan songs is the use of certain vocal ornaments, especially the *cacagan* ornament, which is slow, rather choppy vibrato. One kacapi player described the word rancag as being derived from cacagan, although the dictionary describes rancag as meaning "without adornment" or "stark" (Eringa 1984:617). Three other vocal ornaments are characteristic of this style as well: the use of a slight upturn in pitch at the end of a vocal line (known as *buntut*), long melismas (*reureueus*), and light vibratos (*vibra*).

Rarancagan songs are not only supposed to describe but also provoke certain emotions from the participants. The feelings touched off by hearing rarancagan songs are ideally of a far more personal and individual nature than are those of papantunan or jejemplangan songs. Because so many songs of the rarancagan style are concerned with topics of nostalgia, nature, and love, it is said that one of the true pleasures of performing these songs comes from trying to affect the listeners as deeply as possible. These songs are often described using the term *gagah berani* (strong, brave), appropriate for those texts describing nature scenes such as the sea and storms. In discussions of tembang Sunda by instrumentalists and vocalists, however, it is usually made clear during these conversations that rarancagan songs do not carry quite the same weight or historical depth as do those of papantunan and jejemplangan.

DEDEGUNGAN

Van Zanten classifies dedegungan songs as essentially the same as rarancagan songs, and places the two types together in his discussion of the stylistic divisions of tembang Sunda (1987:137). I have distinguished dedegungan from rarancagan style based on discussions with some of the older singers, the classification system of tembang Sunda competitions, the musical features unique to the dedegungan repertoire, and the contrastive grouping of dedegungan and rarancagan in recordings, competitions, and live performances. Sundanese writers also separate dedegungan from rarancagan; see, for example, Wibisana et al. (1976:727). This style seems to have become even more distinct within Bandung than outside of Bandung, because performances and recordings of dedegungan songs within Bandung are now rare.

The term *dedegungan* is derived from the word *degung*, and the association of dedegungan songs is with the high-pitched Sundanese gamelan of that name. The Sundanese gamelan degung uses, among other instruments, a four-hole suling degung that is of a higher pitch than the six-hole suling panjang ("long suling") normally used in tembang Sunda.[9] Although dedegungan and rarancagan songs have many similarities, several standardized musical features in performances of dedegungan set it apart. One of these main features is the consistently high pitches used in the melodies of these songs. Whereas a normal rarancagan song would have a vocal range with a high end around c (in the upper range of the alto voice in Western terms), a standard dedegungan song has e or f as its highest pitch, a third or fourth higher than the highest pitches of most other pélog songs (van Zanten 1987: 146).

The gelenyu, or instrumental, sections used in dedegungan are standardized in such a way that one single gelenyu is in common usage, and the use of this gelenyu automatically identifies the song as dedegungan to an informed audience. Furthermore, the very beginning of a dedegungan piece uses the opening melodic line from most gamelan degung pieces. A list of other musical features distinguishing dedegungan songs from rarancagan songs includes the lack of pitch borrowing from outside of pélog. One of the characteristic features of songs belonging to rarancagan style is that pitches may be freely borrowed from outside the tuning system, whether the song is in pélog, sorog, or saléndro. This pitch borrowing, either as an integral part of the melody or as an improvisation by the vocalist or suling player, is considered one of the best parts of a rarancagan song. The lack of this feature in dedegungan indicates again that the style is different from rarancagan. One of the reasons for the restriction to songs completely within pélog is because the gamelan degung ensemble (of which this style is reminiscent) is also restricted to pélog.

Like many rarancagan songs, dedegungan songs use the standard Sundanese poetic forms (pupuh) originally derived from Central Java. In the case of dedegungan songs, however, most of them are identified by the pupuh form in the title, followed by the word degung, such as "Asmarandana Degung." Because one of the main features of tembang Sunda songs using pupuh is that lyrics are interchangeable, singers are free to choose any appropriate text within the same pupuh form. Dedegungan songs, like those of papantunan and jejemplangan, are said to belong to a closed repertoire. One reason for this closure is that they are described as very difficult to compose in a way that will cause singers to want to perform them. Another reason is that many dedegungan songs bear similar characteristics to each other and modern composers want to break new ground with each composition (Suarna, personal communication, 1989).

Dedegungan songs are grouped together in performances and on cassettes. For example, two dedegungan songs such as "Sinom Degung" and "Asmarandana Degung" would be followed by the panambih called "Degung Panggung," that bears a similarity in musical characteristics to the other two. Because many Bandung singers—who do the bulk of the recordings of tembang Sunda—avoid the high pitches of dedegungan as too revealing of otherwise hidden vocal flaws, it is very difficult to find cassette recordings with sets of dedegungan songs. Therefore, one of the strongest stylistic indicators of dedegungan (its emphasis on high pitches) is a main reason for infrequency in recordings. Dedegungan songs are not only rarely recorded on cassette, but also they are rarely performed in Bandung.

Cianjur is still the center for songs in dedegungan style, because these songs never really gained popularity in Bandung (Sukanda 1978:8). My requests for songs in this style were usually met with expressions like, "Why would you ever want to study dedegungan songs? We usually don't perform them," or "Go to Cianjur if you want those high songs."[10] As is the case with jejemplangan songs, almost the only time that songs of this style are worked on is in preparation for a tembang Sunda competition (such as the pasanggiri DAMAS), in which songs from each of the five styles are expected to be prepared by the contestants. In cases like this (the necessity of preparing a rarely performed song style), some students will specially seek out those who excel at singing the high-pitched songs.

PANAMBIH

Panambih are markedly different from the previous four styles in almost every way. These songs are performed in fixed rhythm, and the kacapi accompaniment uses techniques of alternating octaves in the right hand and syncopated bass lines in the left. The two techniques together are referred to as *kait*. Panambih are believed to have been composed later than the other styles, and are tacked onto the end of song sets; hence the name panambih, or "addition" (van Zanten 1987:36). Another term for these songs is *lagu ekstra* ("extra tune"), although panambih appears to be the preferred term. Most musicians with whom I spoke about this style believe that the first panambih were purely instrumental. At that time (the beginning of the twentieth century), most of the tembang Sunda vocalists were men, and the panambih were performed to give the men a short respite from singing. In time, however, short verses began to be added to these instrumental panambih, and the gradual participation of women became more common.

Women sing panambih almost exclusively, with a few exceptions such as the inclusion of kawih-style songs (which may be sung by men) in a tembang Sunda set. Kawih singing is closely associated with pop songs and is usually performed to accompaniment of a kacapi siter (in which case the style is called kacapian) or gamelan degung (in which case it is called degung kawih). Panambih are said to give the singers a break from the difficulty of singing mamaos (Sukanda 1978:16). It is believed that if a man sings a panambih, however, it is as if he was imitating a woman or was somehow less than manly (Wiratmadja, personal communication, 1988).

Panambih occur in cycles of *patokan* or standard structural progressions to which a large number of songs may be set. In other words, a single patokan, like a standard American twelve-bar blues progression, can provide the accompaniment to dozens of songs. These patokan are in many cases borrowed from the gamelan degung repertoire, and many of the same terms are used to describe structural elements in the songs. For example, the final pitch of the cyclical pattern is referred to as *go'ong* ("gong"), and the main pitches that outline the colotomic structure and tonal direction of the cycle are referred to as *jenglong* and *pancer*. In Example 7.6, the song "Kingkilaban" is transcribed to include not just the kacapi patokan but also the rincik, suling, and voice for two phrases. In looking at the kacapi line, it is clear that a cadential point (pancer) occurs on the first beat of every second measure, whereas the go'ong occurs only on the first and last beats of the transcription, thereby completing a cycle.

Because of the cyclical structure of panambih songs, it is appropriate that the lyrics to these songs should occur in stanzas instead of in prose. Many panambih lyrics are fixed and only interchangeable if the syllabic count and number of sentences match between songs. The titles, melodies, and lyrics of most panambih are also far more closely linked together than in any other style. It is common to have a song written about a specific situation and to have the lyrics fixed to that situation. For example, the song "Hanjakal Tepang" ("Too bad we had to meet") is *always* associated with the situation in which someone whom the singer did not expect or hope to see again appears at a gathering. It would be inappropriate to use the lyrics

EXAMPLE 7.6 Two phrases of the song "Kingkilaban" for voice, suling, rincik, and kacapi

for another song (for example, a happy love song) in this song, even if the syllabic count were correct.

Certain composers in tembang Sunda are well known for their panambih compositions. Among these composers are Mang Bakang Abubakar and the late Mang Engkos. Mang Bakang Abubakar is still active in Cianjur not only as a composer but also as a teacher, and also has served frequently as a jury member in tembang Sunda competitions (Ischak 1988:4–11). He also is encouraging the use of the saléndro tuning in Cianjur, a city known throughout Sunda for its rejection of saléndro. Some of Mang Bakang's panambih songs have become the top favorites of young singers, and songs like "Lokatmala" and "Lembur Singkur" can be heard at almost any tembang Sunda performance. Mang Engkos is known especially for his romantic and

EXAMPLE 7.6 Continued

melancholy panambih compositions, which is said to be one reason why his songs are still popular among young people today (Sukanda 1983:45).

Some panambih include a chorus (rampak), in which other singers may join in briefly. In panambih of this type, the verses are either sung by a single vocalist or are traded between two or more vocalists. An example is the song "Jangji Asih" ("Love Promise"), composed by Apung Wiratmadja, in which three long verses are alternated with a couplet. These choruses may be fixed so that the same lyrics are sung after each verse, or may change as the story develops. If the lyrics of the chorus play an active part in telling the story, it is likely that those lyrics will change at each repetition of the chorus.

One of the most important musical features of panambih style is the concept of *wilet*, a type of density referent (see also van Zanten 1987:149–

158). In a sixteen-beat structure, a particular song might be in *sawilet* ("single wilet"). This means that the patokan or structural progression of the song may be completed within the duration of those sixteen beats. The duration of the structural progression also may be doubled, and it then becomes a thirty-two-beat structure, without an increase in tempo. The song is then in *dua wilet* ("double wilet").

Like songs of papantunan and other styles, panambih usually include instrumental interludes known as gelenyu. In most panambih, gelenyu occur between verses; depending on the wilet or density referent of the song, the gelenyu may be quite long. Therefore, the wilet of a song determines to a great extent the amount of improvisation that the suling player may perform. If the gelenyu of the panambih is long because the song is in double wilet, the suling player has long periods in which to improvise and explore musical quotes from other songs or from outside the tuning system. Improvisation by the suling player is an essential feature of panambih performance practice.

In panambih performance practice, the fixed rhythm of the kacapi and rincik represents the patokan or structural framework against which the rhythmically freer suling and vocal parts are set. Although the vocalist must conform to the fixed rhythm of the kacapi and rincik, she is allowed considerable freedom in vocal ornamentation and in the manner in which she arrives at important structural or cadential points in the song. The suling player always provides the singer with the first few notes of the vocal line before returning to an improvisatory passage based on the melody. During the gelenyu of the panambih, the suling player always takes greater freedom than in the verse; sometimes the suling player only plays the first few notes of the melody before waiting until the vocal line comes in. The rincik player is careful to coincide melodically with the kacapi player at important structural points. Because the singing style of the panambih is relatively easy to grasp, beginning singers often start by learning a few panambih before proceeding on to the harder rarancagan songs.

PIECES TO OPEN AND CLOSE PERFORMANCES

Performances of tembang Sunda are always opened and closed with a fixed-rhythm instrumental tune played on the kacapi, suling and rincik. If the final song is in saléndro tuning, the suling is replaced by the rebab. The opening piece is called a bubuka (literally, "opener") and is usually the pélog song "Jipang Lontang" although other pieces such as "Jipang Karaton" may be used instead. When an opening piece is used, it is rarely referred to by its title, because the frequency with which "Jipang Lontang" is used makes identification of the song unnecessary. Instead, singers and instrumentalists will signal their readiness to begin by turning to each other and saying "Bubuka," then launching immediately into the tune.

The instrumental playing style for bubuka is similar to that of panambih songs without a singer. That is, the kacapi player performs a repeating patokan or structural pattern, and the suling player improvises based on the melody. The kacapi and rincik players have to play twice as fast as they normally would, however, which in the case of the rincik player causes him to use a different style of playing altogether. Although the suling player does not have to play twice as fast, the intensified energy and double density of the bubuka require more ornaments within a short space of time and proportionally more time spent in the upper register than in some other songs. Because the bubuka is supposed to be quite brief (one or two minutes), the entire patokan of the song is usually repeated only three or four times, slowing down suddenly at the end and proceeding almost immediately into the first pasieup run on the kacapi. The kacapi player then leads the vocalist into the narangtang (bridge) phrase, which leads the audience into the first song of the evening.

One of the most important functions of the bubuka is to act as an introduction, not only to the unique sound of tembang Sunda but also to the particular tuning system being used. This introduction is done not only for the benefit of the audience but also for the singers, who will need to already have the sound of the tuning system in their ears before they begin to sing. The bubuka is also used to signal the beginning of a new tuning system if the instruments have been retuned during a break. Each tuning system uses a characteristic bubuka to begin the next segment of performance.[11] I have attended occasional performances in which a bubuka was not used, and the singers had difficulty staying on pitch because, as they said later, their ears were not quite ready.

Most cassette recordings use a bubuka at the beginning of Side 1. The use of the bubuka is so strongly associated with live performances of tembang Sunda that beginning a cassette (a fictive "live" performance of tembang Sunda) without a bubuka is altogether inappropriate, but the bubuka is almost never listed or timed on the cassette. This exclusion is an indication that instrumental music is generally considered less important than vocal music (Rukmana, personal communication, 1988). In cases where the bubuka is listed, sometimes it is listed simply as "Bubuka" (that is, as a title) rather than as "Jipang Lontang."

In addition to the bubuka, most performances of tembang Sunda close with a similar instrumental closing piece, known as panutup (literally, something that closes). Its characteristics are similar to that of the bubuka, except that the panutup usually begins directly from the final phrase of the last panambih in the performance. In other words, as the last line is performed by the vocalist, the instrumental ensemble slows, then on the final gong tone the ensemble abruptly starts up again without the vocalist, usually at a greatly increased tempo. The duration of the panutup during a live performance is usually less than one minute, during which time the vocalists close their books, straighten their clothing, and prepare to leave. The audience also responds to this signal by preparing to leave as well.

The panutup is not always the same song or even the same patokan as the final panambih. Usually the panutup is a simple patokan related in pitch structure to the previous panambih. For example, the final song of a cassette or an evening might be "Panyileukan," and the panutup following it would be "Banjaran," because of the structural similarity between these songs. Like bubuka, panutup are rarely mentioned on cassette inserts, and the function of panutup is that of a generic piece with which to fade out the recording and fill out the cassette. Some panutup on cassettes may last five minutes depending on the tape. If a tape ends before the panutup is finished (a frequent occurrence), disappointment is minimized because it is not a vocal piece, but "only a panutup" (Rukmana, personal communication, 1987).

KACAPI-SULING INSTRUMENTAL MUSIC

One recent result of urbanization in West Java is the development of the kacapi-suling genre, which evolved gradually during the 1960s and 1970s as a style distinct from tembang Sunda. Kacapi-suling songs are most often based on panambih borrowed from the tembang Sunda repertoire, performed by the standard tembang Sunda instrumental ensemble. Because the basic structure of many of these panambih is derived from the easier tunes of the Sundanese gamelan degung ensemble, many different instrumental melodies may be performed to a single structural outline. This structural outline was initially performed by the gongs, gong-chimes, and metallophones of gamelan degung; in kacapi-suling, it is provided by the kacapi. The rincik (small, high-pitched kacapi) plays the high-density *peking* (high-pitched metallophone) part of the gamelan. The suling takes a correspondingly more prominent melodic role in kacapi-suling than it does in tembang Sunda, frequently shifting from song to song during each piece. Indeed, the suling essentially takes over the role of the voice. Although the suling parts were initially derived directly from vocal compositions, the amount of improvisation has increased over the years until improvisation has become an essential feature of kacapi-suling recordings.

Of those kacapi-suling tunes not derived from panambih, some are near-exact representations of older, highly complex melodies from the classical gamelan degung repertoire. In these tunes, comprising approximately 10 percent of the kacapi-suling repertoire, both the kacapi and suling are responsible for the melody; occasionally the shorter, higher-pitched suling degung replaces the usual *suling panjang* or long suling. These complex classical melodies, known as dedegungan (meaning "similar to degung"), are very difficult for the kacapi player to perform and only a limited number of players are capable of producing them at the tempo required (Rukmana, personal communication, 1988).

The term *dedegungan*, as it is used here, refers to a different style of music from that occurring as one of the five stylistic divisions of vocal tembang Sunda. Both are "similar to degung," but this one is an imitation of the music of the gamelan degung ensemble, note for note. The other has a whole host of associations (such as high vocal range) discussed earlier. As a consequence of the difficulty for the kacapi player in performing these songs, they are not heard nearly as frequently as the more structurally simple panambih. This infrequency of performance also has resulted in a gradual decline in the use of the suling degung during performances of kacapi-suling (Rae Ann Stahl, personal communication, 1991; Suandi, personal communication, 1988).

Kacapi-suling instrumental music occurs primarily on cassettes, and as a prelude or postlude to performances of tembang Sunda. Even more so than in tembang Sunda, the kacapi-suling genre owes much of its current popularity to the expansion of the cassette industry in Indonesia (Stahl, personal communication, 1991). Some evidence supports the existence of kacapi-suling during the early development of tembang Sunda. It is believed that because there were few female singers of tembang Sunda in the earliest days, the fixed-rhythm panambih were originally performed instrumentally to allow the singers a brief rest from performing.

For the musicians, kacapi-suling is an important means of musical expression in which they are freed from the normal stylistic constraints placed on them during performances of tembang Sunda. Because of its inseparable connection with the cassette industry and its origins in Bandung, kacapi-suling is unquestionably an *urban* ensemble. Tembang Sunda, although firmly established in Bandung and also dependent on the radio and cassette industries to a certain extent, is widely acknowledged as deriving not only from another area (Cianjur), but another era altogether.

In the 1970s, a small group of top-level tembang Sunda musicians (Uking Sukri, Burhan Sukarma, and Nana Suhana) began to make tembang Sunda recordings entirely without a vocalist, using their regular group name of Puspa Nugraha. The type of instrumental ensemble featured on these recordings was called kacapi-suling on the cassette covers to reflect—like many Indonesian ensemble names—the primary instrumentation of the group (see Stahl 1987 for a more detailed discussion of kacapi-suling music). Since the first recordings in the 1970s, kacapi-suling has nearly always been used as background music. The repetitive sound of the kacapi cycles, together with the inherent timbral similarity from piece to piece, make many pieces sound alike. The consequences of similarity among kacapi-suling pieces is that the entire genre shifts, for nonmusicians, into a generic atmospheric aid rather than a series of unique pieces. Performers go unacknowledged, the music is considered fairly unimportant in the larger cultural sphere, few people listen carefully to it, and yet it permeates the atmosphere and creates a specific mood.

All the initial kacapi-suling recordings were made at one studio—Hidayat—whose owner, Bill Firmansyah, enjoyed the sound of the ensemble and felt that it might have some commercial appeal beyond the narrow class boundaries of the more aristocratic tembang Sunda. As the Puspa Nugraha group continued to make recordings with the Hidayat recording company, and other tembang Sunda musicians began making similar recordings, people involved in the Sundanese entertainment industry began to take notice. Not only were the owners of other recording studios aware of this new source of competition, but other instrumentalists saw a new direction for Sundanese music as well as a possible set of changes in their own futures.

First, these cassettes were selling well, causing influential people to look again at the low status of the instrumentalists. Second, people who did not belong to the hereditary Sundanese aristocracy and who wouldn't normally listen to tembang Sunda were buying kacapi-suling cassettes and playing them in automobile tape decks and neighborhood coffee stands, thereby recontextualizing music from a particular status level. Third, kacapi-suling cassette inserts began to show new song titles (Stahl 1987), reflecting a new level of compositional creativity and marketing strategy among musicians who had originally been treated as noncomposing servants.[12] Finally, an important change occurred that reflected back on performances of tembang Sunda. Original suling improvisations captured on kacapi-suling cassettes began to appear in live performances as fixed suling compositions between tembang Sunda verses, copied directly from cassettes. The suling player Burhan Sukarma, as a performer in the Puspa Nugraha group and heavily in demand, powerfully influenced the stylistic future of suling performance practice by having his performances fixed on cassette at a crucially influential time (Stahl 1987).

A major development in the history of kacapi-suling was the adoption of kacapi-suling by the regional station of Radio Republik Indonesia as background music for its daily short stories, read aloud in the afternoons. These engaging Sundanese-language tales (called dongeng) are usually concerned with the difficulties encountered by average rural Sundanese people, and generally end with some type of moral lesson. Aimed at the average man or woman who is home in the afternoon, resting from the heat of the day, unemployed, or just returned home from work, these dongeng are a peaceful way of tying the radio listener to home and family and rural Sunda all at once, encouraging good moral behavior and a sense of regional pride. Using the sounds of prerecorded kacapi-suling in the background pulls together all the other associations of the past, the countryside, and calmness identified with the instruments.

The paradox of kacapi-suling's success is that, in spite of radical changes occurring due to its growing popularity, it has only recently reached the stage of live performance. Kacapi-suling instrumental music appeared almost exclusively on cassettes or radio in prerecorded form, and only occasionally as a brief prelude to live performances of tembang Sunda. Since the 1990s, however, kacapi-suling has become significantly more popular as a stand-alone ensemble, particularly in Bandung. Certain Bandung-area hotels and restaurants have begun hiring kacapi-suling ensembles to perform in lobbies and foyers for wealthy foreigners and businessmen. In spite of this new employment opportunity for musicians, the average local Sundanese is unlikely to walk into a fancy hotel or restaurant unless he is wealthy or an employee. Therefore, most Sundanese do not hear kacapi-suling music performed live outside of weddings, when it is a prelude to tembang Sunda.

A cassette of kacapi-suling is the ultimate portable atmosphere. It can be played with no connection in status to the aristocracy, and it does not make the listener appear to be attempting to rise above his rank in society. It provides the listener with an atmosphere symbolic of a more prosperous, calm, rural past, and imparts a sense of nostalgia (wa'as), pleasure, and well-being. The repetitive, fixed-meter cycles of kacapi-suling are far more representative of Sundanese gamelan than of free-meter tembang Sunda, so kacapi-suling walks a thin status line between the free-meter music of tembang Sunda and the fixed-meter music of gamelan. On cassette recordings, it ultimately cuts across several societal layers and serves at least partly as a leveler of social distinctions.

In spite of the large market available for the support of kacapi-suling cassettes, the musicians who regularly make recordings of it can be counted on the fingers of one hand. One possible reason for this is that good musicians who can accompany singers are plentiful, but good musicians who are comfortable playing independent of a vocalist are harder to find. Only those musicians who are assertive about their musical independence make kacapi-suling recordings; the rest say that they don't feel brave enough, are too shy about their playing ability, or are worried about being considered arrogant by other instrumentalists and vocalists.

It appears that kacapi-suling works primarily as a recorded genre, in an urban setting among a heterogeneous audience. It is certainly a favorite of tourists, as it is unencumbered by vocal music and unintelligible lyrics. It also features the undeniably sweet sound of strings and flute. As background music for the urban Sundanese, it evokes pleasant images of the rural past to mitigate the chaotic experience of the urban present.

Musicians—vocalists and instrumentalists alike—make carefully considered choices about which segments of the tembang Sunda and kacapi-suling repertoire to perform in a given context. The relationship between concepts about tembang Sunda, the behavior (musical, social, and verbal) that produces tembang Sunda, and the sound of tembang Sunda itself corresponds to the theoretical construct for ethnomusicological analysis—of physical, social, and verbal behavior—outlined by Merriam (1964:33). In this discussion of styles, I have tried to show how certain sounds are more appropriate for some listeners than for others. Tembang Sunda is listened to in different ways depending on the audience; when it is listened to by audiences separated by class differences, the musical wallpaper of one group may be the sacred bridge to the ancestors and/or gods of Pajajaran for another. It is this exact feature of the conscious and unconscious choices of the musicians and audience that has determined some of the changes in stylistic emphasis in modern urban performance practice. The following chapter features a discussion of some of the musical sounds that determine these styles and that give them the power to appeal or offend, depending again on the choices of the performers.

8

Instrumental and Vocal Characteristics

This chapter describes the musical instruments and vocal style used in tembang Sunda, to clarify any later references to these instruments and to the particular vocal quality of tembang Sunda. As we saw in the previous discussion of stylistic divisions of tembang Sunda, current performance practice compels tembang Sunda musicians to make choices regarding the relative emphasis placed on certain musical features. For example, performances for weddings emphasize more songs from the panambih style than from papantunan style. Other choices discussed in this chapter reflect developments tied specifically to the process of urbanization.

The modern tembang Sunda ensemble consists of one or more singers accompanied by a large zither (kacapi), one or two smaller zithers (rincik), and a bamboo flute (suling). Occasionally (depending on the songs chosen), a bowed lute (rebab) replaces the suling when the ensemble performs in the saléndro tuning. In the following paragraphs, I describe each instrument, using the most commonly used terminology. Some terminology may vary from other sources, and it should be understood that the Sundanese have a wealth of musical and instrumental terms. The reader is also referred to van Zanten's book for more information about the instruments and their terminology (van Zanten 1989:80–111). The kacapi is most thoroughly covered in this chapter, the suling less so, and the rincik and rebab far less. The reason for this disproportionate coverage is that the kacapi is the most important tembang Sunda instrument, the one essential instrument that cannot be left out in a performance. Furthermore, it is the instrument most strongly connected spiritually to Pajajaran. As will be seen in Chapter 10, the kacapi is the ancestral ship of this book's title. Although the suling is also essential to performances of tembang Sunda, it has close connections to other genres and is not tied exclusively to this single genre.

One of the most hotly contested issues among tembang Sunda practitioners is innovation and development. To what extent can a player be creative and still remain within the boundaries of the genre? At what point does the musician or vocalist step outside? The tendency of the late twentieth century was for innovation to occur within a particular circle of musicians (the members of a single lingkung seni, or "arts circle"). A musician might choose to use a particularly innovative playing technique on a single song, or as a type of "spice" or variation within the songs of a tuning system. If the members of the lingkung seni are hired for a performance, that musician can use the innovative technique for performances, and gradually the informed audience members become accustomed to it. The innovation is then associated with that performer until enough younger performers pick it up and standardize it.

Rukruk Rukmana is an example of a kacapi player who introduced a number of innovative techniques in the 1980s, some of which have now become a normal part of early twenty-first-century kacapi playing. His playing contrasts with that of the late Uking Sukri, arguably the finest kacapi player of his generation and certainly the defining figure of late-twentieth-century tembang Sunda kacapi playing. Both musicians have been recorded on dozens of cassettes, and both clearly represent innovation and tradition, respectively. In the larger debate about whether tembang Sunda should continue to develop or whether it should conform to more traditional standards, the two musicians embody the best of both worlds. With two such fine examples of innovation and tradition, there is plenty of evidence for both sides of the argument.

THE KACAPI

The term *kacapi* is used in West Java to refer to several different types of zithers. Among these zithers are the *kacapi siter*, a flat or board zither used to accompany solo voice and also occasionally used in modern gamelan degung ensembles; the *kacapi pantun*, similar in shape to the kacapi siter but used to accompany recitals of pantun (old epic poems); and the *kacapi indung*, used for performances of tembang Sunda. The kacapi indung ("mother" kacapi), sometimes known as *kacapi prahu* ("boat" kacapi), or *kacapi tembang* (kacapi used especially for tembang), is shaped like a boat with the strings parallel to the body of the instrument, stretching across the top. Invariably, it is varnished in black. From end to end, the kacapi indung (henceforth referred to simply as kacapi) is approximately fifty-nine inches long, ten inches wide (not including the protruding tuning pegs), and thirteen inches from the floor to the top of the strings. The wooden ends of the instrument rise several more inches above the strings. These measurements vary depending on the individual maker, the specifications of the person ordering the instrument, and whether the instrument has been fitted with small wooden feet on one end to facilitate sound projection. The basic shape of the instrument is that of a boat, however, as may be seen in photographs of the instrument.

Although there is some debate as to the origin of the word kacapi, several musicians agreed that the word refers to a reflection of oneself. As several kacapi players mentioned, *kacapi* is derived from the three words *kaca* (looking glass), *samarangan* (reflecting), and *diri* (oneself).[1] The kacapi is usually covered with a gold-fringed velvet cloth in dark colors such as green, red, or blue. This covering is meant to honor and protect the instrument.[2]

The average cost of a kacapi covers not only the kacapi but also the rincik, a small, high-pitched zither that accompanies panambih songs. Because the two are considered an inseparable pair of instruments, they are always sold together. My own set of kacapi and rincik cost 350,000 rupiah, approximately U.S. $194 in 1987. Someone else had ordered them but had neglected to pay for them, so I was fortunate to acquire them shortly after my arrival in Bandung. The man who built them, Uding Ruswandhi, sometimes charges up to 500,000 rupiah for a set of the two instruments, depending on the perceived wealth of the buyer. The late Uking Sukri was one of Bandung's other main kacapi builders, and his rates also varied. All the main kacapi builders in Bandung were charging approximately 150,000 rupiah (about U.S. $140) in 1985, according to Wim van Zanten (1989:90).

The kacapi uses eighteen brass strings, arranged on the instrument so that the highest pitch is closest to the player. These strings, known as *kawat*, may be tuned in two different ways: The rough tuning occurs through the twisting of large wooden tuning pegs (*pureut*) on the side of the kacapi opposite from the player. Fine tuning is accomplished through the use of small, individual pyramidic bridges (*tumpang sari*) that slide along the polished surface of the kacapi sounding board (one bridge for each string). These movable bridges are occasionally used to change the tuning system (if only one pitch differs between the systems, for example), but their main purpose is fine tuning and very minor adjustments to correspond with the pitch of the suling, if necessary. The ends of the strings (twisted around the large tuning pegs) are attached to a fixed bridge by means of small screws.

The sounding board of the kacapi has no resonating holes; rather, the single large resonating hole of the instrument is on the underside and is called *aweuhan*. Openings in the sounding board itself are restricted to the pin-sized holes through which the individual strings are drawn. Van Zanten describes the woods used for the construction of the kacapi, as well as the actual method of construction (1987:91–94). The two ends of the instrument (*gelung*) that rise above the level of the sounding board are designed so that they curl inward slightly (reaching slightly over the sounding board) and attach to the sounding board in step-like gradations. The kacapi player normally sits cross-legged at the side of the instrument, and in most playing styles the left hand is responsible for playing on the lower-pitched strings, while the right hand plays primarily on the higher-pitched strings.

Instrumentalists use several different techniques of kacapi playing for tembang Sunda. The choice of technique depends on which of the five major types of song (papantunan, jejemplangan, rarancagan, dedegungan, or panambih) is being performed by the vocalist. Many listeners will "call the tune" (or at least the style) three seconds into its beginning, simply by hearing the technique used and the pitches played. A multiplicity of associations works in the minds of the musicians and the informed audience to cue the selection and recognition of a melody or style. Among these associations are the tuning system, the time of the evening, the previous songs, the identity (including the vocal range and preferred repertoire) of a singer, the identity of the musicians, the performance context, and the playing style of the kacapi, not necessarily in that order.

The recognition by the musicians and the audience of several types of kacapi playing techniques is essential to musical appropriateness. The names of these techniques are *pasieup, pasieup rincik, cacagan, kemprang tandak, kemprang gembyang, téngkép, téngkép jemplang, kait, rofel,* and *takol balik*. In general, the technique determines the song style. This selection of terms is a reflection of the kacapi players with whom I worked, and because each player develops his own set of terms to describe his technique, some of these terms will either vary in some way from van Zanten or expand on what he has discussed elsewhere.

Pasieup, pasieup rincik, and cacagan all have one thing in common: The index finger of the right hand does most of the playing, and the string is always struck in a downward motion, away from the player. For this playing technique, the thumb is parallel to the hand and the other fingers are held straight out, parallel to the strings. Also known as *sintreuk*—from the Sundanese term for flicking a naughty child on the ear—this downward striking motion is used in many of the free-rhythm mamaos songs. The index finger of the left hand fills out the patterns and ends the phrases begun by the right hand, by plucking upward on the string in a rest stroke (resting the fingertip against the next string after plucking) described as *toél* (Koswara 1973:4). No one I knew ever used the term toél, but it does appear in van Zanten (1987:141). When playing pasieup, the performer executes a series of single-note runs in free rhythm (Example 8.1), outlining the basic melodic structure of the song and emphasizing the main pitches.

The pasieup acts not only as an introduction to the song but also leads the vocalist through the song by providing the first pitch of each line and generally following the pitches of each line through to the final pitch of the line. If the vocalist loses his or her place in the song, it is the responsibility of the kacapi player and, secondarily, the suling player, to clue the vocalist

EXAMPLE 8.1 Pasieup technique on the kacapi

EXAMPLE 8.2 Pasieup rincik technique on the kacapi

in to the appropriate pitches until the song is recovered. Several kacapi players referred to their job, when playing pasieup, as one of "bribing" the vocalist (Indo.: *menyuapi si penembang*). In this case, it is not so much "bribing" as leading the vocalist back into place. Pasieup technique is most characteristic of the subgroup of songs known as rarancagan and dedegungan, but also is used occasionally in papantunan ("Papatet") and jejemplangan songs. It is known especially for its use of free rhythm; the kacapi player must gauge his playing so that he and the singer arrive at the song's structural points at more or less the same time. In Example 8.1, the actual pasieup section begins after the first nine notes.

Pasieup rincik is essentially the same technique, but the kacapi player uses equal timing between the pitches so that they do not occur in rapid clusters as in regular pasieup. Because it sounds quite similar to the technique of fixed-rhythm patterns performed by the rincik player, its name is a combination of pasieup (long melodic runs) and rincik (in rincik style). This technique is not arbitrarily chosen by the player but rather is used only in certain sections of particular songs such as "Udan Mas" (see Example 8.2). An important feature of this technique is that although the pitches have equal duration, their exact selection and the duration of the line depend on the judgement of the kacapi player, and are based on the speed with which the vocalist completes each line.

Cacagan playing technique refers to a chopping action. Used most frequently in rarancagan songs, cacagan occurs as an alternative to pasieup and involves striking the strings in a pattern of descending fourths that group pairs of strings. These pairs are in the interval of a perfect fourth, and the pattern is played by striking the highest note of the first pair followed by the lowest, then a second pair is played beginning with the string in between the first pair. This pattern usually only lasts through two pairs of fourths, then is followed by more pasieup runs. The cacagan pattern is also said to occur as a vocal ornament in rarancagan and other subgroups of mamaos, in which the vocalist approximates a "chopping" sound as a particular choice of ornament. Cacagan style on the kacapi is particularly useful when accompanying a song that temporarily strays outside the tuning system. If the kacapi player is following the singer note-for-note, the song will sound out of tune if the kacapi doesn't use alternate pitches as in cacagan. Cacagan is frequently used in the sorog and saléndro tunings, whose songs (all rarancagan) often use pitches from outside the tuning system. The first few notes of Example 8.1 indicate cacagan playing style.

The next pair of playing techniques occurs primarily in papantunan and jejemplangan songs. These are called kemprang tandak and kemprang gembyang. Kemprang is a type of ostinato accompaniment emphasizing the use of a perfect fifth in the left hand. The term also is used in gamelan ensembles to describe the simultaneous playing of pitches in fifths and octaves on the bonang. As with pasieup, only two fingers are used, the index finger of the right hand using the sintreuk (downward) stroke, and the index finger of the left hand using the toél (plucking upward) stroke. The subdivisions of kemprang tandak and kemprang gembyang refer to whether the kacapi plays in a metered rhythm (*tandak* = "dancing"), or whether it is in a free rhythm. In either case, the vocalist is free to adjust the speed of the song according to whim, and the kacapi player must pay close attention to the melody so that he knows where to change his pattern as he follows the song. The vocalist is by necessity less dependent on the kacapi player (but possibly more dependent on the suling player) during songs using kemprang technique, because its repetitive patterns prohibit "bribing" the singer with pitches as in pasieup. Songs in kemprang tandak have a very strong, steady beat, usually emphasizing the two pitches of a perfect fifth in the left hand (Example 8.3), while the right hand either plays a melody or plays a repeating pattern.

Songs using kemprang gembyang, by contrast, have a much freer rhythm and are characterized by a more sparse frequency of strokes on the kacapi. The relationship between the two is their emphasis on open fifths

EXAMPLE 8.3 Kemprang tandak on the kacapi

in the left hand and their strong association with papantunan and jejemplangan songs. Example 8.4 is from the song "Randegan" and demonstrates one single pattern over which the voice sings in free rhythm.

Téngkép and *téngkép jemplang* also belong specifically to rarancagan and jejemplangan, and are used in the performance of other techniques likes pasieup and kemprang. Téngkép refers to the stopping of a string immediately after it has been sounded. In pasieup passages, the thumb of the right hand mutes the strings so that the pitches do not run together and create a discordant sound. Strings must be *diténgkép* to maintain clarity of pitches. Téngkép jemplang, however, refers to a technique used only in jejemplangan songs, in which muting is done by the middle finger of the left hand to stop the note played by the left index finger.

Lastly, the three techniques of kait, rofel, and takol balik are exclusive to performances of panambih songs. It should be emphasized also that the latter two (rofel and takol balik) are variations of kait and are considered to be an essential part of the panambih playing of Rukruk Rukmana and those who imitate his style. They are both new creations and have been popularized through the cassette industry, and because of that popularization are considered by some urban players to be a normal feature of kacapi playing. The two techniques are, however, strongly disapproved of by some

EXAMPLE 8.4 Kemprang gembyang on the kacapi

EXAMPLE 8.5 Kait technique on the kacapi

of the older players, who resent what they consider to be the more flashy, pop-style sounds. Certain older singers also claim to be distracted by all the variation and rhythmic interest created by Rukruk's style.

The kait technique is the accepted standard practice for all kacapi players. To play kait, the right hand of the player performs alternating octaves in the upper register with the thumb and index finger, in the pattern rest—thumb—index—thumb. The left hand (usually the thumb and index or middle finger) plays syncopated patterns on the lower strings, with structural tones called pancer (playing the role of the go'ong, jenglong, etc.) occurring during the rests of the right hand. The octaves and the part played by the left hand correspond to the patokan or structural outline of the piece. This technique is the easiest to learn of all the kacapi styles, and is the dominant technique found in performances of instrumental kacapi-suling. Most beginning kacapi players start with this technique, either by learning directly from a teacher or imitating what they hear on recordings. Its slow tempo and repetitive patterns make it easy to understand, and the patokan may be used in a wide variety of songs. Example 8.5 demonstrates the first few measures of the patokan for the song "Lalayaran."

The rofel technique is similar to kait, except that it is performed at double the density of regular panambih accompaniment. Therefore, it follows the outline of the patokan in the same manner as kait, and the singer still performs the songs at the same tempo, but the right hand plays twice as fast and occasionally uses the thumb and index finger simultaneously to create more sound. For some reason, this technique is considered extremely difficult to master, although it is used in both the bubuka and panutup, the instrumental opening and closing pieces. Perhaps the difficulty is in sustaining the momentum of the song once the player has switched to rofel technique. It is difficult to switch back to normal kait during the panambih unless it is the type of song that features a chorus (and is played *dirofel*) and verses (played *dikait*). Some vocalists feel rushed if the player uses rofel, and I have heard it described as "impolite." Others, however, comment enthusiastically about the upbeat feel of the technique and characterize players who avoid it as "dull." Example 8.6 is from the patokan for "Catrik," and the rofel technique begins in the second measure.

Takol balik literally means "reversed stroke," and refers to right hand panambih technique in which the alternating octaves are begun by the index finger instead of the thumb. The pattern, therefore, is reversed: instead of rest—thumb—index—thumb (as in kait), it becomes rest—index—

EXAMPLE 8.6 Rofel technique on the kacapi

thumb—index. The string played by the thumb is slightly more emphasized, and its high-register pitches create a different sound quality for the panambih. The same controversy surrounds this technique as for rofel, and some critics complain that it is too flashy. Because Rukruk Rukmana is on so many cassettes, however, these two modern urban techniques have gained wide acceptance among urban players, singers, and listeners. Even the minutest details of kacapi playing techniques do not escape scrutiny in the ongoing debate about tembang Sunda. Example 8.7 is also from the patokan for "Catrik," and the takol balik technique begins in the second measure with the pause in the right hand.

The kacapi bears a great deal of symbolic content for the Sundanese, not just because of its position as the primary instrument of the tembang Sunda ensemble, but because it is one of the oldest of the Sundanese musical instruments. A version of the kacapi is played by the Baduy, who are believed to be the indigenous and original inhabitants of Sunda. In Chapter 10 ("Connecting with the Ancestors") I include more detail about kacapi symbolism

EXAMPLE 8.7 Takol balik technique on the kacapi

in the context of understanding tembang Sunda at a level deeper than the technical aspects of performance practice.

THE RINCIK

The core ensemble of kacapi and vocalist was once enough to create a tembang Sunda performance; it still is, if no other instruments are present. The rincik became part of the group beginning in the 1930s, however, and was firmly established by the 1950s (van Zanten 1989:29) Understanding the origin of the name for this instrument is easier than for the other instruments. The word *rincik*, or *rintik*, is used to describe the sound of a light rain or sprinkle. The sound of the rincik, therefore, is likened to a light background pattering of rain, said to add to the pleasant feeling of a situation. It is also called *kacapi rincik* or *kacapi anak* ("child kacapi"), because of its similar shape to the "mother kacapi" or kacapi indung. Only a few musicians specialize in playing the rincik. People who would otherwise be considered peripheral to the tembang Sunda scene can participate in a playing session by quietly playing the rincik (or the second rincik) if no one else is already doing so. No particular song must be mastered before a musician may play the rincik at a rehearsal, but excellent listening and timing skills are required to follow the singer as she progresses through the song. The acceptable standard of good playing on the rincik seems to be one of following the structure of the piece, keeping a very steady tempo, and especially following in close approximation to the melody of the song. People laugh out loud if a rincik player does not conform quite closely to what the singer is doing.

The rincik is similar in shape to the kacapi, although it is much smaller (thirty-four inches long, seven inches tall, and eight inches wide) and is pitched an octave higher. Furthermore, it does not use the tuning pegs (*pureut*) or the structural beam (*cukang beurit*) found on the much larger kacapi. Rather, its rough tuning is accomplished by the turning of simple bolts on one end, using a special tool similar to an autoharp tuner. Fine tuning is accomplished by shifting the position of pyramidal movable bridges, just as on the kacapi. I have seen some rincik constructed in direct imitation of the kacapi; that is, with an entire row of false tuning pegs on the outside of the instrument, opposite from the player. Others omit these but retain the two curls on the long ends of the rincik. My own rincik has a single curl and no false tuning pegs.

The names for the parts of the instrument are the same, although the high tension of the strings requires the placement on the sounding board of round metal washers, referred to as *mata itik* (duck eyes). These washers protect the sounding board from being too deeply cut into by the high-tension strings. Strings used for the rincik are made of steel instead of brass, because—according to van Zanten—the brass is unable to withstand the high tension required to produce pitches an octave above those of the kacapi (van Zanten 1987:96). Some players purchase light-gauge guitar strings for the rincik and sometimes brass-wound guitar strings for the three lowest strings of the kacapi, but most purchase brass and steel wire of different gauges by the kilo at metal supply shops.

The rincik player sits cross-legged in front of his instrument in a manner similar to that of the kacapi player, unless the other musicians are all sitting in chairs or on couches, in which case he may hold the instrument on his lap. The latter position only happens during casual music-playing sessions and never in performance. Unlike the kacapi player, however, the rincik player is limited not only in the times appropriate for him to perform but also in the repertoire of styles available to him. Because the rincik player only performs fixed-rhythm patterns during the opening instrumental piece and in the panambih or "addition" songs of each set, the player simply sits quietly during the other sections and waits his turn to play.

The musician plays a fixed-rhythm melodic line by striking down with his right index finger (in a motion away from his body) and plucking upward (toward himself) with the index finger of his left hand to fill out the notes of the melodic line. There are three different techniques used in rincik performance practice: *carukan*, *biasa*, and *kenit*. Carukan is used only during the very fast bubuka and panutup sections of a performance, and in order to accompany at an appropriate speed the index fingers of the right and left hand alternate every note. Carukan is described in van Zanten as "mixing different things" (1987:185), and the several rincik players with whom I spoke described it as a reference to the interlocking style of two *saron* (metallophones) in the gamelan. This alternation of right and left hand differs from (and is significantly faster than) the approximately three to one ratio in biasa or "regular" style. Van Zanten describes the fast passages that use carukan as using "around 540 notes per minute, and not one is skipped" (1987:185). Example 8.8 is from the song "Jipang Lontang," and is notated an octave below pitch because of the extremely high pitch of the rincik.

As for the biasa ("regular") style, it does not use the same kind of alternation between right and left index fingers as in carukan. Rather, the playing is done mostly by the index finger of the right hand (as in pasieup on the kacapi), and many of the patterns used are simple elaborations of the pitches in the melody of the song. On occasion, a rincik player will add a lower-pitched drone to his playing, by striking the string with the current colotomic tone on the offbeats. This technique is called *rangkep*, and is more

EXAMPLE 8.8 Carukan style on the rincik

EXAMPLE 8.9 Biasa style on the rincik

difficult to play because the right index finger must play all the pitches normally handled by two fingers. The following figure omits the rangkep pitches, because they are not very frequently added, and if a second rincik is present then the duties of performing the drone pitches will be taken over by that player. Example 8.9 is transcribed from the first two lines of the tune "Nimang." The downward-pointing stems in each measure indicate pitches plucked by the left hand.

These two techniques are used by almost all rincik players, except for students at ASTI and SMKI, who usually play exclusively in carukan style. It is said that graduates from these institutions play rincik in this manner because the teachers there are gamelan performers, not tembang performers. In fact, the rincik is sometimes referred to as peking (after the saron peking of gamelan) in these institutions, because of its high pitch and "tinkly" timbre.

An important recent development of rincik playing in the last twenty years has been the addition of a second rincik, sometimes called rincik gender or rincik kenit. This second rincik functions as a timekeeper for the ensemble during the panambih, in most cases playing a very simple rhythmic pattern (kenit) reminiscent of the *kecrek*, a small set of clashing aluminum plates used in gamelan performances. This four-beat rhythmic pattern uses a rest on the first beat, then the primary pitch of the patokan or structural outline, followed by the octave of that same pitch, then the first pitch again. It is a common rhythmic pattern throughout Sunda and is echoed in the right-hand kacapi part during panambih songs. This pattern or variations of it is repeated by the second rincik throughout the panambih, changing only as the structure or patokan shifts. There are many rhythmic variants to kenit-style playing; the example transcribed is one of the simplest. Example 8.10 is from the patokan for the song "Catrik."

Opinions differ among musicians about the reason for the second rincik. According to some, the second rincik is used to provide a more balanced visual appearance onstage. Others claim that the second rincik creates a richer sound and emphasizes the structure of the piece by its focus on the primary pitches in each section of the patokan. It certainly adds to the visual impact of the ensemble and creates more of a dramatic spectacle when

EXAMPLE 8.10 Kenit style on the rincik dua

viewed from the audience. Musicians from other genres maintained that the use of a second rincik was used as a consolation for musicians who showed up and didn't have anything to play, or for when two players were inadvertently hired for the same job. Sometimes the rebab player will perform on a second rincik as he waits for the saléndro tuning to come up. Although it is not certain whether the phenomenon of a second rincik is exclusively an urban one, in the two years I spent researching this genre I never saw a second rincik in performances outside of Bandung. One of my teachers explained it thus: "They can't afford the instruments in the first place; how do you expect them to spend all that extra money on a second rincik?"

THE SULING

The term *suling* and its variants are used in many parts of Indonesia to denote an end-blown bamboo flute. Although not all suling are of the block-flute variety, this characteristic is common to all types of Sundanese suling. The two main types of Sundanese suling are the six-fingerhole *suling panjang* (or long suling) and the four-fingerhole *suling degung*, a short suling used specifically for performing with a gamelan degung ensemble. Several other suling are also used; among them are the short, slender six-fingerhole *suling mandalungan* and the four-fingerhole *suling saléndro*. I have also seen a very long, deep-voiced suling that is sometimes called *suling cello*, but it is rarely used.

For the purposes of this work, I concentrate on the six-fingerhole suling panjang used for performances of tembang Sunda. The suling degung and suling mandalungan are used so rarely in tembang Sunda (the first is occasionally used to accompany songs of the dedegungan style, and the second is used only for the mandalungan tuning system) that most tembang Sunda musicians only think of the suling panjang when they discuss suling performance practice. Further information on the suling degung may be found in *The Music of the Gamelan Degung of West Java* (Harrell 1974). I received almost all of my information on the suling from Burhan Sukarma, and some from Ade Suandi. Ade Suandi took me to visit a suling maker in the Bojong Loa area of Bandung, and I had the opportunity to watch an order for ten suling be filled by the maker within about an hour-and-a-half.

The date of the first association of the suling with the tembang Sunda ensemble is questionable. Van Zanten cites an observation (by van Hoëvell 1845:428) of a suling in an ensemble that included a type of kacapi and a tarawangsa (a type of bowed lute) in the early nineteenth century, among the Baduy people of West Java (van Zanten 1989:103). The Baduy, however, did not actually perform tembang Sunda. Nonetheless, the early association of kacapi and suling is an important one in that it must have influenced the later development of tembang Sunda ensembles among the aristocracy. The earliest use of the suling in tembang Sunda ensembles has been placed (at the latest) at the end of the nineteenth century (van Zanten 1989:103). It is clear from the earliest recordings of tembang Sunda, however, that the suling was already well established in the early part of the twentieth century. In these oldest recordings (obtained from the archives of the Ethnomusicologisch Centrum "Jaap Kunst" at the University of Amsterdam), the suling appears in nearly every song.

Although the suling has a strong role in evoking the nostalgic feelings essential for the true enjoyment of tembang Sunda (van Zanten 1989:105), some Sundanese musicians do not take the instrument very seriously. I heard it described on many occasions as a *mainan* (children's toy), and I heard players of instruments other than suling express surprise that I would even consider studying such an "easy" instrument. I was warned on many occasions not to get too involved with the suling because it is believed that playing the suling ruins the singing voice.[3] My research also confirms van Zanten's claim that the Sundanese suling players view their instruments as female, not as a male or phallic instrument (van Zanten 1989:105).

The suling is sixty to sixty-two centimeters in length, or approximately two feet long. The selection of length (sixty, sixty-one, or sixty-two centimeters) is based primarily on the pitch range of the vocalist and the ability of the kacapi to withstand being tuned up to pitch. If the strings tend to break on the kacapi, a longer suling is selected to lower the pitch and the string tension; similarly, if the vocalist cannot reach the lower range very well, a shorter suling is used to raise the pitch. The bamboo suling is almost perfectly cylindrical and is of a fairly uniform diameter from one suling to another. According to van Zanten, the bamboo used (Indo.: *bambu*; Sund.: *awi*) is either *awi tamiang* (*Schizostachyum blumei*) or *awi bunar* (*Bambusa longinodis*), which van Zanten derived from Heyne (1927:302; van Zanten 1989:99).[4] The musicians with whom I worked mentioned only awi tamiang, but I worked with a suling maker different from the one who worked with van Zanten.

The mouthpiece is encircled by a thin strip of bamboo tied in a ring, leaving a small "tail" with no function except to decorate the suling. The small ring itself is responsible for directing the air over the soundhole, and is not actually attached to the suling except for the fact that it is tightly tied around the mouthpiece. Other suling makers may use rattan for this ring (van Zanten 1989:99). In 1996, I watched a suling maker create the ring by shaving a sharp knife along a length of bamboo until a thin strip came up, and this strip was then shaved down considerably until it was very thin and flexible.

The suling has six fingerholes known as *lubang* (Indo.) (Sukarma, personal communication, 1987) or *liang* (Sund.) (van Zanten 1989:98). The size and placement of these holes are responsible for the basic pitches of pélog and sorog but also may be altered by the fingers of the player (in combination with overblowing) to produce *nada sisipan* or *nada tanggung* (enharmonic tones) or to create certain ornaments. Although the suling also may be used to play in saléndro, this tuning system is usually left to the rebab rather than the suling in tembang Sunda performances. Players occasionally adjust the size and shape of the fingerholes (van Zanten 1989: 99), and the overall length of the suling, to raise or lower the pitch.

When a player buys a suling, he usually buys several at a time. One reason for the purchase of several of these instruments at once is that the creation of a very good suling is actually a matter of chance. A good suling maker may sometimes create a poor suling, and the player takes his chances when he orders several suling from a maker. Another reason to order several at a time is that a suling can be unpredictable and turn bad, or dry out and crack, or go out of tune, or become damaged by insects.[5] While a good player may be able to get an acceptable sound out of a bad suling, most players simply stop using the bad suling and switch to another. A player may become attached to one particular suling, but if that instrument fails in some way the player is compelled to change to a new suling.

In financial terms, it is cheaper (and less bothersome) to order several suling at once than to get them one at a time. Van Zanten lists the price of a suling in 1985 at 1,000 rupiah, approximately U.S. $1 (van Zanten 1989: 99); by the time I was in Bandung between 1987 and 1989 the average price of a suling was between 2,000 and 3,000 rupiah, or about U.S. $1.11 to $1.66. By 1996, suling prices had risen to 10,000 rupiah, or U.S. $4.44. Suling prices also depend, of course, on the bargaining skills of the buyer. A good suling player who is a frequent customer of the maker may still be able to get the instruments for far less than the going rate.

In the performance of free-rhythm or mamaos songs, the function of the suling is to provide the initial pitches for the vocalist, to follow along in heterophony, and to play the melody of the gelenyu or instrumental section if the song has one. In a panambih, the suling player still accompanies the vocalist, but is free to improvise in the gelenyu before and between the verses. He also may change octaves to correspond with the climax of the song, and improvise much more freely during the verses than he would in a mamaos song. So that the suling player does not create pitch trouble for the vocalist, he must stay fairly close to her pitches. The best musical situation for a suling player is one in which he and the vocalist are so comfortable with each other's style that his improvisation is desirable, rather than a problem.

The first three fingers of each hand cover the six fingerholes of the suling. Most players place the left hand above the right hand (in other words, the left hand covers the three highest holes); however, some players reverse this position. The player almost always sits to perform on the suling. He usually sits cross-legged on the floor for performances, but in a latihan also may sit on a chair or couch depending on where the other players and the host are. Most suling players (and other tembang Sunda instrumentalists) who have already achieved a basic level of proficiency do not practice on their own, but simply attend latihan sessions and performances, and maintain their ability within that forum only.

The pitch of the suling may be shifted by as much as a half-step by changing the player's embouchure, depending on how close to the player's body the suling is held. When the suling is brought close to the body, the embouchure shifts and the pitch drops, and the pitch can be raised simply by raising the end of the suling. According to Ade Suandi, this technique is most useful if the kacapi falls or rises in pitch, depending on the temperature of the room or the strength of the lights, or even contact between the instruments and the chilly outside air at night. Another frequently used technique for maintaining an illusion of being in tune is to play rapid ornaments on pitches other than the out-of-tune pitch, which, it is hoped, tricks the audience.

Most of the ornaments and pitch changes on the suling are caused through the movement of the fingers. The pressure (*tenaga*) of the player's breath, however, is responsible not only for which of the two-and-a-half available octaves is selected but also for the stability and accuracy of the pitches. Accidental overblowing can cause a mistake, resulting in laughter among the other musicians. Therefore, the player must keep up a steady level of air pressure; in fact, he may, use his breath to create a light vibrato by varying the pressure just enough to affect the pitch (Sukarma, personal communication 1987). When a suling player is executing very high and very low pitches, he tongues them to get a stronger, more accurate sound. The lower pitches use more of a "d" sound in the tongue than a sharper "t," which would cause the pitch to leap up one octave.

Although there are specific ways of playing the suling for each of the five main styles of tembang Sunda (for example, using a "breathy" sound to accompany jejemplangan style), each player has a stock of ornaments that may be used in almost any of the styles. Ornamentation on the suling does not have to imitate vocal ornamentation even though the basic melodic line is similar; instead, the suling player selects ornaments appropriate to the suling pitch and to the melodic line. According to Burhan Sukarma, the reason for this is that each singer has her own set of vocal ornaments and her own individual version of each song, based on who she studied with and how she has created her style. If a suling player were to imitate all the vocal ornaments of one singer only, his playing style would be inappropriate for the accompaniment of a different singer.

Although some of the ornaments for suling now have terms, these terms are often interchangeable, substituted with terms for vocal or rebab ornaments, or are simply the onomatopoetic sound of each ornament. The musicians care less about the terms (except perhaps for the students and faculty at Bandung's music institutions) than about the proper production of them. Many are unable to separate the melody from the ornament (van Zanten 1989:162). When Burhan Sukarma (the foremost suling player of tembang Sunda) was developing his own style of playing, he never used any of the terms heard today. Instead, he simply played the ornaments as part of his own improvisation on the basic melody (Sukarma, personal communication, 1987). In the following musical transcriptions, the term is indicated for each ornament according to Burhan Sukarma. Because van Zanten derived some of his terms for suling ornamentation from the kacapi player Uking Sukri

EXAMPLE 8.11 Léotan on the suling

(van Zanten 1989:161), the terminology differs slightly from that of Burhan Sukarma. Now, when a student comes to ask about a particular ornament, he may use the term for it but is far more likely simply to sing the ornament he wants to the senior player, and it is up to the senior player to know to which ornament the student refers.

The most common general term for suling ornamentation is *sénggol*, a term that is also sometimes used for vocal ornamentation. A sénggol is a decoration of a preexisting melodic line. *Reureueus* is also frequently used as a term for ornamentation in general, but seems to refer more closely to tremolo-type ornaments than grace notes or glissandi. Ornamentation is said to be the same between tuning systems, although some ornaments may use pitches from other tunings to create the desired effect. For example, a glissando (*léotan*) in pélog may borrow a pitch from sorog as the upper note on which the glissando begins. Creative players are continually perfecting their technique and trying to produce new and interesting ornaments, and each new ornament represents a challenge. One of the most difficult techniques is to keep the suling vibrato very stable; it was recommended to me that I squeeze very hard limes to strengthen my fingers and steady my vibrato.

Among the named ornaments used on the suling are *léotan, betrik, gelik, endag, puruluk, keleter*, and *renghik*. Not all the terms listed in van Zanten have been included here, partly because they were not used by Burhan Sukarma, but also because I did not hear other musicians use the terms in the manner described (van Zanten 1989:162–180). The limitation of this list of suling ornaments resulting from my exclusion of certain terms should therefore be taken into consideration and the reader should be aware that not every ornament or creative musical activity on the suling has an accompanying term.

The léotan ornament is a glissando or slide, both from above and from below the main pitch. It may be played on almost every pitch, and the term is derived from the motion of ironing. A léotan ornament does not have to be within the range of a half-step, but may involve the slow lifting or placing of more than one finger. Léotan is said to occur more often in sorog melodies than in pélog. Example 8.11 demonstrates an upper-to-lower pitch léotan in pélog, notated as a slide from pitch e to pitch c in the first part of the phrase.

The term betrik refers to a very quick touch on a lower fingerhole; for example, if the first three holes of the suling are covered, the index finger of the right hand quickly touches the fourth hole just long enough to create a percussive effect. If the finger remained across the hole, the pitch would

EXAMPLE 8.12 Betrik on the suling

EXAMPLE 8.13 Gelik on the suling

EXAMPLE 8.14 Endag on the suling

lower. The pitch does not noticeably change in a betrik ornament, however, because the desired effect is percussive and not melodic. The betrik ornament often occurs after a keleter ornament but may also occur on its own. Burhan Sukarma refers to the relationship between betrik and keleter as *adumanis*, a sweet relationship, and gave an example of the blending of two beautiful colors to create an even better final result. The ornament is depicted twice in Example 8.12 as the two grace notes on pitch d, enclosed by parentheses because they are only heard very slightly.

The gelik ornament is similar to betrik, in that it is a very rapid flip of the index finger, but it occurs in a different place on the suling than betrik and is an upper grace note rather than a lower grace note. Burhan Sukarma describes it as an upper grace note with a large interval between the grace note and the actual pitch; Wim van Zanten describes it as a double appoggiatura (van Zanten 1989:163). He also acknowledges that gelik is in the same general class as betrik and that the term *betrik* could conceivably be used for both ornaments. The gelik ornament does not occur on pitch four because all the fingerholes are open, and is used almost exclusively to describe the position in which the index finger of the left hand lifts very briefly while the fingers below it continue to cover the fingerholes. This ornament is notated in Example 8.13 as the final grace note of the line, enclosed by parentheses to indicate its very light and quick passage.

Endag is used to define the shaking of leaves by the wind (Eringa 1984: 205) and is one of the vibrato techniques used on the suling. In this technique, the finger does not completely uncover the fingerhole. Instead, only the slightest opening is revealed, that very rapidly and gently shifts the pitch up and down by less than a quarter of a step. This ornament can be very long in duration and is not limited to a fraction of a second, as are some of the other ornaments. The endag ornament is often used as a prelude to a gong tone in panambih songs, and is used in most mamaos as well. Burhan Sukarma described endag with the English word "tremolo" and distinguished it from "trill." In Example 8.14, the ornament is notated with a wavy line after the half-note on pitch a.

EXAMPLE 8.15 Keleter on the suling

EXAMPLE 8.16 Puruluk on the suling

EXAMPLE 8.17 Renghik on the suling

If endag is tremolo in English, then keleter is a trill. Unlike endag, however, the keleter ornament is a very brief and rapid trill in which the fingerhole is completely covered and uncovered by the finger. Therefore, the difference in pitch between the lower and upper pitches of the ornament is greater than in endag. The duration of keleter is only as long as the pitch is held; in other words, the pitch does not abruptly go into the keleter ornament from a straight tone on the same pitch. It is tongued individually and is often followed by a betrik ornament, usually approached from below. In Example 8.15, the keleter ornament occurs as a rapidly oscillating trill between pitches e and c.

The puruluk ornament is also a brief but fast and wide-ranging vibrato. It is quite similar to the keleter, but instead of being a short vibrato in one breath, used as a contrast to other pitches performed in a straight tone, the puruluk is constantly used from one pitch to another without extra tonguing to provide a fluttering sound. The term is onomatopoetic because the short duration of the ornament causes it to sound like the three syllables pu-ru-luk, spoken very quickly. In Example 8.16, the ornament extends from the second group of rapid notes until the betrik ornament just before the half note on pitch e.

Renghik is a term used to describe the action of a very brief grace note spanning a large interval at the end of a phrase. Burhan Sukarma does not use this or any other term for the following ornament; however, I have heard it used by several other suling players and by vocalists. In the following transcription, the renghik ornament occurs for a fraction of a second at an interval of a major third above the previous pitch. In the voice, this renghik ornament is the same except that the singer produces it as a very soft, breathy falsetto tone. The suling player usually plays the renghik very lightly and creates the same light, breathy effect as the singer. In Example 8.17, the renghik ornament is indicated in parentheses to emphasize its soft, breathy quality; it occurs at the end of the phrase on pitch a.

In some of the earliest recordings of tembang Sunda, the vibrato of the suling players is not steady and it appears that the development of a very stable vibrato has only occurred in the recent past as part of the extraordinary influence of Burhan Sukarma. Because few modern Sundanese musicians have access to these early recordings (78 rpm records), it is difficult to assess the degree to which early players were influenced by recordings. The current and very frequent use of cassettes in the learning process (since the mid-1970s) has unquestionably created a broad sphere of influence from the recordings of Burhan Sukarma both inside of Bandung and in the villages. In Chapter 6 ("Learning the Craft"), I discussed some of the ways in which suling players and other tembang Sunda instrumentalists learn how to play their instruments.

THE REBAB

Sundanese music uses two different types of bowed lutes, known as *tarawangsa* and *rebab*. The tarawangsa (differing from the rebab in its construction and the type of music it accompanies) is used in several different types of village music and is usually paired with a kacapi (Falk 1980:1), but is not used in tembang Sunda. The two-stringed rebab is mainly used as one of the instruments of the gamelan saléndro ensemble, but appears occasionally during the saléndro portion of tembang Sunda performances. Not all saléndro songs use rebab; only those derived from the kakawén (wayang song) repertoire. Only a few rebab players are thought to be fully conversant and adaptable to the tembang Sunda repertoire in saléndro; one of the most famous was the late Dacép Eddy, believed to be the most appropriate rebab performer for tembang Sunda in Bandung. Dacép Eddy often doubled on rincik during non-saléndro sections of performances.

The body of the rebab is in the shape of a rounded upside-down triangle, and a long spike extends from the top and bottom of the body. The total length of the instrument is approximately forty-five inches long. Unlike the suling, however, the total length of the rebab is generally not taken into consideration when the instrument is purchased because the length has no effect on the pitch of the instrument. The rebab is broken down into its component sections when it is not in use, and is placed in a small suitcase for easy transportation to latihan sessions and performances.

Although some of the terms used to describe the parts of the rebab are unique to the rebab, others are similar to terms used for the parts of the kacapi. For example, the movable bridge of the rebab is called tumpang sari, the same as the term for the multiple bridges on the kacapi. Similarly, the large tuning pegs extending on either side of the neck of the rebab are called pureut, and are also used on the kacapi. The term *wangkis* is used on both instruments to describe the upper surface of the body's sound board. The two strings of the rebab are called *kawat*, a generic term that can refer to anything made from wire.

The long spike of the instrument is divided into three pieces: the *suku* or base of the instrument (resting on the floor or the edge of a chair), the *tihang* or long neck that extends above the body, and the *pucuk* or top portion of the neck that rises above the large tuning pegs (van Zanten 1989: 104). Rebab players usually use a soft cloth between the strings and the place where they connect to the bottom of the instrument's body. This cloth mutes the sound and, more important, cuts down on noisy interference from the overtones of the vibrating skin. An outdoor gamelan performance does not require a soft sound from the rebab and in fact it must compete against a large number of bronze instruments; however, outdoor performances almost always use microphones and the cloth is now a feature of outdoor performances as well.

The bow of the instrument is called *pangésék* or *pangését* (something that bows). As with many other Sundanese music terms, people do not seem to care when one letter is substituted for another; *gésék* and *gését* are the same. The hair used for bowing should be of very long, fine tail hairs from a horse, but horsehair is expensive and nylon lasts longer. Therefore, many rebab players choose nylon for their bows instead. The more expensive bows are carved at each end in the shape of a *makara* figure, a type of mythical sea-monster, found in many parts of Southeast Asia and Hindu in origin. Inexpensive bows use no carving at all. In 1989, the cost of a fairly good rebab was 150,000 rupiah, or about U.S. $83.

The rebab player almost always sits cross-legged on the floor, except in those circumstances in which everyone else sits on a couch or chair. In those cases, the rebab player must sit on a couch or chair himself to be at the same level as the other players and singers. The player holds the rebab slightly to the left of his body, holding the bow in his right hand and stopping the left of the two strings. Because the strings require only light pressure from the fingers, there are no frets and the strings never touch the neck of the instruments. The right string is used only as an occasional drone and is not stopped by the fingers. All four fingers of the left hand are active, and the thumb of the left hand supports the back of the neck and holds the instrument in an upright position. The right hand holds the bow with the thumb across the top of the end, and the other fingers supporting the bottom of the bow end.

The rebab has been used in tembang Sunda ensembles since the 1960s (Dacép Eddy, personal communication, 1987). The function of the rebab is as a substitute for the suling in saléndro; in other words, the suling is almost never used to accompany saléndro songs, but the rebab is used instead (van Zanten 1989:81). In a manner very much like the suling player, the rebab player precedes the first pitch of every vocal line, following in heterophony to the end of the line. In panambih songs, the rebab cues the entrance of the vocalist and also must improvise during the gelenyu before and between verses. At the beginnings and ends of phrases, the rebab is most likely to perform ornaments that are idiosyncratic to the rebab (Suanda, personal communication, 1990).

During performances in saléndro, the majority of the free-rhythm songs performed are of the rarancagan style, but occasionally songs may be borrowed from the kakawén repertoire. This style is not discussed in the section on stylistic divisions, because it does not officially belong to tembang Sunda; rather, it is a small group of songs that are normally part of the wayang golék song repertoire (see Sukanda 1983:32–33; also Robson 1983 on Javanese *kakawin*). Some of the most commonly performed kakawén songs are "Toya Mijil," "Sebrakan" and "Kayu Agung" (van Zanten 1989:28). Most kakawén songs used in tembang Sunda are in free rhythm and sound similar to those of the rarancagan style; however, they are accompanied by the rebab and kacapi, whereas the rarancagan songs in saléndro are only accompanied by the kacapi. The resulting difference in texture between saléndro songs in free rhythm and sorog or pélog songs in free rhythm is marked; the sparseness of the sound (due to a lack not only of a suling, but even a substitute for a suling) creates a very different feeling for the participants.

As is the case with each of the instruments associated with tembang Sunda, the rebab has its own set of terminology for ornamentation, and its own style of accompanying songs. The very best rebab players like the late Dacép Eddy are able to duplicate the frequency of the vocalist's vibrato as they follow the melodic line. In addition to producing several types of vibrato, the rebab player also imitates the ornaments of the vocalist. For example, if the vocalist uses a slight upward turn (*buntut*) at the end of a phrase, the rebab player is likely to follow. In panambih songs, the rebab sometimes plays both strings at once as he approaches a structural point (such as a go'ong or jenglong pitch) in the cycle of the song, but only if the pitch of the structural point is barang (pitch 1 in the Sundanese cipher notation). This technique is usually only used during a gelenyu or instrumental interlude because it may throw the vocalist off or be too distracting. The glissando ornament is a prominent feature of rebab technique as well as suling technique.

The rebab is only occasionally used in tembang Sunda performances, and rebab players find many more opportunities for employment in gamelan ensembles, commanding higher pay than the smaller tembang Sunda ensemble. Furthermore, the rebab players believed to be compatible with tembang Sunda musicians are comparatively few. When a rebab player is hired for a performance, he only plays as much and is only paid as much as the rincik player, and therefore receives far less money than what he could get at a gamelan or wayang performance. The financial incentive for rebab players in tembang Sunda is minimal. Because they usually play only during panambih, rebab players spend many of their performances simply waiting to play. Some rebab players find a practical solution to this problem by playing the rincik during the pélog and sorog sections of the performance, then switching to rebab for saléndro; at this point, the suling player switches to rincik. This combination is also a happy solution for the sponsor of the group, who needs to hire only three musicians: a kacapi player, a suling/rincik player, and a rebab/rincik player. Because of the rarity of saléndro in most urban performances, the rebab is gradually fading from the urban tembang Sunda scene. Although it is unlikely that use of the rebab in this genre will cease altogether (because it is still needed for tembang Sunda competitions and all performances in the traditional style), it only rarely appears and is not expected to take greater prominence in tembang Sunda (Komariah, personal communication, 1989).

THE *SUARA*, OR VOICE

Sundanese music has many different vocal styles, some of which have been described in Chapter 2. The techniques used for the style of tembang Sunda are considered very difficult and many people who sing tembang Sunda are not able to produce all the vocal ornaments required for an appropriate performance. Furthermore, although most tembang Sunda instrumentalists understand many aspects of vocal technique, they are not always able to produce the ornaments themselves and do not have a unified terminology. The lack of a unified terminology occurs all over Sunda, not just in tembang Sunda; however, when instrumentalists discuss vocal ornaments they often use terms that are applicable only to the instruments, not to the voice.

I have continually asserted that tembang Sunda (especially the vocal aspect of it) is associated with the aristocracy and its descendants through the process of signification. Some of the most famous singers of today use their aristocratic last names with pride, in spite of the official government discouragement of the use of titles and class differences. In the last several decades, however, many singers have risen in importance whose origins are relatively humble. Some of these singers have been able to do so by marrying a member of the aristocracy (sometimes as a second wife) and thereby at least partially assuming their husband's status level. Others have risen through the quality of their voice, their popularity on cassettes, or their connections.

The very existence of non-kinship-based connections in Bandung is a major change in the process of attaining musical prestige for tembang Sunda musicians. By studying with the right person, a singer with talent can in fact attach him/herself to that teacher and to the teacher's prestige and aristocratic position, thereby becoming a peripheral member of the aristocracy. Many young singers choose this route of attachment to a famous teacher to move upward through the ranks of tembang Sunda singers, until they themselves have achieved enough status as a singer to make it on their own. It is accurate to say that the singers with little talent and good connections do not really make it in tembang Sunda, unlike in many vocal genres in the West. A singer of this type may make a recording or even several recordings, depending on who he or she is connected with, but without the validating title of *juara* (first-, second-, or third-place winner, or even runner-up) from one of the tembang Sunda contests, it is difficult to become a successful (active, recording, professional) tembang Sunda vocalist in Bandung or any of the smaller Sundanese cities.

It is frequently said that the old teachers of tembang Sunda used to be extremely stingy (*pedit*) with how many songs they taught, and that nowadays teachers have to lure students in. Several teachers expressed the frustration that none of their children showed any interest whatsoever in tembang Sunda, nor did any of their younger relatives. The greatest joy experienced by a good teacher is the dedication of a good student. I was privileged to watch several outstanding teachers (Euis Komariah, Apung Wiratmadja, A. Tjitjah, Yayah Rochaeti Dachlan, and Enah Sukaenah, among others) bestow some of the secrets of tembang Sunda on their students.

The deepest secrets of tembang Sunda lie in the proper performance of vocal ornaments; however, other factors are taken into consideration as well. For example, it is widely believed that the best singers have undergone (or are always undergoing) some kind of serious emotional hardship in their lives. One singer at the radio station is said to have picked a fight with her husband before each broadcast so that she would sing with tears running down her cheeks (Wiratmadja, personal communication, 1989). Other singers are deeply admired for their ability to express the meaning of the song (*pangjiwaan lagu*) and the hardship of their lives (as someone's second wife, or as an abandoned mother of three) is taken into account in this admiration of their expressional ability. It is also very important to dress well, act appropriately onstage and look good while singing; all of these aspects of performance practice are taught to young singers.

Vocal ornamentation is the most important aspect of good tembang Sunda performance practice. Although other factors such as vocal timbre, depth of expression of the songs, physical appearance, and articulation are also judged to be very important (and are listed for the juries to judge in tembang Sunda competitions), it is the proper execution of vocal ornaments that will win a singer the most praise. Van Zanten quotes musicians in their description of ornamentation as "the flower of tembang Sunda" (van Zanten 1989:161). With their characteristically sharp memory for other musicians' styles, tembang Sunda musicians will discuss the various ways in which a particular ornament can be executed, giving myriad examples from dozens of songs. Singers are known for their ability to perform particular ornaments, and an ornament may be identified as "belonging" to a singer even though everyone else knows how to do it as well. The variation of ornaments between singers is also judged to be an important aspect of individual style, another topic that is thoroughly discussed by musicians.

Tembang Sunda vocal ornamentation breaks down into several large categories. These categories are types of vibrato, types of vocal breaks, types of pressure, and other ornaments (such as melismas and mordents) that do not fall into one of these groups. Van Zanten (1989:167–170) was able to admirably transcribe the different vibrato types and other ornaments through the use of computer-aided analysis that not only recorded pitch frequency but intensity; this has provided him with an extremely accurate

EXAMPLE 8.18 Jenghak ornament in the voice

Su - mo - lon - do ka - nu peng-kuh

rendering of the ornaments. I have chosen to describe here the ornament types verbally and to recommend that the reader closely listen to a recording of tembang Sunda performance to fully grasp the spectrum of ornaments utilized by the vocalists (see Discography). As is the case with kacapi, suling, and rebab performance practice, vocal ornaments break down further into individual types.

The term *reureueus* is sometimes used by instrumentalists to mean ornamentation in general, but it is used by vocalists to describe a heavy vibrato. This heavy vibrato lies in the center of the continuum, flanked on either side by the other characteristic types of vibrato known as cacag (a very strong, choppy vibrato) and vibra, quite similar to a tremolo. Of the three, cacag (from the verb "to chop") is the strongest and most dramatic—to the point that it "chops" the note into short, loud bursts. The musical examples have the cacag ornament as a series of eighth notes separated by apostrophes to indicate the gaps between them (see Example 8.18). Reureueus is slightly less strong and does not use a "chopping" sound, but is very wide and fairly slow, to the point that it is sometimes difficult to identify the exact pitch being performed. Vibra is a very slight vibrato, quite close to a tremolo, and is usually sung at the ends of phrases. It is notated by a slightly wavy line. The farthest opposite end from cacag of the vibrato continuum is a perfectly straight tone, described as *polos*. A straight tone is just as important in the expression of a song as is a vibrato, and singers must cultivate that *polos* tone as carefully as they do the other ornaments.

A second technical skill is the vocal break, a temporary and deliberate manipulation of the point at which the voice breaks into falsetto (discussed briefly in Chapter 2, in reference to older recordings). Instead of smoothing over the breaking point (which happens as well), the singer allows the voice to break upward for only a fraction of a second on a controlled, very breathy pitch as high as a major third above the sung pitch. The three ornaments that use this technique are called *jenghak, renghik,* and *lipat*. Jenghak and renghik are upward vocal breaks, and lipat is a downward vocal break. The jenghak ornament occurs in the middle of a phrase and is almost always preceded by either a straight tone or a reureueus ornament, and followed by a cacag ornament. The example of jenghak is from the song "Sumolondo," occurring on the second syllable of the word *pengkuh*. The jenghak is indicated in Example 8.18 with the graphic symbol of an upside-down v.

The renghik ornament uses the same technique as jenghak, except that it occurs at the ends of phrases and is supposed to land as an almost-silent upper tone, as much as a major third higher than the fundamental pitch of the song. The example of renghik is from the song "Polos," occurring on

EXAMPLE 8.19 Renghik ornament in the voice

Da - un - na

EXAMPLE 8.20 Lipat ornament in the voice

Pa - mi - dang - an   Pa - ja - ja   -   ran

EXAMPLE 8.21 Sorolok ornament in the voice

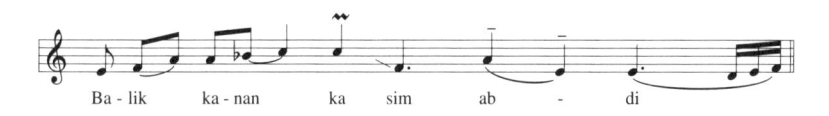

Ba - lik   ka - nan   ka   sim   ab   -   di

the final syllable of the word *daunna* (Example 8.19) The ornament is indicated with a small apostrophe after the final pitch.

The lipat ornament (from the word "to fold") is another type of vocal break and is used just after a vibra or tremolo ornament has begun, and may be conceived of as a simple, single fold in the pitch. The pitch drops for a fraction of a second to an indeterminate pitch (as much as a major third below), then returns instantly to the original pitch and continues the vibra. The example of lipat is from the song "Mupu Kembang," occurring on the last syllable of the word Pajajaran (Example 8.20) The vibra within which the lipat ornament occurs is notated simply by a symbol above the appropriate pitch. The lipat is notated as a grace note in parentheses.

The third type of vocal ornament group has to do with pressure (*tekanan* or *ipiskandel*), that is achieved through the use of the diaphragm. Pressure is one of the most important types of vocal techniques and is believed to make a boring song much more interesting for the listeners. It is also the very hardest of the ornaments to produce. There are several types of pressure-related ornaments, among them *sorolok*, *beubeutan*, and *baledog*. Sorolok, the first type, describes a very brief, tonally unstable vibrato that neither relies on much pressure from the diaphragm nor is loud in dynamics. Its pitch is extremely difficult to control because its pressure fairly light, and it sounds similar to the puruluk ornament on the suling: like a quick oscillation or flutter of sound. The example of sorolok (Example 8.21) is from the song "Ligar" and occurs on the word *ka*. Although pressure is difficult to indicate, the ornament is highlighted below by a jagged line above the second pitch c.

Beubeutan can be considered a generic term for weight or pressure. When used as an ornament, beubeutan stresses a particular pitch and sets it apart from the others. It is caused by an acute but very brief tensing of the diaphragm, and when an informed audience knows that a beubeutan

EXAMPLE 8.22 Spiral ornament in the voice

A - sih sa - nes pu - pu   la - san

EXAMPLE 8.23 Geregel ornament in the voice

Men - ding ba - la   ka ti pa   yun

EXAMPLE 8.24 Lengkung ornament in the voice

geu - ning

ornament is coming, the members of the audience tense up themselves, frowning until the appropriate moment, then acting as if they have been released, sighing and smiling afterward. Beubeutan does not always occur on the highest pitch, but its emphasis of a high pitch is its most characteristic tendency. It is often followed by a lipat ornament when it is at approximately the same pitch level as the pitches before and after it. Baledog is a strongly emphasized straight tone that is used to highlight a beubeutan immediately following it. It is described as a slingshot from which the next ornament is thrown, and it emphasizes the strength and pressure in the following beubeutan by being performed without a vibrato at all.

In addition to these three types of ornaments, tembang Sunda vocal practice also uses mordents, slides, and grace notes. Of the mordents, two are named *spiral* and *geregel*. The spiral ornament is always mentioned in connection with jejemplangan songs, because the spiral is one of the main vocal traits in jejemplangan. It is named thus because its pitches encircle a single central note several times, as in a spiral. The example of the spiral ornament (Example 8.22) is from the song "Jemplang Panganten," on the second syllable of the word *pupulasan*.

The geregel ornament is used repeatedly in every style of tembang Sunda. It is a descending mordent that may go through several cycles of descent in rapid succession before reaching the lowest pitch. The example of geregel (as a single descending mordent) is from the song "Balaka" and occurs on the second syllable of the word *balaka* (Example 8.23).

Lengkung (also known as *léotan*) is a slide. This ornament usually occurs from an upper pitch to a lower pitch in the voice but, when it is played on a suling, it may arrive at the primary pitch from below. It is used sparingly in modern tembang Sunda; however, evidence from earlier tembang Sunda recordings indicates that it was formerly used much more frequently than it is now. One reason for modern tembang Sunda vocalists to avoid it is that this ornament is used quite often in kawih-style singing, and tembang Sunda vocalists tend to avoid sounding as if they bear any influence from kawih. The example of lengkung (Example 8.24) is from the narangtang to the song "Jemplang Panganten," and occurs on the first syllable of the word *geuning*.

The word *buntut* simply means "tail." A buntut ornament is a short upturn (like a cat's tail) of a half-step at the end of a long held note. Buntut is always used with a vibra tremolo, and is approached by a slight dip in pitch before passing the primary tone to the finale tone. Buntut is not always used at the end of every phrase; rather, it is considered a type of spice to be used sparingly.

These examples of vocal ornaments are barely representative of all the creative features of tembang Sunda vocal performance practice. In the greater context of this chapter, the study of ornamentation is only one of the many aspects of musical performance practice in tembang Sunda that is actively discussed among the musicians. The perception of the instruments as well as the construction, maintenance, and tuning of the instruments are all thoroughly brought into consideration in many tembang Sunda discussions, and the songs themselves are picked apart and analyzed line by line, by the singers and instrumentalists both.

In these two chapters on the music of tembang Sunda, I have attempted not only to provide an overview of the genre but also to demonstrate how certain musical features have been promoted and others discouraged as a result of the presence of tembang Sunda in an urban environment. Depending on the performance context, the musicians must choose the appropriate styles, songs, and tuning systems in order to conform to what is believed to be suitable to the situation. Their choices reflect the degree to which they are aware of the many different contexts for tembang Sunda performance, as well as the wide variety of people who now come into contact with the music in the urban setting. Whereas in the traditional setting of the informed, participating audience, the musicians and singers had a much broader range of styles, tunings, and songs to choose from, modern performances must be tailored to fit the audience and the paying host. The final two chapters of this book will examine the deeper meaning of the music, particularly in its twenty-first-century urban context.

IV

THE MEANING OF TEMBANG SUNDA

This final section merges the history and context of tembang Sunda performance practice with the aristocratic Sundanese view of their world. Although not all Sundanese feel the same way about where they live, their history, or their own culture, this section is intended to present a general picture of where tembang Sunda stands in the minds of those who perform and listen to it. I have emphasized the societal division between the urban descendants of the Sundanese aristocracy and the urban middle class who are trying very much to be modern. In some ways, tembang Sunda is the antithesis of everything that it means to be modern in Sunda. By championing the music that is perceived to represent the feudal times, the aristocratic Sundanese reinforce their own heritage and their claim to a spiritual past extending beyond the remote historical fact of Pajajaran and eighteenth- and nineteenth-century feudal life. By continuing to claim the music as their own, the modern aristocrats also claim their higher social position in relation to the *rakyat*, or common people. Indeed, the focus on a local tradition may be seen as at least a surface-level reaction against modernism or globalization (cf. Hall 1997:33).

In spite of the governmental encouragement of relative equality, class divisions in Sundanese society are still strong and their reinforcement through musical means is only one of the subtle ways by which the aristocracy can maintain the status quo. Immanuel Wallerstein points out that "culture has always been a weapon of the powerful" (1997:99), by which he means that the powerful have a way of using artifacts of culture to hang onto their power. The lower strata of society generally feel less positively about the premodern era, because the very events that led to the development of modern Indonesia (and destroyed the colonial way of life for the aristocracy) enabled the lower classes to move upward. Claiming to enjoy tembang Sunda manifests and maintains the difference between oneself and the lower classes, whose music of choice may be pop Sunda, wayang, international pop music, or Indian-influenced dangdut. This statement cannot rest without the caveat, however, that instrumentalists and singers transcend class distinctions. The wholesale claim of tembang Sunda being emblematic of the aristocratic past depends more on the people who listen than those who provide the sounds.

When a type of music is repeatedly said to function as an identifying emblem for a category of people, the statement begins to sound like a universal claim (see Turino 1989:2). Many publications in the ethnomusicological literature have dealt with the issue of regional identity and music; for Central Javanese gamelan, for example, see Sutton's "Change and Ambiguity: Gamelan Style and Regional Identity in Yogyakarta" (1984). In tembang Sunda, the people who identify with the genre most strongly are not only the aristocracy but also those musicians who accompany the singing and are attached to the aristocracy through the formation and maintenance of lingkung seni, or music groups. Some modern aristocrats claim to enjoy tembang Sunda but only listen to it when they have to—pretending to enjoy it but revealing one way or another that they neither enjoy nor understand it—and then only for its political uses. Others truly feel that tembang Sunda is the only appropriate cultural expression of their collective Sundanese soul. The concept of the self as part of a group identity is strongly linked to "public and group opinions about the past" (Appadurai 1996:146), and not necessarily to the individual psyche.

The expression of individual and collective identity through musical behavior has been well examined over the last few decades. In his 1982 work, *Sound and Sentiment: Birds, Weeping, Poetics, and Song in Kaluli Expression*, Steven Feld demonstrates the control with which the Kaluli manipulate social situations through musical performance. According to Feld, the deliberate manipulation of their own metaphors enables the Kaluli of Papua New Guinea to create a type of sonic atmosphere intended to cause a reaction in the listener (Feld 1982: 220). Studies of this type date from the earliest works on "nationalist music" in the nineteenth century, continued through the twentieth century to the work of Alan Merriam in the 1960s, and in the work of others since then. In the case of the Sundanese and tembang Sunda, the music speaks most eloquently to those who identify with it personally. Someone who personally identifies with tembang Sunda does not have to be descended from the aristocracy or even a musician. It is usually someone who feels himself to be Sundanese before any other group (in other words, Sundanese first, Indonesian second), however, and who has a deep-seated conviction that the Sundanese past is a preferred direction toward which one should face.

The reality of someone's economic situation does not necessarily dictate the state of that person's spiritual orientation. If someone lives in Bandung from economic necessity, it does not automatically follow that he is a modern, "developed" (Indo.: *maju*), forward-looking and progressive person in an emerging nation. On the contrary, many people in Bandung long for the village and (privately) wish for the disappearance of all the features that have arrived as a result of urbanization: noisy trucks, pollution, vices such as alcoholism among the urban youth, serious crime, and endless dust. This sentiment is usually expressed as a private wish among friends, because rebelling against urbanization (or even seriously talking about "doing something" to prevent the gradual paving over of the rice fields) goes against the national policy of development and is a risky viewpoint to express in public.

Bandung is not so much a particularly *Sundanese* city as it is a typical administrative Indonesian city that happens to have been used by the Sundanese for their own economic needs. In other words, rather than explicitly expressing Sundanese identity, the city is used as a medium through which Sundanese identity may be expressed. It is up to individual post-Independence musical networks to carve out forms of cultural discourse that speak to the needs of Bandung's diverse population. Tembang Sunda happens to speak to the needs of a particular category of that population, and it also serves the appropriate political purposes for people in power. As a part of developing a twenty-first-century local identity—a movement that Appadurai (1996) refers to as "culturalism"—tembang Sunda has a continuing role to play on several levels of Sundanese life.

9

A Name Is All That Remains

Pajajaran was a Sundanese Hindu kingdom that thrived for almost 250 years, from 1333 to 1579. The kingdom is still widely discussed among tembang Sunda musicians as a particular place to which Prabu Siliwangi (Pajajaran's final king) went when he disappeared.[1] Prabu Siliwangi represents the Sundanese ancestors as the most important one of all; he is the very embodiment of ancestry (Rikin 1973:72). In fact, many Sundanese aristocrats claim to be direct descendants of Prabu Siliwangi (Sutaarga 1965:8). If Pajajaran is home to Prabu Siliwangi, it is home to all the ancestors. Pajajaran is often referred to as the final destination of the aristocracy after death, although such discussions are often clothed in language that also allows for the Muslim trial by fire. Pajajaran is spoken of with reverence, longing, and confidence in the knowledge of a past Sundanese "Golden Era." In his monograph on pantun stories, Andrew Weintraub describes Pajajaran and Prabu Siliwangi as symbolizing "the apotheosis of Sundanese self-rule" (Weintraub 1991:ii). Pajajaran is itself a collective term for an entire constellation of ideas surrounding identity, nostalgia, lost glory, ancestry, spirituality, and pastoral imagery. Located within the larger highland region of Priangan ("abode of the gods"), Pajajaran links closely with modern Sundanese thought about the past.[2] This chapter comprises an examination of Pajajaran's importance in the context of the early twenty-first century, and its representation in the tembang Sunda repertoire.

PAJAJARAN REVISITED

Current Indonesian standards of education call for only national history to be taught in the elementary and middle schools, and the teaching of regional history is left to the elders of each community. Among the upper classes (including the children of those who might be part of the tembang Sunda community), college-level history is generally avoided in favor of income-generating careers in technology, engineering, or medical professions. As a result, few young Sundanese hear anything that might be construed as an "official" (or even recognizable) history of Sundanese culture.

Pajajaran assumes a crucial place in the minds of the Sundanese practitioners of tembang Sunda, yet almost no one seems to know when it existed or many of its details. When asked about probable dates for Pajajaran, several dozen musicians and audience members offered answers ranging from "thousands of years ago" to "just before the Dutch came" to "just before the Dutch left." Yet (and I have Henry Spiller to thank for this observation), it is not the lack of understanding itself that is responsible for inflated views on Pajajaran, but the lack of importance ascribed to historical accuracy that has led to these views. Whether anyone pays attention to the actual dates or not, all respondents point to Pajajaran as being located in a rather generic *zaman dulu* ("olden days") as opposed to *zaman edan* ("crazy time"): the present. In response to questions about the Hindu nature of Pajajaran, several instrumentalists insisted that everyone in Pajajaran was a "good Muslim," and one musician said that all the ancestors converted to Islam after they died.

In conjunction with the apparent lack of common factual knowledge about Pajajaran, nearly everyone not connected with tembang Sunda understands and comments on the connection between the music and the kingdom. For example, whenever I mentioned my object of study to a Sundanese person, the most frequent response would be to dramatically sing a short phrase (*"Pajajaran kari ngaran"*—"A name is all that remains of Pajajaran") from the song "Papatet" (discussed below), to vaguely mention something about *dunia Pajajaran* ("the world of Pajajaran"), or to joke about contacting the ancestors through the tiger spirits "that are all around us." These speakers included a *becak* (pedicab) driver, a policeman, a waitress, a *dalang* (puppeteer), a graphic designer, a batik maker, a Chinese store owner, and various sellers at the local market. Their casual (and often bemused) references either to "Papatet" or to Pajajaran led me to a deeper investigation of the links between the two, and to the recognition that tembang Sunda itself serves as a source of education about Pajajaran.

In his dissertation on wayang golek, Andrew Weintraub argues that "culture in Indonesia emerges as a possible means for people to secure some vestige of control over public life. In the absence of direct political representation, people can still articulate a will separate from the state by participating in the collective process of defining the 'nation,' as these processes coincide with the realm of culture" (Weintraub 1997:4). In tembang Sunda circles, a certain right way of living is asserted by its practitioners, who maintain their sense of authority and power through direct performance of the music and the choice of lyrics. Social constructions of appropriate behavior become represented through an assertion of what "old Sunda" was like. In perpetuating a genre that highlights the feudal era, tembang Sunda performers repeatedly establish and associate power with culture, culture with feudalism, and feudalism with societal divisions. In order to attain social power properly, one should be born to the aristocracy and rise through the ranks of the most aristocratic performance genre in the region.[3]

If an amalgamation of the Pajajaran and colonial eras has come to represent "old Sunda" to the populace, then it is logical that some of the colonial patterns of social order and political representation should come to represent Pajajaran.[4] Lyrics are peppered with honorific words (*juragan* and *raden* both convey honor on the addressee), and continually reestablish a sense of presence in the colonial or older past. Performers dressed in Sundanese formal wear (which is itself historically derived from Javanese formal wear) imitate a popular image of the nineteenth-century aristocracy; this formal wear is also worn by any female attending an event at which tembang Sunda is likely to be performed (such as a wedding or other life-cycle ritual). As John Pemberton points out, the development of such images helps to further establish a sense of regional colonial-era history and a collective image of the area (Pemberton 1994:24). At nearly any formalized performance of tembang Sunda at which outsiders are present (as opposed to the insiders-only malam tembang Sunda or panglawungan, discussed in Chapter 3), the hierarchy and the representation of that hierarchy takes precedence over the music, the event being celebrated, or the actual parties involved.

> Objects with patina [just the right gloss—an implication of time-honored rightful ownership and use] are perpetual reminders of the passage of time as a double-edged sword, which credentials the "right" people, just as it threatens the way they lived. Whenever aristocratic lifestyles are threatened, patina acquires a double meaning, indexing both the special status of its owner and the owner's special relationship to a way of life that is no longer available. (Appadurai 1996:76)

In the case of tembang Sunda, all of the trappings of performance wear, instrumentation, and highly specialized vocal production create just the right sort of patina with the intent of conveying that richness and grandeur on all auditors. For those who do not necessarily dwell within the arena of privilege, the sound of the ensemble is a subtle reminder not only of a collective Sundanese past (in the form of Pajajaran), but also of a heritage to which they do not directly belong.

THE SONG "PAPATET" AS A SUMMATIVE WORK

Many singers claim that "Papatet" is usually the first song fledgling vocalists work on when they begin to study tembang Sunda, although it is more genuinely the case that singers and musicians usually begin with easier songs first, especially those of the panambih style.[5] "Papatet" actually marks the first level that singers strive for when they become serious about studying tembang Sunda. It is believed that once a singer has accomplished a very good rendition of "Papatet," he or she will have minimal difficulty in learning other songs of the repertoire (Sukarma, personal communication, 1987).

Benjamin Brinner discusses the concept of learning a benchmark piece such as "Papatet" in his book, *Knowing Music, Making Music: Javanese Gamelan and the Theory of Music Competence and Interaction* (1995). In focusing on competence generally, he asserts that:

> Since musical competence encompasses all the types of knowledge and skills that a musician may need, it is an organic rendering of the 'systematics' of a musical tradition—the relationships between the things that are known. Grappling with the defining characteristics of a given competence should lead to an understanding of the inner workings of that musical tradition. (Brinner 1995:3)

Brinner notes that musical communities tend to look toward a specific piece, instrument, playing technique or other illustrative point that encapsulates every aspect of what a performer must know in order to be deemed competent. For the Sundanese who play and listen to tembang Sunda, "Papatet" is the very piece that embodies this knowledge. This benchmark piece "implies mastery of all items in [its] class, or at least sufficient competence to master all such items" (Brinner 1995:128). For a young vocalist lacking the ability to perform "Papatet" to the satisfaction of an authority (either a teacher or the participants at a panglawungan), opportunities for further performance or advancement are unlikely.

What makes "Papatet" so essential as a determinant of competence? It contains important and difficult vocal ornaments, all of which are contained in other songs. It lacks some of the hardest ornaments (such as the spiral of the jejemplangan songs), but is thick with *tekanan*—pressure in the voice. It must be performed with confidence and considerable vocal power, and a value-laden line is drawn between the young singer who lays the pressure on thick but lacks the emotional maturity to truly invoke the ancestors, and the older singer who is already perceived to have the blessing of the ancestors. The singer who has not simply picked up the basics of technique, but who has truly absorbed the soul of the song—demonstrated pangjiwaan— is at liberty to perform "Papatet" as the circumstance dictates.

The importance of "Papatet" reaches beyond sheer musical excellence in performance, however. In addition to containing most of the genre's important vocal ornaments and techniques, "Papatet" is also the key piece for explaining Pajajaran, its location, its personnel, and its disappearance. It essentially focuses attention on the key elements of Sundanese ancestry, and so magnifies for the listeners the importance of their historical and ancestral identity. Therefore, it is the combination of the two factors of musical excellence and cultural exegesis that make "Papatet" an important piece not only for aspiring singers searching for musical competence but also for audience members listening for elements of what makes them Sundanese.

Many of the most traditional performances of tembang Sunda begin in pélog mode with "Papatet" unless a lagu rajah is used, in which case "Papatet" is the first song to be performed after the lagu rajah. Prior to the first line of "Papatet" or any other papantunan song, however, the singer must perform the narangtang, or bridge, to the song. Both songs in papantunan and in jejemplangan styles must use a narangtang for a stylistically correct performance in the pélog tuning. Songs in sorog and saléndro never use a narangtang; therefore, this feature is limited to songs in pélog, and only those of the papantunan and jejemplangan styles. Rukruk Rukmana likened the concept of narangtang to the Arabic prayer used before beginning a journey, eating, or any important activity: *Bismi allāhi al-rahmāni al-rahīm*. Like the prayer, a narangtang is used to start a song off properly. Songs within papantunan and jejemplangan styles each use a different narangtang.

The narangtang to open "Papatet" is usually *Daweung ménak Pajajaran*, "Now we will consider the noblemen of Pajajaran." To the Sundanese audience, this one statement is intended not only to transport them back to the time of Pajajaran but also to the emotional space associated with that time. Although *Daweung ménak Pajajaran* is most commonly used, other lyrics may be substituted which use the exact same pitches, such as *Sumangga urang ngawitan* ("Let us begin at the very beginning") or *Gusti, nadapitulung* ("Lord, help me"). The narangtang is also used before the panambih at the end of each set in the pélog tuning: "If we see the *tembang Sunda* evening as a parallel of a ritual sequence, this beginning may be seen as a transition from the normal, social time to the timelessness of music, in which people communicate with the metaphysical world" (van Zanten 1989: 28).

Henry Spiller (personal communication, 1999) suggests that *Daweung ménak Pajajaran* itself may serve as a powerful link to the ancestors: the word *daweung* ("now we will consider") is centered in the present, *ménak* ("noblemen") refers to the people connecting us with Pajajaran, and *Pajajaran* is the historical time period we seek. By the end of the narangtang, we have left the twenty-first century and have slipped back across the bridge of time to the sixteenth century (or earlier). Without this essential bridge, the connection to the ancestors is incomplete and any subsequent performance of "Papatet" lacks spiritual weight.

Similarly, a brief analysis of the kacapi patterns used to accompany *Daweung ménak Pajajaran* reveals the player beginning at a high pitch, close to the body, and executing a series of pasieup-style runs that move from a high pitch 2 (a relatively unstable pitch from which attention is quickly

EXAMPLE 9.1 Daweung ménak Pajajaran

shifted) away from the player's body to a low, grounded pitch 5 (the most frequently used closing pitch for papantunan songs in tembang Sunda).[6] If pitch 5 often functions as a sort of "home" or closing pitch for these types of songs, the kacapi runs from high 2 to low 5 may appropriately symbolize the shift in *Daweung ménak Pajajaran* from the present "crazy time" (zaman edan) to the more stable, calm past represented by Pajajaran. Furthermore, the rather more modern pasieup accompaniment takes us from the present to the past by reaching firm closure in standard papantunan style on the open fifth at the end of the phrase (pitch 5 on the bottom and pitch 2 played at a perfect fifth above).

The vocal performance of *Daweung ménak Pajajaran* echoes the shift from instability in the present to strength in the past as well. In the transcription of the line (see Example 9.1), the vocalist begins the word daweung on a sorog note entirely outside of pélog; the pitch cannot be played on the kacapi. The rest of daweung is then sung with a set of ornaments circling around pitch 2, stopping on pitch 2 with the word *ménak*. Resolution begins to take place as the vocal line begins the word *Pajajaran*—it shifts from pitch 2 to a pause on a very strong 3 at the final syllable, then continues in a rapid descent to pitch 5 at the same time the kacapi reaches 5. The resolution is very powerful for listeners who are following closely; it is even visible in body language. The most avid listeners become physically tense at the beginning of the phrase, relaxing and smiling when the vocalist, kacapi, and suling players reach pitch 5. As Henry Spiller notes, "It [the musical phrase] uses various emblems of the present (in text, modality, accompaniment, and melodic motion) to tie itself first to the present, and then it drags these things back to the past, and those of us listening/singing/playing along with it" (Spiller, personal communication, 1999).

Although the lyrics of "Papatet" are flexible, most singers learn and perform lyrics that summarize an important historical situation, illustrate some aspect of Sundanese cosmology, or describe a feature of nature. The following lyrics provide an example of all three: an explanation of what has become of Pajajaran, together with an implication that Pajajaran is irretrievable. As in many verses of "Papatet," place-names form a very important part of the song.

"Papatet" (Sundanese)	"Papatet" (English)
Pajajaran kari ngaran	A name is all that remains of Pajajaran
Pangrango geus narik kolot	Pangrango has become old
Mandalawangi ngaleungit	Mandalawangi has disappeared
Ngaleungit ngajadi leuweung	Disappeared, become a forest

Nagara geus lawas pindah	The kingdom has long since moved
Saburakna Pajajaran	Now that Pajajaran has gone
Gunung Gumuruh sawung	Gumuruh mountain is so quiet
Geus tilem jeung nagarana.	All has disappeared with the kingdom.

The preceding example should be viewed as representative of the content of many songs in papantunan style. It is historical, describes several features of nature, and discusses Pajajaran, the kingdom that lies at the heart of tembang Sunda. These lyrics are important to the practitioners of tembang Sunda because it is the very "disappearance without a trace" of Pajajaran that has led to its current position as representative of all that the Sundanese lost when the kingdom of Pajajaran ended.

The following three verses of "Papatet" are cited directly with permission from Wim van Zanten's important work, *Sundanese Music in the Cianjuran Style* (van Zanten 1989:196–197). He quotes (and translates) from the notebooks of Uking Sukri and Néndén Asyani:[7]

Gunung Galunggung ka pungkur	Mount Galunggung lies behind us
Gunung Sumedang ka tunjang	Mount Sumedang extends before us
Talaga Sukawayana	As far as Lake Sukawayana
Rangkecik di tengah leuweung	A small frog lives in the midst of the forest
Ulah pundung ku disungkun	Don't be annoyed when treated unkindly
Ulah melang teu ditéang	Don't be anxious when no one visits you
Tarima raga wayahna	Reconcile yourself to it, resign yourself
Ngancik di nagara deungeun.	For you are living in a foreign country.
Gunung Puyuh ti béh kidul	Mount Puyuh forms the southern border
Gunung Salak ti béh wétan	Mount Salak forms the eastern border
Gunung Pangrango ngajogo	Mount Pangrango squats (in the center)
Tetengger nagara mana	Of which state do they form the borders?
Gunung Kendeng keur ngaheneng	Mount Kendeng stands quietly
Déngdék ngalér bahé ngétan	It leans to the north and falls to the east
Banguna galudra ngupuk	Like the mythical eagle that spreads its wings
Pangupukan Pajajaran.	Around the blessed territory of Pajajaran.
Gunung Gumuruh nu nangtung	Mount Gumuruh, standing there
Nangtung ngadeg karatonna	Is in fact a palace:
Dayeuh agung Pajajaran	The royal seat of Pajajaran
Ti jaman Ciung Wanara	Since the time of Ciung Wanara
Nagara turun tumurun	The state was later ruled by his heirs
Turunna nu jadi ratu	As kings his successors
Ciciréna anu kantun	The ruins that remain
Alun-alun séwu cengkal	Form an alun-alun of 3700 square meters.

I provide a transcription of one verse of "Papatet," because its musical features include a veritable catalogue of some of the essential vocal ornaments used in tembang Sunda. The kacapi player begins the performance

EXAMPLE 9.2   Musical transcription of "Papatet"

Pa - ja - ja - ran   ka - ri   nga - ran

Pang - rang - o   geus   na - ri   ko - lot

Man - da - la - wang - i   nga - leung - it

Nga - leung - it nga - ja - di   leu   weung

Na - ga - ra   geus la - was   pin - dah   sa - bu - rak - na   Pa - ja - ja - ran

Gu - nung   Gu - mu - ruh   su - wung   geus   ti - lem

Jeung   na - ga - ra

of "Papatet" by briefly executing a fast series of runs outlining the key features of the melody, then the singer enters with the narangtang ("Daweung ménak Pajajaran"). Finally, "Papatet" begins (Example 9.2).

Whether explaining what has happened to Pajajaran, as in the lyrics offered above, or in assuring the listener that they belong to a larger community than the one present, song lyrics convey considerable historical and cultural information. Robert Wessing notes that the lyrics of "Papatet" provide us with a map of Pajajaran (cf. Noorduyn and Teeuw 1999). Singers must be prepared to confront their ancestry and the noblemen of Pajajaran with great seriousness and strength of character, and it is this exact quality (coupled with the ability to exert tekanan, or vocal pressure) that marks a singer as being both mature and competent enough to face "Papatet."

The acquisition of the psychological competence necessary for the proper performance of "Papatet" and, therefore, the general readiness to appear publicly as a singer of tembang Sunda requires considerable practice, of course (but other features as well). The singer must become attached to a respected teacher; learning from a cassette (see Chapter 6, "Learning the Craft") is not an adequate substitute.[8] According to several musicians and vocalists (including Apung Wiratmadja, Rukruk Rukmana, and Gan-Gan Garmana, among others), the singer should have experienced some kind of direct hardship, particularly in the loss of a loved one through death or abandonment (which would build strength of character and the gravity necessary for correct performance). This standard compares well with Christine Yano's description of Japanese enka singers: "One of the most important aspects of image for an enka singer is that of a person who has endured hardship. Like the genre and particular songs (and its listeners), enka singers are supposed to be those who have learned the value of effort and perseverance through suffering" (Yano 1997:121). Lastly, looking physically aristocratic (pale skin, higher than average nose, clear complexion, refined movements) helps tremendously in the public perception of a singer as being suited toward performance of tembang Sunda in general, and "Papatet" in particular.[9]

The reception of "Papatet" by audience members at—for example—weddings or other performances outside the realm of malam tembang Sunda or panglawungan is not always positive. Its performance can result in guests leaving early or complaining loudly to each other about the feudal nature of the song and demanding more panambih or lighter love songs. On several occasions, singers made remarks about people who refused to listen to "Papatet"—or were seen walking out of a performance—with the assumption that anyone who left during "Papatet" was not of the proper ancestry to appreciate it.

PAJAJARAN AS HOME

The question remains: To what extent do the Sundanese musicians and vocalists consider Pajajaran to be a type of spiritual home?[10] What does a physical home mean in relation to Pajajaran, which is in the forest? In order to uncover parts of an answer, it is necessary to understand what a physical home might be like for an urbanite performer today. The average Bandung-based tembang Sunda vocalist lives in a housing development in a nicer area of town, with the typical urban set-up that includes two separate living rooms—one for guests, the other for insiders (Williams 1998b:74). Many vocalists (particularly if they happen to be female) are very comfortable hosting visitors and are careful to perpetuate the appearance of luxury. Male instrumentalists usually live in less luxurious quarters, often in the less well-to-do regions of town; hosting visitors can be an awkward affair, as the trappings of the aristocracy (brocade furniture coverings or fine teacups, for example) elude the meager salaries of most instrumentalists. In addition, male instrumentalists are limited—even within their own homes—to the public areas of the house in their hosting and general activities.[11]

Aside from yearly trips to see relatives in villages or other event-driven visits, most urban musicians do not appear to visit the villages often; yet, they speak in glowing terms of village life. In fact, their very livelihood depends on perpetuating an idealized image of village life linked strongly to an idealized Sundanese golden era.[12] The Sundanese word *wangsul* means "returning home," and it may be used either for returning home to one's house in the city, or returning to the village—and, therefore, a home more closely tied to one's ancestors. It also may be used as a reference to returning "home" to Pajajaran after death.[13]

Sundanese newlyweds often settle near or even inside the home of the first wife's family when they marry; the man assumes a new sense of home on marriage (Wessing 1997). What constitutes home is challenged by the tendency among some upper-class males to divorce and remarry several times, since Indonesian government officials are no longer allowed to have more than one wife at a time. A new house may be built for the second (or third, or fourth) wife, establishing an entirely different place to live in, for example, the outskirts of one of the larger Sundanese cities. For many Sundanese who live in Bandung or other large cities, a house in the city appears to be just one of several "homes."

Because the Sundanese spend the end of Ramadan[14] (and the Prophet's birthday as well) visiting relatives and tidying up the graves of the ancestors in villages, it might seem likely that the village is a second appropriate image for home. Yet, the discomfort of urban musicians with the life idealized in the song texts they perform is noticeable. The image of highland village life elicits fond exclamations, ideas of peacefulness and relaxation, cleanliness, coolness, and solitude (see, for example, Wessing 1994:63). For more than a few urban Sundanese musicians (and their listeners), however, the image is far removed from reality.

> Although much of this [array of pleasing and nostalgia-generating village sound] is now overpowered by the urban noise of secondhand motorcycles and transistor radios, an aura of hidden richness, nevertheless, lingers in village Java whether rendered acoustically or otherwise, the sense of an incomprehensible complexity concealed just beneath surface clichés of pastoral simplicity and tranquility. This sense of complexity at once attracts and threatens urban Javanese. (Pemberton 1994:237)

At the beginning of the twenty-first century, the village is a site of very difficult labor, minimum comforts, and (for some urbanites) unnerving proximity to nature. Villages vary from one Sundanese region to the next, but they are often most strongly characterized by a single road running through the center of the village, one or two shops, and rice fields in every direction. Most homes are built on a rather small scale (several rooms at most), and an inhabitant can usually see from one end of the village to the other. It is the exact openness and visibility of the villages that contrasts dramatically with the highland forests at the edges of the rice fields.

Tigers, Spirits, and the Primordial Forest

In discussing the song category of jejemplangan, several kacapi players eagerly described the feeling of fear and loneliness (*keueung*) associated with the forest (*leuweung*). In Chapter 7, I mentioned the renowned tembang Sunda master Apung Wiratmadja urging me to go out and fully experience the concept of keueung (fear, worry, uneasiness), saying "Kudu ka leuweung wae" ("You just have to go to the forest"). The forest provides one of the main inspirational points of tembang Sunda, and as a center of spirituality it offers an important locus of home. Indeed, the highland forest, with all its inherent spiritual dangers (darkness, loneliness, and spirits—including those of tigers), far more closely represents the relatively sparse development of Pajajaran-era Sunda than does a modern Sundanese village.[15]

> [Mountains are] a boundary between the civilized and predictable realm of the human and the unpredictable, and thus dangerous, realm of the non-human. This view of mountains as boundaries may include both the hills around a settled area, often forested and full of danger, and the central, cosmic mountain, which may be seen as the boundary between the natural sphere of humans and the supernatural regions of the sky and the underworld. [. . .] While the cosmic, central mountain is associated with kingship and the channeling of cosmic power into the realm, other mountains are often the place where important persons are buried. Such deceased focal figures often take on the role of generalized ancestors to the people living in the area. (Wessing 1988:44)

The forest is a wilder, more remote, lonely, and dangerous place that characterizes the Sundanese homeland. It is a forest in which other spirits dwell and in which the souls of the ancestors are not forgotten. The forest is a classic site for meditation and gathering of magic powers through a hero's quest (see Weintraub 1991, for excellent translations of pantun stories—some of which are set in Pajajaran—that illustrate such quests). The fourth line of "Papatet" itself explains that Pajajaran has gone back into the forest. The highland forest is the final resting place of the souls and the hereditary home of the Sundanese.[16] It is indeed a place to which King Prabu Siliwangi could have disappeared. As Pemberton points out, regarding Central Javanese pilgrimage sites, "The source for supernatural blessings customarily lies elsewhere, far from everyday life" (Pemberton 1994:269).

> In the practical consciousness of many human communities, [the Other] is often conceptualized ecologically as forest or wasteland, ocean or desert, swamp or river. Such ecological signs often mark boundaries that simultaneously signal the beginnings of nonhuman forces and categories or recognizably human but barbarian or demonic forces. Frequently, these contexts, against which neighborhoods are produced and figured, are at once seen as ecological, social, and cosmological terrains. (Appadurai 1996:183)

Prabu Siliwangi is said to have turned into a weretiger (*maung kajajaden* or *maung Pajajaran*) on his disappearance, although a gravesite does exist on Mount Gedogan (Wessing 1988:46). The change in form from human to tiger is not particularly surprising, considering that the spirits of the dead cross a considerable boundary to go "home." Tigers are mentioned only quietly, because it is believed that discussing them out loud will summon a weretiger and disaster could result (Rukmana, personal communication, 1989). The tigers, however, have a compelling presence among those who practice traditional forms of meditation or whose personal spiritual practices extend beyond the boundaries of Islam. These people note the role of tigers as connective spirits to the forest and to the ancestors.

Wessing discusses the importance of rice, in Southeast Asia, in determining one's humanity: that is, upon the consumption of rice, one becomes human (Wessing 1998:47). The cultivation of rice in the Sundanese countryside is far older than any written histories of the era; it certainly predates the Pajajaran kingdom. If rice is an essential determinant of humanity, and the cultivation of rice depends on the clearing away of the forest, then the highland forest represents an era of primordial existence. Several Sundanese stories (including, for example, *Sangkuriang* and *Lutung Kasarung*) include elaborate descriptions of relationships between animist spirits (in some cases, animal spirits) and humans, or at least a lifting of the veil that separates the spirit and the corporeal. Indonesians do not make such a strong distinction between man and animal as elsewhere in Southeast Asia (Wessing 1986:12), and when an animal is considered dangerous, such as the tiger (now close to extinction on Java, if not already extinct in the wild), the danger is not only physical but spiritual as well.

The forest is the spiritual home of the tiger. Ancestral tigers are reputed to maintain a tiger kingdom at Mount Kandana (possibly Kancana) in West Java, and to gather during Maulud (the Islamic month of the ancestors) in Pakuan at Bogor. Wessing points out the resemblance between this gathering and the concept of "coming home" to Pajajaran (Wessing 1986:32 and 99). He also cites a Mr. R. H. Suryalaga, who pointed out that "Sundanese who have passed away become 'residents of Pajajaran' in the form of tigers" (Wessing 1986:32). If the forest is "a place of savagery, antithetical to civilization" (Lombard 1974 as quoted in Wessing 1986:112), then a neatly cultivated rice field (and the long history of such cultivation) represents the ideal of civilized peacefulness. Because the forest is still so close to the edge of the rice fields, however, the dangers of primordial spirituality and behavior are still close at hand. Confronting these dangers through continually evoking the past and the forest in the performing arts is part of the Sundanese fascination with the otherworld in general, and the Sundanese past in particular.[17]

In Chapter 8, I noted that a suling with markings on it (brown spots or stripes—*loréng*) is indicative of special powers. Those powers are connected with tigers and panthers, two animals "thought to be incarnations of the forefathers, in particular of the legendary king Siliwangi" (van Zanten 1989:101). Pleyte (1905:149–162), Rosidi (1977:153–70) and others have noted that the Sundanese tell a legend about a tortoise who has a suling made from a tiger's bone. These important connections should not go unnoticed. When an instrument so central to the performance of tembang Sunda has clear ties to the ancestral tiger spirits, its presence adds even further to the network of linkages to the past and to the forest. Wessing points out that tigers are a manifestation of the "shaman spirit" and are able, as shamans, to cross the boundaries between civilization and the forest: "The prosperity of a society in Southeast Asia depends on the presence of a shaman who can deal with the ancestors. The shaman's soul is the vehicle for communication between the people and the divine, and it is the living shaman who must deal with these souls" (Wessing 1986:112).

When one of the vehicles for the tiger-shaman is the suling, it is no wonder that the sound of the suling is said to evoke powerful feelings of nostalgia, loneliness, and wa'as in its listeners.

The Elements of Keeping Cool

One of the biggest Sundanese complaints about modern urban life concerns the heat of the city. People speak longingly about the good old days when Bandung was *masih dingin* (still cool). Some musicians even recall the previous temperatures (in Celsius) of Bandung during the day and night, contrasting those with the temperatures of today. Bandung's location in the site of an ancient lakebed, coupled with the fact that it is surrounded by volcanoes and filled with factories and traffic, does indeed contribute to its heat. Yet, there is a sense of the "heat" of today referring to the troubles of urban living; the stress, noise, dust, crime, and high-speed lifestyle that characterizes life in downtown Bandung. The highland village, in contrast, is spoken of as being dingin (cool), and as being a refreshing place to recover from the heat of the city.[18] Having a quick temper (easily angered) is referred to as being hot-hearted; becoming calm is referred to as cooling one's heart. Returning to the highland village, which is itself a referent for the cooler past, becomes a way to return to a slightly *more* civilized state than that which is offered by the urban jungle.

The refinement of one's personal coolness (and calmness) of demeanor depends on how much one acts like an upper-class Sundanese man or woman. Appearing calm and cool in the face of adversity is a highly valued trait among the upper-class Sundanese, who try to differentiate their reputation among other Indonesian groups from one of raucous laughter and quick anger (associated with the Sundanese in general) to one of refinement.[19] It is no wonder that the cool image—as opposed to the reality—of village life is most appealing to those who are least likely to "go home" to the village.[20] Although the music of tembang Sunda is not of the village, it nonetheless evokes a semirural vision of home in urban performance practice.

To some urban Sundanese, the highland forest and the many mountain peaks in the Sundanese highlands represent an older form of Sundanese life. If the wilder regions of Sundanese territory, rather than the urban center of

Bandung, represent the pre-Islamic spiritual center of the region, then the urban inhabitants of Sunda are drawn between the two centers—spiritual and economic—and must continually walk the line in their daily lives. As will be seen in the next chapter, tembang Sunda is the intermediary between these two important centers; in keeping with the idea of "center as whole" (Anderson 1972), both centers may then stand for the whole of Sunda.

In view of such disparate issues as the lack of emphasis on accuracy in Sundanese history, the proper execution of "Papatet" by an appropriately prepared vocalist, the audience reception of tembang Sunda, and the image of the forest as the true final destination of departed souls, the confluence of the fourteenth and nineteenth centuries in the minds of tembang Sunda practitioners and casual audience members alike appears to remain constant. Joining the little that is known about historical Pajajaran with the nineteenth century colonial roots of tembang Sunda results in a richly romanticized tool for maintaining the status quo in the name of political, spiritual, and social gain. In the context of Sundanese culture at the beginning of the twenty-first century, highland Pajajaran remains one of the most important historical eras and a crucial reminder both of "old Sunda" and of "home" in the minds of those who listen to and perform tembang Sunda.

10

Connecting with the Ancestors

This chapter encompasses the task of connecting urban tembang Sunda performance practice with the rich heritage of the countryside that surrounds Bandung and the smaller cities. In attempting to draw up a cognitive map for the aristocratic Sundanese, I have found that one of the functions of tembang Sunda is that it acts as the webbing that unites these urbanites with their rural surroundings—not only in the essentially peasant-dwelling countryside but also in the primarily rural Sundanese past (cf. Christine Yano's discussion of enka imagery and its linkage of singers and listeners to Japan's rural past [1997:116]). In the establishment of this connection, the ménak-descended Sundanese are able to strengthen their personal networks, not only with each other but also with those who live neither in the city nor in the present: the ancestors, both real and illusory, who brought Sundanese aristocratic culture to the height of its strength and power.

The Sundanese descendants of the aristocracy are not necessarily those who are wealthy but, rather, those with multisyllabic aristocratic surnames rather than single-word names. These people are acknowledged on several different class levels as having a particular type of cultural power (more so than economic power). Although some aristocratic Sundanese also happen to be wealthy, this wealth is mostly a factor of their willingness to become involved in the Sundanese political arena or in the Chinese-dominated business scene than a factor of hereditary wealth. Many very wealthy Chinese-Indonesians make an effort to acquire certain Sundanese (and Javanese) *pusaka*, or hereditary objects, such as daggers, ivory, or special gamelan ensembles that are believed to contain spiritual power, though almost no ethnic Chinese practice tembang Sunda. The examples given by the aristocratic Sundanese themselves of the necessity of a connection between the urban performers and listeners of tembang Sunda and the rural "outside" demonstrate that the genre is an essential feature of this connection. Urban Sundanese musicians cross a type of spiritual boundary that allows them to keep in contact with nonurban aspects of their psyches. In order to cross that boundary, urban musicians use the intermediary of tembang Sunda.

Boundaries and borders are very important in Sunda and in other parts of Indonesia (Wessing 1988:47); however, I do not intend to imply that immediately on hearing tembang Sunda, in any context, an urban Sundanese musician is instantly (or automatically) transported outside of Bandung and into the collective Sundanese spiritual world of the rural past as it is represented by Pajajaran. On the contrary, the process is neither instant nor automatic. My intent here is to demonstrate that certain aspects of tembang Sunda performance can be activated by its performers and audience as a medium through which a spiritual connection can be established with the past. These aspects include the musical sound of the instruments and the voice performing in various styles, the visual impact of the ensemble, and the song lyrics. Although unequal in importance, each of these three aspects is a product of associating the genre with the rural past: "The Sundanese consider music, dance, and theatre to be the outer manifestations (*lahir*) of thought or inner life (*batin*). . . . The intention, the understanding and the power behind the sounds and movements are considered to be of equal or even greater importance [than technical skill or quality of sound]" (van Zanten 1997:41).

In this statement, van Zanten indicates the importance of pangjiwaan and offers an important clue about how the Sundanese hear music in a broader context. By focusing exclusively on the technicalities of the music, the Sundanese would then miss all of the extra sensations that come from experiencing the totality of the performance—including the talking, the sights, the extramusical sounds, and their own thoughts. This heightened awareness is precisely what allows the association of tembang Sunda with places, people, and events outside the mundane features of a performance.

KACAPI SYMBOLISM

One of the most important aspects of the kacapi is its symbolism in the minds of the Sundanese and other Indonesians. It is described as a boat and also as a woman (with all the necessary features from her hair to her body to her breasts). For the Sundanese, the boat shape evokes not only images of the sea, but also of Pajajaran. Several musicians (not just players of kacapi) described the instrument as the "boat that carries us to Pajajaran." One of the names used to describe the instrument—kacapi prahu—literally means "boat kacapi." Thomas Gibson notes that the boat is one of the oldest of the Austronesian cosmological arenas of ritual practice (2000:47). Although the kacapi was not always constructed in its now-characteristic boat shape, the urban Sundanese in some cases see it as one of their main symbolic links to the kingdom of Pajajaran.[1]

The relationship between the instrument and the player is often described as a marriage (see also van Zanten 1987:98–100). The concept of a marriage between the kacapi (viewed by players as female) and the male player is a powerful image with roots in Sundanese mythology. According to many Sundanese, the kacapi is a symbolic representation of Déwi Sri, the rice goddess, and Nyai Roro Kidul, the goddess of the sea to the south of Java. When a player is performing the music of tembang Sunda on the kacapi, he is physically "marrying" (*kawin*) or engaging in a physical relationship with the instrument, and the music created by the two of them (kacapi and man) is said to be the offspring of this relationship (Rukmana, personal communication, 1988). It will be seen, however, that the relationship itself can transcend the assigned gender of the instrument.

In addition to the manifestation or consummation of the marriage relationship between the player and the instrument in normal performance practice, kacapi teachers were once known to conduct a type of initiation ceremony known as *tawajuh*. According to van Zanten, this ceremony was usually conducted after the pupil had attained a satisfactory level of knowledge and proficiency (van Zanten 1987:60). I had the unexpected opportunity of witnessing this ceremony when I held a very small *hajat*, or ritual ceremony. People hold hajat in their homes for many reasons: as thanksgiving for having successfully completed a complicated task or project, to correct a difficult situation, to ensure good fortune on a journey, as part of a life-cycle ceremony such as a birth or circumcision, or to dedicate a new home. Some scholars describe the hajat ceremony by the term *selamatan*.

This particular hajat originally was planned because I had recently moved into a rented house and began to have trouble with the lights going on and off all the time. Having one's lights go out is not an unusual case in Indonesia, but in my house, one or two light bulbs were going out every day. The problem was blamed on the spirits in my house, who were unsure of my status as a white (and potentially Dutch) person in an all-Sundanese neighborhood. I spoke of this problem to my kacapi teacher, Rukruk Rukmana, who suggested that we hold a hajat to try to straighten out the situation and convince the spirits that I meant well and that I wasn't Dutch. He contacted an older man named Toto, a relative of the late Uking Sukri, one of the finest of the kacapi players. Toto was said to be skilled in magic. We set the event to be held on Jum'at Kliwon (the most important ritual night of the Sundanese/Javanese thirty-five-day calendar), an auspicious night for rituals under any circumstance—particularly the Jum'at Kliwon immediately before the Islamic fasting month of Ramadan, which was scheduled to begin several days later.

My servant was instructed to collect water from the homes of each neighbor in the four directions, and to place the four waters together in a single bowl. Then she prepared a *tumpeng sangu*, a large batch of rice mixed with coconut, curry, potato, chicken pieces, and whole hard-boiled eggs, formed into the shape of an upside-down cone and covered with banana leaves. This was placed on my living room floor next to the kacapi. There were also other items such as uncooked rice (*beas*), unsweetened coffee (*kopi pahit*), and incense, which were arranged next to the tumpeng sangu. In a separate basket woven from fresh banana leaves was placed the *sasajén*, or ritual offering, consisting of several different kinds of blossoms, a cigar, a large and a small banana, and "something sour and something sweet" (*nu aseum sareng nu manis*). I was told to bathe carefully and put on new clothing, and to take a separate outfit of my clothing that I would normally wear for school and place it on a tray, neatly folded. A new pen was requested.

Together with my very few guests, we all sat down on the floor in the living room in front of the sasajén and the instruments. Toto, who led the ceremony, asked me what day I was born. Each day of the week has significant characteristics attached to the people born on those days. In my case (Monday), the important symbol is flowers (as opposed to fire, water, or other attributes) and the number is four. Toto then lit some incense and began with the usual Arabic prayer that begins each ceremony, journey, or physical effort: *Bismi allāhi al-rahmāni al-rahīm*. He explained that he was proud to conduct the ceremony and that, although our religions were different, we believed in the same God. He prayed very quietly to himself in Arabic, and then shifted into a language that I was unable to understand because it was neither Arabic, Sundanese, nor Javanese.

At this point (I was told later by Rukruk Rukmana, my kacapi teacher) Toto had gone into trance, and was being told what to speak and write by a *roh*, or spirit. Toto picked up the pen and held it out to me. I grasped one end of it, and after several seconds he jerked strongly, saying (in Indonesian) "Wah! Kuat sekali!" ("Wow! Very strong!"),[2] took the pen back and wrote six lines on the paper in Arabic, of which he claims not to have any reading ability. As he wrote, he moved spasmodically. I was told to sign my name at the bottom of one side, and he wrote another brief phrase in Arabic under it. Then he folded the paper in half and began writing in the old Sundanese script, of which he also claims to have no knowledge.

Several more brief sentences and foldings of the paper later, he began to say a long prayer. After this last prayer, he turned to me and explained that all life comes from God (*Tuhan*) and through the golden bridge (Indo.: *jembatan emas*) of our parents. He went on to say that King Prabu Siliwangi (the king of Pajajaran) is all around us and that he is the center and the symbol for all that it means to live in Pajajaran. He gave me the folded piece of paper and told me to pray over it, then he took it back and asked me to light a match to it. He held the paper while it burned, then dropped it into a goblet partially filled with coals. He turned to the west and prayed in front of the kacapi, the tray with my clothes on it, and the pen.

Toto turned back, picked up a small bowl of uncooked rice, and discussed the importance of rice in Sunda. Following this, he said another prayer, took a small pinch of rice, and threw it over me as I kneeled in front of him with my head bowed, approximately three feet away. He repeated this action, then went to each room in my house, saying a prayer in each room. After he had sat back down again, he held out the rice spoon to me and together we broke open the tumpeng sangu, flattening the top of it. It looked rather like Tangkuban Prahu, the Sundanese boat-shaped volcano. He took the large bowl with the water in it that had been collected from the four directions, and said a long prayer over it, adding that it was for me to bathe with the next morning.

I was sent to find a handkerchief. When I returned, the kacapi and rincik had been lined up with my suling laid out lengthwise on the kacapi. The instruments were placed so that if I were playing them, I would be facing toward Mecca. I was told to sit in front of the kacapi and place both my palms together on top of the strings, so I did. He then placed the handkerchief on top of my hands and placed his over mine, saying a long prayer. He took my hands off the kacapi, placed them palms together and held them that way, blew on them, said a prayer, blew on them again, gave a long speech in Sundanese about my origin being in America (not in Holland) and my belonging to Pajajaran because of my interest in tembang Sunda, and then he blew on my hands a final time.

We ate the prepared food, and the goblet with the ashes of the paper was placed just outside the door leading to the back courtyard of my house. During the meal, Toto discussed the presence of the spirit of an elderly man in the back bedroom who had once lived in the house itself or had worked in the rice field that had existed before the house was built sometime in the 1970s. The spirit of the old man had evidently been concerned about my motives for moving into that particular house and for attempting to learn tembang Sunda. Toto had assured the spirit that I bore no ill intent and was not Dutch.[3]

Therefore, the event was, a combination of two ceremonies: a hajat designed to appease the spirits in my house; and a tawajuh ceremony for my initiation, not just as a kacapi player but also as a member of the realm of Pajajaran. It was not clear where the hajat ended and the tawajuh began, because each ceremony is slightly different and the entire event could simply have been called a hajat. My kacapi teacher mentioned after the ceremony that he himself had never been married to the kacapi by someone else but, rather, enacted his marriage directly with the kacapi. He also claimed not to have arranged the actual marriage between myself and the kacapi in advance, saying that he had left the planning up to Toto, but Burhan Sukarma, my suling teacher with whom I had discussed the ceremony, was certain that the entire event had been planned between my teacher and Toto. In either case, the ceremony was openly discussed as a "marriage" (*perkawinan*) afterward during the time that we ate the food prepared for it. The next morning, I bathed with the water from the four directions and the flowers from the sasajén, as I had been instructed.

This particular marriage ceremony was definitely unusual in several respects. First, it was conducted between a female player and the kacapi, instead of between a male player and a "female" kacapi. Second, my status as a white foreigner caused the introduction of certain exceptional features into the ceremony, such as the occasional use of Bahasa Indonesia (instead of just Sundanese and Arabic), and the brief discussion of our differing religions. Neither discussion would have occurred if the student were Sundanese. Third, I was at the time still rather new to the kacapi, and could in no way be said to have reached a satisfactory level of competence on the instrument, even by the most enthusiastic praise-giver. Lastly, this ceremony happens so rarely that most players (no matter what their level of proficiency) never experience it and, in the words of my teacher Rukruk Rukmana, "kawin langsung dengan kacapi" (enact the marriage directly with the kacapi) instead.

In spite of these limitations and decidedly foreign elements, the ceremony may still be seen as representative of earlier tawajuh ceremonies and even used as a modern example of how these ceremonies should be held according to someone who frequently conducts traditional ceremonies. Furthermore, my status as a woman did not necessarily preclude my being married to the instrument, because, as Wim van Zanten assured me, it is the *relationship* between the player and the instrument that is essential for good music, not necessarily the gender of the musician (van Zanten, personal communication, 1989). There seemed to be no problem at all that the ceremony was taking place in a very large city with traffic noise going continuously outside, an indication that certain spiritual aspects of Sundanese life may be experienced with as much validity in the city as in the country. It eventually turned out that the lighting problem did not clear up altogether, but I only lost lightbulbs once every two months (instead of every day or so) after the ceremony. Losing a bulb every couple of months is quite common in Bandung, considering the power surges and poor quality lightbulbs available. Much to the disappointment of several of my young male Sundanese friends, the spirit of the old man in my house did *not* supply lottery numbers, even though the hajat was deemed a success.

The kacapi is widely used as a symbol in itself to represent Sunda, not just to the non-Sundanese ethnic groups in other parts of Indonesia but to foreigners as well. Illustrations of kacapi adorn maps of Sunda, restaurant menus, and tourist brochures for West Java. Miniature, nonplaying kacapi have their place as popular domestic tourist items (*oleh-oleh*) alongside wayang golék puppets. Cassettes sold in other parts of Indonesia (particularly Bali) sometimes feature a picture of the kacapi on the cover, even if kacapi music is not featured on the cassette itself. A particularly apt analogy, suggested by David Harnish, is that of the Irish harp: Few Irish musicians actually play it, but its historical significance gives it cultural weight and makes it more important as a symbol than as an instrument. Musicians in other parts of Indonesia tended to mention the kacapi first when they heard that I was studying Sundanese music. Nonmusicians and members of the government, however, more frequently mentioned jaipongan, the popular Sundanese social dance first popularized in the 1970s that swept through other parts of Indonesia by the early 1980s. In his article about popular Indonesian music, Philip Yampolsky mentions that Jakartan producers of pop Sunda tend to insert the sound of a kacapi into a pop Indonesia song if they want it to be a hit in Sunda (Yampolsky 1989:15).

The largest kacapi I ever saw was one outside the Rumah Makan Lembur Kuring (the "My Own Village" Restaurant), between the town of Cianjur and the Puncak Pass. It measured approximately twenty feet in length, was about three feet high, had four tuning pegs on the side and huge wires for strings. It was raised about fifteen feet off the ground and was situated by the main road to Jakarta from Bandung. For years it was painted black but, in the early months of 1989 (before I completed my fieldwork), it was painted a very bright yellow to attract more attention. Workers at the restaurant described the giant kacapi as a type of Sundanese icon (or final outpost of Sundanese civilization) to bring in Sundanese customers who might be on their way to or from Jakarta. One singer described it as the first sign of being inside Sundanese territory again, even though the restaurant is actually well inside the mountain Sundanese or Priangan area. The instrument has since disappeared; some say that the restaurant bowed to pressure from the Javanese visitors! Others speculated that the instrument might have disappeared because it went to Pajajaran. The kacapi, therefore, is a strong symbol of *kasundaan* (what it means to be Sundanese), both to the Sundanese and to other groups.

TEMBANG SUNDA LYRICS

The lyrics of tembang songs are among the most obvious clues toward understanding what is intended in a performance of tembang Sunda. Paying attention to the lyrics orients the listener inward, either toward a very personal expression of emotion, or toward one's own association with the past.[4] One of the most common complaints heard from Sundanese scholars and musicians about the correct performance of tembang Sunda lyrics is that many singers do not pay any attention to how the lyrics should fit the song (Atmadinata 1980:4). Because singers may sometimes substitute one set of lyrics for another (particularly in those songs that use poetic pupuh forms), lyrics about sadness in a relationship may inadvertently be used in a song intended to portray strong forces of nature or warrior-like deeds. Musicians who have a clear idea about the appropriate character of each song simply laugh and criticize those who only know the melody instead of the way the melody and lyrics fit together.

The knowledge of the appropriate selection and expression of lyrics to fit the song is part of pangjiwaan—the inner knowledge or deep-level understanding of a song. Pangjiwaan is, in most cases, much more important than the quality of a singer's voice or facility in the use of vocal ornaments that are believed to be surface features bestowed on a singer by God (Wiratmadja, personal communication, 1988). The ability to move beneath the surface in the proper expression of tembang Sunda is not bestowed by God but, rather, by one's own experiences in life, particularly the hardships. Even though one may use substitutions in certain songs, one may still discuss the larger body of lyrics as representing a kind of collective pangjiwaan among the practitioners of the genre. Although certain aspects of Sundanese poetry—the pupuh forms in particular—are derived from Central Java, their content reflects more of a Sundanese experience than a Javanese experience. In many cases, Sundanese poetic songs are believed to express much more personal and individual emotions than those of the Javanese (Kartomi 1973a:62).

The language used in tembang Sunda mamaos lyrics is generally of the upper three levels of Sundanese: *sedeng* (intermediate), *lemes* (refined) and *lemes pisan* (very refined) (see Wessing 1974). The lower levels of the language (*kasar* = coarse, and *kasar pisan* = very coarse) are never used. Evidently, this selection of language is another factor by which tembang Sunda is differentiated from kawih and pantun, which do use lower level words (van Zanten 1989:76). The choice of words from among the upper strata of language levels is based partially on the basic intent of the song—whether it is intended to be intimate or historic, for example—and partially on what will fit into the poetic form.[5] The Sundanese shift between language levels as a constant form of wordplay, and poets and composers also use it to great advantage. The use of foreign words is generally considered out of place in tembang Sunda. In panambih songs, however, entire verses can be constructed with a conscious, deliberate use of foreign words for variation (see below, *sisindiran*).

The following sketch of the poetry of tembang Sunda outlines some of the basic features of the lyrics, and examines how the lyrics function to support certain performance settings. Those few tembang Sunda songs that use prose instead of metricized poetry or stanzaic forms as lyric material are found primarily in papantunan and jejemplangan. Prose songs are closely associated with the context and history of pantun performance, and tend to carry significant lyric weight. That is, the lyrics are infused with a near-sacred character and are the closest in the hearts and minds of the Sundanese to the perceived original, idealized, premodern classical Sundanese existence.

The Central Javanese are responsible for the migration of Javanese poetic forms into Sunda. It was during the time of Mataram, when Central Javanese cultural influences were felt most strongly in Sunda, that the gradual acceptance of the tembang macapat occurred in the Sundanese upper classes. The Sundanese have taken four poetic forms (pupuh) from the Javanese tembang macapat forms to use in tembang Sunda; each one has unique characteristics. Unlike the Javanese macapat verses, however, Sundanese verses may be switched freely from one song to another as long as the song and the metric requirements of the pupuh match.[6] Javanese macapat may be sung to more than one melody (Kartomi 1973a:38) but are the same in arrangement as Sundanese pupuh forms.

The four most important poetic forms used by the Sundanese are *kinanti, sinom, asmarandana,* and *dangdanggula*. Most tembang Sunda musicians are acutely aware of the metric content of the songs and can instantly identify the form of a song by the time the singer reaches the end of the first line. Knowledge of pupuh is essential during performances, because singers frequently switch from one set of lyrics to another for the sake of variety, so as not to duplicate another singer's set of lyrics, and to fit the context. The use of pupuh is extremely common in songs of rarancagan and dedegungan style. Some jejemplangan songs and a few papantunan songs use pupuh forms as well.

Once a singer has identified a form as asmarandana, for example, any asmarandana text can be selected and sung to the melody of the song in progress. The immediate switching of lyrics is not a particularly easy feat, because, in addition to knowing exactly how the ornaments fit within the boundaries of each syllable, the singer must be aware of all the additions to the text that are used as filler.[7] Words such as *juragan, raden,* and *geuning* are added to certain songs, either to fill out the melodic line, add the appropriate final vowel (*a, i,* or whatever) to the line, or to indicate for whom the song was intended. The addition of these words may also interfere with the syllabic order of the line, and few singers include them in their notebooks. When the singer must quickly find a song in kinanti form, for example, the addition of these extra words may throw him or her off as the syllables, vowels and number of lines are quickly assessed.

Tembang Sunda composition in stanzas occurs most often in panambih songs, in which composers have the freedom to play with rhyming schemes outside the more rigid pupuh forms. One of the features common in panambih that differentiate them from those songs using pupuh forms is an increased use of the syllable *eu,* which I describe above as being one of the hallmarks of the Sundanese language. The great tembang master Apung Wiratmadja noted that panambih have more *eu* words in them because the feelings they describe are more raw and down-to-earth. Others say that panambih are more intense and, possibly, more Sundanese. I was not able to judge the relative degree of "intensity" in panambih songs, except to note that as panambih, these songs are expected to be of a slightly lower level than mamaos (free-rhythm) songs. Therefore, borrowings from the lower levels of Sundanese vocabulary are acceptable for panambih.

Panambih texts often draw from sisindiran, four-line stanzas in which the first two lines bear a strong relationship in rhyme and sentence structure to the second. The first two lines (*cangkang*—"skin"), however, are fairly meaningless in that they do not discuss the main point (*eusi*—essence) of the verse, which is always contained in the second two lines. The verbs, which the two couplets usually have in common, contribute to the verse's coherence. For example, one frequently used sisindiran (in Indonesian rather than the more customary Sundanese) is the following, selected because the similarities are so very strong between the two sections.[8]

Dari mana datangnya lintah?	Where does the leech come from?
Dari sawah, turun ke kali	From the rice field, descending to the river.
Dari mana datangnya cinta?	Where does love come from?
Dari mata, turun ke hati.	From the eyes, descending to the heart.

Because sisindiran are used in many types of Sundanese music (and bear a close relationship to Malay pantun couplets),[9] foreign words can be incorporated into the songs as well as Sundanese and Indonesian words. In performances for Dutch visitors, for example, singers always choose a panambih that will enable them to use the one Dutch/Sundanese verse that everyone knows.[10] Tembang Sunda singers are always careful to emphasize the Dutch-sounding consonants in the verse, and everyone watches the guests closely and hopes for a reaction. Similarly, whenever a Japanese guest is being entertained, a Japanese verse is added. In both cases (the Dutch and the Japanese), the accuracy of the language is less important than the insertion of the foreign vocabulary and the fact that the verse rhymes.

Other words that are not so foreign to the Sundanese yet that are not strictly Sundanese also have found their way into tembang Sunda. Arabic words, for example, are in common usage in Sunda, and their occasional incorporation into tembang Sunda (such as in the song "Hamdan") is spread more evenly across the styles than words from Dutch, Japanese, or English. Words from Javanese are usually restricted to those songs that are overtly Javanese in sound or character. On occasion, words from Indonesian will be used to fill out the metric line or the needs of the song, but, in general, the song lyrics are almost exclusively in Sundanese. Tembang Sunda also uses other poetic forms (such as *wawangsalan* and *paparikan*) in sisindiran, incorporating complicated allusory wordplay and elaborate rhyme into couplets that may be inserted into a wide variety of songs (see van Zanten 1989: 70). In tembang Sunda, however, most of these are associated only with panambih.

As has already been mentioned, many of the older tembang Sunda lyrics have to do with historical events or figures. Older phrases that recount the far-off sound of a suling (which could only be heard in a quiet place), or discuss the glittering of stars (generally invisible in the city because of polluted air and bright lights) can create powerful images in the minds of the listeners. Most of the newer lyrics, however, are about various kinds of love, which is now becoming the most frequent theme in the songs (van Zanten 1989:73).

The following lyrics are selected from a variety of tembang Sunda songs and are translated here to demonstrate the evocative use of imagery—either in invoking a feeling of the past or a sense of the outdoors. Van Zanten has published an article exclusively on the poetry of tembang Sunda (1984:289–316) that may be examined for further evidence. Although most song lyrics are about love, the older songs are less about love and more about historical events or nature scenes, which is one of the most important features of a song that can cause it to be accepted or rejected by a tembang Sunda audience. Depending on the selection of lyrics, the audience can be caused to feel nostalgia or simply be entertained. The examples below belong to the type that evokes nostalgia.

In Chapter 9, I included translations of verses from the song "Papatet" and focused on the song as the core piece of the tembang Sunda repertoire. "Papatet" contains some of the most essential lyrical information as well as all the important aspects of tembang Sunda vocal ornamentation discussed in Chapter 8. It is songs of this type that ground the music in the Sundanese past, and repeatedly evoke the image of the glorious lost kingdom in the hearts and minds of the practitioners and their audience. It essentially reaffirms, as Christine Yano notes for Japanese enka, "not only the past, but a particular conceptualization of their pasts. These persist, if nothing else, in this recreated, nostalgic form" (Yano 1997:126).

The papantunan song "Salaka Domas" discusses the strength and power of the aristocratic ménak or god-kings of Pajajaran. The imagery in these lyrics is of a very powerful man (the child of King Prabu Siliwangi) who wants to fight against everything that assails him. According to several musicians, the song lyrics represent the modern Sundanese man, hampered by his current circumstances but ready to spring into action at a moment's notice to defend himself and his *nagara*, or Sundanese nation-state. Because most aristocratic Sundanese claim descent from the ménak, any one of them may be considered a "child of King Siliwangi" or even a "child of Pajajaran."

Kadia banteng bayangan	Like a fabulous [mythical] water buffalo
Sinatria pilih tanding	A heroic figure without peer
Toh pati jiwa jeung raga	Sacrificing his soul and his body
Seja angkat mapag jurit	Ready to depart in search of war
Najan di luhur langit	Even at the highest reaches of the sky
Hamo burung rek disusul	It will be sought out
Sumujud ka ingkang rama	He will pay his respects to his father
Prabu Agung Siliwangi	The great King Siliwangi
Layang domas, layang domas	[a type of powerful *pusaka* or heirloom]
Didamel jimat nagara.	Made as a symbol of the *nagara*.

Songs of the historical and spiritual type are closely tied to those descriptive aspects of nature, because of the close association of Pajajaran and the more recent past with the rural outdoors. In the following selection from the panambih song "Kingkilaban," descriptions of stars evoke the feeling of being in a place where you can actually see the stars, which has to be outside of an urban area (see the transcription of two phrases of "Kingkilaban" in

Example 7.6 of Chapter 7). In Sundanese songs, happy and sad images are usually tied together in the same song, and it is difficult for the Sundanese to discuss one without the other. As a result, some of the very saddest songs of the repertoire (including those about broken marriages, orphans, lost loves, and unrequited love) are the most popular at weddings.[11] The dried-up stream of the final line of the song refers to a technique of catching fish by drying up their water supply, and the whispering sound is said to be the aural equivalent of a visual mirage. The song uses images of nature to convey feelings of sadness, love, hope and despair all in one verse.

Ting gurilap lir salempay kingkilaban	Glittering like ignited white handkerchiefs
Rek nyaangan kanu keur katunggaraan	Brightening up the sad one
Sakedapan alam padang narawangan	Briefly lit up as if at daybreak
Nu kasmaran lir bentang anu baranang	The one in love lit up like thousands of stars
Kakupingna ngaharewos lalaunan	Listening for a very quiet whispering sound
Ngan seahna parakan baranang siang	It is only the voice of a dried-up stream.

The following selection is from the papantunan song "Goyong," and describes a long view in several directions, including out toward the ocean. The most important lines of this verse are the last two: "Mount Gedé seems to beckon you home," and "It nearly makes me faint." According to several vocalists with whom I discussed these particular lyrics, the feeling of being away from home is not so much connected to one's physical home in Bandung but to one's spiritual home in Pajajaran. The concept of being beckoned home by a mountain makes the singer or listener "feel faint," because it is as if one is being beckoned toward death. The word *kapiuhan* ("fainting") even reaches outside of pélog mode for a single, stressed note in sorog, rather like the beginning of the line *Daweung ménak Pajajaran*. Furthermore, the imagery of the sea is connected very strongly with the underworld and death, and one singer told me that lyrical imagery of this type—which includes the ocean and spiritually important mountains—symbolizes the singers' own confrontation of his or her own mortality.

Laut Kidul kabéh katingali	The southern sea is completely visible
Ngembat paul siga dina gambar	Blue extending out like a picture
Ari rét ka tebéh kalér	If you look to the north
Betawi ngarunggunuk	Batavia is flattened out
Lautna mah teu katingali	You cannot see the ocean
Ukur lebah-lebahna	Just the whole area
Semu-semu biru	An expanse of blue
Ari rét ka kalér-wétan	If you look to the northeast
Gunung Gedé siga nu ngajakan balik	Mount Gedé seems to beckon you home
Méh baé kapiuhan.	It nearly makes me faint.

In the following phrase from the rarancagan song "Bayubud," the singer is told to stay close to home simply by observing the appearance the mountains, which seem to speak through their presence.

Matak wa'as keur waktu ningali	Feelings of wa'as while observing
Gunung gunung bangun narembongan	Mountains displaying themselves
Dicipta jiga ngaromong	As if they were speaking
Basana ulah jauh	They say, "Do not stray far"

The term *wa'as*, which is often used to describe the feeling that comes over listeners when they hear a good performance of tembang Sunda, represents all the feelings of nostalgia, loneliness, reminiscence, wistfulness, awe, reverence, and admiration. It is said admiringly when one sees a beautiful, quiet rural view, such as a sun setting behind a volcano with the sun rays reflecting off the rice terraces and illuminating isolated huts (*pondok*) scattered in the fields. The feeling of wa'as can move people to tears and cause their hearts to ache, and tembang Sunda creates wa'as. That tembang Sunda lyrics should frequently describe breathtaking rural and outdoor settings in gentle, refined language is only in keeping with the function of the genre: to act as a bridge between contexts.

The essential feature of the lyrics of tembang Sunda is that they speak directly to the experience of being Sundanese. In addition, they draw attention away from current events and current situations. By emphasizing the pleasant feelings associated with being in the village (cool, quiet, calm, enjoyable sights and sounds) and with the past (Pajajaran, lifestyles of the regents), the lyrics transcend the ordinary frame of reference for the listener. The many layers of messages conveyed by the sound, the sight, and the setting of tembang Sunda take the practitioners of this music into a spiritual setting created by their own needs. These needs include longing to link up with their strong and independent past, finding a way to cope with the disturbing changes in modern urban life, and giving themselves cultural vitality and individuality in the face of increasing nationalization.

THE CREATION AND MAINTENANCE OF SUNDANESE IDENTITY

The highland (Priangan) Sundanese have established for themselves an identity distinct from their powerful neighbors, the Central Javanese, and also from all other Indonesians and even lowland Sundanese or Cirebonese. By choosing to emphasize certain features of their culture in the early twenty-first century (such as language, music, dance, and performance wear), the Sundanese are expressing what it means to be Sundanese. Anderson proposes that a nation (or, in this case, a regional ethnic group) is "an imagined political community—and imagined as both inherently limited and sovereign" (Anderson 1983:15). In the case of the Sundanese, their nation limits itself to the borders of West Java or, in the case of the aristocratic Sundanese, to the borders of the Priangan. It is sovereign, in spite of its obvious incorporation into the Indonesian national boundaries, because it once boasted a powerful trading kingdom, Pajajaran. Finally, it is a community, because a comradeship exists between the Sundanese that crosses status boundaries when confronting outsiders.

In the maintenance of this Sundanese nation, boundaries must be drawn that separate the Sundanese from the non-Sundanese, and connections must be established that connect and legitimate the present with the past. The Sundanese feel this need to maintain continuity with the past, and speak of *kokolot* ("the old people," one's parents, but also in the greater sense of "the ancestors" or "how the ancestors did things") when they refer to some aspect of culture, knowledge, or authority. In maintaining this continuity, the Sundanese tend to glorify those aspects of the past believed to be better than the present. Most types of musical performance are believed to have been of a much higher quality in the past, and there is a general overall sense of "the good old days" when the Sundanese were free and proud. These "good old days" belong to a rather hazy general notion of the past: pre-Independence and, more specifically, of the era of Pajajaran.

Some musicians unhesitatingly point to the time of Pajajaran as the best time in Sundanese history (*zaman emas* or "golden age"), while others blend together the images of a time—any time but the present—that was not nearly as out of control (zaman edan) as it is now. This is not to imply by any means that the Sundanese were somehow better off under Dutch hegemony; rather, that the harsh reality of the pre-Independence era has already faded for many Sundanese into the more distant past represented by Pajajaran. It is believed that in the troubled and confusing era at the beginning of the twenty-first century, people may derive considerable knowledge and benefits (either spiritual or monetary) through the establishment of contact with the old days and the ancestors that lived in those times.

In order to obtain guidance from ancestors of the general past—that is, those ancestors who are not necessarily the direct relatives of those who wish to contact them—the Sundanese usually must go through an intermediary.

> The Sundanese feel it difficult to approach someone whose status and power are much greater than their own. They say they are *isin* (embarrassed) in the presence of such a person or entity. In going directly to God the petitioner is skipping two intermediary or "buffer" levels which creates quite a social distance between him and the addressee. The problem is implicit in the Sundanese language itself. It is difficult for common people to speak to persons of very high status, such as royalty. (Wessing 1978:97)

The person who is responsible for contacting the spirits at a sacred grave or other spiritual site is known as a *kuncén*. Spirit possession is very common in Sunda (see Wessing 1978), and was once used to get numbers for the

TABLE 10.1 Tembang Sunda on the cognitive map

Wessing: Status relations in spiritual contact		Status relations in musical contact with the ancestors and Pajajaran	
Allah	= high	Allah	= high
Spirit	= low/high	Ancestors	= middle
Kuncén	= low/high	Tembang Sunda	= middle
Petitioner	= low	Practitioner	= low

lottery when such a lottery was still legal in the 1980s. It is standard practice to obtain the services of someone who has been to Mecca (a *haji*) or who is considered deeply religious with a strong trace of traditional animism. For example, the man who conducted the hajat/kacapi wedding ceremony at my house wore the typical *peci* (men's Islamic hat) and said numerous prayers in Arabic, then went into trance to conduct the ceremony. During the trance, he contacted the spirit who lived in my back bedroom. For some people, however, the use of a human intermediary is not always the ideal solution for profoundly personal contact. Music is an alternative means by which an individual or group may approach their ancestors.

Tembang Sunda is a type of kuncén or spiritual intermediary. In Table 10.1, I have duplicated Wessing's analysis of intermediaries (Wessing 1978: 97), and next to his work I have placed tembang Sunda in the position of kuncén, and its practitioners (the Sundanese aristocracy) in the role of petitioners. The spirits, who are one step below Allah, are not only the noblemen of Pajajaran (ménak Pajajaran) but also the creators and supporters of tembang Sunda, all of whom came hundreds of years after the fall of Pajajaran. Whereas Wessing has placed not only the kuncén but also the spirits on the border between low and high, I have placed both tembang Sunda and the ancestors in a medium area, neither high nor low. Almost all practitioners of tembang Sunda are also followers of Islam, and Allah is above everyone else. Within the cognitive map of aristocratic Sundanese cosmology, the god-kings of Pajajaran and the aristocratic line of descendants from the last several centuries belong more or less on the same plane.

The conceptualization of music—not just as a means by which the ancestors may be contacted but also as a manifestation of the ancestral heritage itself—is demonstrated in many different types of Sundanese music. Through the use of music, various kinds of contact may be established. Some Sundanese use music to go into trance; others are able to put horses into trance (known as *kuda renggong*) as they themselves are empowered by the music. In a performance of *debus* (a type of accompanied trance performance) that I witnessed in 1988, music was used to cause the trance to occur. As soon as the participants were in trance, they began to push very thick needles completely through their limbs, throats and upper torsos (with no resulting blood loss) to demonstrate the strength of their religion and personal power. Others can fry an egg in a pan placed on top of their heads, ostensibly through the heat generated by the energy of the trance.[12] In debus and many other types of Sundanese trance-related performances, trance is entered and controlled at least partially through music (for a non-Sundanese discussion of music and trance, see Kartomi 1973b, Porter 1987, and Rouget 1985).

Although not directly used to cause or control trance, tembang Sunda performance has a related function. As a manifestation of Sundanese ancestral lineage, music allows the modern urban Sundanese aristocracy to keep "in tune" with their ancestors. The words *nyurupkeun* (tuning) and *kasurupan* (possessed) are derived from the same root word, *surup* (Baier 1988: 2). As described above, performers who use music to create the appropriate sonic atmosphere for trance are then controlled by that music so that they may stay in contact with the spirits. In order to properly attune themselves to their heritage, the aristocratic Sundanese—although not becoming possessed themselves—establish themselves as part of a longer tradition that aligns them with their own ancestors through the performance of tembang Sunda.

> Tone relations are not without their genealogical counterparts, because the basic descriptive Sundanese image for low/high or for large instrument/small instrument is mother/child (*indung/anak*). On an *angklung*, for instance, commonly two bamboo tubes tuned an octave apart, the mother represents the fundamental and the child represents the octave. To take this one step further, Pak Yoyo always described the shape of *angklung* as representing a line of ancestors, a *keturunan*, with the fundamental tube (the larger) being on the side of the past. In this sense, the *angklung* tubes become the physical manifestation of a line of otherwise invisible ancestors and descendants. (Baier 1988:2)

As is indicated by the arrangement of music described above (in which the larger instrument comes to represent the collective Sundanese past and the smaller one the Sundanese present), the Sundanese are aware that the music they perform today is only a single point on the direct historic line that leads back to the time of the ancestors. The brevity of the present compared with the depth of the past is also represented in the instruments of tembang Sunda; from the size of the "mother" kacapi (and the relative musical and spiritual weight that it carries) to the size of the "child" rincik (and its comparatively lightweight duties in tembang Sunda). The musical ensemble as a whole carries a considerable cultural and historical burden when the events and people with whom it is connected are examined. Its connotations with the past and the aristocracy give it a strong visual image as well, through which a host may raise his own prestige by hiring even a mediocre ensemble. The image of the ensemble (no matter what the music sounds like) is strong enough to indicate high status.

In the case of the aristocratic Sundanese, the ancestral past with which they come into contact through the performance of tembang Sunda is not a particularly Islamic past. That is, although the Sundanese have been in contact with Islam for several hundred years and are believed to be one of the most strongly Islamic ethnic groups in Indonesia, the past recalled in the songs of tembang Sunda is that of Pajajaran, the distinctly pre-Islamic kingdom of the fourteenth and fifteenth centuries. Furthermore, the god-kings who are immortalized in the songs are those who disappeared when Pajajaran collapsed, and who are believed to be residing in the kingdom of Pajajaran until they are ready to reappear. Immortality through rebirth (disappearance until an eventual reappearance) is one of the essential features of Hinduism, not (Sunni) Islam.

By claiming that the Hindu and animist features of pre-Islamic Sundanese life are strong in modern urban Sunda, I do not deny the strength of Sundanese Islam. On the contrary, there seems to be no doubt that Allah is the unquestionable Supreme Being, even for the most aristocratic Sundanese. In fact, Pajajaran was never described to me as a Hindu kingdom but, rather, as a *Sundanese* kingdom. Its Hinduism was less essential to my informants than the scope of its rule and the fact that it was Sunda's biggest kingdom. As many aristocratic Sundanese are quick to point out that they are good Muslims and pray five times a day, it is less politically correct to speak of the time of Pajajaran as the "good old days back when we were still Hindus" as it is to speak of the time of Pajajaran simply as the "good old days." The other (partly Hindu, partly animist) aspects of Sundanese cosmology that play a strong role in modern Sundanese life are said to be merely an incorporation of *adat* ("custom"), allowable and in direct accordance with the Islamic principle of *ijma'*, consensus of the community (Denny 1985:219; Wessing 1978:87).

THE KEY TO POWER

The organization of pre-Islamic Indonesian states (even those that were only partially Hinduized, like Pajajaran) around central ritualized figures is a fact of history (Anderson 1972:25; Wessing 1978:27). The Sundanese seem to conform to Anderson's concepts about Javanese history: that is, it is viewed by the Javanese as "one of cosmological oscillation between periods of concentration of Power and periods of its diffusion" (Anderson 1972:20)—in other words, that the way Indonesians (but particularly the Javanese, in this case) view history is not as a series of concrete starting and ending points but, rather, the waxing and waning of power that is concentrated in the person of a particular ruler or set of rulers. The closing years of the twentieth century saw significant upheavals in the distribution of power in Indonesia, as the Suharto regime fell and the Sukarno era was recalled through the appointment of Vice President Megawati Sukarnoputri, Sukarno's daughter.

> In each period of concentration new centers of Power (dynasties, rulers) are constituted and unity is recreated; in each period of diffusion, Power begins to ebb away from the center, the reigning dynasty loses its claim to rule, and

disorder appears—until the concentrating process begins again. The historical necessity of diffusion is no less compelling than that of concentration, since Power is immensely hard to retain and has perpetually to be struggled for. The slightest slackness or lack of vigilance may begin the process of disintegration, which, once it sets in, is irreversible. (Anderson 1972:21)

The capitalization of the *p* in Power stems from its use by Benedict Anderson, who does this to indicate the Javanese—as opposed to the European—view. Similarities between Javanese and Sundanese views on this topic (Wessing 1978:26) warrant deeper exploration of the concept of Power. Benedict Anderson's analysis of how Javanese and Europeans each conceptualize power illuminates our understanding of why Pajajaran—and some of the regents in later positions of authority in Sunda—should hold so much spiritual weight in the minds of modern, urbanized Sundanese people. For Europeans and those trained in European thought, power is "an abstraction deduced from observed patterns of social interaction; it is believed to derive from heterogeneous sources; it is no way inherently self-limiting; and it is morally ambiguous" (Anderson 1972:7). For the Javanese—and, by association, the Sundanese—power is "something concrete, homogeneous, constant in total quantity, and without inherent moral implications as such" (Anderson 1972:8). Power may be accumulated through the enactment of ritual ceremonies such as the selamatan or hajat, which also brings life into balance and bestows well-being (*selamat*) on the participants.

> Power exists, independent of its possible users. It is not a theoretical postulate but an existential reality. Power is that intangible, mysterious, and divine energy which animates the universe. It is manifested in every aspect of the natural world, in stones, trees, clouds, and fire, but is expressed quintessentially in the central mystery of life, the process of generation and regeneration. In Javanese traditional thinking there is no sharp division between organic and inorganic matter, for everything is sustained by the same invisible power. This conception of the entire cosmos being suffused by a formless, constantly creative energy provides the basic link between the "animism" of the Javanese villages, and the high metaphysical pantheism of the urban centers. (Anderson 1972:7)

For the Sundanese, the kingdom of Pajajaran was the pinnacle of Sundanese power in comparison with other dynasties and their rulers. The kings and noblemen of Pajajaran are the names that appear most frequently in pantun, or epic recitals (Heins 1977: 11), and tembang Sunda texts contain many references to that era (see also van Zanten 1989:70–75.

The way some Sundanese think of Pajajaran in the modern urban Sunda of the early twenty-first century (and described it to me) is like an acknowledgment of a separate state of existence. Pajajaran has become, in the minds of some aristocratic Sundanese, the place from which all Sundanese descend when they are born, the place where their souls belong while they are alive, and the place they return to when they die. Van Zanten mentions the concept of *pulang ka asal* (going back to the beginning) in connection with the idea of Sundanese life occurring in cycles (van Zanten 1987:15). The concept of Pajajaran (a strong, peaceful, independent nation) as a state of mind is further reinforced by the Indonesian national policy on elementary school teaching of history, in which the national history takes precedence over the local. Pajajaran finally becomes more a concept of historical power and prestige than a reality.

The practice and performance of tembang Sunda is a medium through which the aristocratic Sundanese may tap into the power symbolized by the kingdom of Pajajaran and its descendants through the lines of regents and other members of the aristocracy to the present. Although tembang Sunda itself dates only from the mid–nineteenth century, it has maintained a continuous association with the aristocracy since its early development.[13] The tendency has already been noted in Java for current rulers to try to associate themselves with past dynasties through the collection of relics (pusaka) associated with or inherited from the person or dynasty in power, thereby empowering themselves by association (Anderson 1972:26). Ernst Heins describes the acquisition of pusaka of sound as an aural expression of power (Heins 1977:35). On the one hand, tembang Sunda represents a type of pusaka that the aristocratic Sundanese gather to themselves for the purpose of their own empowerment. On the other hand, knowledge and appreciation of (or better yet, skill in singing) tembang Sunda is itself a key to that power.[14] In this sense, the rare skill of being able to perform tembang Sunda in a society filled with people who neither perform nor understand it is akin to a type of literacy.

> The literacy of the ruling class was a symbol of Power largely because it presupposed the ability to make the qualitative leap out of illiteracy. The literati were not just better educated—they were the educated in a society of uneducated. Their power derived not from their ability to disseminate new concepts through society, but from their ability to penetrate to and conserve old and secret knowledge. (Anderson 1972:47)

The Sundanese recognize that only a few designated people are able to call on the power of the ancestors, and that an intermediary is necessary. In a difficult or dangerous stage in life, such as in the process of a life-cycle event (birth, death, weddings, circumcisions), a powerful intermediary should be present to aid in the crossing of the boundaries of these cycles. Music functions as this powerful intermediary in many cases, adding a strong regulating force to the proceedings by communicating the proper norms of behavior (refined and elegant actions onstage by the singers) and psychological orientation (vis-à-vis the ancestors) as it is embodied by the music. In the appropriate performance of the music, "musicians gain prestige through their display of cultural competence, and have an important influence on the flow of interaction" (Coplan 1982:120). It is the exact expertise of tembang Sunda musicians in this communication that makes them the ideal culture brokers between the Sundanese audience and the ancestors.

Singers in particular see themselves as the musical and cultural representatives of the kingdom of Pajajaran. By performing the music of the premodern aristocracy, these singers and musicians are acting as a bridge to that era. The legitimacy of this claim of "belonging" is strengthened by the fact that some modern singers of tembang Sunda still carry their aristocratic names, demonstrating their heritage as descendants of the ménak, or old nobility.[15] The world of tembang Sunda can be set in contexts as divergent as a wedding or disco dance floor in Bandung or the small living room of a singer in Sumedang, because its true setting is a spiritual one. Physically, it belongs in Bandung of the present century. Spiritually, this comparatively new ensemble belongs to the collective rural past that extends not only outside of Bandung and beyond the volcanoes but also back in time to the fourteenth-century kingdom of Pajajaran.

CONCLUSIONS

This book has followed the progression of tembang Sunda from its roots in Cianjur and its dissemination in the various kabupaten (regencies) of the region with the teachings of Raden Etjé Madjid to its regrouping in Bandung. This regrouping of tembang Sunda musicians in Bandung caused a revitalization of the genre during the 1950s and 1960s after the chaos caused by Indonesian Independence. Existing traditional authority systems around which the music was organized before Independence were replaced by new, urban institutions after many of the tembang Sunda practitioners moved to Bandung. It is exactly the urban environment in which modern tembang Sunda is situated that provides for its current vitality.

Many changes have taken place in tembang Sunda performance practice as a result of urbanization. Older, historical songs have been supplanted in many cases by newer compositions about love, and the styles most closely associated with traditional tembang Sunda performance (papantunan, jejemplangan, and dedegungan) have been replaced by the comparatively new styles of rarancagan and panambih, which allow greater compositional freedom. As a result of urbanization, modern performance contexts for tembang Sunda are far more diverse than in the past. In each context, the performers select an appropriate repertoire based on the situation and the audience. Certain styles are emphasized and others are restricted in accordance with what is now considered standard urban performance practice.

Sponsored performing groups provide a necessary structure within which the music continues to develop; these lingkung seni have at least partially replaced the old tradition of tembang Sunda patronage by members of the aristocracy. Juried tembang Sunda competitions provide a learning atmosphere in which practice sessions (latihan) may last all night as contestants prepare the required songs for months in advance. Weddings and other life-cycle ceremonies, as well as building dedications or military functions, provide the backbone of financial support for many of the lingkung seni, and these performance venues are able to support a small but active group of professional singers and instrumentalists. The tembang Sunda groups that have had the opportunity to travel abroad have brought home fame and a good reputation, in addition to increasing the stature of tembang Sunda within the music-playing community in Bandung and the rest of Indonesia.

For many of the aristocratic urban Sundanese, the performance and enjoyment of tembang Sunda is the means to the creation of a personal bridge between themselves and both the ancestors and setting of the past. Although tembang Sunda is a fairly recent genre in Indonesian musical history, its relative age and its association with the aristocracy of the nineteenth century give it the necessary connections with the past—both near and far. By gathering together the images of the fourteenth-century kingdom of Pajajaran, the colonial era when the Sundanese aristocracy were at least partially financially supported by the Dutch, and the early stages of tembang Sunda development (all of which occurred before Indonesian Independence), the aristocratic Sundanese seek to contact the power of the Sundanese past. The representation of strength and independence that was a part of the kingdom of Pajajaran is an important function of tembang Sunda performance; it reminds the listeners and performers of the glorious Sundanese past from which they are descended, allowing them to take pride in their culture. As such, it also functions as the necessary spiritual intermediary or kuncén between the modern, urban aristocratic Sundanese and their heritage in the semirural past. Lastly, tembang Sunda performance acts as a transformative reproduction of hierarchy to reinforce the separation of aristocratic Sundanese from the rest of the Sundanese.

The gathering together of many tembang Sunda singers, instrumentalists, and connoisseurs in Bandung has resulted in the development of intricate and extensive networks that center on the performance and continual discussion of tembang Sunda. These musical networks based primarily on occupational grounds also have led to personal competition, political and social maneuvering, and constant experimentation among musicians in their attempt to carve out individual styles in the urban milieu. Without its support and dissemination through these urban institutions following its establishment in Bandung in the 1950s, tembang Sunda might well have remained an obscure musical genre of the noblemen of late-nineteenth-century Cianjur. In its current state, tembang Sunda functions as a large-scale expansion on the concept of the kacapi as the ancestral ship: Not only does it speak using the voice of the ancestors, but it also offers the assurance of a final resting place in Pajajaran.

NOTES

INTRODUCTION

1. Books, theses, and dissertations in English that deal specifically with Sundanese musical culture include the writings of Baier (1986), DeVale (1977), Falk (1980), Foley (1979), Fryer (1989), Harrell (1974), Heins (1977), Weintraub (1985, 1990, and 1997), Williams (1990), and van Zanten (1987, 1989). Many authors have developed articles on Sundanese music, including Baier (1986 and 1988), Burman-Hall (1993), Cook (1993), Foley (1984, 1985, 1986, 1990, and 1993), Harrell (1975), Heins (1980), Hugh-Jones (1982), Natapradja (1975), Spiller (1993 and 1996), Stahl (1987), Weintraub (1993a and 1993b), Williams (1990, 1993, 1998a, 1998b, and 1999), Young and Kaufman (1993), and van Zanten (1986, 1993, 1994, 1995a, 1995b, and 1997).

2. I originally traveled to Bandung intending to study kacapi-suling, a type of instrumental music used to accompany the singers for tembang Sunda. I was fortunate to meet with Euis Komariah, who graciously agreed to be my vocal teacher. I was encouraged to focus on tembang Sunda rather than kacapi-suling for many reasons, including the fact that at the time kacapi-suling was only rarely performed in a live setting.

3. My generic Western European features also led to my frequently being mistaken for a Dutch woman by many Indonesians, not just the older Sundanese.

4. For more information about Sundanese humor, see my 1993 article, "Our Laughter Balances Our Tears: Humor in Sundanese Arts."

CHAPTER 1: SUNDANESE CULTURE IN TRANSITION

1. Wessing writes that "The mountainous Priangan region of West Java is the abode of the spirits of the Sundanese ancestors (*para hiang*)" (Wessing 1999:62). The term *parahiangan* is often used to describe the highland area. In fact, the train route between Jakarta and Bandung is called the "Parahiangan."

2. In an effort to call back the last rebels of the Dar'ul Islam movement from their hiding places in the hills, a special tembang Sunda verse was composed to the melody of "Jemplang Karang," and broadcast hourly on Bandung radio to implore the rebels to return home (van Zanten 1989:75).

3. The traditional Sundanese *selendang*, a six-foot-long scarf usually worn over the right or left shoulder, can also be draped around the neck and head, giving the illusion of being a Muslim head covering. "You see," said one famous singer, demonstrating her selendang as a shoulder scarf, "when you wear it like this [over the shoulder] you can be as sexy as you want. But then, when you go to a meeting, you can wrap it like this [demurely covering her hair and neck] and be the perfect Muslim!"

4. In 1996, I finally had the opportunity to learn "Hamdan," which had significantly increased in popularity since my initial visit to the area in 1987. I was at a tembang Sunda session filled with young women in Islamic dress (hair completely covered, long close-fitting dress and leggings), and they shrieked with laughter as I went through the Arabic words. While it is normal for Sundanese people to laugh uproariously when foreigners attempt something new, this particular event held greater meaning because the song is quite explicitly Islamic. The spectacle of someone from a culturally Christian area such as the United States earnestly studying an Islamic song was simply absurd.

5. Experiencing violence in the streets may seem like nothing new to someone raised with a healthy sense of caution and awareness. In spite of its size, however, Bandung was not known for its crime rate. The most common crime was theft; therefore, the idea of demonstrations and violent police reactions to those demonstrations is quite extraordinary.

6. An e-mail message arrived from Indonesia during the height of the economic crisis with this carefully phrased sentence: "It is never boring here."

CHAPTER 2: THE ANTECEDENTS OF TEMBANG SUNDA

1. The forced cultivation system (*Cultuurstelsel*) existed from 1830 to 1870 (Sears 1996:85); it ensured a continuing supply of coffee and tea to the Dutch, with little attention paid to the dire consequences it forced upon the Indonesians. Profits from Indonesian coffee alone are said to have financed the entire Dutch navy.

2. The Dutch are still viewed rather fondly by certain older members of the Sundanese aristocracy, who remember what it was like to be subsidized by the Dutch.

3. Comparatively few works have been published on pantun; however, the reader may refer to writings by Danasasmita (1979), Rosidi (1959, 1973b), Pleyte (1910), Falk (1978, 1980), and van Zanten (1993) to explore further historical references in Dutch, Indonesian, and English. The most up-to-date study on the genre is "Pantun Sunda: The Music of an Epic Narrative Tradition in West Java, Indonesia" (Weintraub 1990). In addition, several pantun narratives have been transcribed, analyzed, and published (Rosidi 1970, 1971a, 1971b, 1973a and Weintraub

1985), and the epic narrative "Lutung Kasarung" has been analyzed in detail (Eringa 1949).

4. Raden Etjé Madjid posthumously received an award in 1972 from the Republic of Indonesia for his work in the field of tembang Sunda (Sukanda 1983:30).

5. In 1996, I was kindly invited to dinner at Endo Suanda's home in Bandung, together with Euis Komariah, Philip Yampolsky and his family, and Henry Spiller. After dinner, Philip suggested that we listen to some older recordings of tembang Sunda. He was interested in the reactions of Euis Komariah and Endo Suanda to the recordings. Both of them exploded with laughter at the *lengking* sound of the singers, the extra pressure in their voices, and the unusual ornaments. Our baffled requests for an explanation of what was so funny led to interesting speculation about what constituted current ideas about the old ways of singing, and how very different the recordings were from all the usual discussions of the *tempo doeloe* ("olden days").

6. In addition, Sundanese musical notation (using ciphers) is reversed so that it is read exactly the opposite from Javanese cipher notation.

7. It was suggested to me many times that the job of foreign researchers should be to preserve disappearing styles, not to promote vital, healthy genres such as tembang Sunda, *jaipongan* social dance, or *pop Sunda*.

CHAPTER 3: CONTEXTS FOR PERFORMANCE

1. An article about tembang Sunda listed 178 *lingkung seni tembang Sunda* in West Java, compared with only twenty a decade earlier (Gelanggang Mahasiswa Sastra Indonesia 1975:14). Note, however, that in 1965 Indonesia was in the midst of bloodshed and chaos as part of the process that brought Suharto to power.

2. Because Western-derived rock, jazz, popular, and classical concerts customarily require an entrance fee, however, no one questions paying for those events.

3. It is polite to use someone's name when addressing them directly in Sundanese society, particularly when others are listening.

4. Tembang Sunda uses three primary tuning systems: pélog, sorog, and saléndro. These tunings are discussed in detail in Chapter 7.

5. It should be noted, however, that runners-up do actually try again. It is possible that Pa Apung was speaking about his experiences in the more distant past. Some musicians complain bitterly about the chilling effect that competitions have on diversity and development within each performing arts genre. The standardization of the repertoire (and the lexicon of ornaments) has arguably led to a minimization of the regional differences that characterize performances of tembang Sunda. In a climate in which Sundanese pride themselves on their many diverse genres and regional styles, it is ironic that competitions should be embraced so forcefully by the people in power.

6. A photograph of young Fitri singing tembang at the age of six, accompanied by her father, graces page 52 of van Zanten's *Sundanese Music in the Cianjuran Style* (1989).

7. Pemberton presents this trait as particularly Javanese, but it also shows up among the Sundanese élite and middle class in formal settings. It is not so far-fetched to link this behavior to other aspects of Javanese cultural holdovers.

8. My 1989 article on Sundanese popular music discusses the emergence of pop Sunda as a blend of the urban and rural, and as a means for the Sundanese to maintain their sense of identity in the face of modernization.

9. The rules were never clearly spelled out as to which musicians would be acceptable for performances, or which genres were "most valuable." It was clear, however, that a number of musicians abruptly had fewer gigs that year.

10. The tendency to consider only the events in one's immediate area is a trap that befalls not just local musicians, but even the most diligent researchers.

11. My own light brown sanggul cost 15,000 rupiah (about US$8 in 1988), because the hair used for it had to be purchased from a Dutch tourist by the wig-maker. Combed thinly over a heavy base of black hair, it almost matches my own reddish-blond hair.

12. Both men and women like to joke about those unfortunate women who are obviously wearing too much whitening makeup. These women are likened to moldy *dodol*, a type of dark brown soft Sundanese rice candy that goes bad very quickly and develops a white mold through which the dark candy is visible.

CHAPTER 4: MUSICAL INTERACTIONS BETWEEN MEN AND WOMEN

1. By contrast, Apung Wiratmadja claims that he never cried while singing, and no one questions the depth of his pangjiwaan.

2. The Balinese, Javanese, and Sumatrans note this purported "strict adherence to Islam." It is also frequently commented on by outsiders, because of some of the outward religious trappings of clothing or behavior in the presence of mosques. Nonetheless, significant variation of the amount of strictness occurs within Sundanese society. Nearly everyone will claim to be a "good Muslim," yet some are quite comfortable shrugging off the required five daily prayers or the injunction to fast at Ramadan. Performers number rather high in this category.

3. For more information about gender issues in the home, on stages, and in repertoires beyond the boundaries of tembang Sunda, see Williams 1998, "Constructing Gender in Sundanese Music."

4. In the early part of a married Sundanese woman's childbearing years, she is frequently beholden, one way or another, to her husband. As her children grow to independence, she often does as well. Women with grown children—especially post-menopausal women—may be asked to serve as host for a performing arts event or wedding reception that would have been out of the realm of possibility were she to be in her twenties with several young children. She also is able to discuss money matters openly with men and to speak to men more as an equal rather than as a subordinate or potential sexual partner.

5. One kacapi player proudly told me that his newborn daughter was now "clean," and that he could ease his mind, knowing that she would not be any trouble when she grew up. Although I had to approach this subject rather circuitously with the men, for obvious reasons, several mentioned rather directly that performing circumcision on women made sex more dry, and therefore more pleasurable, for men.

6. This issue may never have previously come to (academic) light outside of Indonesia, simply because no one bothered to ask. Given the important connections between performance and sexuality, however, it seems reasonable to further examine the impact of female circumcision on male-female relationships and, to a certain extent, on the issue of heightened sexuality of the female vocalist.

7. Jane Sugarman and others have noted this representation of a nation in the body of women: "Within the logic of nationalist constructs, women often come to

symbolize the (mother)land that is being fought for or the 'honor' of its people" (Sugarman 1999:446).

8. Note that in earlier chapters I have discussed the importance of the kacapi as another symbolic representation of Sundanese culture. The kacapi, however, represents the cultural region more than it does the people. It is worth pointing out that the kacapi is locally considered a female instrument, as is the suling.

9. This idea came up at a performance, when my kacapi teacher Rukruk Rukmana said that a particular patron just wanted to hear everyone call him "Raden." Rumor had it that the man wasn't really of the aristocracy at all. He did keep asking for particular songs, however, and all of them included honorifics.

10. Regarding the issue of Central Javanese women traders, Suzanne Brenner writes that "their 'danger' lies in their ability to control their own passions, even as they awaken those of others" (1998:166).

11. Rumors abound of audience members "hit" by songs. The most interactions I witnessed were between people who were already connected or at least rumored to be having an affair. I nearly set off a firestorm when I accidentally let my gaze stray to a platonic male friend (a nonmusician) during my performance of a rather torrid love song. The poor man nearly jumped out of his skin, a reaction noted by about half the people present. It took considerable negotiation on my part afterward to convince several eager inquirers that I was a clueless Westerner and hadn't thought about what I was doing at the time.

CHAPTER 5: THE MEDIATION OF SOUND

1. Although some compact discs have been recorded (mostly by foreigners rereleasing previously recorded master tapes), few people own them or the machines capable of playing them.

2. Late at night, after one particularly successful recording, the Jugala studio owner (Gugum Gumbira) called for "beer floats." The resulting concoction was unlike anything any of us had ever tasted.

3. It came as a tremendous surprise to Uking Sukri, a kacapi master in the traditional style, when he discovered that his playing had been replaced by that of Rukruk Rukmana on the cassette "Panyileukan."

4. A suling player, who was under contract and who specifically asked that I not mention his name, pointed out nine different cassettes on which he had played. On each one, he had either some variation on his contract name or played a different instrument, or was deliberately unlisted.

5. In a 1996 latihan, the kacapi was tuned to saléndro before all the singers had had a chance to try out their sorog tunes. Rather than retune the kacapi, the singer in charge simply had everyone sing their sorog tunes over saléndro accompaniment. As the *raja laras* ("king of tunings"), saléndro may be used for anything.

6. "Listening" means a variety of things in the Sundanese context. Under the conditions described in Chapter 3 (see malam tembang Sunda), everyone present is deeply connected to the community of vocalists, instrumentalists, and audience members. No one speaks once someone has begun singing; everyone focuses intently on the lyrics, the melody, the skill of the performers, the accompaniment, and (most important) the pangjiwaan or inner feeling associated with each song. Participants seem to breathe with one breath, to join on a noncorporeal plane, and to share a powerful experience not open to outsiders. At a panglawungan, by contrast, the politicians or businessmen present might lean forward intently as if listening, then

after a minute or two begin their usual business of lobbying and maneuvering. Other audience members appear to "listen" to be considered part of the group, but most of their activities are directed toward people watching and searching for fodder for gossip. Wim van Zanten's excellent article on this very topic highlights the importance of both hearing and listening, incorporating the outward manifestation of sound with the inner feeling (van Zanten 1997).

7. This placement of tembang Sunda outdoors links up with the Hidayat recording company's use of nature scenes on cassette covers; the scenes usually convey a bit more "nature" than the musicians or their audiences care for.

8. Issue No. 1264 (1990) of *Manglé* included a number of anonymously written articles, all of which dealt with some aspect of the jury rigging scandal. The articles focused on several different angles of the controversy, included photographs of participants, and significantly enlarged the issue in the community.

9. Sobirin's 1987 collection is called *Lagu-Lagu Mamaos* (mamaos songs) and *Lagu-Lagu Panambah* (panambih songs). They measure just four by six inches and fit neatly into a purse or pocket. It is customary to carry them when attending a performance, in case one is asked to kaul or in case a performer forgets a songbook. This publication has not resulted in the setting of lyrics into stone in connecting them with melodies, but it has resulted in certain lyrics being favored over others when the books are present. As for the panambih lyrics, most are linked to specific melodies and are not nearly as interchangeable as the mamaos lyrics.

CHAPTER 6: LEARNING THE CRAFT

1. One male singer—as he lit one cigarette while putting out the previous one—asked me what my secret for possession of *nafas panjang* ("long breath") was. I tentatively mentioned that quitting smoking might help, and he shook his head in disbelief.

2. As a result of his own frustration with attempting to notate Sundanese music, Wim van Zanten developed a clear and helpful article called "Notation of Music; Theory and Practice in West Java" (van Zanten 1995a). Van Zanten develops the problems associated with understanding tunings much more thoroughly. See also Simon Cook's 1993 article, "Parallel Versions of Tembang Sunda Melodies."

3. See Williams 1993, for more information about Sundanese performing arts humor generally.

4. The exception to this rule occurs with musicians such as Ajat Sudrajat, the 1996 winner of the pasanggiri DAMAS competition. He was always considered a vocalist, not an instrumentalist, and although he plays kacapi quite well on a few recordings, he is accorded the status of a vocalist.

5. Most of the latihan I attended were held at the home of Euis Komariah, one of the finest tembang singers of Bandung. The latihan described in this section are certainly representative of those held at her home, but I also found them to be similar to those held at the homes of Apung Wiratmadja, Mamah Dasimah, Enah Sukaenah, and Yayah Rochaeti Dachlan as well. The latihan gatherings at Euis Komariah's home (also the site of the Jugala studio) were lively affairs with anywhere from three to fifteen participants, comprising mostly female vocal students and male instrumentalists.

6. I was able to fit into the latihan situation there mostly because I participated as a regular voice student with several other women, and asked Ibu Euis to at least try not to treat me differently from the others. She complied graciously although she

usually had to double-check my spelling of the Sundanese lyrics and correct my pronunciation. This strategy only worked until guests or politicians arrived, who insisted that I be paid more attention and commanded to sing more songs than the others.

7. Neneng Dinar, my fellow student at Euis Komariah's latihan sessions (and now a fine singer in her own right), never bothered with a tape recorder because she felt that she would pay better attention if she was required to use her memory. "The songs go in more deeply," she said.

8. I used the method of private lessons for both kacapi and suling for several reasons. Among these reasons is that I simply couldn't stand to have a large crowd of people listening to me and laughing while I made loud mistakes on the suling. At the time I didn't care whether they were just being Sundanese and using humor as part of the learning process. I needed the privacy just to get my work done.

9. Some day jobs are more enjoyable than others. The Bandung tax office (Kantor Pajak), for example, has a disproportionately high number of musicians, singers, dancers, and teachers in its employ. Walking into the tax office is rather like seeing a large lingkung seni in matching government uniforms, with frequent humming, singing, and surreptitious hand gestures from dance. The members of the office attend each other's performances, buy copies of each other's cassettes, and discuss the performing arts almost continuously; some work also gets done.

CHAPTER 7: THE PARAMETERS OF STYLE

1. Some of my worst performing faux pas were in selecting the wrong style to sing. Audience reactions to my music were always abundantly clear, ranging from beaming approval to awkward embarrassment on my behalf.

2. Another example is *sisingaan*, an extraordinary lion dance held in honor of a young man's circumcision. A week after his circumcision, the young man is dressed in aristocratic costume and hoisted onto the back of a life-size lion figure (*singa*), which is carried through the village with great cheers and congratulations. The lion is the symbol of the Dutch, and the implication of the performance is that by sitting on top of the lion (read: Dutch), the youth of Sunda will eventually conquer the Dutch.

3. Please note that the Sundanese conceptualize their scales as beginning at a high pitch and proceeding downward. The following table gives a basic summary of the three main tuning systems, together with their cipher equivalents, Sundanese solfège names, string names, and relative Western equivalents, noting that a plus sign next to a pitch raises that pitch somewhat:

Pélog scale					
pitch numbers	1	2	3	4	5
solfège	da	mi	na	ti	la
string names	barang	kenong	panelu	bem	galimer
Western pitches	f"	e"	c"	b flat'	a'
Sorog scale					
pitch numbers	1	2	3	4	5
solfège	da	mi	na	ti	la
string names	barang	kenong	panelu	bem	galimer
Western pitches	f"	e"	d"	b flat'	a'

Saléndro scale					
pitch numbers	1	2	3	4	5
solfège	da	mi	na	ti	la
string names	barang	kenong	panelu	bem	galimer
Western pitches	f"	d+"	c"	b flat'	g+'

4. Social and political issues have long divided the Chinese-Indonesians from the native Indonesians. Dating from the colonial period when the Dutch offered greater economic advantages to the Chinese, the tension has frequently boiled over into violence. The most recent manifestation of this tension was in 1998, when Chinese-Indonesians bore the brunt of the frustration felt by the native Indonesians. Shops were looted and burned, people were killed in their homes, and reports of rape were widely disseminated on the news and through the Internet. In the relatively mild-seeming arena of tembang Sunda, a joking reference to a tuning system "smelling Chinese" is only the tip of an enormous iceberg.

5. This common inability to tell the difference in saléndro performances means that a kacapi player easily may take advantage of a singer as part of periodic competitions over who is in charge. By giving the wrong pitch as the first note of the song, the kacapi player may throw the vocalist completely off, with the possibility of causing her to go out of her vocal range and embarrassing her. I observed this happening at least twice; the first time, the vocalist was unaware of the pitch problem until it was too late and she was growling on a pitch far too low for her. The second time, the singer (Euis Komariah) knew instantly that the pitch was off and shot a lethal glance at the kacapi player, who covered his "mistake" by performing a series of cascading patterns until he came to the right place.

6. Kakawén songs are drawn from the wayang golék repertoire. As the only saléndro songs to be performed using a rebab, they are a favorite in late-night performances. The rebab takes the place of the suling in these kakawén songs, and a good rebab player must be able to cross the line between wayang golék and tembang Sunda easily and sensitively. The rebab players Uloh and the late Dacép Eddy are particularly fine rebab players in the kakawén style.

7. The epic narratives characterizing pantun performances do not use any of the four Sundanese poetic forms most common in tembang Sunda. Although some papantunan texts do use these forms, most use prose instead. Even those texts that do use poetic forms always include extra words or phrases (such as *Raden* or *Juragan*, terms of respect for the aristocracy), which effectively disrupt the form and identify the song as papantunan.

8. The gelenyu for jejemplangan songs are notoriously difficult to perform.

9. It is not unusual in performances of dedegungan songs for the regular suling to be temporarily replaced by the suling degung (Tatang Subari, personal communication, 1988). Its use is not just to emphasize the higher pitches in dedegungan songs, but also to incorporate the unusual timbral quality of the suling degung, normally only heard in gamelan degung. Ade Suandi, the suling player for the tembang Sunda ensemble at RRI Bandung in the late 1980s, mentioned that if the suling degung is not used, then the style of playing the regular suling should be very strong (*gagah*), with short, high-pitched phrases on the suling in imitation of the suling degung (Ade Suandi, personal communication, 1989).

10. The exception was one singer (Yayah Rochaeti Dachlan), known for being most comfortable with high-pitched songs, who frequently performs dedegun-

gan songs and prefers them to some of the lowest songs whose lower pitches are unattainable to her.

11. If the set is in pélog, the bubuka is "Jipang Lontang." If it is in sorog, the bubuka is "Samarangan." The usual bubuka for saléndro is "Macan Ucul."

12. The treatment of instrumentalists as servants survives from the days of Sundanese history when Javanese administrators were sent to colonize Sunda. Small courts were set up in each Sundanese regency, and each regency was then headed by a Javanese regent who imported symbols of power, including musical instruments. When the Dutch colonized Indonesia and replaced the Javanese regents with members of the Sundanese hereditary aristocracy, the Javanese returned to Central Java, leaving some musical instruments in Sunda. Once the Sundanese gained at least partial self-determination again, the Sundanese regents used certain Javanese-style techniques: gathering musicians and musical instruments to represent political and spiritual power, except that this time the musicians and ensembles were Sundanese. Musicians attached to the Sundanese regencies performed according to the desires of their patrons, the members of the Sundanese hereditary aristocracy. The old pattern of instrumentalists being at the beck and call of the upper classes persists today.

CHAPTER 8: INSTRUMENTAL AND VOCAL CHARACTERISTICS

1. Andrew Weintraub (personal communication, 1991) notes that it is also said to derive from the words *kaca* (glass) and *pikiran* (thought). Van Zanten discusses kacapi etymology as well (1987:98).

2. Unfortunately, the results of honoring and protecting the instrument with a soft, attractive cover may be somewhat the opposite of what was intended. The soft velvet covering also happens to attract cats, which sleep on the instrument and break the strings one by one as they step across it, turning around to find the ideal sleeping spot.

3. Although I did not find that my voice was ruined by playing suling, perhaps my voice was not ruined because I simply did not practice often enough, and in fact spent far more time practicing for my voice lessons than practicing my suling.

4. Wessing writes that awi tamiang is one of several different kinds of offerings made at Sundanese rice fields (Wessing 1999:62).

5. My own order of thirty sulings (shipped to the United States) included several that had become infested with insects and large Indonesian spiders, several that were cracked, and one or two that were out of tune. I also was lucky, however, to receive several "tiger" (loréng) sulings, the striped or spotted markings of which are perceived to indicate special power (see also van Zanten 1989:101).

CHAPTER 9: A NAME IS ALL THAT REMAINS

1. Andrew Weintraub describes Prabu Siliwangi as "the popular name for Sri Baduga Maharaja, who ruled the Pajajaran kingdom from 1482 to 1521." In addition, Weintraub notes that there could have been more than just one king (Weintraub 1991:1). Mohammed Amin Sutaarga refers to Prabu Siliwangi as an important writer (Indo.: tokoh sastra), meaning that his popularity in Sundanese consciousness has made him a major character in Sundanese oral and written literature (Sutaarga 1965: 8).

2. See Weintraub 1990:4, for more about the specific geography of highland Sunda.

3. In post–New Order Indonesia, listening to tembang Sunda or attending panglawungan gatherings has increasingly become a means by which one has the potential to rise through the ranks of urban Sundanese society. One may simply appropriate the trappings of aristocracy without actually having a blood relationship with the noblemen of Pajajaran.

4. Even the word *Pajajaran* itself is intensely symbolic, carrying with it a host of underlying meanings. See H. Ten Dam's discussion of Pajajaran for an interesting set of perspectives, as well as a map locating Pajajaran directly south of Jakarta, in the highlands near Mount Kancana at the mouth of the river Ciliwung (Ten Dam 1954).

5. Etjé Madjid Natawiredja (1853–1928) is said to have composed "Papatet," placing the song at a significantly later date than that claimed for it by some of the musicians. See van Zanten 1989:25, for more information about "Papatet."

6. Although it may be a risky premise to posit that a movement away from the kacapi player's body represents a kinaesthetic shift in time, when taken together with the rest of the evidence, it does not seem nearly as far-fetched.

7. Every tembang singer's notebooks include the lyrics for "Papatet." The song is in public domain. Van Zanten's translation, however, is the first of its kind in print, and is reprinted by permission here from the Koninklijk Instituut voor Taal-, Land- en Volkenkunde.

8. Henry Spiller correctly points out that claiming a particular teaching lineage for oneself appears to be restricted to tembang Sunda practice. In other Sundanese genres, it even may be a point of pride for an accomplished musician not to have studied with anyone in particular, or to joke about having learned whatever art form *secara alam* ("naturally").

9. While pale-skinned and possibly underprepared foreign researchers may chafe at being asked to perform tembang Sunda under almost any Sundanese circumstance imaginable, it is true that the physical attributes of being of European descent lend themselves to functioning as a pale reminder of aristocracy. The exceedingly high nose of Europeans even shows up in light entertainment-type songs, as in "I've got a flat one, I want a tall one."

10. I am indebted to my teaching partner Joe Feddersen and the students of my 1998–1999 yearlong program, "Envisioning Home: Finding Your Place through Art and Music" at Evergreen State College, for inspiring me to further develop this line of thinking.

11. For further information about the culturally defined roles for each Sundanese gender, see "Constructing Gender in Sundanese Music" (Williams 1998b).

12. See also Jane Sugarman's work on "imagining the homeland" in Albania, particularly the romantic distancing of rural life (Sugarman 1999).

13. My kacapi teacher, Rukruk Rukmana, spoke of expecting go home to Pajajaran after his death, saying that all tembang Sunda musicians go home to Pajajaran.

14. Sundanese people refer to Ramadan more frequently as *bulan puasa* ("fasting month") than by the name *Ramadan*. The end of Ramadan is called *Lebaran* ("freeing"), *Idul Fitri*, or *Hari Raya* ("big day"), which is when everyone goes "home."

15. Robert Wessing (1994:52) notes that today, only 20 percent of Java is actually taken up by forested territory.

16. The Sundanese regard Prabu Siliwangi as the ancestor of all Sundanese ancestors; therefore, all Sundanese are at least spiritually descended from the king of Pajajaran, regardless of their social standing in early twenty-first-century Indonesia (Rikin 1973:72, as cited in Wessing 1986:109). Wessing also notes that weretigers tend to appear during the Islamic month of Maulud, the month of the ancestors (1986:93); they also appear at gravesites (1986:88).

17. One of the most interesting features of Sundanese men's classical dancing is that the male dancers often add significant amounts of painted-on body hair to their faces and chests. The representation of past glories through the addition of body hair (adding, according to several dancers, masculinity, power, sexual potency, and nobility) could lead one to conjecture about the ancestors as being more hairy and/or possibly being slightly more connected the animal world. John Pemberton writes that body hair is a sign of invulnerability in the area surround Solo (Surakarta in Central Java). The Sendhang Teleng ("deep pool") in the Wonogiri district is a place to "bathe for, or in, power" (Pemberton 1994:272). The topic of body hair (relative lack of it on the part of the Sundanese and the overabundance of it on the part of Westerners) comes up rather frequently in the course of conducting field research. Comparisons between people with excessive body hair and monkeys or other animals are often a part of these discussions.

18. The tembang Sunda panambih song "Lembur Singkur" ("My Village") speaks eloquently about life in the village, including viewing it as a place to calm the "heat of one's heart" (*panasna hate*).

19. This trait is also important among the Javanese (not necessarily just the members of the upper class).

20. Paradoxically, the upper-class Sundanese are more mobile than most others in the city. The actual temperature in downtown Bandung (elevation approximately 1,000 feet above sea level) varies from a low of about 68° Fahrenheit at night to about 85° or 90° during the day. The surrounding hills are cooler by about ten degrees. The peaks of the highest volcanoes in the region rise as high as 9,000 feet above sea level, and are considerably colder.

CHAPTER 10: CONNECTING WITH THE ANCESTORS

1. Van Zanten (1987:100) also describes it as "the ancestral ship," a description for which I am (obviously) very grateful. Mircea Eliade also includes a brief passage about the Indonesian propensity for the creation and use of "death ships":

> The "boat of the dead" plays a great role in Malaysia and Indonesia, both in strictly shamanic contexts and in funerary practices and laments. All of these practices are connected on the one hand with the custom of loading the dead on canoes or throwing them into the sea, and, on the other, with the funerary mythologies. The practice of exposing the dead in boats might well be explained by vague recollections of ancestral migrations; the boat would carry the dead man's soul back to the original homeland from which the ancestors set forth. But, these possible memories lost their historical meaning; the "original homeland" became a mythical country and the ocean that separates it from inhabited lands was assimilated to the Waters of Death. . . . In Indonesia the shaman conducts the deceased to the beyond, and he often uses a boat for this ecstatic journey. (Eliade 1964:355–358)

2. John Pemberton points out that Central Javanese *dhukun* tend to discuss this kind of phenomenon as a connection through electrical charges, rather than seeing this kind of connection as a moment of spirit possession. He quotes one medium as follows: "The transmission of a spirit from the third stratosphere . . . is received in a moment of coincidence between two wavelengths: one produced by the medium's concentration, the other generated by the spirit. This momentary contact emits an electrical charge, zap!" (Pemberton 1994:298).

3. "Bearing ill will" and "being Dutch" are separate issues here. Although some of the older people may view the Dutch with concern because of their long history of colonization in the area, most Indonesians appear to have more current concerns. The spirit in my house had not yet "moved on," as it were, and was still worried that a Dutch person might be living there.

4. As Yano writes regarding Japanese enka, "These are not emotions of jubilation, but of longing, heartache, sorrow. In its commodification of these, the genre becomes a site of negotiation of Japanese identity. What this expression of the 'heart/soul of Japanese people' does is offer up a bounded version of Japaneseness situated in the past" (Yano 1998:125).

5. The Sundanese use four different verse forms (pupuh) in certain tembang Sunda songs. Some tembang songs use prose instead. The four primary forms are called *asmarandana, dangdanggula, kinanti,* and *sinom*. Please note that these spellings are Sundanese, not Javanese (e.g., *kinanthi*). Each form uses a specific pattern of numbered syllables and the final vowel in each line, read below, for example, as "8a." Eight is the number of syllables per line, and "a" indicates the final vowel of that line. The forms most commonly used in tembang Sunda are listed below in alphabetical order, with their syllabic count and final vowels included.

Asmarandana:	8i–8a–8é/o–8a–7a–8u–8a
Dangdanggula:	10i–10a–8é/o–7u–9i–7a–6u–8a–12i–7a
Kinanti:	8u–8i–8a–8i–8a–8i
Sinom:	8a–8i–8a–8i–7i–8u–7a–8i–12a

One example of a song in a pupuh form is "Goyong," in dangdanggula, discussed later in this chapter.

6. My thanks go to Philip Yampolsky for clarifying my understanding of Javanese poetic verse. He notes that Javanese texts are usually excerpted from long literary works in macapat forms. Because they are excerpts, the sequence and content of the stanzas is invariable.

7. I was, unfortunately, not able to switch lyrics as quickly as my friends, and on several occasions was told to sing "any asmarandana" or "any sinom" within seconds of my performance time. My blank stare at the point of my entrance caused plenty of laughter, but also caused several people to take me aside and kindly suggest that I get to know the poetic forms better.

8. This particular sisindiran has been recorded on the Smithsonian/Folkways CD *Music of Indonesia 2*, "Indonesian Popular Music: Kroncong, Dangdut, and Langgam Jawa" (SF 40056).

9. Malay pantun are ubiquitous verses with four lines and eight syllables per line, with an a–b–a–b rhyme scheme. They are the most popular type of verse in Malaysia (Matusky and Chopyak 1998:435).

10. That Dutch-Indonesian verse (often used in the song "Panghegar") is as follows, translated with corrected spelling by Dr. Robert Wessing:

Ular naga dat is overlang	The naga snake that is quite long
Putih putih bunga malati	White, white jasmine flower
Mijn ogen zien, mijn hart verlang	My eyes they see, my heart desires
Vergeet dat niet, si jantung hati	Do not forget that, heart of hearts.

11. My reaction of shock at the suggestion that I perform what I perceived to be an extremely depressing song at a wedding was met with casual laughter and a reassurance that a sad song would not be bad luck for the newlyweds. Given the comparatively high rate of divorce, however, perhaps reconsideration might have been in order.

12. It should also be noted that placing a well-oiled wok under the hot (say, 95°F) Indonesian sun for a couple of hours would have a considerable effect on one's egg-frying capabilities.

13. For that matter, the concept of "Sunda" dates only from the mid–nineteenth century. In the oral literature, place-names are quite specific (Pajajaran, Galuh, Tarumanagara, etc.). My thanks go to Robert Wessing for pointing out this idea; he further believes that "Sunda" is probably a creation of the Dutch, possibly as a way to create further opposition between the Sundanese and Javanese (personal communication 2000).

14. See the section on networks of power and influence in Miller and Williams 1998:8–10.

15. One of my servant's friends asked her whether she had developed a taste for tembang Sunda after living with me for so long and listening to it every day. She laughed out loud and said, "You must be joking! Me, listening to that ménak music?" Though it is correct to seriously question the extent of ménak culture and influence today, the perception remains that tembang Sunda belongs to the ménak class (see Alisjahbana 1954, for an interesting discussion of class issues in postindependence Sunda).

GLOSSARY

asmarandana   one of the four main poetic meters used in tembang Sunda compositions, this meter uses seven lines with the syllabic count of each line arranged as 8, 8, 8, 8, 7, 8, 8. The final vowels for each line are *i, a, e/o, a, a, u,* and *a.*
beluk   village performance style read and sung by a group of men.
bendo   small, folded batik cap worn by men.
biasa   generic word for normal; describes the usual way of playing rincik.
bismi allāhi al-rahmāni al-rahīm   Arabic phrase blessing the upcoming effort.
bubuka   instrumental opening piece used before vocal music. The bubuka used in pélog is "Jipang Lontang;" in sorog, "Samarangan;" in saléndro, "Sinyur Panelu."
buntut   literally, "tail." A vocal technique in which a long note (with a slight vibrato) is ended with a brief upturn; may also describe rebab technique.
cacag   one of several kacapi playing techniques, using the right hand to produce a skipping pattern across two strings in a gradual descent to lower-pitched strings.
cacagan   vocal ornament with strong accents on a single pitch, preceded by a long note.
carukan   rincik playing reminiscent of the saron in the gamelan ensemble; the rincik plays very quickly using alternating index fingers.
Cianjuran   old name for tembang Sunda, reflecting its origins in Cianjur.
Cigawiran   unaccompanied free-rhythm Sundanese vocal music using religious texts.

dangdanggula one of the four main poetic meters used in tembang Sunda compositions, this meter uses ten lines with the syllabic count of each line arranged as 10, 10, 8, 7, 9, 7, 6, 8, 12, 7. The final vowels of each line are *i, a, e/o, u, i, a, u, a, i,* and *a*.

dapur rekaman recording studio (literally, "recording kitchen").

dedegungan one of the five stylistic divisions of tembang Sunda. This style is in pélog and related to rarancagan because it uses poetic meters in free rhythm.

gamelan Indonesian gong-chime ensemble generally performing in cyclic patterns punctuated by a gong. Sundanese variants include gamelan degung and gamelan saléndro, used to accompany theater, dance, and songs in saléndro tuning.

gelenyu instrumental interlude or introduction.

hajat special ceremony to mark a life-cycle change, such as circumcision or marriage.

jaipongan popular form of social dance derived from ketuk tilu performance practice, penca silat martial arts dance, and several other regional styles.

jejemplangan one of the five stylistic divisions of tembang Sunda. This style is in the pélog tuning and is one of the oldest styles in tembang Sunda.

kabaya tightly fitting, front-closing, long-sleeved women's blouse.

kacapi eighteen-string boat-shaped zither, also called kacapi perahu ("boat kacapi") and kacapi indung ("mother kacapi").

kain length of batik that is tightly wrapped around a woman's legs and hips.

kait kacapi technique using octaves in the right hand and syncopated patterns in the left hand; used to accompany panambih songs.

kakawén small groups of saléndro songs normally performed as part of the wayang golék repertoire, but periodically used in tembang Sunda.

kaki feet; in the kacapi, the two small feet that lift the instrument off the ground.

kawat strings used on a kacapi, rincik, or rebab.

kawih vocal music in fixed rhythm, sometimes used as a panambih to close the free-rhythm mamaos section of tembang Sunda sets.

kecrek a small cymbal used in gamelan and other ensembles as a timekeeper.

kemprang kacapi technique using a repetitive pattern emphasizing two pitches a fifth apart.

kenit rincik playing that uses alternating octave patterns in varying rhythms; usually played by the second rincik.

ketuk tilu small Sundanese village ensemble from the north coastal area.

kinanti one of the four main poetic meters used in tembang Sunda compositions, this meter uses six lines with the syllabic count of each line arranged as 8, 8, 8, 8, 8, 8. The final vowels of each line are *u, i, a, i, a,* and *i*.

kliningan vocal music used in performances with gamelan saléndro.

kuncén a spiritual intermediary between humans and the spirit world.

lagu song; in tembang Sunda, more characteristically a melody to which a type of poetic structure may be sung if it is appropriate to the meter or number of syllables.

latihan public rehearsal, lesson, or jam session.

lipat vocal technique involving a brief drop in pitch before a return to the original pitch.

lubang holes on the suling.

mamaos free-rhythm parlando rubato vocal music; the backbone of tembang Sunda.

GLOSSARY 249

mandalungan   one of the more unusual tuning systems used in tembang Sunda.
mata itik   small washers that protect the rincik's sounding board from string damage.
ménak   indicating aristocratic descent.
narangtang   introductory vocal passage, acting as a bridge to the following song.
pamirig   tembang Sunda accompanist.
panambih   fixed-meter "addition" song, performed at the end of each tembang Sunda set. Panambih may be in any tuning and also may be instrumental.
pangajian al Qur'an   the vocal recitation of Qur'anic texts.
pangését   bow used for rebab playing.
pangjiwaan   inner soul or deep-level meaning in a song.
panglawungan   formal gathering of people who perform tembang Sunda.
pantun   epic narrative performance in which a blind bard sings and recites ancient epics, while accompanying himself on the kacapi.
panutup   instrumental closing piece, performed after all vocal activity has ceased.
papantunan   one of the five stylistic divisions of tembang Sunda. Papantunan are performed exclusively in pélog tuning and often use prosaic texts rather than poetic meters. They are derived in part from pantun epic narrative performance.
pasanggiri   Sundanese musical competition.
pasieup   free-rhythm kacapi technique.
patokan   playing pattern on the kacapi or other instruments during a panambih.
pélog   one of the three main tuning systems used in tembang Sunda.
pélog wisaya   one of the unusual tuning systems used in tembang Sunda.
penca silat   martial arts dance form.
polos   generic word meaning plain; a vocal technique using a completely straight tone.
pucuk   top portion of the neck of the rebab, rising above the tuning pegs.
pupuh   poetic meter derived from Central Javanese poetic meters.
pureut   pegs used for rough tuning on the kacapi or rebab.
rajah   invocational song that opens a traditional performance.
rarancagan   one of the five stylistic divisions of tembang Sunda. Rarancagan are performed in free rhythm and usually use pupuh or poetic meters; they may be performed in any tuning system.
rebab   two-string bowed lute used to replace the suling during saléndro songs derived from the wayang golék repertoire (kakawén).
rekaman   recording.
reureueus   vocal ornament using vibrato; also a generic term for vocal ornamentation.
rincik   small fifteen-string zither used in the fixed-rhythm sections of performances.
rupiah   Indonesian national currency.
saléndro   one of the three most common tuning systems used in tembang Sunda.
sanggul   type of hairpiece worn by Sundanese women at formal occasions.
sarung   length of batik sewn into a tube, worn by men in performances.
sasajén   offering (of food, incense, rice, and other ingredients of spiritual significance) to the gods, used at selamatan and other ceremonies.
selamatan   special ceremony involving food and guests, which is intended to bring goodwill and blessings to the participants.
selop   strapless high-heeled sandals used by tembang Sunda vocalists.

sénggol   generic term for ornamentation.

sinom   one of the four main poetic meters used in tembang Sunda compositions, this meter uses nine lines with the syllabic count of each line arranged as 8, 8, 8, 8, 7, 8, 7, 8, 12. The final syllables of each line are *a, i, a, i, i, u, a, i,* and *a.*

sisindiran   poetic form using a pair of couplets similar in both structure and rhyme.

siter   small board zither with twenty strings, often used as a substitute for a kacapi.

sorog   one of the three most common tuning systems used in tembang Sunda.

sorog-saléndro   one of the unusual tuning systems used in tembang Sunda.

suara   voice, of humans or musical instruments.

suku   base of the rebab.

suling   six-hole end-blown bamboo flute, from 58 to 62 centimeters when used for tembang Sunda.

takdir   Islamic concept meaning "fate" or "it is written."

takwah   morning coat worn by men in performances.

tarawangsa   bowed lute, usually paired with a kacapi and used in pantun performances.

tawajuh   special initiation ceremony for kacapi players.

tembang   generic word meaning "to sing," often applied to tembang Sunda.

téngkép   technique of muting a string immediately after it has been struck.

tihang   neck of the rebab.

tumpang sari   movable bridges on a kacapi or rincik; the single bridge on the rebab.

vibra   vocal ornament that uses a very small vibrato, like a tremolo.

wa'as   feelings that include nostalgia, reminiscence, wistfulness, awe, and admiration.

wayang golék   rod puppet theater accompanied by gamelan saléndro.

BIBLIOGRAPHY

Acciaioli, Greg. 1985. "Culture as Art: From Practice to Spectacle in Indonesia." *Canberra Anthropology* 8/1:148–172.
Alisjahbana, Samiati. 1954. "A Preliminary Study of Class Structure among the Sundanese in the Prijangan." M.A. thesis, Cornell University, Ithaca, N.Y.
Anderson, Benedict. 1965. *Mythology and the Tolerance of the Javanese.* Ithaca, N.Y.: Cornell University Modern Indonesia Project, Monograph Series.
———. 1972. "The Idea of Power in Javanese Culture." In *Culture and Politics in Indonesia*, ed. Claire Holt, pp. 1–69. Ithaca, N.Y.: Cornell University Press.
———. 1983. *Imagined Communities: Reflections on the Origin and Spread of Nationalism.* London: Verso.
Appadurai, Arjun. 1988. "Introduction: Place and Voice in Anthropological Theory." *Cultural Anthropology* 3/1:16–20.
———. 1996. *Modernity at Large: Cultural Dimensions of Globalization.* Minneapolis: University of Minnesota Press.
Atmadinata, Kosasih. 1980. "Penjiwaan Lagu." Paper presented to the Yayasan Pancaniti, Bandung.
Baier, Randal E. 1986. "Si Duriat Keueung: The Sundanese Angklung Ensemble of West Java, Indonesia." M.A. thesis, Wesleyan University. Middletown, Conn.
———. 1988. "Is Trance Tuning Theorized? or, One Musician's View of the Ancestors in West Java, Indonesia." Paper presented at the annual meeting of the Society for Ethnomusicology, Tempe, Ariz.

Barmara and Ida Achman. 1958. *Perkembangan Tembang/Kawih Sunda*. Bandung: Dua-R.

Benda, Harry J. 1963. "Continuity and Change in Indonesian Islam." Paper presented at the Institute of Asian and African Studies of Hebrew University, Jerusalem.

Boland, B. J. 1971. *The Struggle of Islam in Modern Indonesia*. The Hague: Martinus Nijhoff.

Bradley, Margaret. 1993. "Kecapi Siter and Kecapi Perahu: Two Major Contributors to the Development of Sundanese Musical Styles in West Java, Indonesia." M.M. thesis, University of New South Wales, Australia.

Brenner, Suzanne A. 1998. *The Domestication of Desire: Women, Wealth and Modernity in Java*. Princeton: Princeton University Press.

Brinner, Benjamin E. 1995. *Knowing Music, Making Music: Javanese Gamelan and the Theory of Musical Competence and Interaction*. Chicago: University of Chicago Press.

Burman-Hall, Linda. 1993. "Nano S.'s *Warna*: A Life in Music." *Balungan* 5/2:24–29.

Cobban, James L. 1974. "Uncontrolled Urban Settlement: The Kampong Question in Semarang." *Bijdragen tot de taal-, land- en volkenkunde* 130/4:403–427.

Coedès, George. 1968. *The Indianized States of Southeast Asia*. Honolulu: University of Hawaii Press.

Cook, Simon. 1993. "Parallel Versions of Tembang Sunda Melodies." *Oideion: The Performing Arts World-Wide*, ed. Wim van Zanten, pp. 55–84. Leiden: Centre of Non-Western Studies, Leiden University.

Coplan, David. 1982. "The Urbanization of African Music: Some Theoretical Observations." *Popular Music* 2:113–129.

Danasasmita, Saleh. 1979. "Latar Belakang Sejarah, Sosial dan Budaya Seni Pantun." *Buletin Kebudayaan Jawa Barat* 23/1–3:5–12.

Danasasmita, Saleh and Atja. 1981. *Sanghyang Siksakandang ng Karesian*. Bandung: Proyek Pengembangan Permuseuman Jawa Barat.

de Lauretis, Teresa. 1990. "Eccentric Subjects: Feminist Theory and Historical Consciousness." *Feminist Studies* 16/1:115–150.

DeVale, Sue Carole. 1977. "A Sundanese Gamelan: A Gestalt Approach to Organology." Ph.D. dissertation, University of Hawai'i, Honolulu.

Denny, Frederick M. 1985. *An Introduction to Islam*. New York: Macmillan.

Drewes, G. W. J. 1968. "New Light on the Coming of Islam to Indonesia?" *Bijdragen tot de taal-, land- en volkenkunde* 124/4:432–459.

Durban, Irawati. 1989. "Women's Dance among the Sundanese of West Java, Indonesia." *Asian Theatre Journal* 6/2:168–178.

Eliade, Mircea. 1964. *Shamanism: Archaic Techniques of Ecstasy*. Princeton: Princeton University Press.

Endang. 1979. *Pangajaran Tembang Sunda*. Bandung: Pelita Masa.

Eringa, F. S. 1949. *Loetoeng Kasaroeng: Een mythologisch verhaal uit West-Java; Bijdrage tot de Soendase taal- en letterkunde*. 's-Gravenhage: Nijhoff.

———. 1984. *Soendaas-Nederlands woordenboek*. Dordrecht/Cinnaminson: Foris.

Errington, Shelly. 1990. "Recasting Sex, Gender and Power: A Theoretical and Regional Overview." In *Power and Difference: Gender in Island Southeast Asia*, ed. Jane Monnig Atkinson and Shelly Errington, pp. 1–58. Stanford: Stanford University Press.

Falk, Catherine A. 1978. "The Tarawangsa—A Bowed Stringed Instrument from West Java." In *Studies in Indonesian Music*, ed. Margaret J. Kartomi, pp. 45–103.

Monash Papers on Southeast Asia, No. 7. Victoria, Australia: Centre of Southeast Asian Studies, Monash University.

———. 1980. "The Tarawangsa Tradition in the Priangan, West Java." Ph.D. dissertation, Monash University, Victoria, Australia.

Feld, Steven. 1982. *Sound and Sentiment: Birds, Weeping, Poetics, and Song in Kaluli Expression*. Philadelphia: University of Pennsylvania Press.

Foley, Kathy. 1979. "The Sundanese Wayang Golék: The Rod Puppet Theater of West Java." Ph.D. dissertation, University of Hawai'i, Honolulu.

———. 1984. "Of Dalang and Dukun-Spirit and Men: Curing and Performance in the Wayang of West Java." *Asian Theatre Journal* 1/1:52–75.

———. 1985. "The Dancer and the Danced: Trance Dance and Theatrical Performance in West Java." *Asian Theatre Journal* 2/1:28–49.

———. 1986. "At the Graves of the Ancestors: Chronicle Plays in the Wayang Cepak Puppet Theatre of Cirebon, Indonesia." In *Historical Drama*, ed. James Redmond, pp. 31–49. Themes in Drama, 8. Cambridge: Cambridge University Press.

———. 1990. "My Bodies: The Performer in West Java." *Drama Review* 34/2:62–80.

———. 1993. "Linking Past and Future: Asep Sunandar Sunarya, Irawati Durban Arjo and Endo Suanda." *Balungan* 5/2:19–23.

Friedl, John, and Noel J. Chrisman. 1975. "Continuity and Adaptation as Themes in Urban Anthropology." In *City Ways: A Selective Reader in Urban Anthropology*, ed. A. Southall, pp. 1–22. New York: Oxford University Press.

Friedmann, John. 1961. "Cities in Social Transformation." *Comparative Studies in Society and History* 4:86–103.

Fryer, Ruth M. 1989. "Sundanese Theory and Practice in the Performance of Gamelan in Bandung, West Java." Ph.D. dissertation, Queen's University of Belfast, Northern Ireland.

Geertz, Clifford. 1960a. "The Javanese Kiyayi: The Changing Role of a Cultural Broker." *Comparative Studies in Society and History* 2:228–249.

———. 1960b. *The Religion of Java*. Chicago: University of Chicago Press.

———. 1980. *Negara: The Theatre State in Nineteenth-Century Bali*. Princeton: Princeton University Press.

Geertz, Hildred. 1963. "Indonesian Cultures and Communities." In *Indonesia*, ed. Ruth T. McVey. New Haven: Yale University Southeast Asia Studies.

Gelanggang Mahasiswa Sastra Indonesia. 1975. "Sebuah Tanggapan Atas: Diskusi Tembang Sunda." *Buletin Kebudayaan Jawa Barat* 3(II-I):14–16.

Gibson, Thomas. 2000. "Islam and the Spirit Cults in New Order Indonesia: Global Flows vs. Local Knowledge." *Indonesia* 69:41–70.

Goffman, Erving. 1956. "The Nature of Deference and Demeanor." *American Anthropologist* 58/3:473–502.

Graaf, H. J. de. 1949. *Geschiedenis van Indonesië*. Den Haag/Bandung: W. van Hoeve.

Gronow, Pekka. 1981. "The Record Industry Comes to the Orient." *Ethnomusicology* 25/2:251–284.

Haan, F. de. 1910. *Priangan: De Preanger-Regentschappen onder het Nederlandsch Bestuur tot 1811*. 4 vols. Batavia: Kolff.

Hall, Stuart. 1997. "The Local and the Global: Globalization and Ethnicity." In *Culture, Globalization and the World-System: Contemporary Conditions for the Representation of Identity*, ed. Anthony D. King, pp. 19–39. Minneapolis: University of Minnesota Press.

Hannerz, Ulf. 1980. *Exploring the City: Inquiries toward an Urban Anthropology.* New York: Columbia University Press.

Harrell, Max. 1974. "Music of the Gamelan Degung of West Java." Ph.D. dissertation, University of California at Los Angeles.

———. 1975. "Some Aspects of Sundanese Music." *Selected Reports in Ethnomusicology* 2/2:81–100.

Heins, Ernst L. 1977. "Goong Renteng: Aspects of Orchestral Music in a Sundanese Village." Ph.D. dissertation, University of Amsterdam.

———. 1980. "West Java." In *The New Grove Dictionary of Music and Musicians*, ed. Stanley Sadie. New York: Macmillan. Volume 9, pp. 207–215.

Heyne, K. 1927. *De nuttige planten van Nederlandsch-Indië.* 2nd ed. Batavia: Ruygrok. Three volumes. [First edition 1913–1917.]

Hidding, K. A. H. 1935. *Gebruiken en godsdienst der Soendaneezen.* Batavia: Kolff.

Hoëvell, W. R. van. 1845. "Bijdrage tot de kennis der Badoeinen, in het zuiden der residentie Bantam." *Tijdschrift voor Neêrland's Indië* 7/4:335–430.

Hugh-Jones, Jonathan. 1982. "Karawitan Sunda: Tradition Newly Writ; A Survey of Sundanese music since Independence." *Recorded Sound* 82:19–34.

Ischak, C. Aah. 1988. *Mang Bakang dan Tembang Cianjuran.* Bandung: Binakarya.

Jackson, Karl D., and Johannes Moeliono. 1973. "Participation in Rebellion: the Dar'ul Islam in West Java." In *Political Participation in Modern Indonesia*, ed. R. William Liddle, pp. 12–57. New Haven: Yale University Southeast Asian Studies, Monograph No.19.

———. 1978. "Urbanization and the Rise of Patron-Client Relations." In *Political Power and Communication in Indonesia*, ed. Karl Jackson and Lucien Pye, pp. 343–392. Berkeley: University of California Press.

———. 1980. *Traditional Authority, Islam, and Rebellion: A Study of Indonesian Political Behavior.* Berkeley: University of California Press.

Kartomi, Margaret J. 1973a. *Matjapat Songs in Central and West Java.* Canberra: Australia National University Press.

———. 1973b. "Music and Trance in Java." *Ethnomusicology* 17/2:163–208.

Keeler, Ward. 1987. *Javanese Shadow Plays, Javanese Selves.* Princeton: Princeton University Press.

Kern, R. A. 1898. *Geschiedenis der Preanger-regentschappen; kort overzicht.* Bandung: De Vries en Fabricius.

Keyfitz, Nathan. 1976. "The Ecology of Indonesian Cities." In *Changing Southeast Asian Cities: Readings on Urbanization*, ed. Yue-Man Yeung and Fu-Chen Lo, pp. 348–354. Singapore: Oxford University Press.

Koentjaraningrat. 1978. "Twentieth-Century Rural-Urban Changes." In *Dynamics of Indonesian History*, ed. Soebadio and Sarvaas, pp. 345–376. Amsterdam: North-Holland.

Kornhauser, Bronia. 1978. "In Defence of Kroncong." In *Studies in Indonesian Music*, ed. Margaret J. Kartomi, pp. 104–183. Monash Papers on Southeast Asia, No. 7. Victoria, Australia: Centre of Southeast Asian Studies, Monash University.

Koskoff, Ellen. 1987. "An Introduction to Women, Music, and Culture." In *Women and Music in Cross-Cultural Perspective*, ed. Ellen Koskoff, pp. 1–24. Urbana: University of Illinois.

Koswara, Koko. 1973. *Pelajaran Kacapi, etude jeung tehnik.* Bandung: Balebat.

Kroef, Justus M. van der. 1953. "The Indonesian City: Its Culture and Evolution." *Asia* 2:563–579.

Kunst, Jaap. 1973. *Music in Java: Its History, Its Theory, and Its Technique*, 3rd ed., rev., trans. and enlarged by Ernst Heins. Two volumes. The Hague: Martinus Nijhoff.

Kusumadinata, R. Machyar Angga. N. D. *Ringkesan Pangawikan Rinenggaswara*, 2nd printing. Jakarta: Noordhoff-Kolff.

———. 1969. *Ilmu Seni Raras*. Jakarta: Pradnya Paramita.

Legge, J. D. 1965. *Indonesia*. Englewood Cliffs, N.J.: Prentice Hall.

Lombard, Denys. 1974. "La vision de la Forêt à Java (Indonèsie)." *Etudes rurales* 6/53–56:473–485.

Manuel, Peter, and Randal E. Baier. 1986. "Jaipongan: Indigenous Popular Music of West Java." *Asian Music* 18/1: 91–110.

Matusky, Patricia, and James Chopyak. 1998. "Peninsular Malaysia." In *The Garland Encyclopedia of World Music*, Vol. 4: *Southeast Asia*, ed. Terry E. Miller and Sean Williams, pp. 401–443. New York: Garland.

McClary, Susan. 1993. "Reshaping a Discipline: Musicology and Feminism in the 1990s." *Feminist Studies* 19/2: 399–423.

McTaggart, W. Donald. 1982. "Land-Use in Sukabumi, West Java: Persistence and Change." *Bijdragen tot de taal-, land- en volkenkunde* 138/2:295–316.

Merriam, Alan P. 1964. *The Anthropology of Music*. Evanston, Ill.: Northwestern University Press.

Miller, Terry, and Sean Williams. 1998. "Southeast Asian Musics: An Overview." In *The Garland Encyclopedia of World Music*, Vol. 4: *Southeast Asia*, ed. Terry E. Miller and Sean Williams, pp. 2–23. New York: Garland.

Mitchell, J. Clyde. 1966. "Theoretical Orientations in African Urban Studies." In *The Social Anthropology of Complex Societies*, ed. Michael Banton, pp. 37–68. London: Tavistock.

Mitra Sunda. 1988. *"Seni Buhun" Beluk*. Bandung: Kecamatan Banjaran.

Modleski, Tania. 1991. *Feminism Without Women: Culture and Criticism in a "Postfeminist" Age*. New York: Routledge.

Natapradja, Iwan. 1975. "Sundanese Dances." *Selected Reports in Ethnomusicology* 2/2:103–108.

Nettl, Bruno. 1978a. *Eight Urban Musical Cultures*. Urbana: University of Illinois Press.

———. 1978b. "Some Aspects of the History of World Music in the Twentieth Century: Questions, Problems, and Concepts." *Ethnomusicology* 22/1:123–136.

Neuman, Daniel M. 1976. "Towards an Ethnomusicology of Culture Change in Asia." *Asian Music* 7/2:1–5.

Noorduyn, Jacobus 1978. "Majapahit in the 15th Century." *Bijdragen tot de taal-, land- en volkenkunde* 134/2:207–274.

Noorduyn, Jacobus, and Andries Teeuw. 1999. "A Panorama of the World from Sundanese Perspective." *Archipel* 57:209–221.

O'Connor, Richard A. 1983. *A Theory of Indigenous Southeast Asian Urbanism*. Singapore: Institute of Southeast Asian Studies.

Pacholcyzk, Józef M. 1986. "Music and Islam in Indonesia." *World of Music* 28/3:3–12.

Panitia Seminar Tembang Sunda. 1976. "Seminar Tembang Sunda." *Buletin Kebudayaan Jawa Barat* 10/2–3: 3–5.

Park, Robert E. 1952. *Human Communities*. Glencoe, Ill.: Free Press.

Peacock, James L. 1973. *Indonesia: An Anthropological Perspective*. Pacific Palisades, Calif.: Goodyear.

———. 1979. "Dahlan and Rasul: Indonesian Muslim Reformers." In *The Imagination of Reality: Essays in Southeast Asian Coherence Systems*, ed. Alton Becker and Aram Yengoyan, pp. 245–268. Norwood, N.J.: Ablex.

Pemberton, John. 1987. "Musical Politics in Central Java (Or, How Not to Listen to a Javanese Gamelan)." *Indonesia* 44: 16–29.

———. 1994. *On the Subject of 'Java'*. Ithaca, N.Y.: Cornell University Press.

Pleyte, C. M. 1905. *Soendashe schetsen*. Bandung: Kolff.

———. 1910. "Drie pantoen-vertellingen: 'Njai Soemoer Bandoeng,' 'De lot-gevallen van Tjoeng Wanara,' 'De legende van den Loetoeng Kasaroeng,' een gewijde sage uit Tjirebon." *Verhandelingen van het Bataviaasch Genootschap van Kunsten en Wetenschappen* 58: 1–263.

Porter, James. 1987. "Trance, Music, and Music/Trance Relations: A Symposium." *Pacific Review of Ethnomusicology* 4: 1–38.

Preminger, Alex, ed. 1965. *Princeton Encyclopedia of Poetry and Poetics*. Princeton: Princeton University Press.

Redfield, Robert. 1947. "The Folk Society." *American Journal of Sociology* 41:293–308.

Redfield, Robert, and Milton Singer. 1954. "The Cultural Role of Cities." *Economic Development and Cultural Change* 3:53–73.

Rikin, W. Mintardja. 1973. "Ngabersihan als Knoop in de Tali Paranti. Bejdrage tot het Verstaan van de Besnijdenis der Sundanezen." Ph.D. dissertation, Leiden. Meppel: Racmo Offset.

Robinson, Francis. 1982. *Atlas of the Islamic World*. Oxford: Equinox.

Robson, S. O. 1981. "Java at the Crossroads: Aspects of Javanese Cultural History in the 14th and 15th Centuries." *Bijdragen tot de taal-, land- en volkenkunde* 137/2:259–292.

———. 1983. "Kakawin Reconsidered: Toward a Theory of Old Javanese Poetics." *Bijdragen tot de taal-, land- en volkenkunde* 139/2:291–319.

Rosidi, Ajip. 1970. *Tjarita Nyi Sumur Bandung: Dipantunkan oleh: Ki Endjum (Ujungberung, Bandung) seri ke-4*. Bandung: Projek Penelitian Pantun dan Folklor Sunda.

———. 1971a. *Tjarita Munding Kawati: Dipantunkan oleh: Ki Atma (Banggala-Subang), seri ke-11*. Bandung: Projek Penelitian Pantun dan Folklor Sunda.

———. 1971b. *Tjarita Panggung Karaton: Dipantunkan oleh: Ki Atjeng Tamadipura (Situradja-Sumedang), seri ke-7*. Bandung: Projek Penelitian Pantun dan Folklor Sunda.

———. 1973a. *Carita Ciung Wanara Dipantunkan oleh Ki Subarma (Ciwidey, Bandung), seri ke-14*. Bandung: Proyek Penelitian Pantun dan Folklor Sunda.

———. 1973b. "My Experiences in Recording Pantun Sunda." *Indonesia* 16: 105–112.

———. 1977. *Si Kebayan dan Beberapa Dongeng Sunda Lainnya*. Jakarta: Gunung Agung.

———. 1984. *Manusia Sunda: Sebuah Esai tentang Tokoh-tokoh Sastra dan Sejarah*. Jakarta: Inti Idayu Press.

Rouget, Gilbert. 1985. *Music and Trance: A Theory of the Relations between Trance and Possession*. Chicago: University of Chicago Press.

Rycroft, D. 1977. "Evidence of Stylistic Continuity in Zulu 'Town' Music." In *Essays for a Humanist*, ed. K. Wachsmann Festschrift Committee, pp. 22–54. New York: Town House Press.

Samson, Allan A. 1968. "Islam in Indonesian Politics." *Asian Survey* 4:1001–1017.
Satjadibrata, R. 1953. *Rasiah Tembang Sunda*, 2nd ed. Jakarta: Balai Pustaka.
Scott, James C. 1972. "Patron-Client Politics and Political Change in Southeast Asia." *American Political Science Review* 66: 91–113.
———. 1976. *The Moral Economy of the Peasant: Rebellion and Subsistence in Southeast Asia*. New Haven: Yale University Press.
Sears, Laurie J. 1996. *Shadows of Empire: Colonial Discourse and Javanese Tales*. Durham, N.C.: Duke University Press.
Sekolah Menengah Karawitan Indonesia (SMKI). 1981. *Diktat Karawitan Sunda*. Bandung: SMKI.
Sobirin. 1987. *Lagu-Lagu Mamaos, Lagu-Lagu Panambah*. 4 vols. Bandung: Self-published.
Solie, Ruth A. 1993. "Introduction." In *Musicology and Difference: Gender and Sexuality in Music Scholarship*, ed. Ruth A. Solie, pp. 1–20. Berkeley: University of California Press.
Somawidjaja, Ny. Karman. 1982. *Nyukcruk Galur Nu Kapungkur*. Bandung: Mimitran Tembang Sunda.
———. 1983. "Neuleuman Jiwa Lagu Tembang Sunda Cianjuran." *Buletin Kebudayaan Jawa Barat* 37/3–5:25–27.
Spiller, Henry. 1993. "Sundanese Dance Accompaniment: The Career of Pa Kayat." *Balungan* 5/2:15–18.
———. 1996. "Continuity in Sundanese Dance Drumming: Clues from the 1893 Chicago Exposition." *World of Music* 38/2:23–40.
Stahl, Rae Ann. 1987. "Transformations in *Kacapi-Suling* Instrumental Music." Senior thesis paper, University of California at Santa Cruz.
Stapel, Frederik Willem. 1930. *Geschiedenis van Nederlandsch-Indië*. Amsterdam: J. M. Meulenhoff.
Sugarman, Jane C. 1999. "Imagining the Homeland: Poetry, Songs, and the Discourses of Albanian Nationalism." *Ethnomusicology* 43/3:419–458.
Sukanda, Enip. 1978. *Pangeuyeub Ngeuyeub Kareueus kana Dunya Seni Mamaos (Tembang Sunda Cianjuran); Gambaran Sabudeureun Ngadeg Katut Sumebarna*. Bandung: Panitia Pasanggiri Tembang Sunda DAMAS.
———. 1983. *Tembang Sunda Cianjuran*. Bandung: Proyek Pengembangan Institut Kesenian Indonesia.
Sukanda, Viviane. 1978. *Sekelumit tentang Tembang Sunda*. Jakarta: Lingkar Mitra Budaya.
Supandi, Atik. 1976a. "Tembang Sunda Cigawiran." *Buletin Kebudayaan Jawa Barat* 9/2–3:33–35.
———. 1976b. "Penyelidikan Secara Musikologis dan Kemungkinan Standardisasi Lagu-Lagu Tembang Sunda." *Kumpulan Hasil-Hasil Seminar Tembang Sunda 1976*. Bandung: Yayasan "Lembaga Pancaniti" Bandung.
———. 1985. *Lagu Pupuh, Pengetahuan dan Notasinya*. Bandung: Pustaka Buana.
Suryana, Tatang. 1978. "Ciawian Menanti Giliran." Text of speech presented to the *Daya Mahasiswa Sunda* (DAMAS). Bandung: Yayasan Cangkurileung.
Susanto, Astrid. 1978. "The Mass Communications System in Indonesia." In *Political Power and Communication in Indonesia*, ed. Karl Jackson and Lucien Pye, pp. 229–258. Berkeley: University of California Press.
Sutaarga, Mohammed Amin. 1965. *Prabu Siliwangi, atau Ratu Purana Prebu Guru Dewataprana Sri Baduga Maharadja Ratu Hadji di Pakwan Padjadjaran 1474–1513*. Bandung: P. T. Duta Rakyat.

Sutton, R. Anderson. 1984. "Change and Ambiguity: Gamelan Style and Regional Identity in Yogyakarta." In *Aesthetic Tradition and Cultural Transition in Java and Bali*, ed. Stephanie Morgan and Laurie Jo Sears, pp. 221–245. Madison: University of Wisconsin Center for Southeast Asian Studies.

———. 1987. "Identity and Individuality in an Ensemble Tradition: The Female Vocalist in Java." In *Women and Music in Cross-Cultural Perspective*, ed. Ellen Koskoff, pp. 111–130. Urbana: University of Illinois Press.

Ten Dam, H. 1954. "Verkenningen Rondom Padjadjaran." *Indonesië* 10:290–310.

Turino, Thomas. 1987. "Power Relations, Identity and Musical Choice: Music in a Peruvian Altiplano Village and among Its Migrants in the Metropolis." Ph.D. dissertation, University of Texas at Austin.

———. 1989. "The Coherence of Social Style and Musical Creation among the Aymara in Southern Peru." *Ethnomusicology* 33/1:1–30.

Wallerstein, Immanuel. 1997. "The National and the Universal: Can There Be Such a Thing as World Culture?" In *Culture, Globalization and the World-System: Contemporary Conditions for the Representation of Identity*, ed. Anthony D. King, pp. 91–105. Minneapolis: University of Minnesota Press.

Waterman, Christopher A. 1990. *Jùjú: A Social History and Ethnography of an African Popular Music*. Chicago: University of Chicago Press.

Weintraub, Andrew. 1985. "A Manual for Learning Sundanese Gamelan." Senior thesis in music, University of California at Santa Cruz.

———. 1990. "Pantun Sunda: The Music of an Epic Narrative Tradition in West Java, Indonesia." M.A. thesis, University of Honolulu.

———. 1991. *Ngahudang Carita Anu Baheula (To Awaken an Ancient Story): An Introduction to the Stories of Pantun Sunda*. Southeast Asia Paper No. 34. Manoa: Center for Southeast Asian Studies, School of Hawaiian, Asian and Pacific Studies, University of Hawai'i.

———. 1993a. "Creative Musical Practices in the Performance of Pantun Sunda." *Balungan* 5/2:2–7.

———. 1993b. "Theory as Institutionalized Pedagogy and 'Theory in Practice' for Sundanese Gamelan Music." *Ethnomusicology* 37/1:29–40.

———. 1994. "Tune, Text, and the Function of *Lagu* in *Pantun Sunda*, a Sundanese Oral Narrative Tradition." *Asian Music* 26/1:175–211.

———. 1997. "Constructing the Popular: Superstars, Performance, and Cultural Authority in Sundanese Wayang Golek Purwa of West Java, Indonesia." Ph.D. dissertation, University of California, Berkeley.

Wertheim, W. F. 1956. *Indonesian Society in Transition: A Study of Social Change*. The Hague: W. Van Hoeve.

Wessing, Robert. 1974. "Language Levels in Sundanese." *Man* 9/1:5–22.

———. 1978. *Cosmology and Social Behavior in a West Javanese Settlement*. Papers in International Studies, Southeast Asia Series No. 47. Athens, Ohio: University Center for International Studies, SEA program.

———. 1984a. "Parameters of Economic Behavior in West Java, Indonesia." *Journal of Anthropology* 3/2:28–49.

———. 1984b. "Sundanese." In *Muslim Peoples: A World Ethnographic Survey*, vol. 2, ed. Richard Weekes, pp. 727–732. Westport, Conn.: Greenwood Press.

———. 1986. *The Soul of Ambiguity: The Tiger in Southeast Asia*. Monograph Series on Southeast Asia, Special Report No. 24. DeKalb: Northern Illinois University Center for Southeast Asian Studies.

———. 1988. "Spirits of the Earth and Spirits of the Water: Chthonic Forces in the Mountains of West Java." *Asian Folklore Studies* 47:43–61.
———. 1993. "A Change in the Forest: Myth and History in West Java." *Journal of Southeast Asian Studies* 24/1:1–17.
———. 1994. "Which Forest? Perceptions of the Environment and Conservation on Java." *Masyarakat Indonesia* 20/4:51–70.
———. 1997. "Constituting the World in the Sundanese House." Paper presented at the international workshop on "Transformations of Houses and Settlements in Western Indonesia: Changing Values and Meanings of Built Forms in History and in the Process of Modernization." Leiden.
———. 1998. "Bamboo, Rice, and Water." In *The Garland Encyclopedia of World Music*, Vol. 4: *Southeast Asia*, ed. Terry E. Miller and Sean Williams, pp. 47–54. New York: Garland.
———. 1999. "The Sacred Grove: Founders and the Owners of the Forest in West Java, Indonesia." In *L'Homme et la forêt tropicale*, ed. Serge Bahuchet, Daniel Bley, Hélène Pagezy, and Nicole Vernazza-Licht, pp. 59–74. Marseille: Société d'Écologie Humaine.
Wibisana, Wahyu, Apung S. Wiratmadja, Atik Supandi, and Uking Sukri. 1976. "Mencari Ciri-Ciri Mandiri Dalam Tembang Sunda." *Budaya Jaya* 103:705–743.
Williams, Sean. 1989. "Current Developments in Sundanese Popular Music." *Asian Music* 21/1:105–136.
———. 1990. "The Urbanization of Tembang Sunda, an Aristocratic Musical Genre of West Java, Indonesia." Ph.D. dissertation, University of Washington, Seattle.
———. 1993. "Our Laughter Balances Our Tears: Humor in Sundanese Arts." *Balungan* 5/2:11–14.
———. 1998a. "Sunda (Java)." In *The Garland Encyclopedia of World Music*, Vol. 4: *Southeast Asia*, ed. Terry E. Miller and Sean Williams, pp. 699–725. New York: Garland.
———. 1998b. "Constructing Gender in Sundanese Music." *Yearbook for Traditional Music* 30:74–84.
———. 1999. "Competition in the Sundanese Performing Arts of West Java, Indonesia." *Current Musicology* 63:27–45.
Wiratmadja, Apung S. 1964. *Sumbangan Asih kana Tembang Sunda*. Bandung: Purnamasari.
———. 1996. *Mengenal Seni Tembang Sunda*. Bandung: C. V. Wahana Iptek.
Wirth, Louis. 1938. "Urbanism as a Way of Life." *American Journal of Sociology* 44/1: 1–24.
Young, Gary, and Marcus Kaufman. 1993. "Tembang Sunda Poetry." *Balungan* 5/2: 8–10.
Yampolsky, Philip. 1987. *Lokananta: A Discography of the National Recording Company of Indonesia, 1957–1985*. Madison: University of Wisconsin Center for Southeast Asian Studies.
———. 1989. "Hati Yang Luka, an Indonesian Hit." *Indonesia* 47:1–17.
———. 1991. *Music of Indonesia 2: Indonesian Popular Music*. Washington, D.C.: Smithsonian/Folkways SFCD 40056. [Liner notes.]
Yano, Christine. 1997. "Inventing Selves: Images and Image-Making in a Japanese Popular Music Genre." *Journal of Popular Culture* 31/2:115–129.
Zanten, Wim van. 1984. "The Poetry of Tembang Sunda." *Bijdragen tot de taal-, land- en volkenkunde* 140/2–3:289–316.

———. 1985. "Structure in the Panambih Pélog Songs of Tembang Sunda." In *Teken van Leven, Studies in Etnocommunicatie*, ed. Ad Boeren, Fransje Brinkgreve, and Sandy Roels, pp. 187–198. Leiden: ICA.

———. 1986. "The Tone Material of the Kacapi in Tembang Sunda in West Java." *Ethnomusicology* 30/1:84–112.

———. 1987. "Tembang Sunda: An Ethnomusicological Study of the Cianjuran Music in West Java." Ph.D. dissertation, Rijksuniversiteit Leiden, Instituut voor Culturele Antropologie en Sociologie der Niet-Westerse Volken.

———. 1989. *Sundanese Music in the Cianjuran Style: Anthropological and Musicological Aspects of Tembang Sunda*. Dordrecht, Holland: Foris. [Demonstration cassette tape with the same title is also available and is sold separately.]

———. 1993. "Sung Epic Narrative and Lyrical Songs: *Carita Pantun* and *Tembang Sunda*." In *Performance in Java and Bali; Studies of Narrative, Theatre, Music and Dance*, ed. Ben Arps, pp. 144–161. London: School of Oriental and African Studies.

———. 1994. "L'esthétique musicale de Sunda (Java-Ouest)." *Cahiers de Musiques Traditionelles* 7:75–93.

———. 1995a. "Notation of Music; Theory and Practice in West Java." *Oideion* 2: *The Performing Arts World-Wide*, ed. Wim van Zanten and Marjolijn Van Roon, pp. 209–233. Leiden: Centre of Non-Western Studies, Leiden University.

———. 1995b. "Aspects of Baduy Music in its Sociocultural Context, with Special Reference to Singing and Angklung." *Bijdragen tot de taal-, land- en volkenkunde* 151:516–544.

———. 1997. "Inner and Outer Voices: Listening and Hearing in West-Java." *World of Music* 39/2:41–50.

DISCOGRAPHY

Classical Tembang Sunda: Music from West Java. Ida Widawati and Lies Setiawati, vocals; Ajat Sudrajat, kacapi; Iwan Mulyana, suling; Heri Suheryanto, rincik and voice. Celestial Harmonies 13134-2, compact disc. 1996.

Holding Up Half the Sky: Voices of Asian Women. Euis Komariah, vocals; Rukruk Rukmana, kacapi; Burhan Sukarma, suling; Uloh S., rebab (one tembang Sunda "set" only). Shanachie SP222, compact disc. 1997.

Java—Tembang Sunda: Sundanese Sung Poetry. Lingkungan Seni Malati. Ida Widawati and Neneng Dinar Suminar, vocals; Rukruk Rukmana, kacapi; Iwan Mulyana, suling; Adjat Sudrajat, vocals and rincik. Inedit W 260056, compact disc. 1994.

Sundanese Classical Music. Enah Sukaenah and Didin S. Badjuri, vocals; Rukruk Rukmana, kacapi; Ade Suandi, suling; Riskonda, rincik; Nandang Barmaya, rebab. King Record Co. KICC 5131, compact disc. 1986.

Tembang Sunda: Sundanese Classical Songs. Imas Permas and Asep Kosasih, vocals; Gan-Gan Garmana, kacapi; Endang Sukendar, suling; Kondin Herdinan, rincik. Nimbus NI 5378, compact disc. 1993.

Trance 3: Zen Shakuhachi, Mbira Spirit Ceremony, Sacred Tembang Sunda. Euis Komariah, vocals; Rukruk Rukmana, kacapi; Burhan Sukarma, suling; Nana Suhana, rincik (one tembang Sunda "set" only). Ellipsis Arts CD 4330, compact disc. 1999.

Udan Mas: Ensemble/Lingkung Seni "Malati." Ida Widawati and Iyad Sumarnaputra, vocals; Iyad Sumarnaputra, kacapi; Toto Wahyudi, suling and rebab; Tisna Wangsa, rincik. Pan Records 4004 KCD, compact disc. 1996.

INDEX

ancestors
  connecting with, through music, 226
  obtaining guidance from, 224
  Prabu Siliwangi, as ultimate, 243 n16
  using intermediaries to contact, 224–226
aristocracy
  cognitive map for, 211
  influence on the Sundanese, by the Javanese, 26, 33, 43
  maintaining one's position, 199
  names of, 211, 230, 237 n9
  seeking to connect with the past, 231
  usage of tembang Sunda by, 199, 229, 231
audience members
  foreign, 70–71
  in hotels, 71
  at a panglawungan, 62
  and regional/historical identity, 201
  relative status of, 53
  as targets of tembang Sunda songs, 90–92
  understanding of tembang Sunda, 58–59, 90
  at weddings, 67

Bandung
  as administrative center, 32, 34
  avoidance of dedegungan in, 154
  as a center of teaching and learning, 136
  description of, 22
  early development of, 23
  as home of radio stations, 108
  as a "hot" place (vs. the "cool" village), 209
  Islamic practices in, 27
  lingkung seni in, 54
  location of, 20–21
  as a location for the expression of identity, 195

INDEX

musical influence on smaller towns, 17, 73, 107
as the "Paris of Java," 32
performance of papantunan in, 146
as physical (vs. spiritual) location of tembang Sunda, 230
population diversity of, 34, 49
shift of musicians to, 19, 33
style, spreading as a result of the cassette industry, 107
Batavia, 31–32
beluk, 45–46
Bojong Herang style, 43
bubuka, 103, 106, 158–160, 241 n11

cassette recordings
bubuka and panutup on, 159
covers and inserts of, 98–99, 238 n7
creation of, 95–98
fadeouts on, 160
job market and, 94
of kacapi-suling, 161–163
leading to codification of suling performance practice, 45
as linkage between Chinese-Indonesians and Sundanese, 94
marketing, 101–104
results of their proliferation, 106–107
and stylistic changes, 106–107
in teaching and learning, 134–136
and tuning systems, 104–106
use of female vocalists to sell, 42, 82
use of new songs on, 102
Chinese-Indonesian (people)
acquisition of special objects by, 212
as cassette store owners, 102
linkage to Sundanese, through cassette industry, 94
migration to Indonesia, 31
prejudices against, 144, 240 n4
role in establishing commercial districts, 31
Cianjur, 38–39, 154
Cianjuran. *See* tembang Sunda
Cigawiran, 45
circumcision, 88–89, 236 nn5–6
cities
Batavia, 31
Dutch concepts of, 31

as "home," 50
Javanese, 26
types of, 7
clothing
and body hair, 243 n17
in imitation of nineteenth-century aristocracy, 74, 77, 199
impact of lighting on, 74
Islamic, 29, 234 n3
for performances, female, 74–76
for performances, male, 76–78
as a symbol of ethnicity, 89
trends in, especially for performance wear, 73–79
used to accentuate sexual attributes, 88, 234 n3
and wigs, 75–76, 236 n11
colonization, 25, 30–33
competitions
Daya Mahasiswa Sunda as sponsor of, 42
description of, 63–66
development by RRI of, 112
juries for, 64
mechanics of, 64
mention of, on cassette inserts, 99
and photographs of winners, 98
positive and negative aspects of, 65
preparation for, 66
of pupuh, 65–66
and standardization of the genre, 235 n5
stimulation of performance because of, 66
composition, 102, 156–157
cosmology
and contacting the ancestors, 224–225
importance of volcanoes in Sundanese, 20
Pajajaran in, 197–206

Dachlan, Yayah Rochaeti
high pitch range of, 44, 240–241
on pop Sunda, 68–69
as primary singer of Simpay Tresna, 54
DAMAS. *See* Daya Mahasiswa Sunda
Daweung ménak Pajajaran. See narangtang

Daya Mahasiswa Sunda (DAMAS)
  as general patron of the arts, 63–64
  membership in the military and government, 70
  as sponsor of competitions, 42
dedegungan
  description of, 153–154
  distinction from rarancagan of, 153
  gelenyu in, 153
  grouping of, on cassettes, 154
  high pitch range of, 154, 240–241 nn9–10
  and kacapi-suling, 161, 163
  lack of pitch borrowing in, 154
  lyrics in, 154
  relationship to gamelan tunes, 153
  use of special suling for, 153, 240
Dutch (people)
  colonization of Indonesia, 30–33
  development of colonial cities, 30–31
  Dutch East India Company, 30
  image of colonial city, 31
  influence on early tembang Sunda, 39
  relationship to Sundanese people, 244 n3
  Verenigde Oost-Indische Compagnie (VOC), 30

Eddy, Dacép, on rebab use and technique, 183–186

forest
  amount of land taken up by, 242 n15
  as ancestral home, 207
  as home to tiger spirits, 207
  as location of Prabu Siliwangi, 207
  as representing primordial existence, 208–209

gamelan degung, 10, 155, 160–161
gelenyu
  for dedegungan style, 153
  definition of, 148
  for panambih, 158
  for papantunan style, 148
  transcription of, 148
gender roles
  and cultural politics, 89–90
  divisions of, in urban setting, 82
  in performance of panambih, 155
  and power associated with female performers, 85
  of women, as group leaders, 85
  and women's independence, 236 n4

hair
  body, 243 n17
  and wigs, 75–76, 236 n11
hajat. See tawajuh
"Hamdan"
  as expression of Islamic belief in Hindu context, 29
  as performed by a non-Muslim, 234 n4
hotels and restaurants
  ambience at, 71–72
  as settings for tembang Sunda, 71–72
  use of kacapi-suling ensembles at, 162–163
humor
  importance of, 14
  at latihan sessions, 129
  in the learning process, 124–125
  as a method of social and musical control, 124

identity
  creation and maintenance of, 223
  as distinct from the Javanese, 223
  national vs. regional, 20
  of Sundanese on a national scale, 89–90, 224
instrumentalists, female, 42, 84, 130
instrumentalists, male
  bribing of, before competitions, 64
  emotional connection of, with vocalists, 83
  interchangeability of, in lingkung seni, 55
  knowledge of vocal repertoire, 83
  lack of photographs of, 98
  lower status of, 62, 82
  teaching and learning, 130
intermediaries
  haji as, 225
  kuncén as, 224
  musicians as, 230
  necessity of, 224
  tembang Sunda as, 225–226, 229, 231

INDEX 265

Islam
  and animism, 20
  categories and diversity of, 27–28
  conflict with Hindu Pajajaran, 226–227
  Dar'ul Islam rebellion, 28, 234 n2
  and disruption of latihan sessions, 127
  dissemination of, through Cigawiran, 45
  and hajis as intermediaries, 225
  and outside impressions of the Sundanese, 236 n2
  practices in Bandung, 27
  and respectability of performers, 84
  spread of, in Indonesia, 28
  in Sundanese culture, 27–30
  and use of Arabic prayers, 201, 214

Javanese (people)
  competition with the Sundanese musicians for gigs, 69
  expulsion of regents from Sunda, 32–33, 38, 241 n12
  influence on Sundanese aristocracy, 26, 33, 43
  rejection of, musical, 44
jejemplangan
  closed repertoire of, 149
  description of, 149–151
  difficulty of ornaments in, 122, 151
  intervallic relationship between kacapi and voice in, 150
  linkage to sense of keueung, 150–151
  lyrics of, 149
  similarity to papantunan, 149
  transcription of narangtang for, 150
  vocal ornamentation of, 149

kacapi
  analysis of patterns for *Daweung mênak Pajajaran*, 201–202
  as ancestral ship, 4, 212–213, 231, 243 n1
  associations with style, 167
  for the bubuka, 159
  description of, 165–167
  difficulty of playing in jejemplangan style on, 151
  gelenyu transcription of, 148
  as image of Sundanese culture, 172, 216–217
  in kacapi-suling, 161
  levels of difficulty, 123, 151
  and marriage to the instrumentalist, 213–216
  origin of the term, 166, 241 n1
  performance techniques, 167–173
  private instruction on, 130
  purchase of, 166
  and recording fees, 100
  relationship to vocalist, 168, 240 n5
  siter, as accompaniment for kawih, 10, 46–47
  style in early recordings, 44
  symbolism of, 212–217
  teaching of, at music institutions, 132
  use in cassettes, 217
  use in mandalungan tuning, 105
kacapi-suling
  as accompaniment to dongeng, 109, 162
  description of, 160–163
  as generic background music, 161, 163
  in hotels and restaurants, 162–163
  marketability of, 162–163
  relationship to gamelan degung, 161, 163
  as result of urbanization, 160
  use of panambih in, 160
kakawén, 47, 61, 185, 240 n6
kawih, 10, 46–47
keueung
  Apung Wiratmadja on, 207
  inappropriateness in urban performances, 151
  in jejemplangan songs, 150–151
  linkages with the forest, 207
  production of, by kacapi and voice, 151
  as a quality to reproduce in song, 122
"Kingkilaban"
  as example of panambih, 156–157
  transcription of, 156–157
  translation of, 222
kliningan, definition and status levels of, 47
Komariah, Euis
  as host of latihan sessions, 126–128, 238 nn5–6
  as student of Bojong Herang style, 43

lagu rajah
  appearance prior to "Papatet," 201
  description of, 144–146
  at a malam tembang Sunda, 60
  as the opening song, 144
  transcription of, for kacapi, 145
language
  in differentiating tembang from kawih, 218
  Dutch, use of, 13, 244–245 n10
  Indonesian, use of, 25, 38
  Javanese, use of, 25, 38
  levels, in mamaos, 218
  in sisindiran, 220
latihan
  description of, 126–128
  hosting of, 126
  impact of television on, 116
  as a teaching tool, 125–129
  use of humor in, 124
lingkung seni
  description of, 53–55
  innovation in, 165
  mechanics of hiring, 54
  naming on cassettes, 54
  number of, in Sunda, 235 n1
  outside of Bandung, 54, 58
  at weddings, 68
listening
  to cassettes, 107
  at hotels and restaurants, 71–72
  at a malam tembang Sunda, 60–61, 237 n6
  at a panglawungan, 61–63
lyrics
  association with history and nature, 220
  confusion of happy and sad, 222, 245 n11
  in dedegungan, 154
  discussion of, 217–223
  in Dutch, 244–245, n10
  examples of, 221–223
  in Indonesian, 220
  infusion of, with sacred character, 218
  in jejemplangan, 149
  linkages with village imagery, 223
  in panambih, 155–157
  in papantunan, 146, 149

  of "Papatet," 202–203
  prose vs. metricized poetry, 218
  in rarancagan, 152
  substitution of, 217
  use of honorifics in, 199, 219

Majapahit, conflict with Pajajaran, 24
malam tembang Sunda, 60–61, 237 n6
mamaos
  function of suling in relation to, 178
  as a more specific term for tembang singing style, 37
  performed in sets, 4
  relationship to panambih, 128
  use of specific languages in, 218
mandalungan (tuning system), 105–106
maps
  cognitive, 225
  cultural, of Indonesia, 21
  of Sunda/West Java, 21
Mataram
  ceding of Priangan area to the Dutch, 30
  Dutch/Mataram treaty of 1705, 32–33
  influence on Sundanese pupuh meters, 38
  and the mataraman tuning, 104
  takeover of Sunda, 25
military and government performances, 69–71
modernization
  and access to a restricted genre, 120
  ties with the media, 93
money and remuneration
  control of, by Chinese-Indonesians, 32
  difficulty in verifying amounts of, 100
  economic crisis of the 1990s, 35
  financial advantages for the regents, 33
  flowing from the Dutch to the Sundanese, 32
  as incentive for television appearances, 114
  for new compositions, 102
  paying to watch a performance, 55–56, 235 n2
  for playing rebab, 185
  for purchase of instruments, 166, 178, 184

INDEX

and recording contracts, 99–101
reformasi in the twenty-first century, 36
sponsorship and remuneration of musicians, 55–58
for teaching, 125, 130
types of compensation, 55–58
use of, for studio bookings, 95
"Mupu Kembang," transcription of kacapi gelenyu for, 148
music institutions, 131, 133–134, 175

narangtang
  analysis of kacapi and vocal patterns for, 201–202
  Daweung ménak Pajajaran as, 201–202, 204
  exclusivity of use for pélog songs, 201
  Islamic prayer as a type of, 201
  for jejemplangan songs, 149
  as link to the ancestors, 201
  linked to bubuka, 159
  for papantunan songs, 146, 201
  for "Papatet," 201
  transcription of, 150
Natawiredja, Raden Étjé Madjid
  award for his work in tembang Sunda, 235 n4
  as composer of "Papatet," 242 n5
  as disseminator of tembang Sunda, 41
  influences of, 44–45
  students of, on early recordings, 42
notation
  individual development of, 13
  in instruction books, 135
  in music institutions, 312
  Sundanese vs. Javanese, 235 n6

Pajajaran
  conflict with Majapahit, 24
  connection with tembang Sunda, 23, 198, 229
  as explained in "Papatet," 201–205
  fall of, 24–25, 203
  founding of, 24
  Hindu emphasis in, 198, 226–227
  as home, 205–209, 228, 231, 242 n13
  image of, 25, 197, 226–227, 231

lack of public knowledge of, 23, 198
location of, 242 n4
power and influence of, 25
presence in pantun performance, 39
as representation of ancient Sunda, 199, 231
singers as representatives of, 230
as spiritual location of tembang Sunda, 230
as a state of mind, 229
as Sundanese "Golden Era," 197, 224, 227, 231
as symbol of power, 228, 231
panambih
  accessibility to urban audience, 81
  associations with aristocracy, 81
  description of, 154–158
  difference from other styles, 154–155
  exclusive performance by women, 81
  gender issues in performance of, 81, 155
  inclusion of chorus in, 157
  lyrics in, 155–157
  rebab performance in, 185
  relationship to mamaos songs, 128
  relative ease of performance of, 155, 158
  rincik performance in, 174
  suling performance in, 158
  transcription of, 156–157
  use of kait technique on the kacapi for, 170–171
  wilet in, 157–158
Pancaniti, Dalem
  appreciation of the performing arts, 39
  as original sponsor of tembang Sunda, 38–39
  as regent of Cianjur from 1834 to 1864, 38
  role in early development of tembang Sunda, 39
pangjiwaan
  deepening of, 83
  demonstration of, through "Papatet," 200
  difficulty of accessing, 122
  discussions of, in teaching songs, 127
  and proper vocal performance, 187

pangjiwaan (*continued*)
    through understanding of the lyrics, 218
    Wim van Zanten on, 212
panglawungan, 62–63
pantun
    associations of, with feudal times, 145, 149
    contexts for, 40
    derivation of lagu rajah from, 144
    description of, 39
    earliest references to, 39
    influence on early development of tembang Sunda, 40
    literature on, 234 n3
    recording of, 40
    as source material for tembang Sunda, 38
    stylistic subdivision of, 40
    texts of, 240 n7
    transcription of, for kacapi, 144
    urbanization of, 40–41
    usual performers of, 145–146
panutup, 103, 158–160
papantunan
    appropriateness in performance, 142
    classification of lagu rajah as, 145
    closed repertoire of, 147
    description of, 146–149
    grouping of, into sets, 147
    lyrics of, 146, 149
    origins in pantun performance, 40
    style of performance, 146
    transcription of, for kacapi, 144
    vocal ornamentation in, 146
"Papatet"
    as key piece to explain Pajajaran, 201–202, 204
    as litmus test of ability, 121–122, 200, 204
    lyrics of, in Sundanese and English, 202–203
    resistance to, 205
    as a summative work, 200–205
    as taught in the music institutions, 132
    transcription of, 204
    unique style of kacapi playing for papantunan tune, 148–149
pasanggiri. *See* competitions

patronage and patrons
    of the arts in the nineteenth century, 33
    disruption of, by Indonesian independence, 33
    disruption of, by the 1990s economic crisis, 35–36
    interest in female vocalists, 92
    necessity of, for making recordings, 101
    of panglawungan, 62
    relative status of, 53
    requesting specific songs, 91
    system developed by the regents, 33
    of tembang Sunda musicians, 55–58
    by urban institutions, 93
pélog (tuning system)
    description of, 239–240 n3
    frequency of use on cassette recordings, 104
    in malam tembang Sunda, 60–61
    in particular styles, 143–144
    on the radio, 108
    use in pantun performance, 39
pélog wisaya (tuning system), 104
pitch level
    in beluk, 46
    in dedegungan style, 153–154
    disadvantage of changing, 44
    in early recordings, 42–43
    impact of amplification on, 43–44
    in kawih, 46
    in kliningan, 47
    lowering of, 42–43, 47
    on the suling, 177
    status related to, 44
polemik
    about gending karesmen, 59
    among musicians, 14
    about Qur'anic chant and tembang, 30
    at seminars on tembang Sunda, 79–80
pop Sunda, 46, 104
power
    accumulation of, 26, 33, 212, 228–229
    attributes of, 86
    and control of desires, 86
    differences in conceptualization of, 228
    and influence of musicians, 85
    of musical performance, 47

and organization of pre-Islamic states, 227
Pajajaran as symbolic of, 228
of the regents, 32
symbols of, 26, 33
of transvestites, 87
waxing and waning of, in Sunda, 227
printed matter
books, 119
magazines, 118
newspapers, 117
significance of, 118
song lyrics, 119
pupuh meters
competition in, 65–66
in dedegungan, 154
explanation of, 244 n5
and flexibility of switching meters, 219
influence of Mataram culture on, 38
in live performance, 219
in rarancagan, 152

Qur'anic chant, 29–30, 45

radio
in Bandung, 108
broadcasting of kacapi-suling on, 162
broadcasts, 110
creation of a pasanggiri, 112
criteria for selection of performers on, 108
first singers of tembang Sunda on, 108
private stations, 108–109
programming changes, 109–110
Radio Republik Indonesia (RRI), 108, 112
as a site for teaching and learning, 134
support of tembang Sunda, 110
rarancagan
description of, 152–153
distinction from dedegungan of, 153–154
lyrics in, 152
pitch borrowing in, 153–154
popularity of, at paid performances, 147
provocation of emotions by, 152
use of pupuh meters in, 152
vocal ornamentation in, 152

rebab
description of, 183–184
in kakawén, 185
purchase of, 184
and recording fees, 100
in saléndro, 184
terminology for ornamentation, 185
use in tembang Sunda, 184–185
recording studios
and 78 rpm recordings, 95
and the choice not to record, 101
and contracts, 99–101
and equipment, 96
Hidayat, 98–99, 161
Jugala, 94
and kacapi-suling, 161–162
Lokananta, 95
Odeon, 95
and the recording process, 96–98
and subcontracting, 95
terminology of, 95
recordings
early (1920s and 1930s), 42–45, 235 n5
suling style in, 177
regents
changes in the system of, 33
Cianjur, as site of tembang Sunda development, 38
economic advantages for, 32–33
expulsion of, from Sunda, 38
Javanese, 26–27, 32
patronage system developed by, 33
performance of beluk for, 46
Sundanese, 32
remuneration. *See* money and remuneration
rice, 20, 208, 215
rincik
for the bubuka, 159
description of, 173–174
origin of the term, 173
and recording fees, 100
skills in performance of, 173
teaching of, at music institutions, 132
use of second, in performance, 175
Rukmana, Rukruk
influence on other kacapi players, 165, 172
as an innovator on the kacapi, 165

Rukmana, Rukruk (*continued*)
  on learning jejemplangan style, 151
  on "marriage" to the kacapi, 213
  on the use of male photos on cassettes, 98

saléndro (tuning system)
  description of, 239–240 n3
  difficulty in tuning the kacapi to, 144
  and near-equidistance of notes, 240 n5
  frequency of use on cassette recordings, 104
  in malam tembang Sunda, 61
  use in pantun performance, 39
  in particular styles, 143–144
  on the radio, 110
sex and sexuality
  accentuation of, through clothing, 88, 234 n3
  as an attribute of personal power, 86
  control of, through circumcision, 88–89
  dynamics of, in performances, 82, 90–92, 237 nn10–11
  in female performers, 86–87, 91–92
  of transvestite performers, 87
Siliwangi, Prabu
  disappearance of, 24–25, 197
  as embodiment of Sundanese ancestry, 197, 243
  as historical figure, 241 n1
  as last king of Pajajaran, 24
  located in the highland forest, 207
  metamorphosis into weretiger, 207
  as omnipresent being, 214
  as symbol of Pajajaran, 214
sisindiran, 219–220
sorog (tuning system)
  description of, 239 n3
  frequency of use on cassette recordings, 104
  in malam tembang Sunda, 61
  in particular styles, 143–144
  on the radio, 110
  use for foreign performances, 143
spirituality
  connected to urbanism, 194
  crossing a spiritual boundary, 212
  location of tembang Sunda, 230
  relationship to trance, 225–226
  and Sundanese cosmology, 225, 229
  use of lagu rajah to bless an event, 145
sponsors. *See* patronage and patrons
stage behavior and etiquette, 78–79
status levels
  of audience members, 53
  of instrumentalists and vocalists, 62, 82
  among tembang Sunda performers, 52–53
Sukarma, Burhan
  influence on other suling players, 162
  as member of Puspa Nugraha, 161
  on suling technique, 179–183
suling
  for the bubuka, 159
  connection with tigers, 208–209, 241 n5
  in dedegungan style, 153
  description of, 176–177
  early associations with tembang Sunda, 176–177
  evoking wa'as with, 209
  as a female instrument, 89, 177
  in kacapi-suling, 160–161
  levels of difficulty, 122–123
  in mandalungan tuning, 105–106, 176
  materials for construction of, 176
  in panambih style, 158
  playing techniques on, 178–183
  private instruction on, 130
  purchase of, 178
  and recording fees, 100
  as representing the voice, 89
  restrictions of style in papantunan, 148
  style in early recordings, 44, 177
  terms to describe ornaments, 179
Sunda
  annexation of, 25–26
  concept of, 245 n13
  control of, by Javanese, 26
  eleventh-century kingdom of, 24
  location of, 19–20
  representation of, in music, 89–90, 199

tarawangsa, 39–40, 176, 183
tawajuh, 213–216
teaching and learning
   in Bandung, 136
   changes as a result of the cassette industry, 107
   at grade school level, 131
   with instruction books, 135
   of instrumentalists, 130
   at latihan sessions, 125–129
   lessons, formal and informal, 129–130, 187
   levels of difficulty, 121–122
   in music institutions, 123, 131–134
   of new material, 127–128
   of tuning systems, 123
television
   as competition for rehearsal time, 114
   music videos, 114
   musicians watching television, 110
   privatization, 113
   recording process, 115–117
   role in Indonesia, 113–115
   scheduling, 113–114
   TeleVisi Republik Indonesia (TVRI), 113–117
tembang Sunda
   as ammunition, 90, 193
   as antithesis of modernization, 193
   appropriateness of setting for, 115–116
   association of suling with, 176–177
   connection with the rural past, 198, 211
   crossing a spiritual boundary through, 212, 225
   description of, 3, 17
   and feelings of wa'as, 99
   as intermediary, 212, 225, 229
   kacapi-suling and, 161
   methods of learning, 121–137
   name change, from Cianjuran, 37
   origins and early development of, 38, 41
   performance as a consummation of relationships, 83
   performance settings, 58–73
   psychological weight of, 205
   relationship to trance, 226
   resistance to, 17, 133, 147
   shift from rural to urban, 19, 33–34
   styles of, 141–163
   as a symbol of power and status, 68, 133, 136, 193, 199
   understanding, importance of, 229
tigers and tiger spirits
   dead people turning into, 208
   gathering during Maulud, 208
   located in the forest, 207
   maintenance of kingdom by, 208
   as manifestation of the shaman spirit, 209
   metamorphosis of Prabu Siliwangi into, 207
   sulings and, 208–209, 241 n5
   as vehicles to contact the ancestors, 198
trance
   in debus, 225–226
   of horses, in kuda renggong, 225
   related to electrical charges, 244 n2
   related function of tembang Sunda, 226
   in tawajuh ceremony, 213–216
transmission. See teaching and learning
transvestites as female performing artists, 87–88
tuning systems
   and the cassette industry, 104–106
   description of, 239–240 n3
   in each style, 143–144
   as established by the bubuka, 159
   at malam tembang Sunda, 60–61
   at military/government performances, 70
   opposition between Sundanese and Javanese, 123
   on the radio, 110
   in rarancagan style, 152
   and the rebab, 185
   and the suling, 177–178
   in teaching and learning, 123, 129
   use of rare, 94, 104–105

urban networks
   in Bandung, 34, 49
   among musicians and sponsors, 10, 51–52
   as replacements for kinship systems, 7

urbanism
  connected to spirituality, 194
  economic factors and, 93
urbanization
  in African music, 51
  in clothing, 73–79
  under Dutch control, 30–33
  of gamelan degung, 10
  of jaipongan, 10
  in kacapi-suling, 160
  of pantun, 40–41
  process of, 5–6
  relevance to the current work, 4
  research related to, 13
  of tembang Sunda, 9, 230–231

villages
  absorption by expanding cities, 31–32
  as "cool" places (vs. "hot" cities), 209–210
  as fictive kinship systems, 32
  idealization of, 206
vocal ornaments
  description of, 187–191
  difficulty of, 186
  in early recordings, 42–43
  in jejemplangan style, 150
  in kawih, 46
  mastery of, 122–123
  in papantunan style, 146
  in "Papatet," 200
  proper performance of, 187
  in rarancagan style, 152
  as taught in music institutions, 133

unique to mandalungan tuning, 106
vibrato, 181–183, 188
vocalists, female
  as bearers of a musical culture, 84, 89
  dependency on instrumentalists, 83
  as early performers of tembang Sunda, 41
  emotional connection of, with instrumentalists, 83
  increase in the numbers of, 41–42
  knowledge of the repertoire, 83
  and recording fees, 100–101
  respectability of, 84, 92
  visual impact of, 82
vocalists, male
  on cassette covers, 96
  as indication of serious performance, 82
  kawih singing by, 46
  as performers of the lagu rajah, 60
  restrictions on singing panambih by, 46

wa'as
  associated with tembang Sunda, 99
  as evoked by the suling, 209
  and imagery, 223
  as imparted by kacapi-suling, 163
wilet, 157–158
Wiratmadja, Apung
  on concept of keueung, 207
  on early malam tembang Sunda, 61
  on panambih, 219
  on pangjiwaan and tears, 236 n1
  on tembang Sunda competitions, 65

NOTES ON THE CD

Rekaman ini tidak untuk mendapat keuntungan buat penulisnya. Lagu-lagunya dilampirkan disini atas alasan penelitian saja. [This recording was not made to obtain a profit for the author. The songs are presented here for research purposes only.]

These compact disc selections were drawn from recordings made between 1987 and 1996 in West Java. Most of these recordings took place at events typical of tembang Sunda performance, which means that audience members talk, children call out with excitement, roosters crow, and traffic roars past. In each case except the first, I have keyed selections to comparable commercial recordings listed in the Discography so that readers may hear a more idealized (and/or "perfectly engineered") sound for each type of song or tuning system. I was unable to get a high-quality recording of dedegungan singing, but the CD *Java—Tembang Sunda* includes an example. The first example was chosen to represent the solo voice in all its artistic complexity, without instrumentation and with as little extra noise as possible. Examples 2 through 7 were chosen to represent a typical all-night performance, from the pélog "Lagu Rajah" through the saléndro song asking permission to leave, "Gunung Guntur." The kacapi-suling example is at least partly typical of what one might hear in a restaurant or hotel lobby, and "Kingkilaban" (the final example) is popular at weddings and life-cycle events. Total running time: 70:41.

1. "Polos," solo mamaos performance in rarancagan style, pélog tuning, performed for the author to learn the song. Euis Komariah, vocal. Recorded in Bandung,

February 10, 1988. In this example you can hear most of the important vocal ornaments, from the very long melismas to multiple types (and pressure levels) of vibrato. Running time: 1:34.

2. "Lagu Rajah / Jipang Lontang," pélog tuning, performed for a panglawungan. Asep Kosasih, vocal; Tarman, kacapi; Ade Suandi, suling; Nana Suhana, rincik. Recorded in Bandung, August 6, 1988. This begins with part of the "Lagu Rajah," often performed at the start of a formal evening performance. At 2:43, the musicians shift into the bubuka or instrumental opening piece, "Jipang Lontang." The use of sound systems with significant reverberation, even in small rooms, is quite common. Running time: 4:03. All commercial CDs of tembang Sunda include a bubuka; for the "Lagu Rajah," the CD *Sundanese Classical Music* has a good example.

3. "Narangtang / Papatet / Pangapungan / Lembur Singkur," pélog tuning in papantunan style, performed for a panglawungan. Dadang Suleiman and Tintin Suparyani, vocals; Rukruk Rukmana, kacapi; Ade Suandi, suling; Nana Suhana, rincik. Recorded in Bandung, July 16, 1988. The narangtang (often "Daweung ménak Pajajaran" but in this case "Gunung tanpa tutugan" or "Mountains without End") is a short phrase leading directly into "Papatet," possibly the most important song in the repertoire. At 1:49 the instrumentalists shift briefly into the introduction to the song "Pangapungan," but at a signal from the singer they lead directly into "Mupu Kembang" instead. "Pangapungan" follows at 3:14, sung by Dadang Suleiman. Tintin Suparyani begins the final song of the set at 4:24 with "Lembur Singkur," a panambih. At the beginning of the cut, some confusion appears among the instrumentalists about whether to shift to sorog or remain in pélog. The quick tuning and retuning that occurs is typical of performances and often continues right through the first few seconds of a song. Running time: 9:27. Compare with "Papatet" and "Mupu Kembang" on the CDs *Classical Tembang Sunda: Music from West Java*, *Sundanese Classical Music*, and *Java—Tembang Sunda*.

4. "Narangtang / Jemplang Panganten / Jemplang Cidadap / Jemplang Pamirig / Kembang Bungur / Reumbeuy Bandung," pélog tuning in jejemplangan style, performed for Japanese guests. Recorded in Bandung, April 6, 1988. Asep Kosasih, Euis Komariah, and Teti Affienti, vocals; Rukruk Rukmana, kacapi; Ade Suandi, suling; Nana Suhana, rincik. Jejemplangan songs use a narangtang or opening section different from those of papantunan style. Asep Kosasih performs this narangtang, followed by Euis Komariah on "Jemplang Panganten" (0:33), Asep again on "Jemplang Cidadap" (1:51), and Teti Affienti on "Jemplang Pamirig" (3:49). At 5:24 the set shifts to the panambih "Kembang Bungur" (performed by Euis) and "Reumbeuy Bandung" (performed by Teti) at 8:36. Note the shift on the kacapi from the kait style to the lively, double-density dirofel style at the entrance to "Reumbeuy Bandung," corresponding to the cheery nature of the lyrics. Running time: 9:55. The commercial CDs *Java—Tembang Sunda*, *Trance 3*, and *Tembang Sunda: Sundanese Classical Songs* include examples of jejemplangan.

5. "Bayubud / Liwung / Kembang Bungur," pélog tuning in rarancagan style, performed for a panglawungan. Apung Wiratmadja and A. Tjitjah, vocals; Tarman, kacapi; Ade Suandi, suling; Nana Suhana, rincik. Recorded in Bandung, August 6, 1988. This recording is of a rare performance by Pa Apung and Ibu A. Tjitjah; as two of the most important elders of the tembang Sunda community, they choose carefully when to appear "onstage," even in a setting as intimate as a panglawungan. Note the audience clapping; applause is rare, especially at a panglawungan. Pa Apung was an early winner of the pasanggiri DAMAS and wrote two books on tembang Sunda (see the Bibliography). His wife, Ibu A. Tjitjah, sings "Liwung" at 2:21 and

the panambih "Kembang Bungur" (also heard in example 4) at 3:58. Running time: 7:37. These pieces are not duplicated on any commercial CD.

6. "Udan Mas / Kapati-pati / Asmarandana Ros / Peuting Panglamunan," sorog tuning in rarancagan style, performed for a wedding reception. Multiple female vocalists; Rukruk Rukmana, kacapi; Tatang Subari, suling; Nana Suhana, rincik 1; Adang Dachlan, rincik 2. Recorded in Bandung, March 20, 1988. Rarancagan is the most commonly performed of all the styles; examples 5, 6, and 7 are all representative of this style but in three different tuning systems. This particular set of songs is interesting for its combination of complex fixed-meter kacapi passages and free-rhythm vocal lines. The kacapi player shortens or lengthens his sections according to the needs of the vocalist in an admirable blend of fixed composition and improvisation. As is often the case, however, it is difficult to plan precisely during a performance: the kacapi player begins the pattern for "Asmarandana Ros" rather than going into "Kapati-pati." He quickly covers for it and starts "Kapati-pati" at 2:33, playing scalar patterns until the vocalist is ready. "Kapati-pati" moves almost seamlessly into "Asmarandana Ros" at 4:52 (because the kacapi pattern for "Asmarandana Ros" started at 4:25), and the tension generated by the kacapi finally dissipates with the start of the panambih at 5:55. The presence of wedding guests is notable in this example; audience reactions to tembang Sunda performances differ strongly between weddings and panglawungan or malam tembang Sunda. Running time: 11:09. "Asmarandana Ros" was recorded on *Tembang Sunda: Sundanese Classical Songs*, and most of this set (all except the panambih) are on *Classical Tembang Sunda: Music from West Java*, *Java—Tembang Sunda*, and *Udan Mas: Ensemble/Lingkung Seni "Malati."* "Udan Mas" is also on *Sundanese Classical Music*.

7. "Gunung Guntur," saléndro tuning in rarancagan style, performed at a malam tembang Sunda. Two unknown males and Enah Sukaenah, vocals; Rukruk Rukmana, kacapi; Dede, rebab; Encep, rincik. Recorded in Sumedang, October 3, 1987. Saléndro sets are relatively rare and are almost never performed at paid gigs. The closing song for this set (beginning at 3:42) is actually a kakawén song from the wayang golék repertoire and is a request to the audience, sponsor, and ancestors to allow the singer to stop performing for the night. Running time: 8:12. A sorog version of "Gunung Guntur" (listed as "Sekar Duaan") is on *Tembang Sunda: Sundanese Classical Songs*, and saléndro sets appear on *Holding Up Half the Sky: Voices of Asian Women*, *Sundanese Classical Music*, and *Udan Mas: Ensemble/Lingkung Seni "Malati."*

8. "Palwa / Catrik," pélog tuning for kacapi-suling, performed at a wedding reception. Rukruk Rukmana, kacapi; Tatang Subari, suling; Pepen S., rincik. Recorded in Ciamis, March 12, 1988. This example of kacapi-suling includes "Palwa," a song of the gamelan degung repertoire. Degung tunes played by the kacapi-suling ensemble are sometimes called dedegungan, not to be confused with the high-pitched subset of rarancagan style also called dedegungan. Only advanced kacapi players perform dedegungan tunes. The shift to "Catrik," a conventional panambih, occurs at 5:07. Rukruk switches back and forth between standard kait technique and takol balik or "reversed stroke" beginning at 7:51. The heightened noise of the audience during this performance is typical of attitudes toward kacapi-suling; it is regarded as musical wallpaper. Running time: 13:32. The CDs *Indonesia: Music from West Java* (UNESCO D 8041; not listed in the Discography) and *Tembang Sunda: Sundanese Classical Songs* include kacapi-suling.

9. "Kingkilaban," sorog tuning for panambih, performed at a reception for Gambia's head of state. Euis Komariah and Neneng Dinar Suminar, vocals; Gan-gan Garmana, kacapi; Iwan S., suling; Kun-kun, rincik. Recorded in Bandung, December

8, 1988. The song is discussed and partly transcribed in the Chapter 7 section on panambih songs and is translated in Chapter 9. In this performance, Euis Komariah sings the first verse, followed by Neneng Dinar Suminar (her top student at the time, and now a significant performer and pasanggiri DAMAS winner) in the second verse at 3:06. Running time: 5:11. "Kingkilaban" is also found on the commercial CD *Udan Mas: Ensemble/Lingkung Seni "Malati."*